M000289389

It Will Change You
Your Spiritual Truth Revealed

Marco Governali Ph.D.

Copyright © 2017 by Marco Governali.

All rights reserved. No part of this book may be reproduced, copied, stored, shared, distributed or transmitted in any printed or electronic form, or by any means whatsoever graphic, electronic, or mechanical, including but not limited to photocopying, scanning, recording, or information storage and retrieval system without the prior written permission of the Author.

*Because of the dynamic nature of the Internet, any web address or link contained in this book may have changed since publication, and may no longer be valid.

*The views expressed in this work are solely those of the author and do not necessarily reflect the views of the publisher, and the publisher hereby disclaims any responsibility for them.

*This book is meant for educational purposes only. Any resemblance to real persons, living or dead is purely coincidental. Any names or people depicted within this book are for illustrative purposes only.

*All Bible quotations are taken from the King James Version.

*All materials contained in this book, including text, graphics, photos, and images, are the property of their respective owners.

First Edition, June 2017, manufactured in USA
1 2 3 4 5 6 7 8 9 10 LSI 17 18 19 20 22
Set in Garamond and Times Roman

Book Cover Concept: Marco Governali

International Standard Book Number: 978-0-9913381-6-0

A Seth Teachings Book

For Contact information, News and upcoming Books, visit our Website:
www.SethTeachings.org

Visit our YouTube and Facebook Channels - Search for:
"Marco Governali"

I dedicate this book to all my Fellow Humans. Especially those who seek to know the truth and find the courage to ask the difficult questions." ~

—Marco Governali

Contents

Acknowledgements

W hen way back in 1993 I first started writing this book, I would have never imagined that it was going to take the better part of 25 years to complete. Clearly, I did not have the faintest idea at the time of the enormity of the task I was taking on. Not only was I learning more and more everyday, but I was most importantly evolving everyday, forcing me to restart writing from the beginning over and over, many times. But it was all worthwhile in the end I believe, for I can now take a deep breath, knowing that I too have given my modest contribution. I too have a place in the marvelous realm of All-That-Is!

This work however, could have never been completed without the help and support of many dear friends and family.

Starting with my Wife, who always supported me, but also kept me humble and most of all grounded, preventing me from flying too far off into the esoteric realms. Thank you!

And my Son, the smartest, most good-hearted young man I know. For the encouragement and support, for the many questions he asked along the way, pushing me, motivating me to look deeper and deeper, helping me to ever refine and crystallize my own understanding of the subject. Thank you!

And to my dear friends and associates. Starting with Valana, the classiest and most graceful lady I have ever met. For her tremendous insight and advice and for helping me in fine tuning this book. Thank you!

To Sidney, for the long nights of never ending questions. For supporting—but also for challenging me, forcing me to look at both sides of the coin. Thank you!

To Laverne, for being always there for me. For asking the questions, for the friendship and the unwavering believe that it would eventually all come to fruition. Thank you!

To my friend Thomas, who passed away almost 25 years ago. Question: What do you get when you combine Einstein and Tesla? You get my friend Thomas—who a week before passing gave me a special gift, "Seth Speaks," the book that started this whole experience of mine. Thank you Thomas for entrusting me with your knowledge, I know that (as you said) it was your decision to leave. The world was not ready for what you already knew back then. Rest in peace my dear friend.

Author's Note

This book contains a great amount of challenging information.

If you are dependent upon your present belief system, you are advised not to continue reading. If you do choose to read this book, do so with an open mind.

The purpose of this book is to share information—which will, should you so wish, give you the opportunity to expand your way of thinking.

From a human perspective, we're accustomed to think that a "good versus evil war" is constantly being waged in the heavens—and by extension, here on Earth.

Think about it, what if it were all One-Conscious-Intelligence, experimenting within, wanting to experience the full range of all that can be experienced? ~

—Marco Governali.

It Will Change You

Your Spiritual Truth Revealed

Preface

At the tender age of twelve I was the victim of a very serious automobile accident. As I was getting out of school, a speeding car lost control and rolled over three times, ending up upside-down, pinning me beneath it.

As I found out later, in that accident I had actually died and obviously came back. I recall hovering in midair, looking down at my body trapped under the overturned vehicle. It was a very strange sensation indeed. I, the thinking me was up in midair, while my physical body was down on the pavement under the overturned car.

Perplexed and confused, from above, I saw a number of folks lift the vehicle off me. Then I saw the paramedics placing my body in the ambulance to then speed away toward the hospital. However, strangely, as the ambulance left the scene, I felt as if I had to make a decision of sorts. I had to choose between staying there—suspended in midair, and rejoining my body as it was being taken away in the speeding ambulance.

I don't know if I can say that it was a decision that I made, I simply felt compelled to return to my body, and I instantly found myself in the ambulance.

Several years of rehabilitation later, at age 24, the accident now a remote memory, a Spirit calling himself "Seth," who claimed to be my Spirit Guide and Teacher, contacted me.

Initially my interactions with Seth started as "Dream Visitations," later they developed into full blown "Ethereal Guided Tours," Out of Body Voyages, Time Travel, as well as visiting another inhabited planet.

These interactions continued for about seven years. Their purpose (Seth explained) was to share information on a multitude of subjects including: Creation; The Purpose of Life; Life after Death; The Spirit World; Re-Incarnation; The True Nature of the Universe; UFOs; and the "Mechanics" of how things and events are brought forth and materialized here in the physical world.

Seth further explained that I was not the only one he was sharing this information with. He revealed that he was simultaneously communicating with about two thousand other individuals throughout the planet, who he liked to call "Speakers."

He also mentioned that he was not the only Spirit Guide doing so.

Apparently— we the "Speakers" were being prepared. The purpose (he explained) was to in turn share, *via a variety of mediums,* this information with the wider audiences.

Some would go on to write books, some would make movies. Some would use paintings, music and other mediums. Some would give speeches at seminars.

And some would go on to become heads of state.

Introduction

This book, the result of much personal experience, soul searching, and research, was not intended to be an exhaustive attempt to convince anyone about anything in particular, or to influence anyone's point of view or belief system.

For over twenty years I struggled with the idea of writing this book. This struggle had nothing to do with the writing process itself, but more with the subjects this book would endeavor to address. Subjects such as Creation, The Big Bang Theory, Life After Death, and UFO's for instance, which have proven both challenging as well as controversial. These are profound intricate subjects, so intricate in fact that all throughout history it has proven virtually impossible to develop any conclusive theory that would end all theories. For every time a piece of the puzzle was found, the puzzle simply grew exponentially.

Thousands of books have been written on any one of these subjects, and while I'm far from implying that this book will give you the ultimate answer, I am confident that by the time you are finished reading it you will be a changed individual. How changed and to what degree, I do not know, but you will see the world and life itself in a new—wider, more positive perspective. In my case, the information I am sharing with you clarified a great deal of issues, opening my eyes to an unknown—unseen world. For it turns out that it is not the Universe out there one should endeavor to understand, but instead our inner personal universe. As nothing comes closer to truth, closer to the Creative Source, than that little spark of consciousness we all carry within. For your "True Source" is an inner source, not an external-accidental influence.

Consequently, regardless of religious or cultural background, regardless of what geographical corner of the world we hail from, whether we like to admit it or not, we all carry within the farthest corner of our mind, the most crucial of all questions, "What is the ultimate force responsible for everything in the Universe?" Man is innately curious. Curiosity is in fact vital to our survival, a necessary drive without which there would be little progress.

However, one of the biggest hurdles has always been that the moment someone tries to investigate the so-called "higher questions," they are immediately and inevitably faced with fierce opposition and ridicule. A researcher, who musters enough courage to step out of the proverbial box, will not only be faced with merciless ridicule, but also run the risk of losing their job in the process—and in some cases even worse. Truth be told you simply cannot introduce a new theory unless you've got "the whole story"—and you'd better have tangible proof to back it up, for it would be pointless to propose anything, unless you could prove it in a measurable and detailed fashion. Organized religions would have a field day labeling you by all sorts of undesirable names and titles.

Then why in the world would anyone take-on such risks, when their chances of success are next to nil? It should come as no surprise then if the vast majority of researchers spend their entire career studying much less controversial issues. Like for instance the one I saw on TV one night, where a researcher described being assigned a government funded study, where the objective was to find out of all things, "What was the best time of the day to squash a fly." Two years of research and $250,000 later, the researcher concluded, *and I forewarn you this is going to surprise you,* that the early afternoon hours were the best time to do so. It turns out that "that's when the fly's reflexes are at their slowest." Are you just as un-surprised as I am about the finding?

Mainly the result of an ill-informed mind set, anyone who tries to investigate the so called "higher questions" will invariably find themselves fighting a losing battle from the very start; but not because of their inability to substantiate their findings, but because they're inevitably bound to step on someone else's toes.

Science and religion are huge businesses; they generate untold amounts of money and employ thousands of individuals. They play a huge role in the world's economy, and every time a new technology is discovered, it inevitably renders another obsolete. This often causes the disintegration of whole industries—and thousands of positions, not only at the lower levels but also at the upper levels are lost. Managers, directors, shareholders, as well as political positions can be lost or created literally overnight. Thus, companies that enjoy stability and security one day—can be completely wiped out the next. Routinely, governments allocate millions to scientific projects, like for instance the Large Hadrons Collider in Cern, Switzerland. (Initial cost estimates of $2.2 billion, final bill in excess of $13 billion.) Allegedly, the 27 Km long apparatus is used to study super-accelerated sub-atomic particles whilst colliding one against the other. In so doing, researchers hope to glimpse into what our Universe *supposedly* looked like, the very instant following the hypothetical Big Bang. Completed in 2009, over 10,000 researchers from around the world take part in the experiments. I don't know if it is just me, but I feel a bit uneasy knowing that day-in-day-out, these nice folks play with an apparatus that could—as many experts have cautioned, cause a catastrophe of worldwide proportions. And all to study something that is nothing but a theory. "It's all under control," they assure us, but then how do they explain the potentially catastrophic accidents listed below?

—**March 2007.** *A cryogenic magnet support broke during a pressure test. Director Pier Oddone stated, "In this case we are dumbfounded that we missed some very simple balance of forces. This fault had been present in the original design and during 4 engineering reviews. Analysis revealed that its design was not strong enough to withstand the forces generated during pressure testing."* (Source: Wikipedia)

—**September 2008.** *During powering tests, problems occurred when an electrical fault caused a rupture and a leak of six tonnes of liquid helium. It is believed that a faulty electrical connection caused an arc, which compromised the liquid helium containment. With the cooling layer broken, the helium flooded the surrounding vacuum layer with sufficient force to break 10-ton magnets from their mountings.* (Source: Wikipedia)

—**July 2009.** *Two new vacuum leaks were identified.* (Source: Wikipedia)

What concerns me is that each of the 27 million millimeters that make the system is a potential catastrophe waiting to happen! What if, we in the near future discovered that we could have achieved the same in a desktop computer simulation? Call me critical, but to me constructing a 27 Km long apparatus to study something so small no human eye can see, plainly makes no sense. However, that said, it is neither the cost nor the size that troubles me most about the project, but the fact that the enormously expensive—enormously dangerous system was built based all on pure assumptions and speculations. But don't take my word for it; here is how one of their websites puts it.

"The LHC allows scientists to reproduce the conditions that existed within a billionth of a second after the Big-Bang, by colliding beams of high energy protons or ions at colossal speeds, close to the speed of light. This was the moment, around 13.7 billion years ago, when the Universe is believed to have started with an explosion of energy and matter."

"During these first moments all the particles and forces that shape our Universe came into existence, defining what we now see."

But did you happen to notice the word "believed" in the above article? What this means is that despite maintaining that it is only a theory on the one hand, the enormous apparatus was built and these experiments conducted, *as if the Big Bang actually took place* on the other, and they are trying to duplicate it. While the very same people who designed the system are the first to acknowledge that it is nothing more than a best guess.

Now, when I first started writing this book, the question I struggled the most with, was: Why would a Spirit Guide deliver material of such complexity to someone who is not a scientist? The information was not only very complex but also very hard to verify, especially when one lacks the appropriate background. I do hold two Ph.D. degrees, but they are one in chemistry and one in computer sciences. It was much later that I realized that this was not by accident. As Seth himself puts it, "Nothing in the Universe is accidental or coincidental."

Seth later explained that he chose someone, who precisely because of his non-affiliation to any pre-established doctrines, would deliver the information unchanged and unbiased. Someone, who wouldn't skew the information for financial gain or to favor this or that sponsor. Someone with a solid understanding of life in general, but most importantly, someone with an open mind. By giving me the material, Seth knew that it would be delivered in a plain and simple fashion and in a style that anyone from the scientist to the theologian, to the unstudied average, but curious Joe could relate to.

As you can imagine, an enormous amount of research went into writing this book. To make sure I was not just "dreaming" the information Seth delivered, I had to triple-check every minute detail. Couple that with the fact that as I am sure you've noticed, English is not my first language, and you can start to appreciate the enormous effort involved. Overwhelmed and frustrated I gave up many times, sometimes throwing dozens of completed pages away. I once discarded over 120 pages of material. "This is it, I am done! Sorry Seth! This is too much for me," I yelled, only to regret doing so a few hours later, having to start from scratch all over again.

Then about three years ago, after a couple of year's break, while driving on the highway on a gorgeous Sunday afternoon, a sudden eureka moment, "Why am I worried about 'how' to write the book?"

"Why am I worrying about how folks are going to receive it? This is not my information in the first place, why don't I simply write it without questioning it—in the same manner it was given to me and let the chips fall where they may?"

Suddenly, it felt as if a ton of bricks were lifted from me. I couldn't wait to get home and start writing again, and I have rarely skipped a day since.

And if I've learned anything during this whole process, it is that in life, no matter what you endeavor to do, there are always going to be those who do not agree. Some have even questioned Seth's legitimacy, which is incidentally what I did when he first contacted me. Some don't believe in the existence of Spirits, but similarly to those who are afraid of skeletons—forgetting that inside they're dragging one around all day; they forget that they themselves are Spirits—wearing an Earth suit. For where would their thoughts and consciousness, or even their feelings, come from, were they not a Spirit first and then a body?

Then there are some—especially those who read other Seth's books before—who seem to reason that once Jane Roberts (who back in the '70s wrote Seth's original books) died, Seth died with her. Well, for starters Seth was already "dead" for he is a Spirit. And as he himself put it, "While it is true that Jane had signed contracts with publishers and so on, I personally never signed any such agreement with neither Jane, nor any publisher."

Now, the vast majority of the material in the book comes from Seth, thus it is not I who should take credit for it, for I am just the writer, while Seth is the source. Without Seth's input this book would've never materialized. On my own, I could have never come up with this information. It was given to me over several years of channeling, dream messages and out of body encounters. And while I spent two decades piecing it all together, studying dozens of books, researching every piece of information I could find, had he not contacted me—simply put, I would have never written this book.

The process was extremely tiring but also amusing. Each time I needed information, as if by magic, the right book or documentary would popup in front of me, on the web, on TV, or while browsing at a bookstore. To the extent that before long, I was no longer surprised by the continuous chain of coincidences. For example, I was browsing at a bookstore one day, standing a couple of feet from the shelves, lazily scanning through hundreds of books, when for no apparent reason one of the books just fell flat on its side. Instinctively I picked it up; it was exactly what I needed! Just the night before, Seth had given me some information. The book's title fitted like a glove. Then the mother of all validations, I randomly opened the book and the first thing I saw was Seth's name, as an Egyptian god. A coincidence?

Recently, a client of mine who is a retired naturopath practitioner recommended a book on body detox and general wellness he had just finished reading. The book titled, *Clean Gut* by Alejandro Junger, is a great read for anyone. Jim wrote the book's title on a business card, which I placed on my desk, with the intention of ordering the book later that week. But before long, the card got lost under the usual mountain of paperwork. Out-of-sight-out-of-mind, I forgot all about it.

A few days later, Laverne, another client of mine, stopped by to visit, and he had a book in his hands. He had ordered the book for himself from Amazon he said, but they had somehow sent him an extra copy by error, so he gave it to me. I gave the book a quick glance, the title looked somewhat familiar, but I did not make anything of it. I put the book on my desk. But when Laverne left my office that title was really bothering me. I kept wondering where I had seen it before? I looked and looked on my desk and I finally found the business card with the title of the book I was planning to buy. My jaw dropped. It was the exact same book Laverne had just given me. Another coincidence?

I can always tell, for instance, when someone's coming to visit, a day or even a few hours before. Coincidences? Out of the blue I happen to mention someone's name—and they call a few minutes later, more coincidences?

As I am sure it must be yet another coincidence the fact that the driver of the car that almost killed me, has the same first name as mine!

What about this little episode that just happened a few days ago? I was in the hospital for a minor day surgery. After the surgery, a nurse came to check my vital signs. Her face looked very familiar.

"Do I know you from somewhere?" I asked her.

"No, I don't think so," she replied.

I was convinced otherwise, but for the life of me I could not remember how I knew her. And that's the precise instant when my phone beeped. It was an incoming text message.

"Hi Marco, this is Kim. I know we haven't talked for years, but I am having trouble with my computer, can you help?"

And bang—it suddenly came to me. "Are you Kim's daughter?" I asked the surprised young nurse who was about to leave.

"Yes, I am," she hesitantly replied, "...but how did you know that?" She asked confused.

"Well, here I was, breaking my brain trying to remember where I knew you from, when out of the blue, your mother—after we haven't talked for years—sends me a totally unrelated text message!" I said.

She was just as mesmerized as I was. "Isn't life interesting?" She said.

"It sure is," I replied. Another coincidence?

Here is another interesting one. Years ago I worked in IT. A customer called me to her house one day as her computer wouldn't start. But once there, I pressed the power button and it started just fine. But while in her house, I could feel a very heavy—negative feeling in the air. So much so that once I got out of the house I felt as if I could finally breathe again. I sat in my car for a few minutes trying to make sense of that sickening sensation I had felt inside, but in the end I decided that it was none of my concern and I drove back to my office.

But not even an hour later she called back. She said that as soon as I had left, the computer had stopped working again. I tried helping her over the phone, but the computer would not cooperate. Somewhat reluctantly I went back, but once there, once again the computer started on the first try. I checked a few things, but there was nothing wrong with it. Just as that morning however, the feeling in the house was so sickening that I couldn't wait to get out. Now in the entrance putting my coat on, fighting my gut feeling telling me that I should say something—while my brain told me that I should keep it professional and just leave. In the end I couldn't help it. I gathered enough courage to ask her a simple question.

"Are you alright?" I said.

No sooner had I finished the sentence, the woman, as if hit by a bolt of lightning, collapsed on the floor like a rag doll. I had to literally pick her up and help her to a chair. With tears pouring out of her eyes and a very surprised look on her face, she said, "How did you know?"

"How did I know what?" I asked.

Her life had been a life of pain brought on by a devastating third degree burn she had suffered as a child, she explained. She then confessed that she was planning to take her own life that evening and that she needed the computer to write a goodbye letter to friends and family.

This took me by total surprise. She was an attractive young lady in her mid-thirties. Her body however was another story she said, completely disfigured from her neck down.

We had a long talk. I reminded her that if she so wished no one could stop her from taking her own life, but to keep in mind that she the Soul had chosen that specific life, together with all its victories as well as challenges for a reason, to learn something specific!

She told me about everything that was wrong with her life—and it was a lot. "Now tell me about what is right with you instead," I said.

So she started talking about her family, and the things she enjoyed doing. It didn't take long for her to realize that, overwhelmed by negativity, she had lost touch with her inner-self: Her talents, her hobbies, painting, and piano playing, her friends, her two little nieces, the beauty of life itself.

"I will now leave," I said, "but you must promise that you will call me tomorrow."

The strange thing was that now the room felt totally different. The sun came shining through the window melting that fog that just a minute ago made the air non breathable, replacing it with a joyous positive light. I could now see a spark in her eyes, where I saw the look of death a minute before. She hugged and thanked me. I left, and when she didn't call the next day I feared the worst. I went on the Internet looking for news. I was worried, but I resisted the urge to call her. Something inside told me that I didn't have to worry.

She called four months later. She started by thanking me for intervening—when professionally speaking I shouldn't have. In the end she decided that despite the challenges, life was well worth living.

Since our talk, things had totally turned around for the better, she said. She received several high paying job offers, many of her friends she hadn't heard from for years got back in touch, and she had also found a boyfriend—who didn't mind her disfigured body, and that they were planning to marry within months. She now had a whole new outlook on life she said, and she even said that her scars didn't look that bad after all.

Some may see this as yet another coincidence; but to me it was an opportunity to help someone in need.

And allow me to tell you about another interesting little episode that happened a couple of decades ago. At the time I owned a large automotive service business. It all went very well for a decade or so, and then we got hit with a recession. I had to lay off half of my 16 employees. Things got even worse when my largest customer (a fleet rental outfit) went out of business. I was still able to manage paying my bills and pay my guys, but my bank decided to change my bank account manager.

Fresh out of training, the newbie—having no experience whatsoever, went strictly by the book—and the book told him that unless the economy turned around I could be closing my doors within six months. He got nervous and basically demanded that I offered more security on my loan.

This meant that I had to go elsewhere to find new money to secure their money—thing which I was not comfortable doing, as this would have exposed me to too high a risk. I asked him to leave things the way they were but he did not want to cooperate.

I received a call from his boss, telling me that I needed to go see him. I went in, resigned to the possibility that—should they have called the loan, I might have had to hand in the keys to my business. I sat down in his office and the older bank manager, head down busy looking through my paperwork, did not say a word for five minutes or so. Looking at his bald head, from where I was sitting, he actually reminded me of Seth, about the same age and a similar appearance.

When he finally raised his eyes, he said, "Hello Mr. Governali, so I have been going through your loan papers and all—but to be totally honest, things don't look very promising."

"I am aware that things are not going great right now. But as you know recessions do not last forever. If I can only get another six months or so, I can pull it off," I said.

"Well, let me tell you my plan instead," the old banker, replied. "Today, happens to be my very last day here at the bank, and I do not wish to retire on a negative note. What I am going to do for you instead is that I am going to refinance your existing loan, with a lower monthly payment, and no payments for the first three months." He surprised me with.

"Wow, I surely did not expect that, you do not know how much I appreciate that," I said shaking his hand.

And that is when, hidden behind a book, I saw his name tag on his desk—and I almost fainted. I did not say anything of course, but I was laughing on the inside. His name was Mr. Seth Ball. "Thank you for playing ball Seth," I thought.

There are times for instance when I need a car mechanic or a dentist, and the next day one walks into my office. I plan to mortgage a home, and a mortgage broker calls me to see if I need anything.

Could these all be coincidences? Interestingly, when I asked Seth why had my life become such an endless chain of coincidences, all that he could say was, "Why do you ask that question, when you already know the answer?"

And I am sure you, the reader, must be wondering why am I telling you all this. "I too can sense when someone is about to call me. I too have gut feelings warning me of things before they happen," you're probably thinking. My point exactly! I am telling you, to remind you that it is all totally normal and nothing extraordinary, an inherent spiritual side everyone has within. There's nothing special about me, nor do I possess any special powers. All I want is to awaken you to the realization that you are a Soul first—and then a body. For when you come to accept this fact, or at least allow for the possibility, the advantages are many. And since we are on the topic of "gut-feeling" allow me to elaborate a bit.

I was very surprised when Seth explained that what we call "gut feeling" is a lot more important than we give it credit for.

"When you find yourself in a precarious or dangerous situation, where do you suppose that uncomfortable—at times painful feeling in your gut comes from?" Seth asked.

"I do not have a clue," I replied.

"Your medical scientists correctly attribute it to 'chemical-bacterial reaction' but, what causes those bacteria to react to impending danger I ask?" Seth said.

"I really never thought of that, please explain," I asked.

"In what you call 'your near future' your doctors will discover that the so called 'gut' is a lot more important and is responsible for a lot more—a whole lot more in fact, than previously thought," he said. "In some ways, it can be said that your gut is actually more important than your brain is," he continued. "Information, which I am sure will raise many eyebrows in the medical community," he said. "Yes, your brain is what coordinates physical data—but where do you suppose the brain gets its 'guidance' from?" He asked. "The gut is where!" He continued. "The gut, which can be likened to an 'antenna'—or more precisely a 'human antenna'—(and this is going to surprise many)," he said, "can sense and pick-up signals from as far out as six kilometers (about 3.7 miles) around you."

"Wow," I said, "this is getting really interesting, and I am starting to see where this is heading," I said.

"Indeed Marco," he said. "So, when you feel moody or uncomfortable for no reason of—or doing of your own, your 'antenna' may very well be picking-up negative energy from the house next door or from a kilometer down the street. It goes without saying that 'like-attracts-like,' thus, the more 'negative' the neighborhood, the more negativity you will experience. Also it goes without saying that people's health will be very much affected —thus these are the areas of the city or neighborhoods where you will find the highest incidence of crime, infrastructural deterioration, cancer, and all sorts of other forms of lower vibrational states," he continued.

"Wow, that is just incredible, but it does make sense" I said.

"Have you ever wondered why—while for instance driving your car at night, you feel more comfortable in some areas of the city than you feel in others? Why do you—while driving, instinctively roll up the car window in some areas and open it in some others? That is why, because your 'antenna'—your 'gut feeling' senses the negative (or positive) ions in the air—again up to six kilometers around you, how is that for an early warning system?" He said jokingly.

"That's a hell of a self-preservation device we all have," I said.

"Yes, and that is by the way, the reason why over time, a city—any city, develops so called 'good areas' and bad areas. For folks will instinctively— and in most cases without realizing it—gravitate toward 'like vibrations,' hence they will instinctively buy or rent a home in those areas that match— resonates with their own personal vibrational level—their state of mind.

But there is more than just 'folk's state of mind' at play here," he continued. "Unseen to the human eye, but very visible to animals and discernible to certain equipment, cities are crisscrossed by invisible 'energy lines'—lines that end up dividing the city into 'sectors'—square sectors to be exact, and the same applies all the way from the 'atomic' scale to Nations and Continents, and everything in between.

"Wow, this is going to surprise a lot of people," I said.

"Indeed, but it will become common knowledge by the mid 2030's," he said.

"What else can you tell me about this?" I asked.

"Well, these are the same 'energy lines' animals follow when migrating from North to South and vice versa, and this is also the main reason why every city on the planet has a so called 'East-end," he surprised me with.

"What do you mean by "East-end," I asked?

"Pick a city—any city," he replied, "New York, Chicago, Miami, London, Rome, Tokyo, Sydney and so on, and tell me if their respective 'East-end' is not where most of the trouble takes place. Crime, poverty, sickness, etc."

"What?" I said. "So does that mean that every city's East-end is predisposed to 'trouble?'" I asked.

"Indeed, Marco, indeed. The planet is naturally divided by intersecting energy lines, which form of course 'grids'—at all levels, from the atomic to the planetary scale. And once you start paying attention and know what to look for, you will see these patterns everywhere you look, for they are in fact very visible to the eyes that care to see them. Go out in your yard later, and tell me if you cannot see what we just discussed." He said.

"What should I look for?" I asked.

"Squares, square patterns—of all sizes. And squares within squares. Try using your so-called 'third-eye,' your instinct, instead of your regular eyes, and you will be amazed at what you will be able to see," he said.

"I can't wait to go out in my backyard and report back," I said.

And so I did. The next day I went out in my backyard and I started looking at the grass, almost an acre of it. I could not see a thing, it all looked the same. Disappointed I was going back inside. But then as I went up on my deck, which is about 5 feet off the ground, I looked back and my jaw dropped when I saw something strange in the lawn. I noticed an area where the grass appeared to be twisted almost, and more yellow than the rest of the surrounding grass.

This is when I remembered what Seth said, "Use your third eye." And so I tried and tried. Instead of looking with my regular eyes, I tried to un-focus my vision—and instead let my 'mind' do the seeing. And after a couple of minutes things really started to look different. For starters the grass became brighter, almost florescent. And I could now discern patterns in the lawn that I had never noticed before. Seth was right. I could see "squares" in my lawn, and the grass conformed to them. It was pale, yellowish and unhealthy looking on the right upper corner, and very luscious and deep green toward the left (West) side of the square. Also in-between the two extremes I noticed a combination of the two. I was amazed. I could actually see that even grass—nature itself, responded to these invisible energy patterns. And then it hit me, we Humans are also part of nature of course, and that is why (as Seth said) we are also affected by these energy patterns. I could not wait to report back to Seth. So that evening, I mentally asked him to visit me in my sleep. And so he did.

"Hello Seth, I see what you meant," I said, "I could see the 'energy squares' you mentioned in my lawn."

"Yes indeed, and once you start paying attention to them, you will see them everywhere," he said.

"But what does this mean in the larger picture?" I asked.

"Well, this information will gradually make its way into the scientific community. It will be fought tooth-and-nail at first, but as it will become more understood, it will gradually become more and more accepted and further developed. The biggest obstacle is that it cannot be seen by regular eyes, hence a heightened-spiritual approach is needed, which is of course considered 'taboo' amongst mainstream science," he said.

"Slowly but surely, your scientists will begin to connect the dots— literally. And they will begin taking seriously, study and understand what was common knowledge to previous civilizations. How else could you explain the fact that many so called 'sacred sites or structures where in fact built on those intersecting points?"

"Such as?" I asked.

"The Great Pyramid of Giza, for instance, Easter Island, Stonehenge, and many, many more sacred sites. And other so called 'high-energy' areas— or areas with the highest incidence of strange phenomena or anomalies are also located on these intersecting lines. The Bermuda triangle being the most well-known among them," he said. "In addition, many areas on the planet, Countries included, that happen to be on these intersecting lines, are going to be naturally unstable" he replied.

"What do you mean by 'naturally unstable?'" I asked.

"Countries which happen to be on the East intersecting corner of the square or grid—what I like to call 'the busy corner,'" Seth said, "are going to experience extreme changes and instability. They can be the center of civilization and very wealthy one century, and in total ruin the very next. Iraq being a perfect example," he said. Countries that are instead located on the 'quiet' stable side of the square or grid—the West side that is, will instead have a more stable, linear, predictable, healthier history. Your Country, Canada being a perfect example," he said.

"And is that way the Canadian province of Alberta seems to have all the oil in the Country," I asked?

"Good observation indeed Marco!" He said. "Yes, that is why, for do not forget that in reality these so called 'squares' have more than one side to them—for they are in fact not squares but cubes, energy cubes to be precise. Hence the same rules that apply on the ground's surface also apply to the ground below—or underground. And so these are the areas where not only the biggest oil, diamonds, and gold deposits will be found, but also, socioeconomically and demographically speaking, the most 'unstable' areas," he said. "And these are the areas that will be caught-up in a seemingly never ending cycle of boom-to-bust!" He said.

"But why has this information not been passed down to us? I mean this could have really made a difference, empower us," I asked.

"For millennia you've been brainwashed into believing the exact opposite. 'You're a mere human-sinner' you have been told over and over, outcast and abandoned to steer an existence on a hellish devil's ruled Earth, as punishment for a sin. Sin that is not only metaphoric in nature, but that you had nothing to do with!" Seth said.

"But why would anyone want to do that to us," I asked?

"On the surface it may appear to have all to do with 'gaining control over the masses,' distance you from the Sacred-Self that you really are, but there is more to the story. It is all part of your collective grandiose movie script!" He said.

"But who's benefitting from it," I asked?

"Again, on the surface it may appear that those making a hefty living from the nefarious indoctrination—is who! And in the short run it may very well appear that way, but not in the long run, not in the larger design. So, when you hear 'We're under a constant terrorist's threat,' 'You're sick and getting sicker—buy our medicines,' or 'an Armageddon is coming,' which is always supposed to happen within a month's time, but that for some reason never does, remind yourself that that's only the surface of things, window dressing if you like. The truth is, 'that's how you grow as a society,' that's how you grow Spiritually! By facing your lower vibrations, recognize them, make the necessary adjustments and become a better—

more spiritual society, thus closer to Source," Seth explained.

"So, I should not be scandalized when I see well-meaning folks falling for these seemingly unscrupulous quacks' quackery and take money from their children's mouth and send it to them. "Send us money," let me correct that, "donate us money, so that we can mail you a small vial of blessed (faucet) water, or some green colored handkerchief that will make you supernaturally wealthy and healthy," they chant on TV every night," I said.

"As I said, it is all part of the movie script you have chosen as a society. It is your preferred path to enlightenment. And so you shall!" Seth concluded.

Now, back in the mid-'90s, Discovery Magazine ran an article titled "The Nature of Time," by what it labeled "The three most qualified physicists in the USA." An excellent article, but one that in the end fell short of shining any new light on the subject. What I found particularly fascinating was that in the closing paragraphs the three luminaries ended the article by almost admitting defeat, when they frankly stated:

"The truth is that we're at a standstill. The study of physics has reached a point where something radically new is needed. We wouldn't be surprised if something new will come out in the near future, which will radically change pretty well everything we know!"

As they put their names at the end of the article, I wrote a short email to one of them. Thinking back, I might've perhaps been looking for validation from an expert. Naturally, I didn't expect a reply, but to my surprise, a few days later, the renowned astrophysicist telephoned me. For obvious reasons I will refer to him only by his first initial, "C."

C must've seen something interesting in the message, as he called me all the way from France where he was giving a lecture. What I would estimate to be a $150 one-hour phone call at the time. As both C and I happened to be of Italian background, we started by breaking the proverbial ice. I'm sure he was trying to find out if I was only partially or certifiably insane.

Then once he assured himself that he wasn't talking to an E.T., C confessed that the subject of "Time" was in fact his lifelong fascination and that he had dedicated his entire career researching that single but most important topic. And when I shared my interpretation of the subject, he replied that he had long suspected a similar model, but that he would be unable to demonstrate it practically, simply because no instrument existed able to demonstrate the "invisible side" of the physical, the half that completes the unit, what our scientists call "Matter/Anti-Matter."

And to my surprise C didn't hang up the phone, even when I revealed that the source of the information was a Spirit. Obviously he must have heard something interesting in what I (and Seth) had to say. It was a constructive conversation indeed.

And finally I asked him, in his opinion, why was this information given to me and not to a scientist like him.

"No one really knows why some folks get information before others do, Galileo being a good example," he said. "He understood 'Gravity' and all that it entailed, centuries before everyone else did. And how do we know if Galileo and other great minds of the past got their information from a spirit also?" C concluded.

At the time, the pope had in fact excommunicated Galileo, threatening to burn him at the stake, unless he stopped spreading rumors that our Solar System was (building upon Copernicus' earlier theory) "Heliocentric" (Sun centered) and not "Geocentric" (Earth centered) as the church wanted folks to believe.

It is only recently that Rome issued a symbolic apology to Galileo, finally recognizing his findings as valid.

"Three things cannot be long hidden, The Sun, The Moon, and The Truth." ~

—Buddha

About the Author

My name is Marco. Mine was a fairly normal childhood. Then at age twelve, in one instant, everything changed when I became the victim of a very serious automobile accident.

February 28th 1972, a day I shall never forget. Yes a very unfortunate day, but a day that in many ways, turned out to be a blessing. It became the starting point of a life-changing experience.

I suffered over a dozen bone fractures in that accident; and in between surgeries I was hospitalized or bedridden at home for over three years. By the time my late teen-years rolled around, life had gradually returned to relative normality. Then at age 23 I moved to Canada, where shortly after I took ownership of a large automotive business. Fully immersed in work, other than the daily family-work routine, life seemed to flow normally, until one day, Thomas, a friend and customer of mine, gave me a book as a gift. The book was titled "Seth Speaks, The Eternal Validity of the Soul."

A week had passed from the moment Tom gave me the book, when one afternoon his son Glenn came to see me. But as soon as he stepped into my office, a thought immediately flashed in my mind. "Your father is dead!" I said out of the blue. "…I am really sorry." I immediately corrected myself, "Why in the world would I say such a thing? That was terrible of me," I apologized. I felt horrible. I had no idea why I had said such a terrible thing, but the thought just came out on its own.

"…But my father did die last night," Glenn replied surprised, "He had a heart attack in his sleep. But the question is—how did you know?" Glenn asked perplexed.

My heart sank. "I'm really sorry to hear that, please forgive me, I don't know how, but the thought just came to me," I said.

"My dad did talk about a special connection between you two, now I know what he meant. I just came to inform you about his passing, but I see that he had obviously already done so himself," Glenn said.

With my friend Tom's passing, in my mind it became even more important that I read the book he had given me only a week prior. And I felt bad for not having found the time to start reading it. So I couldn't wait to get home that evening, and after dinner I started reading the book.

But the interesting thing was, that from the very start, from the very first pages in fact, it felt as if the book was talking about my own life, as if I had somehow participated in writing it. It was as if, page after page, I had previous knowledge of what was to come next. I simply couldn't put the book down, and when I had finished reading it, I read it again, four times. And what was even stranger was that a couple of days after I started reading the book, "Seth" the Spirit Guide and main protagonist in that book, started appearing in my dreams. At first, there was no doubt in my mind that I must have processed in my dreams, what I was reading in the book. But as night after night the dreams continued, and Seth the Spirit started to actually interact with me, initiating a dialogue of sorts, I realized that there was more to it. These dreams just didn't feel the same as all the other dreams I had.

Raised in a catholic household at the time, I was accustomed to believe that things could only belong to this or that side of the fence, "godly" or "ungodly." I concluded that Seth had to be bad news. Very uncomfortable and scared, at first I didn't even want to talk to him. However, as time went on, realizing eventually that I had nothing to fear and out of sheer curiosity, I agreed to participate in what Seth called, "a series of teaching sessions and guided tours."

The first few sessions, took place in what resembled a school classroom, complete with blackboard, desks, and a wand Seth used to point out information on the blackboard with. However, the peculiar thing about the classroom was that it felt as if it floated in midair. The walls and the checkered black and white floor seemed to shift and sway from side to side as if made of rubber.

Seth did not walk; he hovered slowly at about a foot off the ground. A woman by the name of Jane, (more about her later in the book) participated in at least three of these encounters. In one instance, Jane entered the classroom from a door to the far right corner and came hovering toward me, but all I could see at first was an empty black dress with no one in it. Then, as it got closer to me, she suddenly materialized inside the dress, scaring the hell out of me.

In the end, these encounters served to not only open my eyes to an unseen world, allowing me to see that there was more to life than what we think, but also gave me, if you will, a new—wider perspective.

Seth and I explored a wide variety of subjects. He informed me, for instance, that I was now living my 49th Earth life of the current Earth

Civilization. This was, he said, only but a small portion of the more than 12,000 lives I had apparently lived both in other Earth civilizations as well as on other dimensions. Out of my present 48 other Earth lives, Seth and I visited 17.

Now, all throughout this book you may find information that will likely surprise you, some more than others. Please keep in mind that I too, *during the course of my interactions with Seth*, found relating to some of the information he shared, challenging and difficult to accept, as it went against everything I knew. For instance, when I learned about my past lives, when he said that I had lived a total of 12,000 lives, I simply laughed. So I totally understand if you also laugh. Seth, as usual, eloquently resolved the question by simply stating:

"Whether you believe what I tell you or not, it does not change the facts, it only delays your understanding—in the larger scale of things, for I have neither the reason nor the time to talk about untruths. You find it difficult to believe that you've lived 12,000 lives roughly speaking, and yet, you could not give me a single reason why you couldn't have!"

Similarly, some folks may scoff at the idea that other civilizations beside ours could have existed on Earth before, but propose to pay them a million bucks—if they can give you one single reason "why not"—and they wouldn't have a clue! The truth is that thinking outside of the box upsets everything we know. It forces us to "think," thus, we refuse to even allow other possibilities. This type of narrow approach has always puzzled me. How could we be so shortsighted and believe that no one else existed prior to us—ever?

One day, I was having a conversation with a well-studied friend of mine. As soon as I mentioned the possibility that other civilizations could have walked the planet before us—some of whom possibly "Giants," he abruptly ended the conversation saying that it was getting "too spooky" for his liking.

But, "define a giant," I asked him.

"I wouldn't know where to start," he replied, "that is why I am ending the conversation, as it goes against everything I've studied and believed all my life. I don't want to re-learn everything I know," he said.

"Even if what you've learned is wrong?" I asked.

"Yes, because I am comfortable with the status-quo," he replied.

But let's look at this a bit further. What would we call "a giant" I ask, if everyone on Earth were twenty feet tall, our homes and our means of transportation—all accordingly proportionate, would we be giants then? Are we giants now? Depends who you ask, from our standpoint we're not—again because we're all more-or-less similarly built, but does an ant see us as giants, when from their perspective, relatively speaking, we appear to be roughly 3,000 feet tall? Think about it!

My interactions with Seth continued for about seven years. Then he informed me that he was going to leave this realm and focus on other realms where his help was needed most. But he assured me that despite shifting his attention onto other systems, our fundamental connection would endure nevertheless. This, not only because all dimensions are inherently interconnected, but also because I apparently am myself part of the larger "Seth Entity." He also informed me that I was not the only one he was interacting with. He explained in fact, that he was simultaneously "guiding" about 2,000 other individuals. We (the two thousand, he said) were actually a "projection" of him "the source."

"I am the trunk, you the branches," he explained. "Together we form the tree. As such we will never be separated. I am going to focus on other realms—where I have other 'branches.' I would like to explain to you about these other realms, but they wouldn't make any sense to you if I tried."

The purpose of it all, *Seth explained*, was to disseminate information and spread the good news about the true magnitude and beauty of "All-That-Is." This is necessary, *he went on*, as we are now, (our frequency is), at the tail end of our "Industrial-Technology-Religion" driven phase. We are now at the doorstep, as I am sure you've heard before, of a New Age, an age of Spiritual Unity and cooperation. Many thousands of so-called "Light Workers" have volunteered to be born at this specific time, to help in the process and facilitate in the transition. Some will hold seminars, he explained, some will write books, communicate through paintings, movies, songs, and a multitude of other mediums.

Seth said that although he would put an end to our sessions, I would still be able to feel his presence. By simply thinking about him, *he said*, a switch of focus or "tuning" on my part would take place. Similarly to dialing different channels on the radio—thinking of Seth would bring forth our underlying connection. True to form, *until recently, to answer a question I had asked,* I haven't dreamt of him since, Encouraged and fascinated however, curious to push the envelope a bit further, I went on having many experiences on my own, ranging from Out of Body Experiences to Astro-Travel, to excursions to the so-called "Other Side, as well as—though briefly, "switching channels." And as you will learn later in the book, I also had a Ghost, intentionally appear right in front of me in my living room—not once, not twice, but three times.

Together with several O.B.E. inducing methods, Seth described a technique allowing me to visit, what we call, "The Other Side," but what he ironically calls, "Home." It is a somewhat elaborate procedure, but it allowed me to deliberately travel, or better, "shift" there, on three separate occasions. And if you think you've seen a lot here, let me say that you haven't seen anything yet. If you also asked me to somehow quantify it, I would have to say that this Earth dimension we're so concerned with, would only amount to 5% of what I have been shown. Then, taking it one step further, Seth mentioned that what he had shown me thus far only amounted to roughly 5% of "All-That-Is." Should you really wish to make your brain spin, he went on saying that "All-That-Is"—as he understands it, might only be a portion of yet a larger Gestalt. In fact many other Gestalts might exist—parallel to, or as part of an even larger one. That larger Gestalt being the ultimate, "All-That-Is." However, this is irrelevant information to us, *himself included*, Seth explained, as we will never know the true magnitude.

Now, as I said Seth calls the other side "Home." As it turns out, what we call the "other side" from here, is in-fact our "Home Side," where we normally reside as Souls, our natural state of being. This "Human side" we're all so concerned with here on Earth, is instead nothing more than a "temporary sojourn," a temporary-self. If you were able to see this concept, *as you should*, from your Spirit's standpoint—because that is what you are first and foremost, then this "Earth Projection" would actually become "the other side." At home, where no such a thing as the "passage of time" exists nor is of concern, is where we always reside as immortal Souls. It can in fact be beneficial if you tried making a small effort to detach yourself from the idea that everything must somehow "die" or "end," for that only applies here on Earth. There, at home, we simply exist! From there, as Souls, we project portions of ourselves onto a multitude of systems, while we the Soul, remain completely unaffected by how many times we "die" in this or that system. Thus, as Souls, we never leave our Home-level—we instead project our energy onto other systems, such as planet Earth.

We do so mainly for learning purposes; we seek experiences, events that we are unable to experience there at Home. And depending upon "where" we project onto, we must wear a "suit," so-to-speak, or assume a "form" that will allow us to exist and function in that specific environment.

And as far as the UFO subject is concerned, Seth explained the fascinating phenomenon as best as I could relate to it. And although this is far from being a book about UFOs, later we shall discuss the topic in some detail. Allow me to just mention, for now, that about 15 years ago, perhaps in an attempt to appease my own doubts, I was—together with a friend, the unwilling witness of a "UFO encounter." While driving in the Canadian Boreal forest, and in broad daylight, my friend and I both saw two Unidentified Flying Objects slowly coming out from the row of trees to our left and in front of us, then stop in the middle of the road. They remained there motionless for about half a minute. They then took off into the sky at an inconceivable rate of speed. Seth went on to explain that event and much more on the subject, which I will share with you later in the book.

I could undoubtedly tell that Seth had his hand in all of these more recent experiences, as if still giving me long distance lessons. If I, for instance, formulated a question in my mind and directed it to Seth, I would—focused somewhere slightly above my right shoulder, immediately feel his presence. I would ask a question and I would hear his voice in my head, together with the answer, in most cases even before I had finished formulating the question. Most of the times however, Seth would reply with what eventually became a familiar and somewhat humorous answer. "Why do you ask that question, when you already know the answer?"

"Cut me some slack Seth, I am only a Human!"
Or am I a Soul, energizing a Human body?

"I know God won't give me anything I can't handle. I just wish he didn't trust me so much." ~

—Mother Teresa

Prologue

Who is Seth?

By his own definition, Seth is a personality who no longer focuses in physical reality.

Now, chances are that if you are reading a book of this genre, you have most likely read other books about Seth before. Some of you may have heard about Seth from the so-called "Seth Material," a series of manuscripts Seth dictated through Jane Roberts while in a trance state, over a period of time from 1968 to 1984—until Jane passed away. Both Seth and Jane gained much popularity during that time. A large movement of Seth scholars followed, still going strong today. And strangely, all throughout that material, Seth referred to Jane as Ruburt and her husband Rob as Joseph—names (he said) that better described their greater selves and previous lifetimes. The many thousands of pages of information were later translated into a series of books; some of the better-known titles include, "Seth Speaks, The Eternal Validity of the Soul," "The Nature of Personal Reality," and "The Unknown Reality." The range of topics covered in the Seth books is extensive and runs the gamut from Out of Body Travel to Life after Death, Biblical and Religious History; Astro Travel; E.T.s and UFOs; Other Dimensions of Existence; Parallel and Probable Selves; and the Behavior of Subatomic Particles.

While on the surface, many of Seth's revelations may appear as too in-depth and technical—thus not likely to be grasped with a quick read through, he wrote with a sharp sense of humor, frequently reminding the reader that things are literally, "only as complicated as we expect them to be." Throughout all the material, two main themes return again and again, specifically: "You create your own reality" and "You get what you focus upon." If you haven't already done so—as a starting point, I strongly suggest you pick up a copy of "Seth Speaks." Many of Seth's ideas were explained in simple terms in his earlier books, and only later did he give fuller, more intricate explanations. You would do yourself a disservice if you jumped into his later books without first having a basic understanding of these theories. In fact, over the years, I have given Seth Speaks as a gift to a few people, whenever I felt a friend was in need of spiritual guidance, or simply put, my "gut feeling" told me to do so. But neither I nor anyone I know has ever tried to force this information on someone else, or convert them over to Seth's teachings. Seth's information is not a religion, far from it; no "Seth dogma" exists. You do not need to worry about anyone trying to change who you are. Simply put, you cannot "change" until you are ready and most importantly, willing to do so. Out of mere curiosity however, here is a small teaser for what you might learn in the process.

"The intensity of a feeling or thought or mental image is, therefore, the important element in determining its subsequent physical materialization. If a man wants to change his fate, desire is not enough, but expectation is. Desire may grow into expectation, but alone is not enough. Expectation is actually the main trigger that switches inner data into the realm of physical construction. Without it, no physical construction can result."

"Expectation is then the force that triggers physic realities into physical construction. Expectations are formed by the emotions, then, it is obviously the basic emotions themselves that must be manipulated, since expectations are the frameworks formed by the emotions. This is the starting point. Emotional power behind your expectations, powers your expectations into physical reality. If you have faith in your inner-self and direct it to steer you through your physical existence, it will do so. If you concentrate upon difficulties, you will not allow it to do so." (Source: The Seth Material).

When understood, this is truly priceless information!

Now, one nice evening of about twenty years ago, I was having a conversation with a good friend of mine. Daniel and I exchanged views about the so-called "higher topics." At the time, AIDS was front-page news. The epidemic disease was on everyone's mind. I dared to suggest to Daniel that if we truly wanted to eradicate the disease—in my opinion, the best approach was to simply "stop talking about it!"

I was fully aware, of course, that at first examination this type of approach might have seemed senseless, even foolish. "How could I even suggest that," you might ask? "How could stop talking about a disease, make it go away?" My good friend Daniel, an unwavering J.W., dismissed the concept altogether, laughing it off. Twenty years later, this is what U.S. President Barack Obama speaking at a conference on AIDS, said:.

"U.S. President Barack Obama heralded the 'beginning of the end of AIDS' on Thursday as he renewed America's commitment to defeating the pandemic that has killed 30 million people. He said the world had come a long way from being unable

to imagine solving the crisis to talking about a 'theme of getting to zero.' Who could imagine we would be talking about the possibility of an AIDS-free generation, because that's what we are talking about,' he said at an address in Washington."

You might argue that billions have been spent on the disease and you would be right, but as you know, we have yet to find a cure. But then, what is finally ridding us of the disease? People's increasing disinterest, the un-focusing of our attention from the subject as a whole, that's what's going to eventually totally eradicate the disease! I fully realize that this seems to go against everything we know. We are conditioned to believe that the only way to defeat a disease is by taking medications—drug companies do not discourage that idea of course. But if we truly grasped how the process of "creating" works, we would also see that what we really need to do *if we wanted to defeat—not only AIDS, but every other disease*, is to "un-focus" from sickness and instead put our focus on becoming a healthy society. For it turns out that, "whatever you focus upon, you get more of."

One of my all-time heroes, Magic Johnson, a world-class athlete, has lived with the HIV virus since 1991. Well over two decades later, not only is he living a healthy lifestyle, but he is in a better frame of mind today than before he first learned about the illness. What Magic did, was to make the conscious decision that he was going to be stronger than the disease itself—and that he wasn't going to be defeated by it. He focused on being "healthy" not being sick! Conversely, what do you suppose would've happened if he had instead given up and confined himself to a hospital bed, feeling sorry for himself? Think about that.

Now, because AIDS is a "collective disease," a collective approach is needed. And although on a different "scale," the same principles also apply on a personal level. "Somatic" is the term doctors use to describe physical disorders that originate in the psyche. To better illustrate the process, below is an article taken from *http://patient.Info* (a medical website.)

'When mental factors such as stress cause physical symptoms the condition is known as somatization. Somatoform disorders are a severe form of somatization where physical symptoms can cause great distress. However, people with somatoform disorders are usually convinced that their symptoms have a physical cause.

—What is somatization? Somatization is when physical symptoms are caused by psychological or emotional factors. For example, many people have occasional headaches caused by mental stress. But, stress and other mental health problems can cause many other

physical symptoms such as: Chest pains, Tiredness, Dizziness, Back pain, and nausea.

*—**How can the mind cause physical symptoms?** The relationship between the mind and body is not fully understood. When we somatize, somehow the mental or emotional problem is expressed partly, or mainly, as one or more physical symptoms. However, the symptoms are real and are not imagined. You feel the pain; have the diarrhea and so on.*

*—**How common is somatization?** Very! Sometimes we can relate the physical symptoms to stress or a mental health problem. For example, you may realize that a bout of neck pain or headache is due to stress. Anxiety and depression are also common reasons to develop physical symptoms such as heart palpitations, aches and pains, etc. Often the physical symptoms go when emotional and mental factors ease. However, often we do not realize the physical symptom is due to a mental factor. We may think we have a physical disease and see a doctor about it.*

*—**Somatization and functional symptoms.** Doctors use the term "functional" when no known physical cause can be found for a symptom. A functional symptom means a function of the body is faulty for example, there may be pain or diarrhea but we don't know the cause. The cause may be due to mental factors (somatization), physical factors not yet discovered, or a combination of both. Another term that is sometimes used for such symptoms is "medically unexplained symptoms".*

To this point, allow me to tell you about two short personal episodes. The first, I was only a witness, as it happened to my aunt, and the second happened to me personally.

Several years ago, on a nice Sunday afternoon, my parents, my sister and I were invited to my uncle's home for dinner. My uncle's wife Maria had prepared a beautiful dinner for everyone including several types of pasta, entrees, desserts, and all the trimmings. She appeared to be in perfect health. I recall my Mother asking her how she was doing, and Maria replied that other than a minor stomachache, she had had for the last couple of days, she was actually doing very well.

"I am going to see my doctor tomorrow. It is probably something to do with my digestion," Maria said.

The next day we received a phone call from my uncle. Crying, he explained that his wife was found to have cancer in her stomach, which had spread so far throughout her organs in fact, that it was too late to do anything about it. Maria was given about six months to live. But tragically, the following day (Wednesday) Maria passed away. She died so suddenly and unexpectedly, leaving everyone in disbelief. How could someone appear to be in perfect health only three days earlier, be told they have cancer—and die immediately after, everyone wondered?

I am not disputing the fact that she would have died within months regardless, but a couple of questions have since lingered in my mind. Specifically, how could someone die so quickly upon learning they had cancer? Did she decide—realizing perhaps that she had no hope, to avoid going through all the pain and suffering caused by the breaking down of her body organs? But what's even more perplexing, I kept asking myself this question, "What would have happened if she hadn't gone to the doctor on that Monday morning, if she was never told that she had cancer?" Still today, I really wonder.

The second short story is a personal one. Twenty or so years ago, I asked my family doctor to perform a complete blood check. Now middle-aged I wanted to know if I needed to make any changes to my diet, vitamin deficiencies and so on. The doctor called me a couple of days later and said that he wanted to see me as soon as possible. Concerned I asked what was the urgency about, but he assured me that despite the urgency, there wasn't anything like cancer or the like, to worry about. So I went in the next day. He said that the tests had come back positive for Hepatitis-C. Unprepared, I asked him to elaborate.

He said that I most likely contracted the virus in the many blood transfusions I received after my accident decades earlier, but that he was surprised that it appeared to be totally asymptomatic—meaning, I did not show any signs of having it. And while it is true that someone can in some cases have Hepatitis-C for 10 or 15 years with no appreciable signs of the virus, in my case it was over thirty. He suggested we did some in-depth tests and go from there. So we did. The lab technician took several more vials of blood from my arm, and two days later the doctor called me again. I had once again tested positive for Hepatitis-C, he therefore made me an appointment with a blood specialist.

A month and several blood vials later, the blood specialist called me in. He confirmed what my family doctor had said all along. I did have Hepatitis-C he said, but he was also surprised that after so many years I didn't show any signs of having it. I asked him what I would have to do, and if I would have to change my diet or take medications. He informed me that unfortunately (at the time) no definite cure yet existed for Hepatitis-C, but that—just like my family doctor, he was very surprised that I did not show any signs of having it.

"I do not wish to alarm you however," he said, "but unfortunately hepatitis of the "C" type is the worst one can get, and basically untreatable (this was 1995.) You will most likely experience some difficulties in the near future," he concluded, "but we will manage it as needed. Start by taking these pills for now, and come back to see me in six months," he said, handing me three prescriptions.

This is going to sound strange, but while talking to both my family doctor as well as the specialist telling me what they had found, in my mind, it felt as if they were not talking about me—but someone else instead. It was as if we (the doctors and I) were talking about a totally different person altogether, if it makes any sense. In other words, there was a sense of total "detachment" from the subject. In plain English, I wanted nothing to do with it! But not out of fear, but out of pure "detachment," a decision I made—right there and then, wanting literally nothing to do with it. "It does not apply to me," I said, that simple!

So, prescriptions in hand, I sat in my car for a minute reexamining what I was just told. I knew what they had said, but in the end I reached a simple conclusion. If it were true that, unknown to me, I had the disease for thirty years, without any symptoms, then all I needed to do was to keep myself from knowing. Therefore, I made the mental decision that they couldn't possibly have been referring to me. Not that they had misdiagnosed me of course, but that they must've been talking about someone else all along. Even further, I instantly decided that this whole episode never happened! This whole day as a matter of fact, never took place, I told myself. I took the prescription and threw it in the garbage, and I totally and utterly forgot all about that incident.

About five years later, I was browsing in a store one day, when I met my family doctor. "How are you Marco he said, and by the way what did you do about your hepatitis" he asked?

"Well, I feel ashamed to admit it doctor," I said, "but I did nothing at all! As a matter of fact, I threw away the prescriptions the specialist gave me that day, and forgot about the whole incident."

"What Marco?!" He said somewhat irritated and visibly perplexed. "The specialist gave you a prescription for a reason. You are supposed to take those medications, or your condition will only get worse," he said. "Come to my office as soon as possible, we need to run some new tests immediately, to see how far has your hepatitis gone."

And so I went to see the doctor and he ran a whole new set of tests. The nice doctor called me back the next day, telling me that we needed to do another test as there was something wrong with the last one. So we repeated the tests again. A couple of days later he called me back and said that he wanted to see me. I went in, but this time, he had an even more perplexed look on his face. The doctor, plain and simply said that the hepatitis had completely vanished, so completely in fact that they could not even find a single trace of it. Totally gone!

"But how did you do it? What in the world happened here?" The doctor asked.

I don't know what happened" I said, "all I know is that when you told me about it back then, quite frankly and with all due respect, I did not believe you! Have you heard of the saying 'what you don't know won't hurt you?'" I asked him.

"I can't believe this," he said laughing. "Well, whatever you're doing, just keep on doing it! But don't forget to get checked again in a few years," he said.

"Why would I do that doctor, if there is absolutely nothing wrong with me?" I said.

"Whatever you say Marco," the doctor said, while shaking his head.

Fifteen years later, December 2015, as I needed to do some other tests, I asked my new family doctor to check for any signs of hepatitis. So, the good doctor checked not only for hepatitis, but also for antibodies—antibodies that (if you had the virus at any time in the past) are supposed to stay in your system for life. No trace of the virus, but even more strangely, no antibodies were found! And if you think I am surprised, I'm not, for based on what I've learned about the marvel that the Human Mind is, that's exactly what should've happened. But for the sake of the discussion, let's look at the other side of the coin for a moment. What do you think would've happened if I had instead started feeling sorry for myself and cocooned myself into a self-pitying, "I'm dying" mindset, and started taking medications, waiting for the illness to take its course? Do you think I would still be here writing this book today?

Here is a simple experiment you can try for yourself.

The next time you feel a mild headache coming on, focus on the pain and see what happens. Intentionally worry about the headache and tell everyone around you that you have a headache. I guarantee you, without doubt, that puny little headache will grow into a full-blown migraine, putting you out of commission for the day. But what do you suppose would happen if you did the exact opposite?

So the next time you feel a mild headache coming on, take a whole different approach to it. Simply dismiss it! Start singing your favorite song; watch something funny on TV, something that makes you laugh. Go out for a walk. I guarantee you that the headache will be gone in no time flat. It goes without saying that there is a physical side to it, namely that laughing and feeling happy in general, causes your body to produce so called "feel-good chemicals," such as Serotonin, Endorphins, etc.. But aside from that, would you like to know my little secret, a secret no doctor would ever recognize as factual, but that I know is the real reason why I've never had a single headache in my whole entire life?

As a child I saw my Mother experiencing daily paralyzing migraines. I can still see her contorting on the floor from the pain. One day, with my Mother in tears from the tremendous pain, feeling helpless, and out of fear perhaps, I walked into another room and uttered a simple statement. "I will never-ever have a headache," I said! Perhaps afraid to go through it myself, without realizing it, I must've formulated that simple statement in a way that precisely because of its simplicity and directness, it came out as a "command" of sorts, which obviously made a long-lasting impression onto my psyche. I cannot prove any of it of course, but what I do know is that at the age of 55 now, I still do not know what a headache feels like, even a hint of it. I simply have never had a headache in my life, period—finito!

How many times have you heard the saying "Watch what you wish for," or "Garbage in - garbage out," or "You are what you think" or even "You create your own reality?" The problem is that though commonly used, very few truly understand the meaning and implications. Fewer still put them to use. Most of us think of it as "too profound" and we proceed to sweep it under the proverbial carpet and mind the easier things in life. Constantly immersed in a seemingly infinite sea of negativity, bombarded from all sides, television, newspapers, coworkers, even our own friends and family, we all seem to be engaged in a competition of sorts, to see who can add more to that mountain of rubbish. Then, we go on complaining about how unfair life is, thus further reinforcing the idea. Not realizing, that the very action of complaining about what we do not want, is precisely what invites more of the same. We concentrate on negativity thus granting it more validity. We feel it physically. We attach emotions to it. This can only amplify it, making it ever more real. Allow me to propose a simple scenario if you will, to illustrate "how" this fascinating process works.

Imagine the following. A poor child, somewhere in a third world country, is only days away from succumbing to starvation. Because of the lack of food, the poor child is under a constant state of physical discomfort. Starving and with his tummy in pain, the poor child is unable to rest even at night. His brain is busy thinking about the food he does not have, hoping some good samaritan just might offer some much needed relief.

But what the child cannot possibly realize is that by so doing, he will unfortunately have to endure even more of that suffering, and likely perish from it. It may sound cruel, and it breaks my heart knowing that so many children are dying of starvation every day, but from a Universal-Creation standpoint, unknown to him, when concentrating on hunger—the symptoms of starvation and the resulting discomfort, the child is unfortunately inviting—not the relief, he so desperately needs, but more of that same desperate condition. And understandably so, without a doubt, the child's mother, who may also be experiencing much of that same anguish, represents—unknown to her, even more of a negative magnet than her child. For she is convinced—she is sure in fact that no one could possibly care about their unfortunate situation. Accustomed to the daily suffering, over time she has gradually come to accept that unfortunate condition as their way of life—their "destiny." Unaware, that by so doing she is in fact attracting even more of that same condition she is so desperately trying to avoid.

How could this be possible you ask? Later in the book, we will look at the mechanics of this fascinating all-powerful Universal law in detail, but in simpler terms, for now, let it suffice to say that:

There are certain Universal laws at play governing our existence!

In a nutshell, the Universe simply cannot decide for us—and neither can it discern between what is "good" and what is "bad" for us.

The Universe's only role is to give us what we focus upon, to manifest any   scenario we envision, and experience the consequences—good or bad regardless. There is no exception to this rule! For Earth is nothing more than a "Learning Play-Ground." We're here to experience conditions that simply put, we cannot experience in the realm we reside in as Souls. Thus, the Universe simply manifests whatever we focus upon, but it is not "what we verbally ask for" that it manifests, but instead what we mentally focus on. When you say, "I want food," you would think the Universe would give you food. But by saying "I want," you are implying that whether a minute—or a day from now, it is sometime in the "future" that you want that food. The problem is that the Universe cannot manifest something in terms of "future," as from a Universal standpoint; "Time" simply does not exist. The Universe always operates in terms of "now"—in-the-moment; thus, it interprets your request, not as you wanting that food, but as you being hungry now. Thus, it (the Universe) keeps you so.

The Universe responds in kind, by matching whatever frequency you focus upon, and delivers more of the same, in this case more hunger! It matters not whether the outcome is good or bad for you, the Universe does not question—nor second-guess your thoughts, as you always create your own experience, with no exceptions! The Universe's only purpose is to respond with the matching means or circumstances. Mostly without realizing it, we in fact do this continuously, not verbally but mentally. Each and every moment of our lives, we continuously manifest our thoughts outwardly into physicality. Though unaware, we do this by simply thinking of the next moment. Thus, moment-after-moment, the Universe simply complies, therefore manifests!

What we have just discussed here is but a short simplified introduction to the mechanics of physical manifestation. Of course, there is a lot more to the process. Later we shall revisit the subject in more detail. Just like grass under the soil awaiting one more drop of water to emerge above ground, so is our Physical Universe manufactured from a less dense, invisible to our eyes, "layer," residing in a slightly altered frequency.

The whole Universe is made of Intelligent Energy. Energy that accelerates or decelerates in oscillation accordingly, to make one object or a whole scenario appear more-or-less material, depending upon the layer of existence it resides in. But this most fascinating "building process," or more precisely, the "Transmutation of Energy into Matter," needed some kind of "Driving Force"—a common method of control, allowing it to work via a simple "unified blueprint." This is self-evidently true despite the infinite number of different probabilities. Our scientists are becoming more and more aware and accepting of this truth. As incredible as it may sound, the "driving force" that makes it all possible and makes the entire "energy-into-matter" process work, is, simply put, Thought!

On the surface, it is really as simple as that. It is, however, not a simple task to explain, much less understand the mechanics. "Thought" is the "method of control" the Creative Source sat in place when it *coincidentally,* first "thought" of the Universe. But not because it so decided, but because "thought" is the only "ingredient" one has at their disposal when "thinking" of building or creating anything! Hence, still now, we simply cannot make, build, or create anything, *no exception*, into physical manifestation, unless we first build it or create it in our mind! The more intense and focused the thought is, the faster it will manifest into physical reality. We can safely say in fact that:

"Thoughts are objects, waiting to become!"

We "create" by simply thinking of something. The Universe cannot bring anything forth into physical reality, without someone, somewhere first thinking about it. This is true both at the personal as well as in the "en-mass" collective level. Thus, you think you're getting sick—the Universe makes it so; you think you're getting better—the Universe makes it so. You think you are losing or gaining weight, buying a new car, losing or finding a job, or even losing or finding a mate… well, I am sure you get the idea.

But please pay attention to what I have just written, notice that I did not write, "You will get sick," "you will lose your job," or "you will gain weight," and so on. In all instances, what I wrote instead was, "you are!" In other words… *now!* Thus, unbeknownst to them, all that the poor child and his mother needed to do, was to envision—not the lack of food, but instead plenty of it before them. But here is the caveat. It is imperative that they do not "desire, hope, wish" for that food—that they do not envision it "coming" to them, but instead already in front of them. For again, desiring, hoping, wishing for something—or seeing it "coming" to them, tells the Universe that they do not yet have that food now, thus the Universe will keep it so, coming—but not quite! Essentially the Universe only understands and operates in the present, "now" tense. What they needed to do instead was to focus upon the sensation of actually eating that food. Taste the taste; imagine the feeling of fullness, having plenty of food to last them a lifetime—and the Universe grants them that experience! It has no choice!

The poor child and his mother couldn't possibly be aware of this universal truth, but that is truly all that was required of them in order to fulfill their wishes. The Universe has no limits and no mind of its own—because, <u>we are its mind!</u> Not only does it not discriminate, the Universe's only purpose is to respond in kind to our thoughts and grant our every wish. The child and his mother needn't worry about how, from whom, or where would the food manifest from, the greater forces at play would have figured that out. It would have inevitably found the way. It would have caused relief caravans to "accidentally" lose their way and "accidentally" stumble upon the needy mother and son. Aid organizations would have "accidentally" learned about them and sent them aid. Whatever it took to fulfill the child's—not "requests" (very important) but <u>present </u>"state of mind!"

The Universe is inherently interconnected, intertwined with our thoughts. Basically, it follows a blueprint from the Creator, and since we are not apart from, but a-part of—and inside the Creator, the <u>Universe must also follow our orders.</u> The Universe spends every moment in fact, reverberating to—matching and responding in kind to every living thing's state of mind. The Universe doesn't have a choice in the matter! For the Universe's purpose is to basically serve as a form of "warehouse" from where everything manifests. This is a directive, actually the main directive, from the Creative Source. This rule, this "Law," is <u>Creation itself</u>, and thus not optional.

Just as you and I are part of Creation, the child is also <u>part of</u> Creation, a spark from the Creative Source, thus part of the Creative Source. How then would the Universe dare not fulfill a wish from the Creator, when that is precisely the reason why it exists in the first place? Could the gasoline in your car's gas tank steer the car for you?

And thus the Universe's only purpose is "to fuel"—thus to obey, to manifest into the physical, anything and everything the Creative Source, and inherently His "Representatives"—us, wish to experience.

"Be kind whenever possible. It is always possible." ~

—Dalai Lama

Chapter 1

Our Current Address in Time

While it is quite normal for all children to be curious, as a child my curiosity went further than most. I always had an insatiable fascination with all things, especially anything of a scientific nature. Growing up, my curiosity simply grew exponentially. I was not satisfied for instance, with merely playing with a toy, or listening to the music coming out of the radio. The only way I could be really gratified with whatever happened to pique my interest, was to take it apart and study its insides, so that I could understand, *or at least pretend to*, its inner-workings, and then try to improve upon it. I had to make everything perform to its utmost potential, or I was not happy.

Take my electric train set for instance, which I got as a gift when I was nine and continued to enjoy well into my thirties. Not only did I love playing with it, I had to find ways to make the locomotives pull fifty or more cars, triple the normal amount. My friends could seldom win a race when playing against me on my electric slot-car set; as I had modified my cars so that they would always stay on the track without having to slow down in the curves. Over time, this earned me the title amongst my friends and relatives, of "the kid who could fix anything." Whenever they had something broken, for instance an appliance or a telephone, they would bring it over to me to fix.

My fascination was not that the blow dryer could blow hot air, but instead how it could generate that hot air. I wanted to know what each component was responsible for—and how they each interacted with the whole. I will never forget at the age of only three or four, the countless hours I spent in front of my grandma's old *GE* radio. Barely tall enough to reach the dial with my eyes, I spent days in front of it, my eyes glued into that illuminated dial convinced that I would eventually see little people singing and dancing to the music inside. One day our small kitchen TV broke down, so naturally I volunteered to fix it. We had just watched a show with Marilyn Monroe and Dean Martin, so I was sure they were still in there. I quickly disassembled the TV, but darn it, to my disappointment they had already left.

I enjoyed taking things apart and studying their inner details, for I was convinced that the outer was always in strict correlation—an external expression of what went on inside. As I learned later in life, this is not true only for gadgets and appliances.

Constantly experimenting, I had read that baking soda made an excellent tooth cleaner. Somewhere else I read that lemon juice was an excellent stain remover. The genius in me automatically kicked-in. If these two ingredients were good on their own I reasoned, why not combine them together? And so I did. I poured two spoonsful of baking soda and half a cup of lemon juice in an empty plastic soda bottle.

Nothing happened at first. I screwed the cap on the bottle and shook it to mix the ingredients. But as I loosened the cap half way, the bottle just exploded. We had suds all over the floor, walls and appliances and even on the ceiling. Needless to say, my Mother was not very impressed.

However, the thing I wanted the most as a child was a microscope. Back then they were quite expensive, so my Father promised me that as long as I saved my weekly allowance and helped my Mother around the house he would buy me one. The day finally came when I had put enough money aside. I was seven at the time; I waited the whole day for my Father to come home and take me to the store. But I had underestimated my Father; he came home with a microscope. And when I gave him the money, he said that I could buy the second thing I wanted the most, a chemistry set. I was in heaven!

I spent countless hours looking into that microscope, analyzing—if only in my mind, everything I could find, a drop of water, a strand of my Mother's hair. I even pierced my little sister's finger with a needle so that I could analyze a drop of her blood. I didn't have a clue what I was looking for, but I kept on looking! I did very well in school. My teachers couldn't decide whether I was going to become a mechanic or a scientist. Today I am a little of both.

But I must confess that growing up I felt a bit different from my peers, as I didn't share most of their interests. At schoolyard time for instance, while they played soccer, I preferred staying aside studying a tree and the intricate lineage of its bark, or observing an ant carrying a piece of bread four times its size, or a flock of birds flying overhead.

And I spent countless hours looking at the shape-shifting clouds in the sky. I had an insatiable thirst for knowledge. Constantly looking for new things to learn, new things to explore. Science, Geography, and History were my preferred subjects, in that order.

Then one day, at age twelve, getting out of school, I was the victim of a terrible automobile accident. A car, taking a curve at high speed, lost control and rolled over three times, ending up upside down, trapping me beneath it.

I almost lost my life in that accident, and as I found out later—if only briefly, I actually died. I suffered many bone fractures in that accident—my legs especially. As a result, I had to endure several major reconstructive operations so that I could regain the use of my legs. However, as I found out over a decade later, that accident turned out to be far more significant than I could have ever imagined. For it was undoubtedly the starting point—what gave birth to this whole adventure of mine, and even more importantly this very book.

February 28th, 1972. My family and I lived on the third floor of a building, and as I did every morning, I raced down the stairs so that I could catch the school bus outside. But something very peculiar happened that morning. My Aunt Josephine, who lived on the floor below us, was out of her suite sweeping the stairs.

"Good morning Aunt," I yelled racing past her.

"Stop, I must tell you something," she replied back.

"What is it?" I asked.

"Be very careful today," she said.

"Why?" I asked.

"Because I had a very bad dream last night, and I know that these types of dreams are a bad omen, something very bad is going to happen today. I do not know to whom, but I know that something terrible will happen to someone in our family today." She said.

"Sure Aunt, I'll be careful," I said. I ran out of the building and I immediately forgot every word she said. Then at 2:20 that afternoon, the terrible accident happened.

Our Phys-Ed. teacher had taken our class to a running track nearby the school. When finished, getting out of the facility, we all lined up in a single line to walk back to the school. I wanted to drink a little water, so I stopped at the fountain just inside the gate for a moment. As I exited the gate and sped up a bit to catch up with my class, similar to what you would hear in a movie in a police chase scene, coming from behind me, I heard the loud noise of a revved up car engine and screeching tires. Instinctively, we all stopped and turned toward the source of the noise. In amazement, I saw a yellow midsize car, about fifty meters behind us, travelling at an incredible rate of speed (120 Km/Hr. in a 50 Km zone the police said). It was a one-way street around a soccer stadium and the car was travelling on two wheels. At first the car appeared destined to hit a cyclist on the opposite side from us. As far as we could tell—and especially because it was a very wide street, we could never have imagined what took place next.

In an attempt, I suppose, to avoid the cyclist, the driver of the car decided to steer abruptly to his right. This caused the vehicle to not only do a 180 degree turn, but to also—because of the high rate of speed, roll over on its side, not once but three times. And while rolling, it was coming straight for me. It all happened very fast. I had nowhere to go but back. Instinctively, I went as far back as I could, until my back stopped against a chain-link fence. If it weren't for the few feet between the rest of the class and me, several of us would have been caught under the rolling vehicle.

I am sure that just as I have, you've probably heard this before. It would appear that when you're about to perish, the passage of time slows down. From the moment I turned around and saw the car on two wheels, until the time when the car started rolling on its side towards me, "time" was perfectly normal, as a matter of fact it all happened very fast. But as the car—still rolling on its side, while flying in midair—got closer and closer to me, as if in a slow-motion movie, time suddenly slowed down. And as if in an old black and white mute movie, all colors and sounds also disappeared. I saw the car suspended upside-down in midair and only a foot and less than a second from crushing me, but from my perspective it felt more like thirty seconds before it made contact with me. As if held by invisible wires and in incredible detail, I saw the car suspended in midair—inching ever closer and closer to me.

The roof of the car now a few inches away from my chest, I instinctively pushed back as hard as I could, but the chain-link fence was as far as I could go. The roof of the car now against my chest, I took a last deep breath and then, as the full weight of the vehicle pushed me and the fence, flat down on the asphalt, I felt a tremendous downward crushing sensation. With the fence under me, I was now flat on the ground, pinned under the full weight of the overturned vehicle.

It didn't feel real; it really felt as if it were a dream. I laid flat on the ground, the upside-down car on top of me, covering my entire body, except my head. From my perspective everything was still happening in slow motion. I will never forget how the car windshield—as if made of rubber, popped out of its frame and slowly flew twenty feet up in the air, to then come down crashing onto the asphalt immediately to my left, exploding in what resembled a silvery shower of hundreds of slow moving sparkling glass fragments, many of which imbedded themselves on my head. It is difficult to describe, but because of the extreme slow motion, I could see all of this in every minute detail.

Then, in a sudden explosion of sounds and colors, everything and "time" itself, returned to normal. I was incredibly confused. Having no idea of what had just happened, all I could hear was a loud buzz-like sound inside my head, mixed with the frantic muffled voices of dozens of people around me. The car engine still revving while still upside-down and on top of me, I lost consciousness, and then regained it again, but something strange happened. While my body was still under the car, "I" was not.

I could not believe my eyes; I could not understand why there where now two of me. I could distinctively see my body under the overturned vehicle, but I—the "thinking me" was floating in midair, at what I would estimate 25 feet from the ground. I saw several folks literally grab and lift the car off me, and then still upside-down; they sat it down on the pavement a few feet from me. A man reached inside a broken side window to shut the engine off, then with the dazed driver still inside, they rolled the vehicle over right-side-up. A man, witnessing how fast he was driving, grabbed and pulled him out of the car. Then he started yelling at him, "What are you doing speeding like a maniac, are you crazy?"

With the car now off me, from above, I could see my lifeless body on the ground. It all felt very strange. Not only could I see myself, but also the top of dozens of people's heads as they all gathered around. Two middle-aged ladies directly beneath me cried for me. "Povero bambino, penso che e` morto," (poor child, I think he's dead) one said.

Confused and overwhelmed, I could not believe what was happening. I looked down toward my feet and noticed that I—the "me" up there, appeared to be made of a cloudy whitish substance, like dense smoke. I could only see my body down to about my stomach; from there down was an undefined smoky silhouette. Unable to make sense of it, I redirected my attention toward my physical body on the ground. It appeared lifeless and flattened—as if by a paving steamroller machine. From the downward pressure, my brown corduroy pants had busted at the seams. And protruding from the sides and through the ripped pants, I could see both my white femoral bones. My teacher kneeled next to me holding my head in his hands; and while crying profusely, he gently slapped my face trying to revive me.

Overwhelmed, and trying to make sense of what I was seeing, I simply did not know what to do. Then, I heard a siren; it was the ambulance racing toward the scene of the accident. Because of the height I was hovering at, I could see the ambulance coming from at least a kilometer away. By now, a hundred or so people had gathered around; they all moved aside so that the ambulance could stop closer. Two paramedics placed my lifeless body on a stretcher and then into the ambulance. My teacher sat next to me in the ambulance. The paramedics closed the back doors, turned the siren back on and left for the nearest hospital.

And as the ambulance sped farther and farther away from the scene of the accident, I didn't know what to do at first, but as it almost disappeared from sight, I felt as if I had to make an urgent decision of sorts. I had to decide between staying there where I was, or rejoin my body as it sped away in the ambulance. This is difficult to explain, but it felt as if—had I allowed the ambulance to get out of sight—I would have lost the ability to rejoin with my body.

It was really not a conscious decision, it just seemed the logical thing to do, and so I elected to go with my body, and I instantly found myself inside it. The strange thing was that for a few short seconds it felt as if I was inside my body—but not one with it, but still separated from it. I could see the ambulance's interior from inside my body, but not through my regular "eyes" as I should have. If you have never experienced anything similar, this can be difficult to visualize. Allow me to clarify it a bit further.

Suppose you're inside a large cardboard box, and so that you can look outside you make a hole on its side. That's what it felt like! Though only for a second, it felt as if I was inside—but not one, with my body. As if my body was a shell. Then a second later, my body and I suddenly became one, and I was now fully aware of my surroundings. However, I wished I hadn't done so because being one with my body meant only one thing; I could now feel all of the excruciating pain, in all of its glory. All I could do was scream at the top of my lungs.

A short while later we arrived at the hospital. Two male doctors and a female nurse attended to my mangled body. The nurse stood at the head of the stretcher, while a doctor cut open what was left of my pants. They then painted my legs in yellow iodine tincture and drilled long rods on the sides of both my knees. My eyes are tearing up as I am writing this, for it brings back very painful memories. I remember screaming until I could no longer scream. The nurse held my head while gently caressing my face. I will never forget the way she looked at me. Her eyes filled with love and compassion, she looked into my eyes without saying a single word, but I could see it in her eyes that she could feel my pain. Then something very strange happened. Suddenly I felt as if I had once again separated from my body. I was still there, fully aware of my surroundings. I could hear the noise of the drill, I could still feel the doctors drilling my legs and the puncturing of the rods as they passed through my knees, but the pain was gone, as if I had once again disconnected from my body somehow. And that's when the nurse walked out of the room.

They kept me in the emergency room for about twenty minutes to stabilize me. Then one of the doctors came back and asked me how I was doing. "I feel terrible, but please do not let my Mother know about what happened," I said. The good doctor smiled. He said that he was going to have someone push my bed into a semiprivate room. I asked him if the blonde nurse could come back in to see me.

"What blonde nurse?" Asked the doctor.

"The blonde nurse who was here before," I said.

"Before... when?" The perplexed doctor asked.

"When you were drilling into my legs," I said.

"But there never was a female nurse in the room with us, it was just me and the other male doctor," he replied perplexed.

And so they pushed my stretcher into a semiprivate room, and transferred me onto a special bed with all sorts of pulleys and wires attached to it. I needed to stay in "traction" for 15 days they said. In the meantime, the doctors had informed my parents that they would do whatever possible to save them, but because of the many fractures, they feared that they would have to amputate at least one, possibly both legs.

Two very long and painful weeks went by. Then the day before my first surgery, a group of doctors and nurses came to see me for a pre-surgery assessment. They left ten minutes later, but as soon as they got out in the corridor they got into what sounded like an argument. Then, with their voices getting louder and louder, a nurse walked back into my room and asked my scared Mother—who had been there by my side fifteen straight days and nights—to come talk to the doctors in the corridor.

Five minutes later my Mother came back in, but her eyes were filled with tears. She didn't want to say anything, but I insisted that she told me what they had just discussed. She had to sign papers exonerating the hospital from any liability, should they—during the course of the complicated nine-hour operation—have to amputate my legs.

"But why were they arguing," I asked.

"Because your femoral bones are totally crushed, the orthopedic surgeon in chief has already decided to amputate your legs," she said, "while the other (second in command) doctor, wants to try a new procedure first," my mother said.

A normal routine today, the procedure consisted of making a metal casing and securing it onto the good upper and lower ends of the crashed femurs. Then, almost like in a puzzle, they would arrange the bone fragments inside the casing as best as they could. The theory was (and it was right) that the bone fragments would naturally seek to rejoin and grow towards one another, forming eventually, new bone where the gaps once were. Then three years later they would surgically remove the metal casing. The orthopedic surgeon in chief yelled, because he felt challenged by a subordinate. He reluctantly approved the new procedure, but he refused to perform it himself, and as he put it, he "washed his hands of the whole thing."

Scared to death, envisioning a life of challenges without my legs, I was speechless listening to my Mother. Then suddenly something incredible happened. A gigantic ball of light entered from the window to my far right. Not knowing what it was, I thought the sun was playing a light trick through the window, but my window faced north, and therefore it couldn't possibly be the sun. In over two weeks there, nothing like that had happened before. The gigantic gold colored ball resembled a huge ball of fuzzy cotton candy. It slowly came floating from the window, hovering over the empty bed to my right, to then stop in midair directly above my bed. The room had a very high ceiling; the ball measured what I would estimate at least two meters in diameter. Not transparent enough for me to see through it, but it truly reminded me of a big cotton candy ball.

In amazement and a little worried, while pointing at it, I asked my

Mother if she could also see it.

"Mom," I asked, "what is that?"

"What is what?" She said.

"The ball… what is this big ball of light over me?"

She turned in the direction I was pointing to, "I cannot see anything," she said.

That was when I realized that I was the only one who was meant to see that beautiful vision. A calming—warm, loving wave came over me. I felt at ease and relaxed. As if by magic the fear of losing my legs had vanished.

"Mom, don't worry, everything is going to be fine. They won't amputate my legs," I said.

"How do you know that?" My mom asked crying?

"I don't know how, I just know," I said.

"Let's pray to God that you're right," said my mom.

Then the gigantic ball of light started to slowly dissolve, until it completely vanished.

Today I couldn't thank that orthopedic surgeon enough; if it were not for his determination; going against a direct order from a superior, I would most likely not have my legs today.

I actually called the brave Doctor to thank him the other day, he immediately remembered me. He is now 97 and he was very happy to hear from me after 42 years.

And as a point of interest, although I have no way to know if there was any connection or if it was just another coincidence. A few days after my surgery, the chief orthopedic surgeon who wanted to amputate my legs got transferred to another city. And the doctor, who instead performed my operation and saved my legs, was promoted to the top position.

I do not hold any grudges toward that doctor who had already decided to amputate my legs without first trying to save them, but I often wonder if he would have done the same, had it been his own son in my place.

"All great changes are preceded by chaos." ~

—Deepak Chopra.

Chapter 2

Looking Back

Where did we come from? I mean, really come from?

Wanting to explore the higher questions is a universal human trait. But far too many folks are too busy trying to make ends-meet and can rarely afford the luxury of contemplating life's higher questions.

Traditional doctrines and an endless number of translations and reinterpretations have all contributed to a substantial distortion of the original information, to such a degree, that today it can be very difficult to discern between what is fact and what is fiction, and what out of sheer convenience, was purposely added along the way. Thus, over the course of many centuries, a parallel corresponding belief system developed and readjusted repeatedly, to mirror whatever the most popular belief system was—or needed to be, at any given time throughout history. Whatever the case may be, it is a system we've nevertheless accepted as valid. We've learned, or better yet, we've been indoctrinated over the centuries, not to "question" and just accept as valid, whatever modality <u>was in fashion at any given time.</u>

A few years ago, I went back to my native country of Italy to visit my family. One afternoon my Mother and I were talking about "religion," when my 95 years old Grandmother walked into the room. Overhearing the conversation, she intervened saying "Of course we know who God is. We even know what He looks like! Let me show you!" And so she went downstairs to her suite and came back with a large illustration of Jesus. Near the bottom of the picture there was an inscription, *"Our Lord and Savior."*

You probably think this was a single case of a confused 95 years old woman who's no longer able to differentiate between God and Jesus, but you'd be surprised how many folks are in the same boat as my dear Grandmother. Most people believe in fact that the two are one and the same. And even most preachers, not only do they have a difficult time deciding where to draw the line themselves, where in other words one ends and the other begins, but they further confuse the masses by habitually referring to Jesus as "Our Lord," or "King," titles usually reserved to address the highest and most supreme. Ask a few of the people you know, and you would most likely discover (mostly because of the so called "trinity" story) that two out of four, believe that Jesus and God are one and the same, or at the very least, part of the same "Trinity Family."

When taking such a simplistic approach, we inevitably end up missing the larger scope. In human terms, Jesus was simply one of many Messengers—with a lot of wisdom and a mission to fulfill. While the main purpose of the "God concept," has instead always been to represent an effort to understand the greater Universe. And throughout history, hundreds upon hundreds of "gods" and "deities" have been adopted, each hatching a corresponding following—hence "religion." Thus, when we assume that the present post-Roman Empire idea of a God is the one that was always used, or even worse "the only real one," we once again fall prey to egotism and arrogance. What about other pre-Roman Empire civilizations? How could they have possibly known? What about the many jungle tribes who have yet to meet anyone outside of their own circle? What about the Mayans, the Aztecs, the Incas, or the ancient Egyptians? What did their god, or gods, look like?

Of course, we could always say that God and the Universe, is one and the same—and I would agree to a degree, but not so fast however, for it is not as clear-cut as that. Not so fast because of one very important reason. It has all to do with "which God you're referring to."

If you're referring to the God—who spends his days sitting on a cloud punishing or rewarding folks, that's one thing, but if you're referring to the "Source-God," then that God is much, much more than just the Universe. For as magnificent as the Universe may be, it falls far short from giving us an adequate description of the "Source-God, All-That-Is. It would be much the same as stating that the "Monna Lisa" (*not "Mona" as it is normally spelled*), represents Leonardo. A magnificent work of art indeed, but far from describing the artist, the creator.

Now, while it is true that I've done a lot of research—that alone does not make me an expert. But let me ask you this question: What is an expert? Does one become an expert, just because they've been studying the same wrong information for a hundred years? If the topic at hand were, say "Geology," then I would agree that we could call someone who's been studying that specific branch more than most— an expert. But when it comes to the true nature of the Universe, how does one become an expert—if the information they've been studying and the tools they've been using were wrong in the first place? Having a diploma on the wall does not help much either. So if you happen to believe that only those with the diplomas are qualified to discuss the higher questions, I suggest you think again, for studying geology is one thing, but if the Universe is what you want to understand, then the real certifications you need are: an open mind and an open heart. And no university can teach you that!

We all know who Einstein was. To date he is still revered as the greatest mind that ever lived. There is no doubt he contributed greatly to science, but while he received many accolades, do you believe he achieved—what he achieved because of the many diplomas he had, or simply because of "who" he was—with or without the diplomas? And interestingly, if you did a little research, you'd find that instead the opposite is often true. True geniuses like Einstein, Tesla, Volta, Marconi, DaVinci, Galileo and Fermi, just to name a few, made the most groundbreaking discoveries, simply because of who they were, regardless of whether or not they had any diplomas.

Now, as we saw earlier, laying a proper foundation is not only the first—but also the most important step in any endeavor—be it writing a book or building a tower. Thus, as you may have noticed, up until this point in the book we've been busy laying if you will—the "groundwork." This was done intentionally, a necessary step, so that a starting point, a "provenance" could be established and then built upon. Then move onward from there, before we addressed the larger subjects.

Earlier in the book we talked about Seth, the Spirit Guide and driving force behind this work. Without his input, this book would never have existed. And although I have no way to know where you stand on these issues, it would be safe to assume that, *knowing that nothing happens by accident,* if you are reading a book of this genre, chances are that you are a fairly open minded individual. Thus, as mentioned, in my mid-'20s I was on the receiving end of a seven years long interaction with Seth. Seven years, followed by another twenty-plus years of mind breaking research. The thousands of hours researching the Internet, reading dozens of books, and watching dozens of TV and YouTube documentaries, in the end, all culminated into an enormous amount of information, which I simply could not keep for myself. Simply put, I had to get it out of my brain, and although in a much-condensed fashion, here in this book, I am sharing with you the reader, what I have learned throughout that process. Basically,

Seth would deliver information, or show me a given scenario—usually in a "dream session," the rest was then up to me. To satisfy my own doubts however, *for believe it or not I am also a human*, but mostly to make sure that Seth was not—bluntly put, "wasting my time," after each session, I tried my best to find anything that could disprove what he was delivering each time. However, time and time again, I would instead end up finding mountains of corroborating material, further reinforcing his messages. And before going into more details about my encounters with Seth, allow me to give you a better understanding of the Seth Personality.

The Seth I interacted with for about seven years *back in the '90s*, looked similar—identical in fact, to the Seth Jane Roberts and her husband Robert Butts interacted with back in the '70s. A man in his mid-seventies, he did not walk, but he instead appeared to "float" at about a foot off the ground, thus, it was difficult to tell his actual height, but I would estimate about five and a half feet tall. Though he appeared to be semi-transparent—meaning that I could see right through him, I could clearly see him. He usually dressed in plain beige pants, and a red and white-checkered logger's style shirt. Seth was quite a character, full of wit but very concise and to the point. Each of his sentences had the meaning of a thousand books—and frankly, I could not keep up with him; he was always one step, *or several*, ahead of me. He was pure experience and knowledge, he could see through me, he could read my mind, and he knew what I was going to say before I could say it. Whenever I asked him a question, the answer would magically appear in my mind, in most cases before I had a chance to start talking. To better illustrate a point, he would orchestrate "scenarios" that when analyzed later, contained answers and clues to multiple questions, answering not one, but two or three questions at once.

In most instances, Seth appeared to me as a "teacher" in a classroom setting, complete with desks and a chalkboard on the wall, on which he wrote information and made drawings. And in some of the encounters Seth took the role of a "tour guide." In most cases I would be the "spectator," meaning—as if watching a movie where I was the main actor in, I observed the other "me" in the scene. Each time however, the "me" in the movie would look completely different than the "me here," but strangely I was instinctively aware that the individual in the movie was also me. Seth would in most cases position himself to my side and slightly behind me, from where I could hear his voice narrating the unfolding scene. This is by the way, how I learned of—and was shown several of my other incarnations.

Now, as you may know, back in the '70s Seth was the driving force behind several books authored by Jane (Roberts) and her husband Robert (Butts.) With Jane in a trance state, Seth channeled the material through her, while her husband took notes. Their combined efforts resulted in dozens of books. Both Jane and Rob have since passed. The peculiar thing is that together with Seth, Jane also appeared in at least two of our meetings. In that environment Seth referred to Jane as his wife, but interestingly—he called her "Ruburt." As some of you may recall from the Seth books, Jane was a friend of Seth's in another life and in that life Jane was a man named Ruburt, hence the name. In one encounter (which I will better describe later in the book) Jane and I had a fairly lengthy interaction. And what she repeated again and again, while staring straight into my eyes, was to "Make sure I made what I knew, available to others."

Now, in all honesty, at first I was not sure of what to make of all this. Before, I had always been strongly opposed to anything about the supernatural. I remember it as if it were yesterday, when my sister asked my opinion about a ghost documentary they were airing on TV. As I had to go to work to make a living every day, I had always been more interested in what I considered "Earthlier matters." "It's not that I don't believe in ghosts," I said, "but since I am not planning to get involved with that subject anytime soon, it is best for me not to comment on what I do not know." Little did I know that not only was I shortly after, going to embark on a lifelong exploration of the so called "Spirit World," but I would also now be the one who asked others to talk about the subject.

When it came to ghosts and the like, I believed them to be nothing more than a figment of the imagination. This was further reinforced when Seth first appeared in my dreams—dreams I was sure I was having as a result of reading, "Seth Speaks," a book my friend Thomas had given me. But as the dreams became more and more compelling, I had to accept the fact that these were not dreams of the conventional type. Totally different from the usual dreams we're all accustomed to. While there, I was fully aware of the fact that I was not only in the dream but also asleep in my bed, here on this side—thing which you certainly do not experience in a conventional type dream. Therefore, I understand if some of you may find this information difficult to believe. Keep in mind that up to a short time before my interactions with Seth started, I too did not believe it, until it happened to me! I also agree that having a Spirit talking to you in your dreams is uncommon to say the least. The fact remains however that what I am writing here is nothing but the truth. I am simply sharing my experience with you, and what I have learned in the process, unchanged. But I also know that those among you who have had similar experiences will fully and truly understand.

Several years back, in an attempt I suppose, to validate what was taking place, I decided to contact Robert Butts (Jane's husband) and ask for his opinion. I was aware that in so doing I was taking a big risk as I could not do so without mentioning his departed wife, thus I had no way of knowing how he would react. I didn't even know if he was still involved with the Seth material, and the last thing I wanted to do was to sadden him in any way. But in the end, I felt that I had no choice, I had to know where I stood—and because of his lengthy involvement with Seth, he was the only qualified living person who could unequivocally clarify things for me. I needed him to tell me whether these two entities (Seth, and his wife Jane) were really who they claimed to be. So after some research I managed to find his address. I sent him a long detailed letter describing my experience.

I also sent him drawings that I had made after each encounter. His wife Jane was portrayed in at least two of them, I portrayed her as close as I could remember, her appearance and the way she dressed, even the way she moved and talked. I put the long letter and the drawings in an envelope and sent it to him. Here is a verbatim transcript of my letter to him.

Dear Robert. Allow me to first express my gratitude for taking the time to read my letter. I hope it finds you in good health. I am not sure if you are still involved with the "Seth experience," thus I have no way to know how you will react to what I am about to share with you. It is certainly not my intention to sadden or upset you in any way, and I hope that you will instead welcome this information.

About two years ago, a friend gave me a book you and your wife Jane wrote, "Seth Speaks" as a gift. Oddly however, as soon as I started reading the book, I felt a strange sensation, as if I somehow belonged in it. This is difficult to explain, but I felt as if what I was reading were preparing me for something bigger. Shortly thereafter, I had my very first encounter with Seth.

He appeared to me in a dream, as he has done many times since. Naturally, at first I was skeptical about the authenticity of these encounters; for I was sure the book itself triggered the dreams. But as they became more and more involving, I had to conclude that something of significance was taking place. Seth was not only answering many of my personal questions, but he was also sharing information of a seemingly "pseudo-scientific" nature. This still continues today.

The dreams resemble "lessons." Most take place in a classroom complete with blackboard and desks. I am the student, while Seth appears to be the teacher. I see the whole scenario from a spectator's perspective, meaning that I am not only in the scene, but also a spectator, like watching a movie in which you are the main actor. Seth appears to be semitransparent, I can see through him, but strangely I can see the color of his clothes. Seth appears to be about seventy-five, he does not walk but he floats instead, about a foot off the ground. One thing I have noticed lately is that since these encounters started, I am no longer having dreams of the regular kind, or if I do, I am somehow unable to recall a single one of them. I've also noticed that just before I go to sleep, a sense of relaxation and peacefulness comes over me, but also a sense of excitement, like a rush of energy, suggesting that I am somehow being readied for the encounter.

The "lessons" are concise and to the point. If there were a way to time them, I would estimate they lasted about half an hour. Interestingly, they often convey messages answering several questions at a time, suggesting that it must be difficult not only to establish, but also maintain a link between the two realities for long periods of time. While I have made sketches of some of the dreams (in case I forgot) - for some reason, these encounters remain impressed in my mind in their entirety. I very clearly remember every word spoken and every detail. And with some uneasiness I must confess, I should also mention that your wife Jane also appeared on three occasions. There, Seth introduced her as "his wife Ruburt." There, Jane appeared to be about 65 years of age, long black hair, and of a petite build. The first time she appeared was only in a symbolic way, but in subsequent instances, Jane played a major role. And, with your permission, I would like to share these with you.

The scenario started with me driving my red sports car on the highway. My car needed fuel, so I pulled into the first gas station. Almost immediately, I noticed something peculiar about the facility; it appeared as an old 1920s style enterprise, a stark contrast with the very modern high-tech highway I had just been on, complete with L.E.D. signage and all. Nevertheless, I pulled up at one of the pumps and asked the gas attendant to fill up my tank. I got out of the car and stood leaning on its side for a minute, when coming from behind me, I heard what appeared to be two female voices. I turned toward the voices but I could only see one woman walking toward us.

And judging from the way the woman interacted with the gas attendant and as he later confirmed, I concluded she must've been his wife. The woman stood to my left, he to my right. I was in the middle of the two, as they kept talking back and forth. Then it occurred to me that I could hear a third voice partaking in the conversation, another female voice to be exact. Intrigued, I looked around, but I could not make out where that third voice was coming from, then much to my surprise I saw what appeared to be a "light form" of some type, hovering about four feet from the ground and that was where that third voice appeared to originate from. It was a very strange sight indeed, oval in shape but with no defined edges, about two feet wide by three feet high, but flat like a sheet, with no depth. It was of a milky transparency with a bright shimmering look to it. It reminded me of the shimmering mirage-like effect you sometimes see far in front of you when travelling on a highway in a hot summer day. It honestly startled me.

Noticing my uneasiness, "don't worry," said the gas attendant, "that's my wife's friend," he reassured me. Then, he politely introduced me to his wife, but strangely enough he introduced her as "Ruburt." I turned a bit to shake her hand, but as she raised her eyes and looked at me, she jumped back as if surprised. Then with wide-open eyes and still holding my hand, she said loudly: "Oh my God!"

"What is it?" I asked.

Still holding my hand, and this time a lot louder, she again said: "Oh my God!"

I did not know what she'd seen, and frankly, at this point I thought she was missing a screw upstairs and I couldn't wait to get out of there, but since she wouldn't let go of my hand and a bit curious I must confess, I asked her to explain. She came so close to me I thought she was going to give me an eye exam. Her black intensely penetrating eyes pierced through my eyes reading my mind through them. I felt as if I could hide nothing from her.

Then still looking into my eyes she said: "You have the Universe in your eyes! I can see the whole Universe in your eyes!"

This was when I really thought she was going berserk, but out of curiosity I asked her to elaborate.

"Come with me," she said while pulling my hand in the direction of a small house on the premises.

Everything was happening so fast, that I could not understand what was going on. I looked at her husband but with a smile he reassured me: "don't worry, go with her while I take care of your car," he said. Before I knew it, the woman, Mrs. Light-thing, and I, were inside the house.

The small room resembled a chemistry lab. There were stacks of books everywhere and a table with several chemists' tools on it. Then the woman put a chair in the middle of the room and asked me to sit. I asked her for an explanation, I wanted to know what was going on and most importantly what she intended to do. This time, with a very calm and reassuring voice, she said that she wanted to do a small experiment.

"What?" I said almost angrily.

"Lady, you must be mistaken, who do you think I am? I just wanted to get fuel in my car, when you pulled me in here without any explanation, and now you want to do an experiment on me? I don't even know you, I am walking out of here right this instant."

She smiled and reassured me that I had nothing to fear. She said that she was not even going to touch me. Still floating in midair, Mrs. "Light-thing" also tried to reassure me saying that it was not going to hurt. "How would you know when you don't even have a body?" I said.

Politely the woman asked me to please sit in the chair. I don't know why, but I did not feel in any danger. While very "unusual" and eccentric to say the least, I at the same time felt that I could totally trust her. I complied.

She asked me to cross my arms. She was going to put on me a set of what she called "invisible mental handcuffs," she said, and she reassured me that it was not going to hurt at all.

So I did. I crossed my arms in front of my chest. While standing at about three feet in front of me she looked down to my arms. She then tilted her head down once, as if sending out some sort of mental message.

Then she asked: "Can you move your arms?"

"Of course," I said, pulling my arms apart.

She was going to try again she said. Only this time, she was going to try at twice the power. So I crossed my arms again, and again she did the same thing as before, only this time she nodded her head twice.

"Can you move your arms now," She asked.

"Of course I can," I said, pulling my arms apart once again.

"Ok," she said, "I am going to try one last time, and I am going to use all of my power, but I am afraid I already know what the outcome will be," she said.

We tried again, only this time she nodded her head three times. Then she asked if I could move my arms. It felt slightly different this time I must say—a very light resistance similar to having a weak rubber band wrapped around my arms, but as I tried a little harder the resistance simply vanished. I stood up. I had enough of this game.

Standing in front of me with her hands on either side of my arms, and while looking straight into my eyes she said: "Marco, pay attention to what I am about to tell you. You have the Universe in your eyes!"

I asked her to be more specific. "What do you mean by 'The Universe in my eyes,' what do you see in my eyes exactly?'" I asked.

The tone of her voice changed, she now sounded very serious. Then she said: "Marco, I see everything in your eyes! You have been gifted with ultimate knowledge. An amount of information not even you are yet aware of. Just make sure it doesn't go to waste. Put it to good use, people need to know what you know. Just remember, nothing can stop you, not even I could!"

She paused for a second, and then she said again: "Do not forget Marco, nothing can stop you!"

I didn't ask any more questions; I somehow instinctively knew what she was trying to tell me. I walked out; standing next to my car, the gas attendant was waiting for me. As he handed me my keys, he smiled. Now I recognized him. Seth!

To my total surprise, two weeks later I received Robert's reply. Not only had he replied, but contrary to what I expected he didn't sound upset in the least, and even more importantly, he had acknowledged that the woman I had met in the encounters was indeed his wife. Here is a verbatim copy of Robert's reply letter to me.

March 2, 1994. Dear Marco: Re: Your most remarkable dreams, to me the most remarkable of all is the long one involving drawings 2+3 "The Universe in your eyes, etc." You seem to dream about Jane, Seth, + Ruburt more than I do, and very vividly. Your drawings add a lot too, quite unique in their individual ways."

To me they translate into paintings. I wish I had the time to go into details about your dreams, ideas, etc., but sadly I don't. I'm always struggling to keep up with the mail, which seldom eases up, so I do the best I can, I hope that my efforts at least acknowledge the caring efforts others send me.

I wish you the very best. Yes, I'm still involved with Jane's work, but here again I have to be careful about what commitments I make, least I promise more than I can deliver. This involves some hard choices! I'm enclosing the notices I usually send to those who write, if you've seen any of them before, please pass them along, or use the circular file. Once again, your dreams + insights are remarkable. This is something I don't tell others so strongly usually. Seems to me that you'll have a great life exploring what you already know!! Rob. *(Actual letter at the back of the book)*.

Now, though not as often, Seth and I still communicate in a number of ways, mostly via psychic messages he sends through books, television, and so on. I may have a question, or I could be researching something, when seemingly out of the blue, I run into information specific to that subject. I would be scanning through TV channels for instance, and a documentary would be airing about that very topic. I would be browsing at a bookstore, and a book would fall on its side on its own, sometimes even on the floor, as if begging to be picked up.

There are times when a book simply stands out from the rest, be it color-wise or some other unique feature, and when I open it, Seth's name would invariably be there, either as the author's name, a contributor or a reference of some type. If the name in question were "John" or "Bill," I could have agreed that they were all coincidences, but as you know the name "Seth," is not all that common. How many people named, "Seth," do you know? Not many, if any at all, right? And that is why I know that finding his name in a book or whatever it happens to be—immediately after I asked a question, has to be connected to the question. I have become so used to this continuous flow of information that I no longer pay attention to it. I simply accept the fact that "this" must be the way I—as a Soul, chose my life should unfold—no more, no less! But it sure makes for a very interesting life.

Now, from the very beginning these "dreams" felt very different from my normal dreams. Not only because they almost always took place in a classroom, but also because they each picked up where the previous one left off. They continued—as if a series of TV episodes. Seth called them "teaching sessions," but very concise and to the point, I would simply fall asleep and suddenly find myself in the classroom. One peculiar thing was that about one hour before each session started, I would invariably feel as if I was somehow being prepared. As contradictory as it may sound, I felt both very excited and at the same time very relaxed. Later I shall describe in detail, what in my opinion, are some of the more meaningful encounters.

Now, in the first part of the book, we touched on "Religion," and since it, *religion*, plays such an important role in our lives and our development as a society, let's look at this fascinating subject a bit further, as this will serve us well if we want to explore possible future directions. Suppose you were making plans for the future, "plotting," in other words where you might or wish to be in say ten years from now. Ideally, you would be wise to first establish where you are standing "now," your so-called "status-quo." And sometimes, doing a little research about your heritage, provenance, etc. could also prove valuable information. For each of us conducts our daily life based on a certain set of beliefs—beliefs we have accumulated over time, and sure of their validity, hold onto dearly.

Perfectly normal you may say—and you'd be right, if it wasn't for the fact that we have somehow managed to convince ourselves that "ours" is the only right belief system out there—and all others must then be wrong. No one, *almost*, takes a pause and questions that idea. It would be much wiser instead to take a step back—and at the very least, try to understand "how" we inherited that present belief system we so dearly hold on to, and most importantly, where it originated from in the first place.

As we said, throughout history, religion has played and still plays a very important role, but it should be pretty obvious by now, that the main purpose of religion has mainly been to try and understand what we couldn't readily explain. And divergences between the various religions were mostly born from the various geographical areas and matching cultural backgrounds. However, the objective was always one and the same: "Connecting with our own id-Entity." This is mainly the reason why, despite the fact that it only represents a mere "best effort," in addressing the higher questions, Religion was—and still is, an absolute necessity.

Throughout history, the process has continued unchanged, and over time, as we evolved and adjusted our way of thinking, religions also evolved and adjusted accordingly. This process still continues today. However, the apparent downside is not religion itself, but the many seemingly unscrupulous opportunistic individuals, who emerge along the way, and proclaiming to be God's representatives, take advantage of the painfully slow progression. This is still taking place today as it did a thousand years ago!

However, as we saw earlier, while on the surface we may call this "the negative side of religion," it has everything to do with "learning," for that is how we learn here on Planet Earth. Thus, this too was—and still is, a "necessary evil," for "learning" is always and inherently positive, no matter what you learn. So the next time you turn on your TV and see this or that preacher trying to take your money—one way or another, simply recognize the fact that they too—despite the appearance, are contributing positively to your life experience, thus, thank them mentally—and instead of money, send them love. For despite the apparent life of careless luxury they live, they are in fact serving a very useful role, they are helping mankind grow, and become better in the process.

Now, you will probably agree that, as we said earlier, not very many folks out there spend a lot of time and effort trying to answer the so-called, "higher questions." There aren't a lot of people who wonder why would someone choose a particular faith—while his neighbor next door chooses to believe in something totally different. Even more puzzling is the fact that not only each one of us rests firm in the belief that our particular faith is the only "right one," *thus labeling all others wrong*, but we go as far as believing that our particular group is the only "chosen group"—the group who will be saved and let into Paradise, while all others will of course perish in a blaze of fire and brimstone. But let's try to understand what's really happening here.

Suppose I asked you to name the best Country in the world, or the best family, or even the best breed of dogs. What would your answer be? Wouldn't you agree, that we're each conditioned, to think that our particular Country, family, or even dog, is the best—period? Should this come as a surprise? Of course not—for that's how it should be! It is perfectly natural for each of us to believe that what's ours, and what we are most familiar with—is "the best." It is part of our self-preservation mechanism. It is normal to believe that what we grew up with must be the only and most accurate version of events. We were each raised by certain customs and rituals, which over time became engrained in our brain! In essence, our "beliefs system" is what we are!

So regardless of whether you were raised in a well-to-do family in a royal palace, or a tribe in the Amazon jungle having to hunt for food every day, with each passing day you became more and more assimilated in that environment. That environment became your environment—your way of life, which you gradually accepted and took for granted. Regardless of your level of wealth and circumstances, your parents did their best to teach you what they knew—their way of life. It should come as no surprise then if we subscribe each to a particular set of beliefs. What I find peculiar, and interesting, is the fact that we stubbornly label everyone else's belief system as wrong! Why do we so easily forget that we're all children of different geo-cultural backgrounds —but children from the same Source nevertheless? Think about that!

Here is a question for the ages. Picture if you will, five people in a room. Each of them is convinced that they are the only "sane" person in the room and that the other four are crazy. The question is: How many crazy people are in the room?

Most of us go through our entire life convinced that we're each on the right track, thus safe and with nothing to fear. We secretly envision a god who will have mercy on those who share a similar opinion to ours, but will incinerate all others whose beliefs stray too far. But who is "us," I ask? If you are a Buddhist, "us" are the Buddhist, but if you are a Jehovah Witness, then "us" are the Jehovah Witnesses! We take comfort in the knowledge that for as long as we say the occasional prayer—and donate a little money on the weekend, we have nothing to worry about. "God is on our side," we reassure ourselves, but mine is a simple question, "What's God's religion?" Or better yet, "Did God start any religion—or it was us humans who did?" Why can't we face the facts, once and for all, and have the courage to be bluntly honest and admit what the real reason for labeling other faiths wrong is? Would you like me to give you a hint? Fear!

Fear is the real reason! Fear of letting a different belief system infiltrate what we perceive our own, whatever it may be, for that would cause a change, and we humans despise changes. For "changes" upset everything about our way of life, our status-quo, everything we know and hold most dear—what we're accustomed to, what we have practiced and lived by all our life. This is the same fear that makes us not only reject other faiths, but also other cultures, religions, skin colors, and last but not least, sexual orientation. So while the racist, the homophobic and the religious zealot— in an apparent display of manhood beat their chest and wave their signs at demonstrations and rallies, wanting to instill fear and intimidation, trying to keep away those who they perceive as "different," what they are really screaming instead is, "I am scared!" Think about that!

One afternoon three of my friends and I were having a conversation in my office, when the subject of religion came up. As my friends happen to subscribe each to a different faith, I asked them, "You all seem to disagree about which is the 'right' religion. You each contend that yours is the real one and all others are wrong, but let me ask you, what religion is God's?" I could see it in their eyes that that question had never crossed their mind before.

"He would be Christian," John promptly replied. "No disrespect to Muslims, but they seem to always be fighting one war after another, God surely does not condone killing I am sure," John concluded.

"But weren't you *Christians* who first killed Jesus and then made Him your King?" Ahmed replied. "...And I've always wondered why you carry a cross around your neck, the very instrument used to kill Jesus. I know you consider it a symbolic reminder of Jesus's sacrifice, but does that mean that if someone I care about is killed by a bullet, I should carry one, *a bullet*, around my neck, so that I don't forget them," my friend Ahmed asked?

"You are both wrong, God would most definitely be Latter Day Saints," our friend Jim startled us with. But since I wasn't overly familiar with that particular faith, I asked Jim if he could elaborate a bit further.

"Latter Day Saints believe that Jesus Christ, under the direction of God, leads our church by revealing his will to our congregation's president, who happens to live in Utah. Our president is regarded to be a modern-day 'prophet, seer, and revelator,'" Jim explained.

This was when I got up and made myself a double espresso. I needed to know if I was awake or if I was having a nightmare.

Judging from that telling exchange, it would appear that we each respond to a self-protection instinct. Very natural—but have you ever wondered what are the possible reasons for inheriting such a mindset— other than sheer survival?

Most folks don't dare to ask, some because they don't have the time, some because they see it as a sacrilegious topic. These are taboos we think. We're afraid to be ridiculed, to be seen as strange by our peers. "They will laugh at us and won't associate with us" we fear. We do not want to be alienated. It is definitely much easier and safer to just occupy our mind with much more mundane subjects, such as, "what am I going to wear today," or, "did you see that girl's hair," and so on.

But an even bigger reason exists, and that's "fear of God." What if we asked questions we weren't supposed to ask? What would God do to us, we worry? Isn't the Bible full of accounts reminding us of how angry He could become when disobeyed? And in fact, out of mere curiosity I wanted to know just that.

It turns out that several Internet websites have taken the time to do just that, they tallied-up all of the killings attributed to the Bible-God. They amount to 2,476,633 in total—almost two and a half million, but that doesn't include en-mass killings like the flood, the Sodom and Gomorrah episode, etc. If we included them, the websites estimate, it would amount to a figure of somewhere between 25 to 50 million killings. How's that for a loving god?

So we keep going on with our lives, our jobs, our mortgages and our hockey games. And while we all undoubtedly carry unanswered questions hidden inside a remote corner of our brain, we simply keep them there— unanswered, as if a foggy thought. "Let the experts worry about it," we conclude. However, I happen to subscribe to a totally different mindset.

Believe me when I say that throughout my teens and early twenties I too went through that very same struggle. On one hand I wanted to know, but on the other—because of past root assumptions, I was very scared. I didn't dare to ask the questions, I went on with my daily life, pretending not to know what I knew in my heart-of-hearts, that there was more to the story. There had to be!

One of my "qualities"—which depending on who you ask could be seen as a virtue or otherwise, is that I cannot leave anything unfinished. Most of all, I cannot just say "yes" to something I do not agree with, or without first fully understanding the subject. I literally despise it when someone tells me, "we are not supposed to know," or even worse, "we are not supposed to ask any questions." Thus, eventually the time came when I had to throw out everything I knew and go back to basics. Only then I could see, "where we all went wrong."

When Jesus said, "Ask and it will be given," or "Thou shall find your Creator within, not without." He meant exactly that! So why are we not heeding to these most basic of teachings?

Undoubtedly, Jesus, as well as all others who similarly tried to influence the masses in a positive way, got their inspiration from a higher source. The misinterpretation of the initial message became a problem only when some folks started taking things way too seriously and got carried away with the rhetoric. They started changing—adding to the original message, and introduced all sorts of, for the most part, self-serving "rules." Over time, this caused us to lose track of the initial purpose and intent of the messages. What started as a simple well intentioned guiding message became a full-blown religious enterprise, an enterprise whose objective gravitated so far from the initial intent that it inevitably ended up achieving the exact opposite.

Thus, in essence, there is nothing wrong with "religion" in itself, the problem is that people become so preoccupied—invested, and scared of doing the wrong thing—that they inevitably lose sight of the intended purpose. This inevitably puts folks on a collision course of sorts. Their inner instinct is telling them one thing, while their religious leaders tell them another. Their inner source tells them to trust themselves and their instinct, while their preachers tell them the exact opposite. "You are a sinner, your inner voice can only come from the devil," they're constantly reminded. What we need to remember is that outside guidance, can never replace inner guidance, that's what Jesus and many others tried to teach us, and that the knowledge, the connection with Source we all seek, is within, not without.

About twenty years ago, the time came when I had to decide what to do about all of the unanswered questions in my brain. I could park them aside for a while and keep my mind busy with more mundane issues, but I could only do so for at best a few days—as new questions kept on coming. I tried very hard not to let my state of mind interfere with my work, but I couldn't switch it off, or more precisely, I couldn't switch my mind off. My office desk, which should have been covered with business related material, was instead covered with books and magazines on the supernatural. I struggled with this for years, until I finally realized that I had to face reality and follow my heart. I asked Seth to guide me in the decision.

The answer came within only three days. At the time I owned a large automotive business, when out of the blue someone approached me and offered to purchase my business. You can trust me when I say that it is not easy to sell an automotive business of twelve employees nowadays— much less someone offering to buy it from you. But I am sure it must've been yet another coincidence! As you can understand, it was not an easy decision. Everyone in my family was completely against the idea. We tend to get comfortable with our steady income, especially when a sizeable one. It is not easy to just throw it all away and pursue what they perceived as a non-serious endeavor—a hobby almost, especially a hobby they did not even understand. I had no choice however, if I wanted to find peace of mind. While my body was in my office every day, my mind was somewhere else—all of the time.

As I said before, I am not implying that because of the many years of research and the information I received from Seth, I now hold the ultimate answer, because no one does. However, what I am saying is that as a result, my interpretation of life has changed drastically. Today I have a totally different and vastly broader perspective. If nothing else, just being able to enjoy the scenery I experienced along the way, was more than worth the effort. So that is why I decided to write this book—to share, *although in a much condensed fashion*, what I have learned throughout my journey, hoping you will benefit from it also.

A while ago, I was having a conversation with a friend about the so-called deeper questions. But after two hours of trying to convince me that his was the right religion, realizing that he could not change my mind, or better—once he realized that I was not going to be another notch on his belt of converts, angrily almost he said: "Marco, what you're saying makes sense, but why would you want to take any chances? Just do what I do and play it safe! There are things we are not supposed to know!" He Said.

There we go again, I thought. But the more I heard this kind of "Put-your-head-in-the-sand-and-don't-ask-any-questions" nonsense, the more I was convinced that the opposite was actually true. For such a system of "don't-ask-questions-or-else" simply should not exist. You cannot have a Creator, create something out of love, to then watch it suffer unspeakable pain and do nothing about it! You cannot have a Creator who on one hand wants you to know Him, while forbidding you from asking any questions on the other. Is it just me, or you too think something is wrong with this arrangement?

Years ago I was in Italy. My cousin Nella wasted no time inviting me over to her house for coffee, but as soon as I arrived there, I discovered why. She immediately started bombarding me with how wonderful her new religion was. Pretty much the same thing as before happened—for it seems that they have all been programmed alike. She did all of the talking, allowing me to only say a few words if any. Not only would she not allow me to talk, but she wouldn't even hear the little I did say.

As if I wasn't even there, she talked and talked nonstop as if she were a robot. She spoke fast and loud—and just like a robot, completely unaffected by anything I said. And what little I did say went right through her. She had a blank stare in her eyes, total emptiness. When I insisted on debating anything, she would pull out a Bible, and aimlessly start flipping pages back and forth.

Then she started reading verses she had bookmarked prior. I couldn't believe my ears, "dragons with seven heads and ten horns, skeleton horsemen riding white and black horses, swarms of locusts that looked like helicopters," and of course the ever-present imminent "doomsday," which had forever been "just around the corner—but not quite yet." Then, realizing perhaps that I was not going to convert anytime soon, in an attempt to sound more "authentic," more "biblical" I suppose, she began talking in ancient Italian (Latin that is.) Being the polite person that I am—and to be honest somewhat amused, but mostly realizing that this was going to be yet another lesson for me, I listened to everything she had to say, until she was finished. But all I could think was, "Dear Lord what did

I do to deserve such punishment?"

Finally, my head abuzz, at the end of "her" two hour long discussion, realizing that she wasn't going to change my mind, as a last ditch attempt she pulled out a piece of paper and on it, she drew a small square with a little stick-man figure inside. Then she said, "Look, I don't know what is wrong with you as I don't seem to be getting through to you. I am really sorry for you because you're my cousin and I don't want you to end up burning in hell. But because you are my cousin—and I want to help you, let me give you a bit of inside information. When God creates someone, He gives them a small space in which they are allowed to dwell. However, that man is not supposed to venture out of that space, ever! Because if he does, he would violate God's will! As soon as that man decides to do things his own way—and ventures outside his God-given space, he automatically steps into devil's territory. This is because, in life, whatever is not from God automatically belongs to the devil. Do you understand?" She asked.

Wow, I thought, so much for the "inside information!" What would you have possibly replied in my place? "I understand fully my dear cousin, I understand more than you might realize," I said.

"So, does this mean that you are going to convert and allow me to be your sponsor-teacher," she asked?

"Well, not at the moment, perhaps some other time," I replied.

What my dear cousin Nella failed to realize is that she has sentenced herself to live a life confined inside her self-imposed—not God-given as she said—but her preacher-given little square. Anything I said, was therefore interpreted as "from outside that little space," thus from the devil. She later admitted, that it was in fact the very reason why she did not listen to a single word I said, for as far as she was concerned, I was speaking from a devil controlled position.

A few years later I returned to Italy. My cousin Nella and her husband had just divorced. As soon as she saw me, she said, "See? What did I tell you last time? My husband decided to have an affair with another woman! He ventured outside of our God-given space and we now both must pay the price! By the way, have you converted yet?" She asked.

"Not yet, I am still thinking about it," I replied.

"Let me know when you're ready because I want to be your sponsor," she concluded.

Trying to make sense out of nonsense, the more I tried, the more

I realized that something important had to be missing. One single contradiction that literally kept me up at night—which in my opinion was the screaming tell-tale sign that there had to be more to the story, was that for every three words they spoke—the fourth was "punishment." They made sure they constantly reminded you of a God who's always ready to administer punishment at the blink of an eye, when to my mind the notion that God would punish us, simply couldn't exist. I asked myself countless times "why would God choose to punish His children, when He could simply teach them about life's rights and wrongs?" *Keep in mind that at this point in my late teens I still subscribed to the idea of God I was raised by and accustomed to, a god who rewarded and punished as needed.* Thus, to those around me, my "questioning" may have appeared I suppose, as an attempt to disprove God, when in reality the exact opposite was true.

What I wanted instead was to find God! But the "real God," so that I could prove His existence! And so after several long and agonizing years of self-examination, sure that that version of God couldn't possibly exist, I started doubting God's existence altogether and I declared myself an Atheist. But this left me with no floor to stand on, so-to-speak. I needed to know whether God existed, and if not, what in His place. I reasoned that no one wants to live in an open-ended Universe. I simply had to find the answer. So one day I decided to have a heart-to-heart talk with God himself. What did I have to lose after all? If He is there I thought, He would hear me, if not, then no harm done. I still remember the words I used almost in desperation.

"Dear God, please forgive me but I want to understand. It is not that I don't believe, but far too many contradictions cause me to doubt. What our preacher preaches does not make any sense. Thousands of children starve to death every day, how could you possibly allow that? Could You please clarify these questions for me? Please give me a sign, show me that You are there, and that You do hear me!"

You may say that I should've simply taken things for granted and not ask questions. But think about it for a moment. What we had here was a confused teenager asking God for direction, so what's wrong with that? Why wouldn't God intervene? What teacher tells his pupils, "Good day kids, today I am not going to tell you the subject we are going to study, you will have to read my mind?" Let's seriously think about this point for a moment. Why would God not want us to know Him?

By my early twenties, *circa 1983*, I had embarked on what would become a mind breaking, two decade long research. Anything I could find on the subject of Creation and of course the Bible, was the first thing I read, three times. What I soon came to realize however, was that nothing out of that mountain of information shed any new light on the real questions. It all amounted to nothing more than a huge collection of stories we had already heard and reheard many times. No book, no documentary, no university course, dared to address the real question, "Is there a God?"

I soon realized that predominately two distinct interpretations existed, the "Creation side," which started every sermon with *"..And God created the Universe..."* and the "Scientific side," which started every lecture with *"..And there was a Big Bang..."* The problem however, was that no one could explain who or what caused that "Big Bang" to bang in the first place! In the end, although more informed about the many interpretations a given subject could inspire, I knew less now—than when I first started. However, what became blatantly clear was that it wasn't certainly God who wanted to keep us from knowing!

In my quest for answers I needed to find a starting point. And at that early stage in my early twenties, I saw it natural to begin my search from what I was most familiar with. As I mentioned before, at the time, we lived close to a church, and being familiar with its daily chores, some questions really started to bother me more than others. Specifically: "Why are there so many contradictions between what the church tells people to do—and what it does?" "Why did the church tell folks to donate from the little they had, while it indulges in such extravagance?" Gold, huge bank accounts, millions of acres in real estate, and investments worth billions. Just one of the Pope's rings, if sold, could feed a whole village for a year. *This did not make sense to me.*

Why would preachers speak of a simple and humble Jesus, who spread the parable—never asking for compensation, while doing the exact opposite? If they truly were, *as they claim*, "His representatives," why didn't they follow His example? *This did not make sense to me.*

"God is most benevolent and forgiving," they preached. Then why would He want us to *as they said* fear Him? And why would He do us harm in the first place? Even further, if, as they said, "God has absolute power over everything," why would He allow us to go astray in the first place, so that He can punish us later? *This did not make sense to me.*

"God only wants good things for us, while the devil wants nothing more than to torment us," they said. Then "why doesn't God simply rid us of the devil once and for all?—And why does He allow the devil to exist in the first place?" Why isn't He stopping wars, diseases, and thousands of children from starving to death every day? Why would God—in a car accident, choose to save one child, but let his little sister sitting next to him, die? *This did not make sense to me.*

One evening, Larry King hosted an interview with one of the most, *if not the most*, well known evangelic faith preachers in America. A very interesting conversation I must say. Larry asked a series of questions, but virtually all of the answers the preacher gave, not only were they very evasive—but totally senseless, some utterly ridiculous. Simply put, not a single intelligent answer was given. It all amounted to a whole hour of "Only God knows the reason," and "God acts in mysterious ways," and "We might not always understand why God does what He does." And when asked about the present state of the world, he attributed anything of a positive nature to God, while needless to say, the devil got credit for everything else. And whenever Larry asked a question, which neither of the two extremes could satisfy, he would save the day with a "there are things man is not meant to understand." How convenient! Could you envision being summoned before a judge in a court of law, and you answer every question he asks you with "We are not supposed to know that your honor." Or "God acts in mysterious ways your honor!"

Then Larry asked him if he could explain the suffering going on in the world. The answer floored me. This is what he said.

"Because of the initial power struggle between God and Lucifer, and because of the original sin Eve committed (women seem to always get the blame) God decided to give the planet to the devil, thus allowing him to rule over it for six thousand years. After which, God will once again reclaim ownership, ridding the planet of the devil once and for all, together with all those who have fallen into temptation. Hence anyone who is born under the present (devil ruled) system is automatically born a sinner."

So according to this reasoning, any and all babies born in the last six thousand years are "automatic sinners," before they even have a chance to take their first breath of air. Then as a final question Larry asked, "If you could have a talk with God, what would you ask Him?"

"Two questions," the preacher replied!

—1) Why does God have to wait that long (six thousand years) to get rid of the devil and end our suffering?

—2) When God created us and planet Earth, why did He have to go through the trouble of creating so many other planets, stars and galaxies just for us, when we do not seem to need the vast majority of them?

Now, as I said, I was still in my early twenties at this stage and still struggling to reconcile my semi-religious upbringing, with the endless series of questions bombarding my mind, questions that simply put, would not allow me to put the matter to rest. Looking back from where I stand today, I can see the spiritually un-evolved young man I once was, trying to make sense of what did not make sense to him. But I can also see how I was, *then unknown to me*, being readied for bigger things to come. Consequently I searched and searched, but the more I searched, the more increasingly clear it became that something had to be missing. I found it absolutely unimaginable that we could have—for so many centuries, been satisfied with such a poor and ridiculous explanation.

It was soon clear to me that the only way I could have begun to understand the issue was to go as far back as possible in what we call "known history," and attempt to shed some light on "how" and "where" could have such a story originated. What circumstances could have contributed to the birth and subsequent dissemination of such an impossible set of beliefs?

As we know, the Bible gives us its own version of "beginning," which frankly, *to use the words of the great Shania Twain,* "Does not impress me much!" There again, what about the other side of the fence? Where did the scientific version of "beginning" stand, I wondered?

So I started investigating anything I could find on the most widely accepted of all theories, namely "Darwin's Evolution of the Species Theory." What was immediately evident was that at first examination it appeared to make much more sense than its Biblical counterpart. It appeared to offer measurable—tangible evidence, but most importantly, this was no magic story. The theory seemed to also address the many archeological finds which the biblical version did not, thus it seemed worth exploring. It soon became evident however, that even with all of its valid points, Sir Darwin also fell far too short from answering some very fundamental questions. But even more disappointing, despite of the fact that he spent virtually all of his life trying to complete the theory, in the end—Sir Darwin conceded defeat, when he failed to address the infamous "missing link."

As you may know, Darwin's Theory of Evolution also begins with the inevitable "Big Bang," which is coincidentally the very part where I found most of the shortcomings. However, before we analyze the theory in detail, let's first try and clarify what it actually proposes.

Basically, in its most concise and much simplified form, the theory implies that: "All matter in the Universe, together with all Galaxies, Planets, Stars and so on—and space itself, *the empty space between Planets and Stars,* all originated from a single 'super compressed spec of matter' commonly referred to as the 'Primordial Grain of Sand.'" The theory maintains that, "this so called 'super compressed grain of sand,' *for reasons that are not known,* eventually exploded—thus creating the whole Universe."

At first look, the above would appear to be a reasonable explanation. I say reasonable because when we do train our telescopes into deep space, or how our astronomers, *erroneously according to Seth,* call it "back in time," all celestial bodies appear closer and closer together than they are today. This logic seems to hold water, for if we were to examine a grouping of fragments each travelling away from a seemingly common point of origin, common sense dictates that at one point they all must've been grouped together in one location. So far so good—if it wasn't for the fact that this model falls far short from explaining many fundamental questions that basically stop the theory dead in its tracks. The interesting part is however, that despite our scientific community being well aware of this, it still adopts the theory as valid nevertheless. This is because, *as they themselves admit,* "they have nothing better to replace it with." Let us look at some of the main hurdles the Big Bang theory fails to overcome.

—1) If we accepted the nonsensical notion that everything in the Universe originated from a "super-compressed grain of sand," which supposedly exploded, *hence the name,* creating everything—space itself included—then where exactly was that super-compressed grain of sand <u>prior</u> to the explosion—when space didn't yet exist? In simpler terms, if space is an after-product of the Big Bang—and therefore post-explosion, then where was the "seed" that supposedly started the explosion located, when there wasn't any space to be located in?

Scientists downplay the *Catch-22* dilemma by suggesting that *"..Prior to the Big Bang, all matter in the Universe was so inwardly super-compressed that it only occupied as much space as a grain of sand."* But do you see the problem?

For starters, it screams of desperation. "If you can't explain where the elephant was hiding, say it was once an ant"—*which is of course much easier to hide*, only that in our case, we must multiply the problem a quad-zillion times, as the Universe is of course much larger than an elephant.

Secondly, is it just me, or you too have a difficult time accepting that—compress it as you will, the whole Universe could fit into a single tiny little grain of sand? But let's for argument's sake, assume that the whole Universe could have indeed been squeezed into a single tiny "grain of sand," the problem still remains, specifically: "Where was the grain of sand itself located, before space itself appeared?"

I think you'd agree that no matter how much we minimize, *literally*, the issue, we still need some type of "space" in order for anything—no matter how tiny, to be "located" in.

—2) Then to the second point, which is—in my opinion, what renders the theory useless. Specifically, as we all know an explosion can only result from one of two processes.

—A) Someone has to set it off.

—B) Something, be it chemical or natural process, superheating and so on, has to set it off.

With that in mind the two-pronged question is: "Who" or "What process" set off the explosion in the first place? But suppose that we will eventually be able to find who—or what set it off, where was that "someone" or "something" located, prior to the explosion itself? For once again, there was nowhere—no-space, to possibly be in!

—3) Furthermore, if the Big Bang "banged" spontaneously, without any intelligent intervention, then where did "intelligence" come from?

—4) Did God cause the Big Bang thus created the Universe? Or are God and the Universe one and the same and there was never any bang?

—5) Are we alone in the Universe?

—6) If—as some maintain, "The Universe was created for our exclusive use," why did it need to be so unimaginably enormous, when it would appear that the only planets we truly needed, were of course Earth, the Sun to give us life, and the Moon to look pretty at night?

Latest estimates place the number of Galaxies in the Universe anywhere from 100 to 500 billion, with more being discovered every day.

On average, each galaxy contains more than 100 billion stars. Even if we used the lesser figure of 100 billion Galaxies, the number of stars would be a staggering ten-billion-trillion. That's a 1 followed by 22 zeros. And if you think that's a lot, scientists recently concluded that the Universe we can see and measure—our "observable Universe" that is, only amounts to no more than 5% of the Universe' probable size. It begs the question, "Why go through the trouble of creating such an enormous Universe, when all that we needed was but a minuscule portion of it?"

Not only do we seem unable to intelligently address any of these questions, but also, because of the inherent shear profoundness, every time someone tries to—the question simply grows in complexity. For each question inevitably brings forth a whole new set of even more complex issues. Issues such, as for instance, "What is the purpose of life?" And once on that road—once we start asking questions about "life," then even deeper questions come up to the surface, such as: "Is there life after death?" "Reincarnation," "Ghosts" and so on.

It is plainly evident that when it comes to any of these so-called higher questions we are basically at a standstill, hence my question. "If we're seemingly unable to answer even one single question—how could we possibly hope to find answers to each and every question?"

What became obvious at the start of my twenty years of research was that the notion of finding to each question a different answer—was plainly unthinkable. Thus, I was convinced that there must exist a single all-encompassing common denominator, *that we are somehow missing*—tying it all together. It couldn't be any other way! Not only must these seemingly different oddities all originate from a common source, but they must've all been part of one and the same occurrence, different facets of the same diamond. And with that hypothesis in mind, it became clear that if I stood any chances of making any progress in finding that elusive common denominator, I would have no other choice but to go as far back as possible—and from there, work my way forward. Thus, similarly to how our scientists adopted the Big Bang as their starting point, I too had to establish my own starting point. But I was also aware of the fact that one should never dismiss anything before all facts are known. With that in mind, I decided to take a serious look at the fascinating Big Bang, and try to determine its true worth. Thus I started by trying to determine, *based on the official theory*, just how far back I could trace it. And to be honest, I would have much preferred, if it, *the Big Bang*, did turn out to be the theory that ended all theories, for it would have spared me from at least a decade worth of research. But unfortunately that was not to be the case.

For starters, the name alone I found, is in itself not only unfitting but also highly misleading. For as you well know, a "bang"—of any type that is, automatically implies some type of explosion—and in this case a big one. That mislabeling alone, throws anyone attempting to shine some light on the subject inevitably off-track from the very get go. For I am sure you'd agree that if a fire marshal wanted to investigate a scenario, where an apparent "bang" of some sorts took place, they would automatically limit their research to only those probable causes that could have caused that "bang"—and nothing else. Chances are that they would logically focus their investigation on "whom" or "what" could have been responsible for the explosion—accidental or otherwise. And that's precisely why labeling our subject a "bang" is not only misleading but also highly erroneous, for <u>what if it turns out that there never was any type of bang in the first place</u>?

Furthermore, the theory proposes that what became the unimaginably large Universe we all see today, *all galaxies, stars, planets and so on*, was once—*for no apparent reason, as no one knows who or what caused the compression,* all tucked—inside and "super-compressed" into an infinitesimally small "point," hence the elusive "grain of sand," to then—again for no apparent reason, simply explode at some point, with an unimaginable amount of force. But once again, no one knows "how" or "what" caused that explosion. Bang! And voila the super-compressed puny little grain of sand, which:

—a) Did not originate from anywhere.

—b) No one or anything placed it there.

—c) Could not have been anywhere, as no space existed at this point.

—d) Already contained within all of the galaxies, stars and so on.

—e) No one caused it to explode.

For no apparent reason, it simply decided to explode! And behold, the Universe was born! Do you, *like me*, find this methodology totally senseless? But since we promised to give the theory a chance, let's agree to disagree, and for now assume that all of these impossibilities were plausible nevertheless and see how far we can walk this dog.

The theory proposes that, *although "time" didn't yet exist at this point,* an enormous amount of Energy was released at that specific point in time. Hence, an enormous amount of energy and matter left the eye of the explosion and started its outward journey. And as it travelled farther and farther, not only did the expelled material "create space" as it went, but also started cooling down more and more, a gradual "coagulation," giving birth to the very first rudimentary shapes of matter, culminating, *eons later,* into a countless number of celestial "fragments"—our beloved Earth being one of them.

At first, due to the tremendous heat, our planet must have been nothing more than a molten rocky mass of metals and other materials.

However, as it progressively cooled, the enormous heat and vapor emanating from its surface formed a thick mantel of vapory clouds, enveloping the entire planet. And as the hot clouds came into contact with the much cooler surrounding space, they became heavy with condensation. And there you have it, the very first form of primordial rain. Copious amounts of water came raining down on the red-hot surface, releasing even more vapor—which in turn formed even more clouds, which in turn caused even more rain to fall on the planet. The first Heat-Vapor-Condensation-Rain cycle was born. This is of course a much simplified version of events, but the cycle itself, although much more stable and predictable, still continues uninterrupted today.

Now, in a nutshell, Darwin's *Theory of Evolution* proposes the following.

"Many millions of years ago the very first microorganisms formed in the seas. In a continuous quest for self-preservation the microorganisms developed into more and more complex and larger living things. In their quest for survival, instinctively searching for food mostly, the microorganisms widened their exploration, some even venturing onto dry land. Accordingly, these first microorganisms or Amoeba went on to develop into everything that is alive today."

And below is that same above "official explanation" once again. Only this time, pay particular attention to the underscored sections.

"Many millions of years ago the very first microorganisms formed in the seas. In a continuous quest for <u>self-preservation</u> the microorganisms developed into more and more complex and larger living things. In their <u>quest for survival, instinctively searching</u> for food mostly, the microorganisms widened their <u>exploration,</u> some, even venturing onto dry land. Accordingly, these first microorganisms or Amoeba went on to develop into everything that is alive today."

But did you notice anything odd? Wouldn't you agree that in order for even a microorganism to have been <u>aware</u> that it "wanted to survive" and undertake any—however short, journey in search of nourishment it must've been able to think? Not only must've it been aware, but most importantly able to reason, <u>thus intelligent</u>! It must've had an in-built self-preservation mechanism telling it: *"I must survive, I must find food or I will dwindle into nothing, or worse, I may end up eaten by my bigger neighbor living under the rock to my right!"* Wouldn't you agree that no matter how microscopic—any bacteria capable of reasoning must possess some type of "awareness?"

Could you envision an unaware lifeless Amoeba, that perhaps pushed by the waves, happened to accidentally bump into a "piece of intelligence" that happened to be growing under a rock, causing it to suddenly become aware and alive, to then go on and "infect" all other Amoeba on the planet with that newly acquired awareness?

Or, would it make more sense to assume that "awareness" was already "<u>a part of</u>," <u>built into every atom</u> so-to-speak, that made the Amoeba in the first place, thus innately aware?

Based on this irrefutable fact alone we have no choice but to conclude that awareness hence "intent" preceded matter and not the opposite! And for the life of me, I cannot fathom how could someone of the caliber of Sir Darwin's—able to conceive such a fascinating and, for the most part, accurate theory (of Evolution) miss the most crucial of all details! He spent his life looking for the infamous "missing link," decipher how we went from the monkey-like beast, to you and I. But he instead failed to recognize that a vastly more important "link" was missing. Specifically, "How did the lifeless Amoeba become aware, and then decide to move about, survive, and procreate?" Had he addressed that question first, the missing link he so fervently searched for—would have automatically "linked" on its own. Later, we will revisit this issue in more detail, but if you were able to truly grasp the significance and implications this next piece of information, *in bold*, is about to propose, *and I am sure you will*, reading the rest of the book would be a "walk in the park." For understanding the significance of the information immediately below is without a doubt the "key" that will make everything else fall into place. So here we go.

The answer can only be one.

The Amoeba had to be inherently aware! An in-built consciousness was the force that made the Amoeba reason and think in the first place. <u>Matter is then the "vehicle" consciousness uses to express</u>

itself and manifest into a world that is material. Consciousness is in fact the force that drives the material world itself. Matter simply could not exist on its own! "Consciousness" then was the primordial force, not Matter!

Or as Seth explains it: *"Nature, without nature's source, could not exist even for a moment. There is no exception to this rule. There's simply no possibility that a chance combining of chemical elements could—under any circumstance, 'produce' consciousness, or the necessary conditions that would give birth to consciousness. A chance combining of a few different chemicals can—and has resulted in say 'Crazy Glue,' but not consciousness! The myth of the great chance encounter that is supposed to have brought forth life on your planet then presupposes, of course, an individual consciousness that is, in certain terms alive by chance alone. It is somewhat humorous that such a vital consciousness could even suppose itself to be the end-product of inert elements that were themselves lifeless—but somehow managed to combine in such a way that your species attained fantasy, logic, vast organizational power, technologies, and civilizations."*

And yet, some still argue that some unexplained explosion created a bunch of rocks—rocks that were either "aware" or became aware, to in turn go on to give birth to intelligence, and not the other way around. And again I am not implying that you should take Seth's word or mine for it. All that I am encouraging you to do is to think with your own brain. Think about what you just read, *in bold*, and then decide for yourself!

But for the time being, let's continue on our journey, and examine the few existing—accepted theories a bit further. It promises a journey full of impossibilities, but for the sake of trying to arrive at some type of explanation, *about how we could've ended up in such a conundrum*, we will have to close one proverbial eye so-to-speak and for now set aside these impossibilities. Thus, we are going to assume that a Big Bang did in fact take place and for as ridiculous as it may sound, even agree, "that rocks did in fact give birth to awareness." Let us also skip the various missing links and assume that the aware-less—thus lifeless Amoeba did somehow go on to become what you and I are today. And let us also, *for the sake of the argument*, park aside the consciousness issue for now, (we will revisit it in much more detail later in the book), as what we are trying to determine for now is, "what is the reason why our scientists—still today, have nothing better to work with, than at best an impossible fable?"

Countless volumes have been written on the subject of evolution, but since we will discuss that topic in more detail later, let us for now leap over our precious Amoeba and its awareness conundrum, and even grant the *Theory of Evolution* validity. Thus, let's continue our journey in an attempt to understand, where could today's various belief systems have originated. What were the possible societal and religious circumstances leading to today's status quo? Let us take a leap forward from the time of the first microorganisms—all the way to the point in history where our ancestors, the so called "cave men," first walked the land, and try if you could, to envision yourself as one of the very first cave dwellers. Try and envision an existence amounting to nothing more than a daily struggle for survival.

So there you are. You have nothing but a spear and a few tools you fashioned from rocks you found by the river. Your home is a hole on a hillside. You must continuously kill or be killed. Volcanoes erupt all around you making the ground shake constantly. The sky is afire and constant thunder and lightning makes your life a living hell. It's a scary environment you live in. You experience nature's rage at its best, but you do not have the slightest idea about what's causing all the commotion, and the enormous forces fiercely pouring down on you. Your life is in a constant state of danger, you don't know if you'll be alive from one moment to the next. Of course, you have no way of knowing that what you are experiencing is nothing more than a young and evolving Earth, basically, nothing more than Mother Nature trying to find its own balance.

You cannot possibly fathom where that wind, capable of eradicating trees from the ground is coming from, or the water coming pouring down on you from the sky. You know nothing of nature's cycles of destruction and self-regeneration. You only know what you can see and touch. You know that fire is hot, because you burned your hand the other day. Over time, you've familiarized yourself with the landscape around you, and as far as you can tell, your surroundings only include others like you, animals, plants, water and rocks of all sizes. Rocks seem to do nothing at all you reason, plants sway in the wind but they can't walk or harm you in any way. Animals can be dangerous of course, but you've managed to outwit most. But then who or what in the world is causing all of that merciless harshness and commotion coming down on you, seemingly from the sky you wonder?

Well, if none of us is responsible, could a powerful "giant" be the cause of it all? But if this giant is able to make water rain from the sky, rocks and fire come out of volcanoes, and make the wind go wild, then he must not only reside somewhere high up there, where he could control everything from, but he must also be able to fly, you reason. This powerful-flying-giant has so much power it seems, that he can incinerate entire forests with a single bolt of lightning, change entire landscapes and with a strange force that makes the ground under your feet shake—make mountains appear from the ground. But if he's able to do as he wishes—and whenever he wishes, you reason, then he must no doubt own it all. And if he can build and destroy everything at will, then he must no doubt be the one who also made everything in the first place. How powerful can this secret-flying-super-being be, you wonder? Could he have also made you? No doubt! For he surely reminds you about who the boss is, constantly it seems. Many of your friends have perished; some in earthquakes, some eaten by animals. Could they have disobeyed him somehow? You'd better behave, or else!

Centuries later you're still being reminded about "who's the master," daily. You have children, and you teach them everything you know, starting with "you must fear the master or else." Your children grow up following your example. They are eventually going to have children of their own—and they are going to teach them everything they know.

Fast forward a few millennia; you've evolved a great deal by now. You even invented the wheel the other day, when you saw that tree rolling down the hill. You've learned to use fire. You no longer have to eat your meat raw. The master is even allowing you to domesticate some animals. You no longer need to risk your life hunting to feed your family. You now have cows and chicken, all thanks to the master. But does the master have a name? How should you call him you wonder? You'll have to pick a special name, a name fitting of the power and magnificence. And so if you lived in ancient Greece you named him Zeus, while your Roman archenemies named him Deus. American and Australian Aborigines called him Great Spirit. In the Far East they named him Shangdi, Kami, and Vishnu.

As time went on, you moved from your caves to more comfortable wooden shacks. You communicate with others; you're now exploring new lands; you trade artifacts and foods. And in the process, you've unknowingly invented the very first rudimentary forms of commerce. However, as it is always the case in the world of commerce, some folks were more honest than others. And while most relied solely on their honest bargaining skills, some saw the opportunity to profit from the less informed. Hence, slowly but surely, folks began to heed to them. For they seemed to have all the answers, and if they did not, they claimed that there were things no one was supposed to know, *"the master acts in mysterious ways,"* they claimed! People had and still have a natural need to feel protected from the unknown forces well beyond their comprehension.

And so they slowly but surely became accustomed to—and even welcomed that arrangement—an arrangement where via the (self-proclaimed) representatives, afforded the ordinary person a sort of indirect link with the master. They welcomed the notion that they could party and do mischief all week-long, to then attend a half hour ritual on the weekend, donate a dozen eggs—and voila have it all wiped clean forgiven, as if nothing happened. It couldn't be any easier! The simple-minded average Joe saw this as a welcomed easy solution to their perceived, dilemma. *"What's a chicken or a few eggs on a Sunday,"* they thought, *"when we can go on and do whatever we like for the rest of the week?"* This caused folks to slowly become accustomed to this never-ending cycle of "sin-donation-absolution." And there you have it! This is where the idea of "Religion"— and all that it entails, most likely originated.

But suppose that the above scenario would never have taken place, what other alternatives could we possibly have in its place? We would most likely have an unorganized, lawless, chaotic society, a society where everyone would do as they wished. A primitive society. Thus, all of the growing pains and tribulations we have experienced were just that, to teach us something, to allow us to "grow." The shaping of our present belief system was therefore not only unavoidable, but also necessary. It is how we learn and progress spiritually.

Now, what we have attempted to do, up to this point in the book, is to establish some type of foundation, some ground to stand on—and to impart meaning to the seemingly senseless, illogical state of affairs we appear to find ourselves in, and what plausible scenarios may've contributed to that process. But "illogical," only when examined from a human perspective. As I mentioned before, this was neither illogical nor unnecessary when seen from a different perspective—the Spiritual perspective. A thing, which I was not aware of at that early stage in my research.

And so, discouraged by the so called "religion approach," I decided to give the other side of the fence a chance—the "scientific side." But I soon realized that the best scientific version to date, namely the Big Bang theory, while partially correct, also did not—and still does not give us, as we saw earlier, a definite and complete answer. Thus, based on these facts, I came to the conclusion, *as I said earlier*, that there must be a point—something we all must be missing, a somehow unseen component that could not only explain the origins of the Universe, but also reconcile the various religious and scientific models. "Easier said than done," you may think.

Believe me when I say that I am completely aware of the enormity and the implications such a suggestion brings forth. An untold number of scientists and theologians alike have been wrecking their brain and spent untold fortunes, trying to achieve that very goal for centuries. I am therefore not taking what I am proposing here lightly. You would be surprised however at how simple it will all become—once you "un-fog" your brain of everything you have learnt thus far, clear your brain from the centuries of misguided conditioning—and grasp the most basic of concepts. What you need to do is basically what I did back then. I started from "scratch" so-to-speak; I erased everything I knew up to that point—and piece-by-piece started to compile and formulate my own "brand-new" interpretation. Only this time, instead of fables and scare tactics, using "common sense." And that's when, with much help from Seth of course, everything started to fall into place. For once you discover what the "common thread" that resides in everything is, once you know what to look for, the rest will automatically fall into its own place—and finally make sense.

It goes without saying of course that there will always be skeptics; those who will never agree with anything, no matter what proof you provide. Some folks have simply made of being a "skeptic" their profession. It is therefore their mission to always and automatically disagree with everything. Thus, they approach everything from a closed-minded—refuting mindset and will readily reject any result from any experiment, even when the results were objectively obtained. Their logic is simply that if the results proved positive, then the experimenter must have been unqualified or the instruments malfunctioned. Thus they will refuse to look at the evidence, they will even manipulate the evidence, and they will refuse to accept any data as valid, and when unable to negate the evidence any other way—as a last resort, they will blame it on "brain chemistry." Interesting!

So what about our scientific community, you may ask? I truly feel for them. Simply put, they are forced to work within the ranks and the clamps of institutionalized science. They in other words, have their hands tied. Scientists, who are employed by, or are part of an organization, laboratory, or university, have no choice but to abide by their rules. Thus, scientists are told what they can—and cannot do.

What they can—and cannot say. They're given guidelines about how far they can push a given research. No out-of-the-box ideas are allowed, as they could potentially embarrass the organization they work for and most importantly the financing body. And in most cases the politician or politicians responsible for allocating the funding.

Because of this sad state of affairs, most of the really important discoveries to date have all been made by scientists who refused to have their ideas restricted—and instead chose to work on their own. TV, Radio, Telephone, the Airplane, the Electric Motor, the Automobile, just to name a few—all came from inventors who in most cases worked from home on their kitchen table. These were individuals of great courage who were using the most basic of tools and often had no means of supporting themselves and their family. To see their dreams realized, they un-hesitantly put everything they owned on the line, sometimes even their own life. They had a vision. They could see things before they existed. They were persistent and unstoppable. And how do we know if they too received information from a higher source?

Often labeled "crazy" or possessed, and fought every step of the way by the establishment, the moment they even as much as mentioned a new idea, they were immediately faced with fierce opposition. Their ideas always delayed by decades, sometimes centuries. And in some cases, they were unable to see their ideas realized, until after their own death. One case in point, which clearly illustrates the above, took place in the 1930s at the Arrow Automobile plant in the USA.

Nikola Tesla, inventor amongst countless other things of the widely used AC motor, had found a way to produce electrical current, by virtually drawing it out of the air somehow. He understood the "golden principles" of Energy, principles our scientific community still wrestles with today; chief amongst them the fact that the Universe is nothing more than a huge ball of Electromagnetic Plasma.

"Everything is made of electricity! Everything including you and me, as well as the air we breathe! Then why not pull the electricity out of the air?" Correctly concluded Tesla.

And so, he proposed a demonstration. He invited the media at the Arrow Automobile plant. Arrow supplied a brand new automobile for the experiment. The stock gasoline engine was removed from the car and replaced with one of Tesla's AC electric motors. At a local radio supplies shop, Tesla purchased 12 vacuum tubes, two graphite rods and assorted wiring. After assembling the whole in a wooden box, he then sat the box on the passenger seat and wired the box to the electric motor in the engine compartment. Tesla went on driving that car on a closed circuit for not one—but seven consecutive days (taking breaks) often at speeds of 90 mph. Remember that he did this without using any conventional fuels or propellants whatsoever. The box he had built was somehow able to draw electricity from the surrounding air, amplify it, to then convert it, and power the car's electric motor.

At the end of the experiment, the press and everyone present were in awe. But when Tesla opened the next morning paper, what he found was a whole different story. He read nothing but negative innuendos, ranging the gamut from trickery to witchcraft. Disappointed, he realized that folks and society itself were obviously not yet ready for the technology. So he completely destroyed every record of it, taking the secret to the grave with him. Just think how different our lives would be today, if we all had a "Tesla box" in our cars, in our homes, and everywhere else electric power is used.

Now, I am sure you have heard of Leonardo Da Vinci. Vinci, a small town of only a few hundred, is situated at the bottom of a hill in the Florentine region, coincidentally only five kilometers from where I grew up as a child. Now a famous museum, I have visited Leonardo's home many times. And although centuries have passed since Leonardo died, the small town still talks proudly of their world renowned citizen, and one of the most talked about passed-down stories about Leonardo is about something peculiar he did every time he was struck by a new idea.

The story goes that every time he had a new idea, before he implemented it, he would go down to the local tavern (a cappuccino bar today) and there, share the idea with as many folks as possible. He used the tavern in other words, as a sort of "market research," or "test-bench," only in this case, a reverse test. Leonardo was convinced—and rightly so, that most people react instinctively to a new idea, even before they understood what the idea itself was. In addition, he was convinced that only a small minority of people could give an unbiased opinion, without being influenced by their personal preconceptions, biases and circumstances. Thus, Leonardo would make note of how most folks in the tavern reacted. If the majority responded negatively, he would return to his shop and start working on the idea. Conversely, if the majority responded positively, he would go back and scrap the project altogether.

We could argue about whether this was a reliable approach or not, but judging from his accomplishments, I am putting my money on Leonardo, as the man seemed to know a thing or two.

The point here is that all great inventors throughout history, had to—before they could see their ideas realized, fight tooth-and-nail with the masses and in most cases their fellow scientists. Imagine how frustrating it would be, having an idea in your head, which you know would greatly benefit mankind, but you're unable to implement it, until others also understand it. Not only must you bring them up to speed, thus enriching their own knowledge in the process, but you must also endure being labeled "crazy," simply because they are unable to understand—what you understand. Need we be surprised then if most geniuses prefer working alone?

I was having a conversation with a good friend of mine one afternoon; we were exchanging views about the Big Bang theory. As the conversation went on, I could see that anything I said simply went in his left ear and immediately out the right. My good friend, who happens to be a certified scientist, as usual, expected me to just listen to him—and agree with everything he said without argument. But could you imagine someone born in Corleone, Sicily—not argue? Finally, realizing that he was unable to change my mind, he abruptly ended the conversation by saying: "Marco, please don't argue with me, I am a scientist!"

Oh dear God!

"Whenever you find yourself on the side of the majority, it's time to pause and reflect." ~

—Mark Twain

Chapter 3

Spiritual Junctions

The question, "Where did our Universe originate from?" is without a doubt one of the most fundamental dilemmas mankind has ever been faced with. Over the centuries many theories have been proposed, but while some appear to make more sense than others, all known theories to date, fall far short from giving us a definite answer.

As I said before, I am not a scientist—at least not in this life, but what I am is a curious individual who has an inexhaustible thirst for knowledge, and most importantly, an open mind. And while reading this book, I urge you to keep in mind, *allow me to remind you once again*, that the information does not come from me—the author.

The information was delivered to me in a series of "scenarios," concise "lessons" if you like. These encounters were, *as I later realized*, all initiated by me, meaning that nothing would happen, had I not taken the first step. If I stopped asking the questions for say a whole month, the information would simply stop coming until I resumed asking questions again. As Seth reminded me many times, *from his perspective*, "time" does not exist, he is thus not under any pressure to deliver the information within a specific time-frame. It is basically all up to us, you will only receive information that you are ready to receive, and nothing is given to you unless you first ask, or at the very least put yourself in the right "flow," demonstrate in other words, that you are ready. For the act of "asking," or watching certain documentaries for instance, or reading certain books etc, proves that you are ready to receive. I couldn't stress this hard enough.

The sayings *"Questions come to those who ask,"* and *"Knock and the door shall be opened,"* mean exactly that! We all have an infinite amount of information available to us—all there for the taking. So if you are not receiving information, you are either not asking, or you are not ready to receive it. And that's exactly what happened in my case back then. Unsatisfied with the status quo, I questioned everything I knew up to that point. I did the work and I did my research, I showed in other words, that I wanted to know more. I asked the questions, knowing instinctively that answers do come to those who do so. For unknown to most, each of us has not only a Higher Self but also a number of Volunteer Guides—there ready to assist us with everything. They couldn't care less if we believe in their existence or not, all they are waiting for, is for us to ask, or show that we are ready. I am sure you will have a better understanding of this concept later in the book, once you discover "who" you really represent.

Now, I am sure you'd agree that this book, *or any other book for that matter*, couldn't possibly satisfy everyone—no book ever has. And neither is this book intended for the reader who is satisfied with the status quo, for "he who is satisfied does not ask questions." This book is certainly not for those who prefer living with their head in the sand, without even knowing why. Neither is this book for those who believe there is a devil waiting for them around every corner, or punishment ready to be administered at the blink of an eye, although they too would greatly benefit from reading it, for as we will later see, a devil—or even "punishment" will in fact be there, waiting for them, if that's what they believe—therefore expect.

This book was instead written for the seeking individual, those who instinctively know something is missing. Those who refuse to accept "magic" as an explanation. Those who are aware of their sacred right to know the truth, and those who refuse to believe that "they are not supposed to know." And especially, those who have personally experienced the so called "unexplainable." My hope is that, in it, they will find that little piece of information that will help them complete their personal puzzle. Those who suffer quietly and fear speaking out, those who for fear of being ridiculed prefer keeping what they know is true—a secret. And those who have been ridiculed for having had the courage to speak out and say what they knew was true. I am referring to those who have "died" and came back, those who have seen UFOs, those who have had Out-of-Body Experiences. Those who have seen ghosts or strange apparitions and are unable to explain them, and those who instinctively know that dreams are not just "dreams"—and wish to know what they really are. Those who wish to shed some light on the subject of "Creation" so that they can better appreciate their Creator and the true reason why we were created in the first place.

And those who are curious to know about the process of departing from the Earth-Channel, and the process of returning, what's usually, *but erroneously*, referred to as "Re-Incarnation." Big changes are at the door, the question is, are we going to pretend we don't hear the knocking? If that were our only reason for being on Earth, we would all have been born ostriches! We need to stop limiting ourselves and give ourselves a chance to—or at least try to understand. Let's all realize once and for all that our only reason for being—this incredibly beautiful Earth Life of ours, is nothing more than a learning experience.

—Note: It is at this point in the book that I will stop referring to the "Creator" as "God." Said title brings forth far too many conflicting ideas. Thus (unless when referring to the "Biblical God") I will henceforth refer to the Creator as "All-That-Is".

We're all here, *and many other levels*, to experience what we couldn't possibly experience (as Souls) in our natural environment. Why do we need these experiences, you ask? Because <u>everything we experience—our Creator experiences through us</u>! "All-That-Is" simply imagines of "Beings and Universes," and Beings and Universes manifest in His imagination. And All-That-Is imagines these Beings having free will—and so they shall. <u>But because they live within His imagination</u>, what each experience—All-That-Is simultaneously experiences, for they are within Him, thus He is in them, and He is them. Thus, Beings and their Universes do not exist outside (as we are told) apart from All-That-Is, cast abandoned to their own devices; but they instead exist <u>within</u> All-That-Is. Thus, not only is all of Creation interconnected from within, but also connected to— and within the All-That-Is Creator. For everything is within All-That-Is, therefore everything <u>is</u> All-That-Is. Thus All-That-Is is everything!

This is no doubt a difficult concept, but that's only because we are accustomed to envision a Creator—a somewhat of a powerful flying-super-being, who lives somewhere up there on a silver cloud. A deity, who creates things and mortals, then throws them away abandoned to fend for themselves on a hellish Earth—and as if that weren't enough—to then punish them as needed. As we shall see, that's not the case.

Now, as it can be proven in a lab, if we were to take a sample of "matter," be it a fragment of metal, rock, human skin, plastic, etc., put it under an atomic microscope and then zoom-in all the way down to its smallest units, what we would find is "Energy," or more precisely, conscious intelligent energy. What this means in layman's terms is that down to its very fabric, even that office chair of yours—or the paper cup you're drinking your coffee in, is alive!

Our scientists know this fact very well. And by that same principle, even a decaying dead corpse is also alive. Allow me to explain.

Suppose that, *using an atomic microscope*, we examined any given sample of matter, zooming in all the way down to the atomic level. What we would find is that at its very fabric, that sample of matter is made of Energy. Protons, Electrons and Neutrons are the basic units that form the Atom. But the fascinating thing is that the atom is in itself "self-powered from within" so-to-speak—the problem is that no one knows from where that power originates. Do you recall what we discussed a few pages prior? Specifically: "<u>Awareness always precedes matter?</u>" That should be our clue! But why does awareness always precede matter? Because, *as we just saw,* we—<u>everything exists inside an aware All-That-Is</u>!

So, if we took an atomic microscope, and zoomed in down to the atomic level, what we would find is a myriad of live little floating "things," frantically moving about, bumping into each other, grouping and ungrouping constantly. This "grouping," this combining of atoms, is what shapes and forms everything in the Universe, including your body—and the Universe itself. Common sense would suggest for instance, that a sharp needle tip would be just that—sharp, but if we looked at that same needle tip under an atomic microscope, we would find anything but. As we zoom-in, we would—much to our surprise, find that that very sharp needle is in fact not sharp at all. The needlepoint would in-fact appear as if it were made of a fuzzy wool-like material. Zoom-in even further and we would find a myriad of atoms, bouncing on and off the edge of the needle tip, intermixing as if in a dance of sorts, with the atoms in the surrounding air. Actually, it would look as though the millions of atoms that make the needles tip, switched places alternately with the atoms in the air. And zoom-in even further and we would eventually be looking inside one of the atoms itself, and that is where we would find the same building blocks, as we would find inside any other atom: Protons, Electrons and Neutrons.

But I am sure you must be wondering about that aforementioned "dead corpse." "How could something dead be alive?" You ask.

It may sound a bit macabre, but it can—and it is indeed! For if we—for the sake of the argument, examined a sample of skin from a cadaver under that same atomic microscope, down to its very fabric, what we would find is that said piece of dead skin is instead very much alive.

Atoms forming that so called "dead skin" would be just as electrically charged as those in your, *living*, skin, or anything else in-fact—dead or alive. They would be just as alive and ready to recombine into a myriad of new things. The corpse appears dead only because its driving force, *the Soul*, has abandoned it to its own, *Earthly*, devices. Hence, the sans-Soul body must now follow Earth's recycling rules. Think of a dead corpse if you will as if it were a dead battery. The physical structure is still in place, but without its energy, *the Soul in our case*, it will decompose into Earth's melting pot, to then recombine into something—or someone else. What our eyes see is a decomposing corpse we promptly label "dead," but what an atomic microscope sees in that dead-corpse, are trillions of atoms disassociating from one structure to reassemble into another, recombining, forming an endless number of other objects, plants, animals, people, even the food we eat. Each and every atom being perfectly aware throughout the process.

Thus, while we customarily label a human body that no longer moves "dead," we do so, without paying much attention to what that label really implies. Thus today, if we were to look up the definition of the word "Death," in a medical dictionary, what we would most likely find would be something similar to this:

[Death]—"The cessation of life resulting from irreversible changes in cell metabolism."

But in thirty years from now, if we were to lookup that same definition again, what we would most likely find is something like:

[Death]—"The parting or separation of the Soul from the body due to irreversible body damage and/or wear."

Let's take it one step further and add another century to it. I would then venture to speculate on something along the lines of:

[Death]—"Archaic term, commonly used by our physical counterparts, prior to the reclassification of the true nature of reality."

But not because we would have by then all turned into Souls, but because we would've understood that what we truly are, is a Soul first and a body second, not the other way around!

As Seth once put it, "You are not a Human Being having a Spiritual experience; you are a Spiritual Being having a Human experience."

The honest truth is that even with today's medical knowledge, we're still not categorically sure at what stage life actually begins and real death actually occurs. Even as recent as a century ago—when we knew relatively little about the brain, doctors all agreed that the heart and not the brain was in fact our organ in chief. The medical community basically decreed, "An individual should be declared dead when their heart has stopped beating for a reasonable length of time." But as doctors gained a better understanding of the inner workings of the brain and its related functions, they realized that if taken in time, they could in most cases restart a stalled heart. And the newly invented electroencephalograph clearly demonstrated that the brain could still send out signals even when the heart had stopped working for a relatively long period of time. This new understanding forced physicians to reevaluate and redefine when a person could be labeled "dead," as old interpretations were no longer reliable. Then the era of human heart transplants began.

On December 3rd, 1967 Dr. Christiaan Barnard performed the first (official) human heart transplant. We now had concrete proof that if an individual with a malfunctioning heart was kept alive artificially whilst their heart was being replaced, that individual could be reawakened to a new beginning. And as heart transplants became more routine, doctor's attention gradually shifted from the heart to the brain.

Today, heart transplants are an everyday occurrence, but I am sure you remember what we all fantasized about when we, *back in the sixties*, first heard about the first heart transplant. While it no doubt was a major achievement, we couldn't help envision a day when we could walk into the local "store" and buy replacement parts for our body.

Today many hospitals have adopted a definition of "death" equivalent to irreversible coma. By this definition a person's brain can be declared dead when it produces a flat encephalographic reading. And in a case for instance, where the brain is damaged as a result of lack of oxygen (anoxia,) or when a brain no longer responds to stimulus, again, that person may be declared dead even though his or her heart and other organs are still functioning. And despite laws requiring that hospitals took a second reading the day after the first declaration of death, there have been many reports of people unexpectedly coming back to life, in some cases in the morgue. But if it were my decision to make, I would replace the label "Dead," with "Clinically Dead" instead. This while we established with full certainty in what circumstances, if any, could an individual really be declared "dead."

What this clearly illustrates, is that we do not yet understand what "dying" really implies. We are interpreting death, in whatever form is the most fashionable and agreed upon at any given time. Just think how surprised we will be, when we will eventually discover that our brain— while in fact being our body's chief organ, is in itself not of much value without its "driving force," the Soul. For the brain is nothing more than the interface, the link if you like, between the Soul and the body, a link we Souls, *being pure Energy*, use to communicate with our material body. Thus the brain acts much like a transformer of sorts, transforming psychic energy (commands) into electrical impulses, impulses that via bio-wiring travel throughout the entire body, a body that is made of atoms, atoms that are inherently charged electrically, thus powered from within. In essence, to put this concept into simple perspective, your body is made-up of a quad-zillion atom-sized, *literally*, "batteries" and because these batteries are not only inherently aware but also "magnetic" in nature, they all "stick" together so-to-speak, thus forming, shaping your body.

To better understand this, we could use the ubiquitous computer as an analogy. For no matter how powerful, if it were not for its brain (the CPU or Central Processing Unit,) a computer would amount to nothing more than a bunch of worthless components. And despite the enormous amount of data a modern computer hard drive can store, that data, without the CPU processing it, would amount to nothing more than a useless bunch of code. But even with its CPU (brain) in place, a computer will not make a single beep until such time as it is plugged into a power outlet, hence "energized."

Likewise, the human body has stored in its cells, an unimaginable amount of information, but without its "Central Processing Unit" (The Brain) coordinating all of that data, *much like a computer*, the body too would not be of much use. But in the end, both the body as well as the brain cannot move a single finger, *literally*, unless "power" is applied to it. And when it comes to us humans, that power is the Soul. Thus, we shouldn't mistakenly assume that what we are is a "body" with, *maybe*, a Soul inside, for in reality the exact opposite is true. What we are instead is a perpetual Soul, vitalizing a temporary—recyclable body. Why you may ask? So that we can experience life on Earth, for if we didn't, *vitalize a body*, we could still appear here, but only as a "ghost."

To better relate to this concept, and start appreciating ourselves for what we truly are, it would be wise to try and think of ourselves—not from the body's side, but instead from the Soul's perspective. We must—in other words, reverse roles, thus observation points. In a much simplified, concise version, a Soul is what we are. A Soul that through the brain sends instructions to the body. The body is then nothing more than the "vehicle" we, *Souls*, elect—to exist here on Earth. The question remains however, "Is the brain and the body we *Souls* energize, also part of us the Soul?"

Absolutely! You the Soul "energize,"—or more precisely "permeate," shape and direct the whole. But how does the process of communication between the Soul and the body take place, you may ask? Is the Soul directing the brain, then "remotely" or "wirelessly" the body?" No, the Soul's energy permeates the whole instead. Your body, *brain included*, is simply an extension, a projection, a "decelerated," thus denser portion <u>of you the Soul</u>. It is what your fingernail is to your finger. The Soul is thus not independent or separated from the body, but one with it. And just as a lake in the winter is made of liquid water, but ice, *which is still water*, on the surface, you are also made of many layers of more-or-less dense Energy. Thus, while it is indeed correct to think of ourselves as a Soul first—then a body, we shouldn't think of ourselves as a Soul separated from our body, but instead, a Soul extending—permeating into our body. The brain then—also inherently energized by the Soul, *not unlike a computer's* CPU, is merely the interface the Soul uses to send psychic commands to the body. The brain then transforms these commands into electrical impulses, which the body can understand and respond to—physically. Let's simplify this a bit further.

Suppose that you, *the Soul*, the "reasoning-part," decide to go to the movies tonight. You send the thought to the brain, the brain then directs the body to get in the car and drive to the movie theater. That is basically, what you do every moment of every day, without realizing it, seamlessly. Every moment of your day, consists of nothing more than a continuous flow of thoughts, you, *Soul*, think and then send to your brain—thus your body. And fascinatingly, the opposite chain of events takes place, when you for instance accidentally burn yourself.

Your hand's receptors, *through the bio-wiring in your arm,* send a signal to the brain, which then translates and sends that signal to you-the-reasoning-partof the whole—you the Soul. A Soul that having access to infinite Universal knowledge, interprets the signal as "painful and dangerous," but dangerous not to you, *the Soul*, but to that portion of you, which is your body. Thus, if you wished to keep living that Earth life a bit longer you'd be wise to instruct your body to remove that hand from that hot surface— and fast! So you send the appropriate signals to your brain, which in turn tells the body to move the hand. In addition, you direct the brain to "locally" store that knowledge in its memory banks (synapses) for future reference. New data is stored there constantly. Similarly to adding more hard drive space (more storage to your computer) as newly acquired information needs to be stored there, new synapses are continuously manufactured. Hence should something similar reoccur in the future, your body—thanks to that previously stored information, would react "instinctively," even before you the Soul realized what just happened. While this may appear to be a long complicated process, it all takes place in a nanosecond.

Now, many attempts have been made to pinpoint "where" exactly the elusive "mind" resides. Still today, most experts will tell you that our consciousness, memories, emotions, thoughts, dreams etc., are all manufactured by and actually reside inside our brain. Only a small number think that another explanation may exist, and some are not exactly sure. And the simplified sequence of events described above, although accurate doesn't even come close to explaining the full mechanics of the process, much less the reason the "process" exist in the first place. So here are a couple of interesting quotes in point, by the genius Nikola Tesla—that in my opinion say it all:

1)— "My brain is only a receiver. In the Universe there exists a core from which we obtain knowledge, strength, and inspiration. I have not penetrated into the secrets of this core, but I know that it exists!"

2)— "The day science begins to study non-physical phenomena; it will make more progress in one decade than in all the previous centuries of its existence!"

Now, of course, it all starts from Source, All-That-Is. But let's for our purposes step down a few "levels" from Source—and instead use the "Entity" as our starting point. And since we are on this topic, allow me to clarify that according to Seth five more levels exist between the "Source" and the body, seven in total.

"I am the Alpha and the Omega," which means just that—not "the beginning and the end," as our dear preachers would like us to believe. "End" of what exactly, another Armageddon?

"Alpha and Omega" in Greek do not mean "beginning and end" but instead "First and Last!" Or in simpler terms, both "Source" as well as "Body" and of course "everything in between!" However, for the sake of our discussion, we need not concern ourselves with all of the seven levels, *for each level is simply a "higher" version (frequency-wise) of the one before—all the way up to Source.* Thus, we will only concern ourselves with Source, level-1 (All-That-Is)—then skip a few levels and looking from the Body's side (level-7) we will discuss the Soul (level-6) and then level-5 (the Entity.)*

The Entity can choose to stay in its natural state within its own environment indefinitely as it does not concern itself with "time." Alternatively, the Entity can choose to "project" a portion, or portions of itself onto other environments. These (projected) fragments are cast so that it can experiment with whatever these environments have to offer. Earth of course, being one such environment.

These, *cast*, fragments become Souls. An Entity can, *according to Seth*, cast up to about a thousand Souls, but it can choose to cast any number of Souls up to that amount. This does not mean that in so doing the Entity becomes smaller or diminishes in "power" in any way. Even if the Entity would in fact choose to cast the maximum number of Souls, the Entity, *at its source*, would still remain unchanged. As it does not "shoot" away Souls, it simply "extends"—projects outwardly and those extensions become Souls, then Soul extends into bodies.

Thus, the Entity does not "subtract" from its energy, but it instead "projects" portions of itself onto different dimensions.

Now, to illustrate the above, I know it may sound a bit funny to use an octopus—as a guinea pig, but the main purpose of this book was to, *whenever possible*, simplify complicated subjects. So how can an octopus help us to better understand the process? Think of the octopus as the Entity. As such it can decide to keep all of its tentacles underwater or extend any number of them above water. If each tentacle represented a Soul, and their tips represented physical bodies, then each body, *being above water*, would experience an environment that— though symbiotic to the environment underwater, were completely unique—hence each a whole new existence. The octopus is thus able to experience environments, both under and above water, thus a multitude of simultaneous but diverse experiences,

(See illustration at the end of the book).

and all without ever living its native environment. And depending upon the environment chosen, a suitable "suit" must be adopted by its tentacles' tips. In Earth's case a "body" is the better-suited vehicle.

And a body is never chosen by chance, for it must not only function in that environment, but it must also provide whatever experience the Entity wished to have in a given lifetime. Thus, if for instance a wheelchair-bound life is chosen, then proper planning is set into place, together with all the events, accidents, etc. that will eventually lead to that intended experience. The Entity never leaves its natural environment, but connected to all of its projected Souls and all of the more-or-less material "vehicles," its Energy permeates throughout, energizing the whole, Entity, Souls, brains and bodies, all at once.

Now, a few years back I decided to take a psychology course. I filled out the university application and submitted the hefty fee. Then I was called in for a pre-assessment interview to decide my most suitable class level. The nice professor asked me many questions. When done, I politely asked him if he could give a concise version of what the yearlong course consisted of.

"The most recent findings about the human mind," he replied.

But then I asked him another simple question—or so I thought. "What is the human mind?" Or at the very least "where does it reside?" My intention was not to embarrass him, but as if caught unprepared he hesitated for a moment, and then somewhat sarcastically he replied, "No one knows the answer to that!"

"But then what is the point in spending a whole year talking about something which we don't even know where or what it is? Wouldn't it all amount to guesses and speculations? I would gladly do so if we were going to at least try to find answers to these questions," I said, "but if all that we are going to do is discuss what we already know—or what Sir Freud said a hundred years ago, all of which can be easily looked up on the internet, then what is the point" I asked?

"My apologies but I can't spend a year learning what I can readily find on the web," I said. I forfeited my fee and never went back.

To the professor's defense however, the problem is that what we loosely label "the mind" or "consciousness," that part of us responsible for thinking, is actually one and the same with the Soul—it is the Soul!

Thus, there is no specific place where it actually resides. The Soul is part of the Entity, thus by extension, *literally*, the Soul and the Entity are also one and the same. We could use "Energy" as an analogy, for as you know Energy is everywhere. The body is Energy; thus Energy is what our body is made of. Thus, energy is in your brain—and it is your brain. It is in your bony skull—and it is your bony skull. Energy is in the water you drink, the food you eat, the air you breathe, and your lungs are also made of Energy. Energy is inside and outside our planet, as well as in all the other planets and stars in the Universe. All planets, galaxies and the seemingly empty space in between—is also all Energy. The Universe makes energy, and yet the Universe itself is made of Energy! Energy that is inherently "aware!" The battery in your TV remote for instance, has not only Energy stored in it, but is itself made by that same Energy. And the remote control is also made of Energy. And in case you're wondering why I am using a capitol "E" for the word "Energy," it is because Energy is inherently Sacred. For Energy is All-That-Is!

But why use Energy as an analogy to the relationship between Mind and Soul you may ask? Because they are one and the same! Every single atom in you, as well as every single atom in the Universe has its own built-in awareness. And every single atom always knows exactly what its purpose is! For Energy is inherently aware. Do not ask me why, because there is no answer to that question—it simply is! Why can you not find non-live electricity? Because no such a thing exists! The same goes for Energy. And years ago, for the fun of it, I asked Seth that very question, "Why are all atoms inherently aware?" I said.

"Because that is the only way they come!" He replied.

From a human perspective, we could always ask "who" inserted the awareness in the atom. You're probably starting to see how one would at this juncture—just want to walk away from the subject, attribute the whole thing to a higher wisdom and close the argument there.

However, for the rest of us, the question remains. Specifically, how could something "be there" without someone or something putting it there?

The answer does not change, "It simply is!" It is essential that we learned to switch focus from a material view, *where everything is "made,"* to a Spiritual view instead. For Spiritual questions cannot be answered in physical terms, as in human terms the answer simply wouldn't make sense. Alternatively it would make a lot of sense, if you were able to see it from a Spiritual perspective. And do not interpret this as an attempt on my part to avoid the question with a, "we aren't supposed to know" answer. When addressing "Spiritual" questions, it would serve us well to reexamine how we normally relate to and perceive our surroundings, think in other words, like a Soul would think.

But how do you do that? Try and see things from a "Spiritual" perspective, how a Spirit would see it and not the usual "materialistic" approach where everything has to be "made" by something else, which was in turn made by yet something else. So, for as difficult as this fact may be to accept in human terms, the answer is quite simple, "No one injected the atom with awareness. Quite the opposite; it was instead awareness that gave birth to the atom—outwardly, hence giving birth to all material things!"

Suppose I asked you to explain "who or what made water wet?" What would your answer be? For as simplistic and pointless a question this may seem, the truth is, that no matter how much money one would be offered they wouldn't be able to give you an answer. Water, is simply "wet." Or as Seth would say, *"That's the only way it comes!"* Thus, "wetness" if you like, is what "makes water," not the other way around.

So in our quest to understand "how could've something been always there," the key is to remember that "always" does not apply here. We use human words because we have nothing better. The problem is that when saying "always," we inherently imply "time," and of course time in the Universal scale of things does not apply, hence the paradox!

We take it for granted that "Humans" is what—and all that we are, thus we automatically think from a human perspective. "When was the Universe created?" We ask. A valid question, but valid only in human terms. For here again, *perhaps without realizing it,* we're asking "when" "time-wise." Thus, "when" automatically implies that the Universe was "created at some point in time." And this is no small issue, as this is actually the very obstacle science is struggling to overcome. Time—or better yet the "measuring of time," is just that—a scale of measurement, a component we humans introduced to make our lives easier, here! A component used only but within a small portion of the Universe, <u>our portion</u>! As far as the Universe as a whole is concerned, or even as far as a Soul is concerned, time does not apply.

"A Soul is immortal" you have probably heard a thousand times. But what do you suppose we mean by it?

It simply means that a Soul is immortal, but not because it has "superpowers" thus it never dies, but because "Time," simply put, at the Soul level (the dimension where Souls reside) again, does not apply! The Universe doesn't need calendars to know what year it is, for the Universe was never intended in terms of "time," the Universe simply is! Thus, time is totally irrelevant in the eyes of the Universe, much less in the eyes of its Creator. Much like meters and kilos, time is just another system of measurement. As such, (Time) is only useful to us, its architects! And on this point, allow me to share yet another very revealing quote by the genius Nikola Tesla.

"To me the Universe is simply a great machine, which never came into being and will never end!" Do we need to add anything to that?

It is fashionable to say that we are in this or that year. We, *mostly for commercial purposes*, use the so-called "Gregorian Calendar" while several other calendars are used by different cultures. Next to the Gregorian, the most widely used are the Islamic, the Chinese and the Tibetan calendars. So my question is, "What year are we in?"

It depends who you ask of course. But let's take this concept a step further and suppose that another inhabited planet existed in the blue yonder, and they also had their own calendar! What year would it be if you asked them? And what year would it be if you asked the Universe? Who's to decide whose calendar is to be taken as accurate in the first place? Are you starting to see how foolish and pointless is to declare that the Universe is 14 billion years old—if we can't even agree what the year is, here on our own planet? But since Humans is what we are, it is almost inconceivable for us to envision something that wasn't made by—or as a result of something else. And as I said before, this is the very reason why our scientists are at a loss when trying to decipher the "time" concept. For let's not forget that they are of course also Humans, thus they think as Humans would. Thus unable to envision a scenario that does not include some sort of beginning. And this is—in my humble opinion, precisely the reason why science is in essence "clueless" when trying to explain the so-called "Big Bang," for how could you possibly explain a "beginning" that never was?

Specifically, in my opinion the problem originates from a small "terminology technicality." The solution is simple; we must do away with the label "Beginning." And this is coincidentally what worries me most about the experiments being conducted in Cern, Switzerland. These extremely complex and potentially disastrous experiments are conducted based on the assumption that there once was a "beginning," which in reality never was. Do you see my point?

Back in 1942 the military commissioned a chemist named Dr. Harry Coover to formulate a type of plastic to make transparent rifle sights. To his total surprise however, he instead accidentally ended up with a very sticky substance—today's ubiquitous "Superglue." But ending up with glue when the intended goal was a type of plastic is one thing, but playing with a piece of equipment that if misused could cause a worldwide disaster, is altogether another matter.

We are a material oriented society. We make, manufacture and build everything. "A car was made by workers in a plant—using plastics that were made by other workers and metals that were made by our planet—in turn made by our galaxy—in turn made by the Universe—and in turn made by God." This is how we allow ourselves to sleep at night. This preconceived "order of construction" accurate or not—is what we automatically accept as valid and live by. We so routinely take it for granted in fact, that we do not pay any attention to—much less question it. These beliefs are so deeply engrained in our culture that we fool ourselves into believing that literally everything must have been "made" sometime, somehow. Therefore, we reject any possibility that something could simply "exist"—on its own, not having been made by someone or something else. Thus, unable to let go of that mindset, we limit ourselves to only one of two options.

The first is to simply wash our hands of it and let someone else figure it out. Too busy with our daily lives we simply avoid the issue altogether. We then go on attributing all good things to a deity and all bad things to a devil. There couldn't be an easier way out.

As an alternative, for those of us who like to think, the only plausible option is to realize—once and for all, that the many hundreds of conventional deities we have incessantly been chasing throughout history, were all based on our misconstrued, uninformed, understanding of the Universe, as we progressed throughout history.

This, coupled with the fact that throughout history—*"a necessary evil," or not*—we've all been grossly misguided by the various religious interpretations, has basically steered us to look for answers in all the wrong places, thus missing the point altogether.

The real God, what I—as well as Seth—like to call "All-That-Is," is far more than that. And I am well aware of the implications this brings forth. I know that if something of this magnitude could be materially, *here we go again*, proven, it would without a doubt rewrite history, as we know it.

But whether we realize it or not, history is in the process of being rewritten. An unstoppable wave of new information is pouring in from all sides. All Nations, All People, are awakening to a new awareness. Just go on the Internet and see what is taking place everywhere on the planet. News folks call it "Spring," "Revolution," "Rebellion," or "New World Order"— but in a word, "Change" is what is taking place! We're fast approaching a most important milestone. Or as Seth would say, "A new address in our voyage on the Universal Highway".

And in the last half century or so, the closer we've been getting to that milestone, the more of a new "mindset" has slowly but surely been trickling down to us, ever so more discernible with each passing day. The process is always the same:

—1) It starts as a fantasy.
—2) Then it becomes fiction.
—3) Then so called futuristic books and movies are made about it.
—4) Then, getting even closer, that fictional data becomes "emerging technology," more feasible with each passing day. But not because the information itself changes, but because <u>we</u>, getting closer, change more and more, becoming more and more "in line with" thus accepting of it.

As it is always the case, what we called "fiction" fifty years earlier, becomes ubiquitous a few decades later. Think what would've happened if say a hundred years ago, you told folks that in the near future we would all be walking around holding a small device in our hands which we could not only communicate with our friends in our city with, but also folks halfway around the world. Even our Grandmothers have cell phones nowadays. Or what do you think they would've done to you if you were to suggest that in only a few decades the United States would have elected a black President? Think about it.

Naturally, we always think from a human perspective, but have you ever asked yourself what causes an idea that is unthinkable or pure sacrilege one day, to become a probability five years later—and a fact soon after? Travelling on the Universal highway causes us to get hints of what's going to happen in the future. These "hints," first appear to us as vague thoughts or fantasies, they then become possibilities, and then blueprints.*

In the early 1900s the idea of a black American President was simply unthinkable, but as we got closer and closer to that point in the "play script" (address) where that possibility resided, the early '90s arrived, and lo-and-behold the possibility of a black President was no longer such a crazy idea. And year after year folks started to warm up to the idea more and more. Then on November 4th 2008, Americans elected their first black President. And watch by the way, for a black Pope coming soon at a Vatican near you! Why am I so sure of it you ask? Simply because of the fact that we are now starting to think about that possibility—thing which we wouldn't be doing, unless we were actually approaching that milestone—the "address" that is, where that specific event will eventually take place. Thus, the closer to that address we get, the more "feasible-probable-reality" the event becomes.

Now, just as approaching a new milestone brings us closer to the data encoded there, leaving one behind understandably causes the opposite effect. As more and more distance is put between previous milestones, thought patterns, and belief systems that were once valid, become less and less relevant and fashionable. So, if you would like to know what the so-called "future" holds, say a hundred or five hundred years from now, you'd be wise to pay a bit more attention to what we today call "futuristic" movies and books. For whether or not the director or author are aware, or even believe it, they are getting that information from—you guessed it, the future. The simple reality is that by merely projecting their thoughts into the future, trying to extrapolate what that future might look like (so that they can produce that book or movie) they are accessing future data. By the way, this is in fact something that every individual can do—and does every moment of every day. The only difference being, that we usually don't venture too far into the future, but very normal nevertheless.

---

*(I strongly suggest you pay special attention to this enormously important point. A blueprint represents nothing less than the very "passage" from the Psychic to the Physical! That is why you should always pen all of your wishes on paper. For the very act of "inking" a thought on paper, is the "necessary step"— what links the nonphysical to the physical!)

Earlier in the book we endeavored to shed some light on the subject of religion and its probable origins, the question now at hand is: "Why do we appear to be experiencing such a high degree of imbalance between the various classes? How could it be possible that a mere 5% of the population could seemingly have control over 95% of the planet's total wealth?"

The reasons are mainly two—and it has nothing to do with "who is to blame," for allow me to remind you once again "it is a very complex play-script we're all acting in." So, on the surface it may appear as if it is a "dog-eat-dog survival of the fittest Earth" we live in. Thus we, *governments and world of commerce included*, seem engaged in a competition of sorts, a struggle for survival in an apparent world full of enemies. And not just "commerce and political enemies," but also racial, cultural, religious, and even class enemies. Actually we seem to find enemies everywhere we look. Thus the world's governments declare new wars even before the last one is finished. All nations seem to be engaged in a race of sorts, to see who can take more of the planet's natural resources, more land, more oil, more diamonds, more gold and so forth.

From a Human standpoint, that is what we may appear to be experiencing, but the second and perhaps most important reason for the perceived imbalance has to do with what Seth likes to call "our movie script." Simply put, these are "scenarios" we had originally included, *by mutual agreement I may add*, in our "Earth Experience Script." As Souls, we wish to experiment with—and learn from, scenarios we are unable to experience there at Home. This is mainly because of the lack of any discernible laws of physics as well as the absence of physical sensations. It is really that simple.

Thus, this Earth experience of ours is nothing more than a "Grandiose Play" which we all agreed to act in, share and participate-in in advance. We're all interacting, in-acting roles we each chose and wished to play in each life-experience. We also chose those, *other actors*, we were going to interact with along the way, as well as those who are going to be affected both positively and negatively by our various roles. They in turn chose to be the victim—or the beneficiary, accordingly. You in turn chose whose victim or beneficiary you were going to be.

So you see, nothing is coincidental or random, these are simply "acting roles," from the beggar to the king and every other role in between— each is a role, each actor had chosen or volunteered to play, for their own benefit, or for the benefit of others. For ultimately we are all here for one single reason, *Learning*!

Now, the biggest misconception hindering us from coming to terms with what All-That-Is truly represents, is the fact that we've somehow managed to convince ourselves that there exists a god, that from somewhere up on a silvery cloud or some other exotic place, spends his days looking down on us. That's probably the reason why we always look up when referring to god. "He's up there somewhere," we think, "disconnected and apart from us, watching every move we make, ready to punish us at the blink of an eye." This is, as it turns out, the single biggest misconception. For when we set ourselves apart from All-That-Is, we can only and inevitably end up envisioning an "external-watcher-punisher" type god.

So, the next time you wish to address your Creator, do not look up to the clouds, for All-That-Is is to be found within instead, or more precisely, "you are within All-That-Is!" Thus, you the body, you the Soul, you the Entity exist within All-That-Is! Hence All-That-Is is in you and thus is you! All-That-Is is not only the "Source" but also you the Entity, you the Soul, as well as you the body! From Source to body, hence where the definition of "the Alpha and the Omega" originates from.

I remember asking Seth years ago, "Tell me Seth, is All-That-Is the Sky too?"

"He is All-That-Is," he replied!

"Is He the mountains and the seas, and the trees, and the birds in the sky?"

"He is All-That-Is," he again replied!

"Is He the cars in the streets and the homes, and all the people inside these homes, as well?" I asked.

"What part of 'ALL' don't you understand?" He replied.

And on that specific point, let me remind you once again what Ascended Masters like Jesus as well as other Prophets have all tried to tell us all throughout history, "*Look for your Creator inwardly, not outwardly!*"

You the Body, you the Soul and you the Entity, live not "connected-to" but *within* All-That-Is. That's why All-That-Is is everything that you are! Thus, you live within a Universe that is also within All-That-Is. A Universe that is, All-That-Is!

Allow me to share with you the single-most important clue that (back in my teens) helped me immensely in grasping this concept.

While our preacher preached that *"God was everything and everywhere,"* he in the same breath also preached that *"we were down here and God up there, separate from us worthless human beings, abandoned in punishment, trying to steer an existence through a labyrinth of sin."*

How could it be possible, I asked myself hundreds of times? How could God be "in us" and yet apart and separated from us? So I asked Seth to clarify this very point for me.

"You are a small spark from All-That-Is, but within All-That-Is. A spark that was granted its own free will, thus, you are not only ever-connected to and enriched by that union, but simultaneously, you also enrich that same union." He said.

Thus, everything you experience as a free-willed-being, All-That-Is experiences. All-That-Is is in you, me, and everyone else. All-That-Is is in our planet, our Galaxy, and our Universe. But All-That-Is is not only in everything and everywhere—He is everything and everywhere. Thus, All-That-Is is you and I, the Earth, the Galaxy, and the Universe, for everything is within All-That-Is, thus everything is All-That-Is!

We couldn't possibly be "outside," or separated from All-That-Is, because there is no outside. And altogether—we and the Universe, or Universes, form All-That-Is. And yet, All-That-Is is more than the total sum of all parts. And because All-That-Is is everything and everywhere, He is aware of everything and everywhere, thus not a single grain of sand or a single blade of grass is insignificant, for All-That-Is is every grain of sand and every blade of grass!

So when you laugh, All-That-Is laughs. When you cry, All-That-Is cries!

And if we truly wish to move forward and progress as a society, we need to first remove this last remaining hurdle. For this is the single biggest obstacle keeping us from closing the gap between our technological and our spiritual growth. For technology, need not concern itself with "punishment;" it simply keeps on expanding. It is we, who must let go of these thousand years old handcuffs.

As Seth once said,

"It is time for mankind to awaken from the nightmare it chose to experience, of a Creator, who one day decided to create a Universe filled with zillions of planets, then place a bunch of humans on but just one of them, to then leave them abandoned, governed by a devil as a form of punishment." He said.

"Replace that nightmare with the following dream instead," he said.

"All-That-Is is not a man or a woman; All-That-Is is not a being. All-That-Is is a "Gestalt!"

"Out of immense wisdom and creativity, and possibly out of solitude, All-That-Is envisioned probabilities within, probable Universes—and Universes appeared."

And All-That-Is envisioned inhabited Universes—and inhabitants appeared."

"And to emphasize the experience, All-That-Is gave these inhabitants free will—but free will always within the All-That-Is Gestalt, not outside, for there is no outside."

All-That-Is created zillions of sparks of creativity within. But if we added all of the parts that make the whole, All-That-Is would be greater still!"

"*The most preposterous notion that Homo-Sapiens has ever dreamed up is that the God of Creation, Shaper and Ruler of all the Universes, wants the adoration of His creatures, can be swayed by their prayers, and becomes petulant if He does not receive this flattery. Yet this absurd fantasy, without a shred of evidence to bolster it, pays all the expenses of the oldest, largest, and least productive industry in all of history.*" ~

—Robert A. Heinlein

Chapter 4

The (Big) Bang That Never Banged

Now, this was certainly never intended to be a scientific book, on the contrary, my intention was to make complex concepts accessible to everyone. This was perhaps the main reason why it took so long to write—over twenty years that is. It certainly hasn't been an easy task, especially when English is not your first language. Though plainly written the studied reader will be able to recognize the profoundness of the issues the book endeavors to address. But most of all, I hope you can appreciate the fact that without Seth's guidance, on my own, I could have never assembled a book of this type. This will become most evident with the next piece of information; for I have never attended a single physics class, and although I have read dozens of books over the years, I have never read one on physics. Physics, simply put, is "too dry a subject" for my liking.

However, what you are about to read next promises, *according to Seth*, to turn the world of physics upside-down. As far back as 1985, Seth suggested that in our next near future (2020-2030) a new scientific formula would replace what's known as the "Holy Grail" of all scientific formulas, namely "E=mc2" Einstein's Formula of Relativity. According to Seth, the revised formula is the answer to what our physicists have been chasing for over a century. And if you happen to be a physicist, you'd be wise to pay some degree of attention to this information, as, according to Seth, that is where the bulk of your future research will be focused on. Seth proposed that the universally accepted granddaddy of all scientific formulas, namely Einstein's E=mc2 will soon be replaced with a much more fitting one:

$$G=mc3/3.$$

In simple terms, while Einstein's old formula proposed that: Energy=Mass@LightSpeed/Squared, our new formula proposes instead: **Gravity=Mass@LightSpeed/Cubed**.

The new formula is obtained by taking Einstein's original formula and multiply it by the Speed of Light (C) once more, thus "cubing" that same speed of light, instead of (as Einstein did) squaring it.

We then divide the resulting value by a factor of 3 to compensate for space's curvature and the effect of relativity. Einstein proposed that Energy (E) is obtained when Mass (M) is accelerated to Light Speed (C) squared. But last time I looked out of my window, I saw not a 2-dimensional—but instead a 3-dimensional world. Thus, Einstein's approach only addresses but one side of a 3-dimensional "cube," falling far short from representing the 3-dimensional Universe we inhabit, hence the new formula. But before going any further and try to decipher what this means in laymen's language, I wanted to point out that while I have been in possession of this new formula since 1985, no scientist to date (2017) has the faintest idea of the impending discovery.

Now, promising you, *the reader*, that we will keep this as short and interesting as possible, let's try and pinpoint the reasons why the present (Einstein's) model couldn't possibly work. Einstein's formula does not and cannot work—this, even when we will eventually have telescopes powerful enough to look as far "back" in space as what our scientists, *erroneously*, call the "Big Bang." But for the sake of the discussion, let's for now assume that there once was a Big Bang. If you're a physicist I am sure you already know where this conversation is heading, for you know very well what the problems associated with the present model are. For the rest of us, let's briefly look at the various obstacles the present model fails to satisfy.

—Question: "Where did the Big Bang theory originate from?"

The theory was introduced when observations and measurements would appear to suggest that all celestial bodies in the Universe are in fact travelling away from a common point of origin, behavior consistent with that of any explosion. This finding proposed that if we were to, *in theory*, reverse the masses' direction of travel—thus reversing "time" itself, we would cause these masses to travel closer and closer together, to then eventually regroup, reforming into the original single mass. In simpler terms, envision an exploding grenade if you will, then reverse the explosion—hence the fragments' direction of travel. Naturally, they would travel backwards, to eventually regroup into the original grenade.

The theory was further reinforced, when recent measurements suggested that all celestial bodies in the observable Universe were indeed decelerating in their respective speed, this (the gradual loss of momentum) being consistent with the aftermath of an explosion. So today you could read a thousand books on the Big Bang, but regardless of how hefty or how visually ornate the book would be, chances are that you wouldn't find anything other than what we just saw in the much simplified last two paragraphs. As you know, you can describe a cup of coffee in one sentence, or you can write a whole book about it, but it is still a cup of coffee. However, what I find interesting is that if you did a web search for "Big Bang," you would discover that despite getting over 470 million results, (I opened the first 50 returns or so) they would all begin in the exact same fashion:

"Approximately 13.7 billion years ago, the entirety of our Universe was <u>compressed into the confines of an atomic nucleus</u> known as a singularity; this is the moment <u>before creation, when space and time did not exist</u>. An ineffable explosion, trillions of degrees in temperature, that was infinitely dense, created not only fundamental subatomic particles and thus matter and energy but also space and time itself. Cosmology theorists combined with the observations of their astronomy colleagues have been able to reconstruct the primordial chronology of events known as the Big Bang."

Now, if we dissected the (official) description above, we would immediately find enough controversy there alone to write not one—but a thousand books. For even the untrained eye can readily see the nonsensical, *underscored*, contradictions it contains. None of the available information on the Big Bang, makes any mention about "how" the so called "primordial atom" managed to contain the whole Universe within it—much less, "where was that same primordial atom, before space itself existed." Nor does it make any mention about "what" or "who" caused the atom to explode in the first place. However, the peculiar thing that you may or may've not noticed in the "official" description is that in formulating it, a specific word was intentionally included—that does not seem to belong there with the rest. That word being "<u>Creation</u>."

In my humble unbiased opinion this can only indicate a conflict of sorts, an attempt to include a theory within a theory, an attempt to satisfy, *though partially*, both the "Evolution," as well as the "Creation" Side.

However, let us for now leave these insurmountable issues aside. Once scientists agreed to adopt that, *inconclusive*, theory as factual, they were immediately faced with another spinoff, *literally*, even greater question, namely: "What will happen to all masses in the Universe, once all of the so-called 'momentum' from the initial explosion was exhausted?" In an attempt to address the question, two scenarios were proposed.

—A) The first scenario proposes that the Universe—together with all masses within, will keep on expanding forever without any possible final address. This is commonly referred to as the "Inflationary Theory," a.k.a. the "Raisin Bread Theory," space being represented by the bread, masses by the raisins.

—B) The second scenario instead, keeps in account the measurable deceleration of all masses in the visible Universe. Hence proposes that once all momentum is exhausted, *just like the aforementioned exploding grenade,* all things in the Universe would re-collapse back onto their point of origin. In simpler terms, "re-suck" itself back to its original state. This theory was fittingly named "The Rubber Band Theory."

Within limits, the two theories do include some truths. But, here is the problem. The unchangeable fact is that: "The readings were taken from a wrong perspective," hence the rest of the "picture" goes unnoticed!

Suppose you're standing before a 30-foot wall. You can of course easily describe this side of the wall, but would it be wise of you to guess what's on the opposite side—sight-unseen? If you had a ladder you could look over the other side, but without one, I am sure you agree that you'd be wise not to take that guess as factual, and you'd be even wiser not to conduct potentially disastrous experiments based on that guess alone.

The above two theories both adopt the "Big Bang" as their de-facto model of "beginning," when it is in fact nothing more than a best guess.

We shouldn't be surprised then if obstacles mar both theories. "What happened in the aftermath" for instance? "Where is the Universe heading?" And so on, for when starting with a "guess," that's the best we could possibly hope for. The grandfather of all obstacles however, lays right there at the beginning, namely, "Where did that Big Bang originate from?"

But let's for now set that enormously important question aside, giving the two theories a chance nevertheless, and let's look at what other problems plague anyone, who despite all, still insists in pushing the square peg into a round hole. Let's start with the so-called "Inflationary—forever expanding Universe Theory," a.k.a. the "Raisin Bread Theory".

As more advanced telescopes keep on sending clearer and clearer photos our way, this theory is fast approaching the end of its lifecycle. Just recently in fact, astronomers discovered that our observable Universe is actually much younger than previously thought. As recent as a couple of years ago it was widely agreed that the Universe was anywhere from 14 to

20 Billion years old, while new evidence suggests that it is instead much younger, anywhere from 8 to 14 Billion years old.

What does this mean, you ask? If you're a scientist it means an awful lot—and it is not good news. The problem lays mainly in the fact that astronomers have clearly demonstrated that some of the stars in the Universe are as old as 22 Billion years. This is extremely bad news for both the Inflationary as well as the Rubber Band Theory, as this finding would imply that the "baby" existed before the "mother." Faced with this new irrefutable evidence, our scientists are now agreeing that we may soon be in for a big surprise. They expect and they are already speculating in fact that the Big Bang theory will soon be replaced with a new more inclusive theory. The problem is that while they acknowledge being on the wrong track, they nevertheless forge full force ahead with the immensely dangerous Cern Super-Collider experiments.

In addition, various other insurmountable obstacles further plague the two theories, one being for instance the problem of "Space." According to the Big Bang theory the Universe creates space "as it goes" so-to-speak. Space is, in other words, part of the explosion itself we are told. To clarify this point a bit, let's make a little experiment.

Join your hands together if you will, as if praying. Your hands representing the "Big Bang." Now slowly separate your hands apart sideways, *as if simulating an explosion*, and observe the "space" that now exists between your two hands—and notice, *as you increase the distance between your two hands*, how you create more and more of it.

But the question is, "where, in what space, were your hands in, before you started 'creating space'?" Similarly, "Where was the Universe located and expanding into, if there was no space for it to be in, nor to expand into?" Confused yet?

"Space," as far as the Universe is concerned, is just as material and interchangeable as the next planet or even your kitchen table. The only difference is the density, or how closely packed together the molecules that make them are. If, *as the Big Bang theory proposes*, after the initial explosion the Universe continued expanding, it would have needed more "space"— to expand into, but in the same sentence that same theory also states that no space existed externally for the Universe to expand into, making this one of the biggest paradoxes ever. It is much like saying that a house was built on a parcel of land before that parcel of land existed. Do you see the problem? But what really puzzles me, is why would anyone suggest such impossibility—and then build a 20 billion dollars apparatus to study it?

And if that wasn't enough, when we look at how "Time" came into the picture, we are again faced with yet another huge dilemma. Namely; according to the Big Bang theory, "Time" started ticking at precisely the very instant of the explosion itself. But here again, we find ourselves facing another huge paradox. For if as the theory proposes, "time did not start ticking until after the explosion," then where was the Universe "before" the explosion itself?

The problem lays in the fact that when stating "before" and "after," we automatically imply "Time." Thus, once again the dilemma we face here is a "chicken or the egg" type dilemma. Namely, how could have the so-called "original atom"—been already there, before the beginning of time itself? Again this is impossible. But are you puzzled yet? Trust me when I say that it is not a game of words I am trying to confuse you with. Two decades ago, when I first tried to make sense of it, my brain almost liquefied. The fact is, that there is simply no better way to describe the issue. Visit the NASA website (the foremost website on the topic) and you will see that they too are stuck at this very point, with no clear solution in sight.

What it really boils down to, the reason why this is so difficult to explain, much less understand, is because we are again trying to make a square peg fit into a round hole! We are attempting to make something that cannot work—work, by merely using fancy terminology. However, fancy terminology alone will not remove the problem. Spin it as you will, you cannot declare that "time started" at some point and in the same sentence also state that some type of "time" existed before that point. Similarly, if space started manifesting after the explosion, you cannot have space before the explosion. This cannot be argued upon! It would be the same as stating that "time started at exactly midnight, but the primordial 'grain of sand' was inexplicably there before midnight." Or likewise that, "Space didn't exist until after the explosion started 'generating' space, but that inexplicably, 'some' space was already there, holding the ingredients that caused that explosion." Do you see the problem?

Why do our scientists adopt this incredibly senseless theory as valid you may ask? The short answer is that regrettably this is the best they have to work with thus far. And that is the astonishingly simple truth.

Now to the second theory. The so named "Rubber Band Theory," is plagued by yet another rather fascinating but equally impossible dilemma.

The theory keeps in account the fact that all visible celestial masses in the Universe can be observed to be travelling outwardly from a common point of origin—thus, gradually losing kinetic energy, or decelerating. At first examination the two observations seem to further validate the "explosion" idea, as this is exactly what should happen in the aftermath of any explosion. This however brings forth yet another huge dilemma, namely, "what will happen to everything in the Universe once all of the original kinetic energy is exhausted?"

Rubber Band Theory subscribers address the question by proposing that all masses in the Universe will eventually run out of steam so-to-speak, reach a momentary standstill a.k.a. "Top-Dead-Center," to then fall back down onto their point of origin. And at first glance this seems to make a whole lot of sense, as after all, if you threw a stone up in the air, chances are that it would eventually decelerate to a point of zero inertia (TDC) to then fall back down, possibly hitting you on the head. This, all thanks to our beloved gravity, which has decided to keep everything as close to everything else as possible. Thus far, this theory seems to make even more sense than the Inflationary (ever expanding) theory, until we run into an insurmountable dilemma that is. And in this case, what we have is an even bigger dilemma than in the previous theory. And once again, "Time" proves to be the elusive factor—which cannot be "factored-in."

Namely, "if time is created as the Universe expands outwardly, hence forcing everything within the Universe to, *what a joy*, grow older and die, what do you suppose would happen, once the whole Universe reaches its maximum expansion point—and then starts collapsing back onto itself—only this time traveling backwards?" Nothing too spectacular I suppose, if it weren't for the fact that everything in the Universe would grow younger instead than older. If it wasn't for the fact that dead people would come out of their graves, un-die, then live their lives backwards to end up, literally, back in their respective mother's womb. Now, that's what I call fun!

Luckily for us, a third less comical option exists, one that our scientists seem unable to see, especially when they are the ones stating that "time" is an after-product of the Big-Bang, thus time shouldn't have started ticking until after the "Bang" itself. I think you'd agree that anyone with an iota of common sense should see that these two theories simply cannot work. But I still wanted to know the reasons for the total disregard of these obvious problems—and still continue on what we knew was a "dead-end," knowing all the while that we would eventually have no other choice but to make a complete U-turn. After much research I discovered what are essentially three distinct factors.

—A) Mostly due to political and/or religious reasons, mainstream scientists, simply cannot question existing accepted theories. For starters, no scientific institution or university wants to jeopardize their funding. In addition, most scientists are—simply put, reluctant to venture into what they perceive as "forbidden territory." Most have personal struggles to overcome; a struggle with their own personal religious dogmas, coupled with a perceived (*self-imposed*) "Einsteinian barrier," which most believe should never be crossed, challenged or improved upon. Namely "Einstein's Theory of Relativity." But to my knowledge, Einstein never stated that the theories he extrapolated were never to be challenged or improved upon! That was simply the best he could come up with, based on the information available to him at that "Time-Space Address." Still, mostly because of fear of ridicule, most modern day scientists are nevertheless very reluctant to cross or even challenge that imaginary (Einsteinian) line.

—B) Most scientists steadfastly refuse to think outside the box, they see, but do not believe that our Universe is made of much more than this or that rock. They refuse to include within the equation the unseen side of the Universe, unseen side that is in reality the more important of the two sides. For the invisible is what drives the visible. For the invisible is where the visible originates. Thus a scientist will study a rock only from its mineral standpoint. The "force within" the rock, the energy, the electrically charged live atoms that form the rock itself are never considered. Despite being aware of the almost magical energy within that rock, the conventional approach is not to acknowledge it, thus limiting the research to only the tangible.

—C) The third and, in my opinion—most important reason, is that scientists are, knowingly or unknowingly, using the wrong instruments. This is as straightforward as it sounds. They're trying to take Spiritual measurements by using material instruments. This is like trying to measure a room's temperature with a measuring tape.

Think for a moment what would happen if people were made aware of something every physicist knows well. Namely, if we could somehow devise a way to extract the energy contained in a single common 1 kg rock—and transform it into usable energy, we would be able to meet a whole year's worth of a midsized city's electricity needs. From a single 1 Kilo rock that is! This is a scientific fact that no one dares to mention.

Thus, until such time as our scientists are going to finally rid themselves of these dogmas, *as Nikola Tesla said*, they will continue limiting themselves but to only about 5% of what they could see. All they need to do is accept what they already know intuitively. Stop ridiculing the courageous amongst them who dare to push the envelope. <u>Accept the fact that a greater invisible force is at play here</u>. They need not doubt, but instead "ask," for answers do come to those who ask.

And that is precisely the reason why I have a great deal of respect for geniuses the likes of Dr. Tyson and Dr. Kaku for instance, for they are not afraid to acknowledge what is plainly evident—the irrefutable fact that there has to be more to what we can see and touch. I refer to the intangible, immeasurable, unchangeable "Life-Force" at the core of everything in the Universe. But not only what we, *from a human standpoint,* label "alive," but everything—even those things we routinely label as "dead."

Every single speck in the Universe, from a Human to a rock to bacteria, from a tree to a mountain, to the moon and the sun and all celestial bodies in the Universe, to the birds in the sky and the fish in the seas, to the prehistoric dinosaur, to the water we drink and the air we breathe! That "Life-Force" is in everything in the Universe, and the Universe too is itself made of that same Life-Force!

Now, the scientific models we discussed earlier are today's most widely accepted. Let us now examine a third possibility.

According to Seth, the Universe is not a "system that was made to appear externally at any specific point in time." The Universe <u>is</u> instead

"The System" that makes everything—within itself! There is no outside in which a Creator or Creative Force made the Universe—and us, to then direct the whole as an orchestra director would direct his musicians. The Universe is not expanding into an external void, for there is no externality to it. All space is instead internal, a closed system. <u>I suggest you read this paragraph a couple of times before proceeding</u>.

But let's look at this concept in a bit more detail, and somewhat the wiser now; let's once again ask that same infamous question.

—**Question:** Where did the "Big Bang Theory" originate from?

—**Answer:** Let us start by saying that scientists needed to insert a finite point somewhere! They simply couldn't keep on researching an unfinished open-ended, *on both ends*, question. They needed a point of origin where supposedly everything started from, thus establishing a sense of direction, a starting point to build upon. For once they established a factual or manufactured—but agreed upon, "beginning," they could then shift their attention to the aftermath, the rest of the story. But did it matter where—who—what—how that manufactured beginning hatched? "No! Let's leave it for later" they decided.

And so this gave them something to further research for the time being, and in so doing, employ thousands and create dozens of whole industries. The one thing however, which I really wish our scientists considered once and for all, is that as we said earlier, they're using "Earth technology," human concepts, human models, to study something that is neither Earthly nor Human! Hence the inability to find answers! And to make things worse, scientists compelled "time" into the equation, insisting on giving the Universe an age. "The Universe is 'x' million years old" they declared, only to a year later, adjust that figure by give-or-take five billion years. And so they continue on that same dead-end road, insisting that the Universe had to have had a beginning, a point of origin in time, while in the same breath stating that "time" could only have started but after that same very point. Interesting!

The elusive truth is that there never was a precise moment, or a precise bang to speak of, where Creation and its aftermath originated from. Instead, the Universe never started at any specific finite point, the Universe manifested <u>whole</u>! You, me, them, everything in the past as well as everything in the future, my house, your house, kitchen sink included! The Universe manifests all-at-once, precisely as it appears today, our perceived Past, Present, and Future included, all from a "Thought!" But not a thought that the Creator manifested outwardly from Himself, but a thought <u>He's having now</u>! For the last time I checked, thoughts happen internally not externally! Here allow me to remind you that the Creator is not a Human—and neither is He a "being." A Human or a being, who first thinks, to then build outwardly. The Creator is instead a "Gestalt," a "State of Being," who imagines—thus manifests within. No outside to the system exists where Universes could manifest into. And the process is not a one time "bang"—and as many believe, then abandon it to fend for itself, the process is an ongoing, ever expanding process. An ever refined perfected ongoing thought. Thus, the Universe was not created once, "Bang"—and there it was, the Universe is instead continuously being thought, thus created whole, Past, Present and Future, all from the NOW point! But continuously, not in terms of time, but in terms of "probabilities!" As this is no easy concept to grasp however, allow me to illustrate it in a much more simplistic fashion, with a personal experience.

I happen to like airplanes. I have flown computer-simulated airplanes for many years. It all started with an idea in my teen years. After decades of fantasizing about flying a plane, finally in my mid-thirties I installed a 50 dollars piece of flight simulation software in my computer. For many years I flew that simple dot on the screen as if it were an airplane. A horizontally split screen, half green—half blue represented the ground and sky accordingly. Today, if you saw these early attempts at flight simulation, you would probably laugh, but back then, folks who like me, liked flight simulators, were in heaven.

Over time the software improved exponentially. The dot had now two protruding lines on either side we called wings. Then I bought a larger screen, then two screens. Ten years later, the software now much better, they gave us credible looking clouds in the sky and trees on the ground, mountains and even lakes. Five years on, and the software was now so advanced that anyone who saw me flying that simulated plane on my computer screen would stand there in awe. I then experimented with a large TV set, then two sets. Some simulation outfits went through the trouble of painstakingly recording real airplane sounds and then coded these real sounds into the simulator. Surround speakers made the simulator sound almost life like. *"And I saw that it was good!"*

Then a few years ago I had to make a game changing decision. Do I continue flying my desk—pretending it were a plane, or do I choose a specific plane and build a realistic cockpit-like structure? And so, I chose a specific plane, and built a replica cockpit. This proved to be both an enormous undertaking, but a very rewarding one. As any serious hobbyist knows the work is never completed, it is a constant process of upgrading and fine-tuning. But when my friends visit me they are amazed.

They call me "a genius" for building such a complex project—all on my own. But I know what it took, years of planning, countless long nights and the meticulous caring effort. One day I install realistic looking but dummy switches and knobs that look pretty but don't do a thing. A few months later I replace them with fully functional ones. One day I use simulated flight data screens; six month later I replace them with working ones. A few months later I connect it to real weather stations on the Internet, so that I fly in real weather. And the work goes on and on—and I know that even thirty years from now, I will never be neither finished nor satisfied. I simply keep on improving upon my original "creation." I pay attention to what it needs, I listen, I look for things that prevent it from performing at its best, and I fix it as I go along. *"And that gives me great satisfaction."*

I saw my "creation" grow from a simple thought, to a full size cockpit look-alike today, so much so that if you sat in the captain seat, and dimmed the lights a bit, you'd swear you were sitting in the real thing. And when folks come and visit—and see my creation, marvel at my achievement, and their eyes lit up. Grownups, who would normally be preoccupied with life's responsibilities, are instantly transformed into careless happy fascinated children. Their inner child takes over, and their heart fills with joy—if only for an hour. *"And it is all good!"*

And I am sure you understand exactly where this is heading, the point I am trying to illustrate. For how could the process of building a flight simulator relate with the Creation of the Universe? But you'd be surprised, for it does relate indeed, wholly and totally! For the process, although infinitesimally smaller in scale, is always one and the same. "But how could it be the same" you may ask? Here is how.

Man resides not outside, but within All-That-Is, within the realm that is All-That-Is! And since we live within All-That-Is, the same rules of manifestation apply to everything and everyone within All-That-Is, the only difference being the scale. Nothing is produced, built or manufactured, that isn't first imagined, then made, then improved upon. The process is always the same—but would you care to guess why that is? Because we reside inside a "Creation" inside a "Creator," thus we became the only thing we could have become, "co-creators!" Thus, we exist, hence "create" by the same rules, by the only rules available in-fact, only the scale changes. For using that same process, All-That-Is created the Universe or Universes.

And "Perhaps out of solitude," Seth said, "simple curiosity, or perhaps for the sole purpose of knowing Himself and His possibilities, All-That-Is thought of experimenting within. He imagined worlds, and still within His imagination, He visualized and refined these worlds, ever more intensely, evermore focused. Thus these 'worlds' started changing in 'vibration.' And these vibrational changes stimulated, initiated even more changes. And All-That-Is liked what he saw, and encouraged, He focused on His Creation even more, refining that initial thought in ever more detail and definition".

"He nurtured it, continuously improving upon His beloved Creation; a Creation He had grown to love. And that process of envisioning and improving upon, His initial Creation still continues uninterrupted today".

"At first All-That-Is experimented with very primordial, primitive life-forms, but again, not in terms of 'time,' but 'probabilities.' From bacteria to dinosaurs, all types of different increasingly intelligent and more creative life forms. And just like a painter uses colors to express himself, All-That-Is also uses colors to express Himself. We can see that colorful love of expression in the plants and flowers, in the animals, in the beautiful landscapes He creates. And just like a Father loves his children whom he created, All-That-Is loves His children, whom He created".

And now that you have this information, think about it—and decide "where" exactly, would you suppose we "placed" the so-called "Big Bang?" At what precise point in this continuous Creation-Process do you propose we should insert it—so that we humans can deal with the enormity of All-That-Is' unimaginably magnificent undertaking?

Are you starting to see how the Big Bang can only represent but a mere attempt to minimize—reduce the enormity of it all, into something we can wrap our heads around? Can you now see how the Big Bang never actually "banged," but is instead an ongoing process—an explosion of creativity?

Thus, going back to my, *in comparison*, insignificant, minuscule little creation—namely "my flight simulator," when did that "bang" take place exactly, I ask? When did my simulator "bang" into being? Was it when I first started fantasizing about it in my own mind? Was it when I started doing research about it? Was it when I started making plans on paper? Was it when I bought the very first small monitor? Was it when I went with the big screen TV? Or was it when I finally decided to build a cabin around the screens and computers? Or will it be when I decide to dismantle the whole thing—and build an even better one? Are you starting to see what I am getting at?

"It was when I first started making plans on paper that it started" you may argue. But that's only because here—in "human terms," we do everything linearly, according to "time." But try and envision an environment—void of that elusive ingredient (time,) and then tell me, when did my little project started? Do you see my point?

Yes, what I have "created" is nothing more than a little computer project—insignificant in comparison, but the process of going from the initial thought to end-product, is still one and the same, only a quazillion times greater! So, the only reason why we're unable to make sense of it, *unless we insert a "bang" of some type—at some point*, is because—unable to envision an environment where "time" is not a factor by which to create, simply put, "we are at a loss." And recognizing the magnitude, so that we can wrap our brains around it, we decided to insert a "starting point" of some type—somewhere. For seemingly immersed in a "material-time based-world" we can only think in linear-material terms.

Our scientists, unwilling, unable, but most importantly, un-permitted to think in a "sacred" intangible fashion, have no other choice but to include in the equation some type of "material" starting point, no matter how ridiculous and senseless. In all fairness however, and this is indeed a very important point, a "transition" for a lack of a better term did indeed take place at some "point," but not a "point in time," for "time" is a man-made measurement, but at some point in the process.

The transition, or better yet "passage," is a transmutation from pure "thought-energy" into "material-energy," what we call "matter." And that represents the point our scientists so fervently chase, the very point they refer to as the 'Big Bang." But again, it was not a momentary "one-time-flash" type of transmutation, but instead a continuous "passage," a "flow," from pure (Light) Energy, all the way to material Energy. No explosion of any kind took place, but a "turning-up" of the light, an "illumination."

So, when our scientists declare, *"from this observation point it appears as if some type of initial "bang" did take place,"* it is only because that is what they see from here—this observation point. What they cannot possibly see is the "other side" of the system. The process, the flow, and the continuous transmutation that from All-That-Is' perspective still continues today and into perpetuity. For All-That-Is does not see His Creation in terms of "when," or in terms of days, months or even millennia, All-That-Is simply sees His Creation, from, our, beginning to end—whole, as "His Sacred Marvelous Work of Art!" Period!

Suppose that you were a painter. Now suppose that a new technology existed allowing you to paint a painting—not gradually but instead all at once, like a photograph. You transfer in other words, whatever you envisioned in your mind, into an immediate all-at-once work of art. Then further suppose that you had the power to make that work of art, not only in 3-D but also alive. Thus, not knowing how they got there, the various subjects in the painting begin extrapolating theories, about probable "makers," probable beginnings, as well as probable ends. And in the process, not only do they come up with some pretty bizarre ideas, but also they unknowingly give birth to the concept of "time" hence "past, present, and future." Not realizing that they were instead all made but in one instant, their perception of "passage of time," their perception of "beginning and end" included.

But, "will this Work of Art still include Humans in the (our) future?

We simply do not know the answer to that question. If All-That-Is decides that He should continue developing and improving upon His original creation, then the answer is yes. But if on the other hand, All-That-Is decides to wipe the canvas clean - and start painting a totally new "painting" from scratch, then the answer is no. But this is how, *when I asked him twenty years ago*, Seth answered that very question.

"Would you wipe your canvas clean, if it included your own children?" I believe Seth may have just given us the answer!

Now, from a scientific standpoint nothing exists unless it can be materially proven. Thus, although I would rather speak in "spiritual terms" if "material" is how we must speak, then so be it!

Envision if you will, two Cones of Energy* joined at their tips, one spinning clockwise, the other counterclockwise.

As for every bit of pull in one direction an equal amount of pull exists in the other, the two equally opposing forces create a perfectly still midpoint. Now, with the two cones joined tip-to-tip, Energy flows uninterrupted through the system, from the lower half to midpoint, to then emerge into the upper half. And it is on this upward journey that Energy gradually loses momentum and decelerates—deceleration, which

(See illustration at the end of the book).

is the very cause of the gradual mutation from Pure-Light to Physical, hence materialization.

Therefore, from the center, Light travels upwards, decelerating, thus materializing more and more, until all momentum is exhausted. At which point it has nowhere else to go but down. Thus, what we call "the top of the upper cone," is in reality nothing more than the "farthest" point the system can travel, for no de-facto "cone"—nor "up-and-down" actually exists, the "cone" is simply the shape the system takes-on in the process.

Thus, once fully decelerated hence fully mutated from Light to Matter, pushed from behind by the continuous outflow from the center, will once again start "falling" out-and-downwardly. And this is when the process itself reverses, only this time on its way back to the center of the system from the bottom. Therefore, what had become "Matter" will again gradually change into Energy, taking on more and more Energy-like properties as it goes, to be finally reabsorbed into a point (the center) of pure Light.

In a nutshell, what came spewing out into the upper half of the system as Pure-Light, will—pushed from behind on one hand, and pulled by the forward-travelling vacuuming centrifugal force on the other—"reach" or better yet "shape" the top of the system.

To then, now fully material, start "falling" outwardly, to then be, re-vacuumed backup from the bottom of the system. Essentially this is a transmutation from Light to Matter, and back to Light again.

Reminiscent (as an example) of clothes being pushed against the walls of a clothes-dryer drum, similarly, Light is spun outwardly centrifugally, except that in this case there are no walls to stop it. Thus, Light will travel "up-and-out" as far as momentum will allow it, thus creating in the process, "space," as well as the System's outermost edge or "invisible walls" if you like. But because it is not a "straight edge" that it produces outwardly, but instead a "cascading-undetectable edge," it is not a defined visible "wall" that it forms, but instead a seemingly never-ending "curvature." This, being the same "curvature" Einstein had correctly predicted many decades ago.

This model clearly explains why everything in the Universe has a natural in-built spin. Everything in the Universe—be it a planet or the water going down your kitchen sink, "spins." No exception.

Now, as we just saw, Light from the center—caught in the spinning vortex, hence spun out and up, is pushed farther and farther from its point of origin, to then gradually lose momentum. This process of deceleration is what gives birth to a process of "gradual solidification," hence materialization. Thus the farther from the center—the more "material" *(what was once pure Light)* will become. Said gradual process of transmutation, running the full gamut from pure transparent Light, to semi-transparent, to semi-physical, to physical. This "last layer,"—the material-tangible portion that is, being the layer of the Universe we Humans are most familiar with and reside in. Or more precisely, where our projected physical bodies reside in. And since this is information few will be able to process at face value, for those of us who are not too scientifically inclined, let's attempt to simplify the process a bit.

Take a large funnel, hold it wide side up, and attach a water hose to its tip. Then while looking inside the funnel, gradually turn the tap on. Observe what happens inside the funnel. At first, the water will start filling the funnel up very quickly, to then (as it reaches the wider part of the funnel) gradually slow down more and more. Interestingly, you may've also noticed that on its way to the top, the water has started spinning. This, as we said before, is due to the fact that everything in the Universe "spins." And once our funnel fills up, and the water will eventually start spilling over the sides, it will have no other way to go but down onto the ground.

But let's now take our little experiment a bit further. Let's take a second identical funnel and crazy-glue it upside-down tip-to-tip to the first. However, suppose that instead of our two upside-down common plastic funnels, what we had instead was a "Sacred System," in the shape of two inverted cones. Self-powered from within by "Divine Intent," the lower half of the system, recycles, or "vacuums-up" for the lack of a better definition, Matter spilling out from the upper half, to then push that matter, compressing it, centrifugally and inwardly, hence causing it to accelerate more and more, until (now at the very center of the system) it becomes Pure Light once again.

This cycle continues in perpetuity, but perpetuity, not time-wise. As far as "Creation" is concerned, the "System" simply exists, period! Then "Time," *since we humans love our watches*, only exists but within a small portion of the whole, the "decelerated-material-solid portion" we live in. Thus, while our poor scientists are literally breaking their brains trying to make sense of the Big Bang, it is in reality a lot simpler than they know. What they call the Big Bang is not (as it appears) "the center of the explosion," but instead "<u>a passage point;</u>" the point where everything comes spewing out from an Energy (Antimatter) realm, into a Matter realm. The only reason why we're unable to see the other half of the system has all to do with "where we are looking from." From here—our observation point somewhere near the top portion of the (material) half, we are only able to see inside but one of the two halves of the whole, the upper half that is. Thus, from this perspective, the opposite side of the system goes completely unnoticed.

And so, based on that observation alone, our scientists logically assume that it is an "explosion" that they are looking at—an "exploding singularity." Wouldn't you? If all that you could see with your telescope was only half of the system? And that is by the way, the very reason why both the "Rubber Band," as well as the "Inflationary" theory can only be half right.

Oblivious to it, they fail to account for the other half of the system, the unseen half, which makes the whole. This is also the reason why are our scientists unable to make these theories work—unless they insert in the equation some type of "beginning." As when Divine Consciousness is excluded, something "material,"—factual or otherwise, must take its place. Simply put, our telescopes couldn't possibly see the other (hidden) half of the equation. That half where everything is continuously recycled into our (material) half from—the half we do see.

To better understand this point; let's again summon our beloved pair of funnels; only this time let's use bigger funnels. We start by again joining the two funnels tip-to-tip, and then hold them vertically. If the funnels were wide enough, imagine putting your head inside the top* funnel while looking in. Look toward the center, and tell me what you see. What you see is exactly what our scientists see when training their telescopes "<u>inside</u>" the Universe. The farther-in you look—the more you see the walls of the funnel coming closer and closer together towards the center—into a focused finite point. Thus, similarly to what you see in your funnel, scientists assume that what they are seeing is "a common point of origin," where everything "<u>appears</u>" to be spewing—"exploding" out from, in a spinning outward motion. But what about the second half—the second

---

*(When stating "upper" or "lower" half of the cone or funnel, or when stating "upward," "up," or "down" etc., it is for illustrative purposes only. In reality, no actual "up" or "down" exists in the Universe, much less in the All-That-Is Gestalt.)

funnel situated just under the one you have your head in. Are you able to see it from where you're looking?

Of course not, hence our conundrum! Thus, in an attempt to explain where all matter in the material-observable Universe, *our half*, originates from, and what causes the outward spinning motion all celestial bodies exhibit, <u>unable to see the whole system</u>, common sense dictates that at some point, some type of explosion must have occurred in that <u>perceived</u> "center." And since common-sense is all that our scientists will consider— hence, what better explanation than that of a "Bang?" A big one in this case. But according to the prevalent theory, "what banged exactly" you may ask? Conventional wisdom tells us that it was "a Super-Compressed Grain of Sand" that banged! But I will let you the reader be the judge of that!

Now, a few pages back, you might or might not have noticed the mentioning of a very subtle but enormously important clue. But in case you missed it, "what is the one unmistakable 'tell-all-clue' that clears all doubts once and for all?" Well, years ago, a good friend of mine who happens to be a geologist, made an interesting comment.

"Marco, what you're proposing makes a lot of sense. It makes a lot more sense than anything else I've seen so far. But the question is—how can it be proven?"

"Firstly," I said, "let me remind you that I am not the one who's proposing this 'theory,' Seth is. I am just the messenger."

"Secondly, the clue is simply this, 'How else could we explain the fact that everything in the Universe spins?'"

"Wow!" He said. "You are right, I never thought of that! If an explosion (the Big Bang) was what made our Universe, fragments would in its aftermath, fly outwardly in all directions. Some would take a linear trajectory, while some would spin irregularly and in every direction. No explosion could possibly create a Universe where all fragments spin instead!" He concluded. So, in case you needed one—that is the clue!

And again, I for the life of me cannot understand why our scientists are unable to recognize this inarguable fact. Namely, if, *as it is commonly believed*, "it was an explosion that gave birth to the Universe," logic would dictate, as I am sure you'd agree, that the resulting fragments would all travel from the center of the explosion in an unorganized outward fashion. But what we have here—our Universe is instead "isotropic," meaning, that everything in it spins! Hence it does not take the Wright brothers to understand that the

Universe itself must be a "spinning system" and not an "exploding system."

Take a dozen tennis balls and put them in your clothes dryer, then turn the dryer on and see how the tennis balls behave. They will all start spinning of course—and so does everything in the Universe. It is therefore not an "Exploding Expanding Universe" that we inhabit, but instead a "spinning-recycling" Universe. A Universe, that simply exists!

But how could something "simply exist," without being "created" by something or someone you may ask?

The Universe was indeed created, but not in terms of "when!" Earlier in the book, we mentioned that at the Universal scale "time" does not exist. Time only exists within our temporary "material sojourn" within the cycle. *This is probably the single-most biggest obstacle preventing us from fully understanding this notion.* We are so accustomed to think of everything being made in terms of "when" that we are unable to think in any other terms. I promise this will become much clearer later in the book. So, what part does "Time" play into the equation? What is "TIME" exactly?

Measurable time only exists in but a small portion of the Universe, <u>our material portion</u>. As decelerating Energy gradually changes into Matter, its vibrational signature also changes accordingly. This gradual process of solidification however, causes it to become heavier and heavier, hence slowing down even further. And this "slowing down process" is precisely what causes—what started as light, to materialize.

We could once again use water's relation to ice as an example, same components—different molecular arrangement. Ice is water in solid form. In ice the molecules stand almost still, while in water they move constantly, and the hotter the water, the more energy the molecules will have—and therefore move faster. So Energy decelerates, and in so doing, it transforms into its counterpart, "Matter." Thus "Light"—the Spiritual side has a material counterpart, the Physical side. Physical counterpart in which inhabitants' decided to invent a system, that allows them to get up and go to work each morning, a system that gives them a sense of direction in an otherwise mysterious existence. We call this system "Time." Then we make watches and calendars, so that we can keep track of it. But "time" is just another "unit of measurement," which <u>we invented</u>, for our own convenience. The last time I checked, the Universe didn't create "time," nor does it care about it. For the Universe does not keep track of time nor does it need to, the Universe simply is! It is the year 2017 for us, but what would you say the year is, as far as the Universe is concerned?

Now, most physicists seem to subscribe to the notion that "Time" and "Gravity" are different aspects of one and the same. But once again, they are unfortunately on the wrong track. Gravity and time are not one and the same, but instead, each a by-product of the same deceleration process. Similarly, just like we invented "time" and watches to keep track of it, we also invented instruments to measure the attraction force that exists between all masses, large or small. So we called this measurement "Gravity," and we made many instruments capable of measuring it, some of the simplest examples of which are right on your bathroom floor, namely your bathroom scale. "Gravity" and "Time" are both by-products of decelerated light, but that's not all. While we normally only associate time and gravity with the process of deceleration, according to Seth, there is a lot more to it.

And I forewarn you that this may sound strange, but, *according to Seth*, a myriad of other factors are also a by-product of that same deceleration process. All forms of "Illness" for instance, "Crime," and even "Negativity" in itself, are all by-products of a decelerated vibration. For the farther from "Light" you are, the "heavier" life itself becomes, in every sense of the word.

I do not wish to confuse you further with information that is almost incomprehensible, however I do want to point out, *I would do you a disservice if I didn't*, that even the above, as magnificent as it may sound, doesn't even come close to describe how Seth defines All-That-Is—truly infinite. But I am not saying this in a religious fashion where mainly out of fear we say things we neither understand nor mean, I say this because the Gestalt most folks call "God," but I like to call "All-That-Is," is truly so incredibly magnificent that we couldn't even begin to imagine. So beautifully complex that it may very well be beyond our ability to fully comprehend it.

As I said earlier, the problem lays in the fact that each time I write the world "God" throughout the book, most readers will automatically evoke a preconceived image of a God, which has resided in their brain for much of their entire life. *And even I must remind myself often that I too am the product of centuries of indoctrination*, thus not only does that "god idea" fall far short from suitably representing what I am attempting to illustrate here, but it is also difficult to replace it, *that centuries old idea*, with the God I am actually referring to. For when one associates "God" with the usual flying magical super-being most of us are accustomed to, not only do we do ourselves a great disservice, but we also do a disservice to (the ultimate) God. All-That-Is.

Now, what if I told you that the Universe—while appearing to be expanding outwardly from our perspective, from God's perspective it actually expands inwardly? We of course, observe and judge everything from our standpoint, but "here-where-we-are" is unfortunately the wrong observation point. Then, to make things worse, we use human made instruments, and with them we measure everything from a star's temperature to gravity, to different light spectrums, and we do so, all within known and accepted parameters. Then, we reason (about what we see) with human brains and human made computers.

Our mind, *our Soul actually*, all the while, hinting very hard, that "there is more to the story,"—but do we listen? Of course not, "We can't touch it, thus it can't exist," we conclude. "We must use accepted agreed-upon parameters," we comfort ourselves with. But agreed and accepted by whom I ask? Weren't we who sat these parameters in the first place—and we did so from the wrong perspective, and based on wrong assumptions? Then we go ahead and design instruments that fall within, and capable of reading within those same preset parameters. But how could we possibly see anything outside those preset limits I ask?

When a new telescope is built, it is not only built upon old existing technology, but it is built to find distances and light spectrums we already know of, just farther! A telescope is not built to look for, or find within an unlimited "open-ended" light spectrum, so how could it possibly show us anything new? What's even worse is that we end up convincing ourselves that those preconceived confinements are all that exists. Thus, the Universe has no other choice—when observed by us, but to appear—to behave in-fact, within these expected confinements.

But before we continue, allow me to extend my warmest congratulations to those of you, who figured it out on your own!

But for those of us who haven't, may I dare to suggest that the Universe we observe behaves exactly as we expect it to?

Every layer of existence is preconceived to behave exactly as each observer expects it will. Exactly as we—the observers believe it should.

"How could that be possible?" You ask.

It can and it does! For as incredible and fantastic as it may sound, this Universe of ours does not actually exist! There, I said it!

The proverbial cat now out of the bag, for surprise-surprise it would appear that our observable Universe is actually and <u>continuously created by us the observers</u>! Moment by moment we "think" hence manifest our Universe outwardly into being, this both at the personal as well as at the en-mass level! But do not wrongly assume that we are also responsible for creating the "System" where our "imaginary" Universe exists-in, for the "System" exists within the All-That-Is Gestalt.

Our "material Universe" represents the opposite end of Creation, "our end" that is, our playground if you like. And I do understand of course the weight these assertions carry; I am fully aware of the fact that some of you reading this are probably screaming "bloody sacrilege" or that I must be missing a couple of screws upstairs.

But that was exactly what I thought when Seth first proposed this to me. "Are you crazy?" I said. But then, as he went on to explain the mechanics in more detail, I realized that it couldn't be any other way.

What if I were to further suggest to you that this dimension of ours, and in-fact all dimensions, do not actually exist, but are "Psychological Dimensions" only?

And even stranger, what if I were to suggest that we are not actually here, but that we actually "pulse" in-and-out of this Psychological Dimension, many times per second. So fast in fact, that it appears uninterrupted thus "physical" to us the observers?

If you ever had a chance to see what a movie-film looks like, then you'd know what I mean. A series of photo stills, that when played in rapid sequence appear to form an uninterrupted movie. The mechanisms are very similar.

And would you believe me if I told you that the instant just prior to opening your eyes each morning, nothing existed around you—and that you, based on your beliefs and expectations, instantaneously manifest your surroundings outwardly? You do so not just each time you wake up, but in fact every instant of your life, no exception! This process takes place uninterrupted moment by moment and all throughout your existence.

And I do realize that from a human perspective this is of course hard to accept, to say the least. However it becomes a whole lot easier, once you remind yourself of the magnitude, the force we are attempting to illustrate here. Do not forget, "<u>Who you are a part of</u>" and "<u>Where you're creating your environment in</u>." Then, what seems unthinkable at first—will appear as child's play.

Now, Earth is presently travelling in space at 107,278.87 Km per hour. From our standpoint this might sound like an enormous rate of speed, but from the system's standpoint it is as slow as it could possibly get. Seth suggested in fact, that we are not only at a point where we are travelling so slow that we had to invent watches and calendars, but that we're actually just starting to re-accelerate. Seth said in fact, that we've already reached and passed our TDC (top dead center), and that we are now starting to fall, <u>outwardly</u>, toward the bottom of the system where we will eventually be "re-absorbed," to be reaccelerated inwardly by the System's other half. However, we need not envision scenarios where we would suddenly fall off any type of "edge" or where we would suddenly be sucked up into a vacuum of sorts. We are attempting to describe an unimaginably infinite system, thus, from our standpoint we will always travel in a straight line.

As our scientists correctly know, the Universe exhibits a natural curvature. Long ago Einstein proposed in fact that if we were to, *hypothetically speaking*, launch a rocket and program it to fly upward in a perfectly straight line and never change course, eons later, that rocket would eventually return to that same exact point. However, the curvature is so infinitesimally subtle that it is basically impossible to detect. The curvature is there, and indeed it does exist, but based on what we can see we can only theorize about it, as to this date, no instrument exists capable of measuring it.

I saw a documentary years ago, where using a similar process a smart pilot fouled an attempted hijacking. While he was ordered by the hijacker to fly to a certain airport, he instead set the plane's autopilot to a one or two degrees turn. Turn which although so subtle that no-one on-board, except the captain, was able to detect, caused the plane to basically return back where it took-off from, and in the process almost run out of fuel. With almost no fuel onboard, the hijacker had no other choice but to allow the plane to land, getting arrested as soon as it did.

Years ago Seth pointed out something peculiar, which some of you may already know. It would appear that although our watches still register 24 hours days, in the last few decades, we have begun to perceive an ever so subtle "acceleration of time." Is it just an illusion or does everything seem to happen faster nowadays? Inventions, illnesses, even heads of states seem to come and go so quickly nowadays. And don't the days seem to be shorter than before? We have to rush through everything it seems nowadays.

I am not in the position of giving a conclusive answer, but according to Seth this is not just our imagination. Seth suggested in fact that one of today's "24-hour days," happens in what was a mere 22.5 hours of say a thousand or so years ago. "But then why are our watches still recording "time" in the same fashion as before?" I asked him.

"Your watches are still registering a 24 hour day simply because, watches, watch wearers, as well as calendars, are all travelling at the same speed as everything else. Thus, watches cannot register the difference," he said. In simpler terms, if you're standing on the ground looking up at an airplane flying overhead at say 900 km/h, you can easily see the speed at which that plane was moving. However, if you were instead on board that same airplane, thus yourself travelling at 900 Km/h, you would then be no longer able to tell if the airplane was moving or not, as from onboard, *minus the turbulence*, the airplane would appear to be perfectly still, as you and the airplane would be travelling together, at the same speed.

Seth explained that the Universe is incomprehensibly big, and that once a certain rate of acceleration is reached, "time" no longer applies. The system is in fact so large, that even if we were to measure it in terms of time, it would take quad-zillions of eons, thus questions we need not concern ourselves with. I also asked Seth if he could give me an idea of just how big the "whole system" is. He replied that there is no way to know.

"Suppose," he said, "that your visible neighboring Universe occupied 5% of the whole, or 0.0000005% of the whole, what difference could it possibly make to you?"

"What if," he continued, "you were to discover that you did indeed occupy 5% of the Universe, but you later discovered that your Universe amounted to no more than 0.00005% of an even larger Universe, what difference would it make to you?"

"What if that larger Universe was only but a small portion of yet another bigger Universe—and so on? What if there was more than one Universe, perhaps parallel, each carrying on with their own 'cycles,' each independent from the next, but all inside an even larger system?"

And then he totally floored me when he said, "What if this unimaginably large system was to amount to nothing more than a passing thought in All-That-Is' mind? But not only that" he continued, "what your scientists are unable to see through their telescopes, is that the farthest reaches of the Universe they observe, while visible to the eye—are not actually there!" He said.

What do you mean by "are not actually there" I asked.

"At its core, the Universe is Energy—intangible Energy that is. And so while your surrounding Universe appears 'tangible' to you, it becomes less and less so—the farther out you look. And only when you will eventually be able to travel far and wide in space—will those unexplored portions of the Universe become 'tangible'—as needed." He explained.

"Wow, this is totally insane," I said.

"No Marco, this is simply how Energy works—no more no less. It comes into being—only and when it needs to—or more precisely, when someone observes it, or a spaceship needs to navigate through it.

"Seth, this is mind-blowing," I said.

"Not when you remind yourself that all exists inside a thought," he said.

And so according to Seth, we simply have no way to know, or need to be concerned with how big All-That-Is is. But since I rarely take no for an answer, I had to ask Seth, "Precisely, how big is All-That-Is?" and "Who or What is All-That-Is in the first place?"

Seth replied that the biggest misconception holding us back from appreciating the true grandiose of All-That-Is, is the centuries of brainwashing we've been exposed to. We've been driven into believing and, in the process, reduced the God idea to a mere flying-super-being figure who spends his days sitting on a shiny cloud, note pad and pen in hand, deciding who to reward and who's going to be zapped each day.

As we said before, this is all by design. This is how we chose to "grow" as a society and learn to know our Source, not all at once, but gradually, from the "outside-in"—starting with the "ugliest" first, and then working our way inward towards the Light. So our un-evolved interpretations give us a corresponding "god idea," along the way to enlightenment. Therefore, in an era of revengefulness, unforgivingness, uncaring violence, we can only envision a matching, revengeful, unforgiving, uncaring, even violent God.

This was egregiously represented, in a conversation I had with a nice client of mine who happens to be a pastor at a local church where she teaches evangelic classes. "Sin," *what else*, was the topic at hand. She assured me that everyone on the planet, newborns included, were made to pay for Adam and Eve's original sin. But when I pointed out what we just discussed here, it was as if a bolt of lightning hit her! With eyes wide open and almost in shock, she said:

"Why didn't I ever think of this before?"

"Well, I don't know," I replied!

"This makes perfect sense Marco, but what this means, is that for over twenty years I have been teaching (to children) that God is uncaring, unforgiving, violent and revengeful. That is terrible! I am so disappointed with myself. My God, can you ever forgive me? Marco what should I do," She asked, almost in tears?

"How about teaching them the truth from now on," I said "How about teaching them that God is caring and loving instead, and that He gave us free will so that we could experiment within all possible scenarios," I said?

"My God, I will have to start all over again. How could I have missed something so obvious," she replied.

"God couldn't possibly allow children to starve to death to make them 'pay for their parent's sins' or for this or that stupid apple! I cannot believe I have been teaching this ugliness for this long and I am going to have a talk with the folks in charge of our organization. This is just terrible..." she concluded.

Then she came around my desk, "How could I ever thank you. Can I give you a hug?" She asked.

"But then what is the real reason why do children starve to death" you may ask?

The real reason is simply that, that is the path of growth that specific Soul chose for their personal Earth experience! An experience, however short, that will not only add to their personal knowledge, but also teach the rest of us a lesson.

Suppose that in another life, you (the Soul) chose to experience a role of pompous wealth and wastefulness, so wasteful in fact that you instructed your kitchen staff to cook enough food for twenty people every day, to then toss most of it in the garbage. Eventually your body became old and died. You, the Soul, from Home (where we always reside as Souls), aided by your Guides, reexamined both the positives as well as the negatives of that life just passed. Hence you decided to relive another life-experience, but this time from the opposite end. For you surely learned what it felt like to be wealthy and wasteful, but what about the opposite side of the coin—not having enough food to even survive, that is. However, this is not to be misconstrued with any form of, *here we go again*, "punishment." There is no "karma" to pay, for that is just another misconception in the long list of "man-made scare-tactics."

Neither will anyone force you to come back, as it is always the case; you always make your own decisions. For it would, no doubt, be useful to know firsthand what it was like to relive that last lifetime once again, but this time from the opposite end. For only then would you have experienced the full gamut, from having your belly full every day, to being so hungry and have so little food that you actually die from starvation. Only then would you have a complete true picture and fully appreciate the totality of that experience. For each of us Souls need—wants to experience the two opposite sides of each and all experiences. The rich and the poor, the loved and the neglected, the healthy and the sick, the athlete and the wheelchair confined, the black and the white, the hater and the hated, the oppressor and the oppressed, the murderer and the victim.

"But Seth," I asked, "why in the world would someone choose to incarnate as say a homeless person, instead of choosing to experience the good life of say a wealthy business magnate?"

"Marco," he replied, "conventional wisdom would suggest that a wealthy business magnate's life would be a much more rewarding life to live, than that of say a homeless individual. But let's look at this from a different perspective." He said.

"The wealthy individual awakens every morning having to follow a schedule of events throughout the day, that was most likely—and for the most part prearranged for him by his staff. His breakfast lunch and dinner are pre-decided in advance, and served to him on a silver plate. His weeks consist of rushing from preset meeting to preset meeting—and from prearranged museum trip, to this and that prearranged golf tournament. And while from the outside he may appear to be in control of his life, the reality is that his lifestyle and work schedule are what control him instead.

"But I am not implying that "wealthy" is not a good place to be," Seth continued, "but let's look at the other side of the coin if you will.

In contrast, the homeless person who has to push a cart full of his belongings all day long, wakes up every morning—if he made it through the night that is, without knowing where his breakfast or lunch are going to come from—this or that trash can, a handout from some nice soul, or throwaway leftovers from this or that restaurant? Then, all throughout the day he has to continuously move from place to place, most likely having to watch over his shoulder all the while, trying to find a place where he is going to spend the next night. Under this or that bridge, under this or that park bench, or even inside this or that cardboard box? And that is the least of his worries, for his only hope is that he makes it through another cold night."

"So, Marco," he continued, "from a Soul's standpoint, or even from Source's standpoint, which of the two life experiences would you say is the most interesting, colorful, varied, and in the end worthwhile living? Especially when considering that from a Soul's perspective, a lifetime goes by but in a blink of an eye?"

"Wow, I am starting to understand, thank you Seth," I said.

"Learning," is Life's purpose, the only reason in fact for coming to Earth! Be it a positive or negative experience, we still learn something—thus, all experiences are positive. And at the end of each excursion, all that information is stored in the Akashic Records, a "Celestial Computer," where everyone's history is photographically stored. I am sure most of you have heard of accounts of near death experiences, where folks, as if in a pictorial slideshow, reported seeing their entire life flash before their very eyes. That slideshow comes from the Celestial Akashic Records.

Have you noticed how everything we do here on Earth, every moment of our life in fact, amounts to nothing more than a continuous learning process? Have you noticed how no matter how hard you try you just cannot stop learning? You're having a conversation with someone—you learn; you watch TV—you learn; you read a magazine—you learn; or you're daydreaming on the sofa—and you're still learning! Our physical system was so conceived, or more precisely "thought into existence" for one reason only—and that reason is learning! Learning through physical experience, things which we cannot do there as Souls. Thus, everything we experience, at all levels, All-That-Is experiences. And there is simply no way to know All-That-Is' true magnitude! For All-That-Is is not a person, but instead a "Gestalt." And if we looked up the definition of that word, here is what we find:

"Gestalt: A perceptual pattern—so united as a whole—and possessing qualities that cannot be described merely as a sum of its parts."

In simpler terms, All-That-Is is everywhere and in everything. "He" is everywhere and everything. "He" is all of the physical and non-physical realms put together. Yet, even if we were able to somehow add together all of these parts, All-That-Is would be greater still! In fact, Seth himself does not know All-That-Is' true magnitude.

But where did "All-That-Is" come from?

All-That-Is did not come from anywhere! For starters, we need to remind ourselves that "time"—and thus "when," does not apply anywhere else but within our small "sector" in the whole system!

All-That-Is is the System! Thus, All-That-Is never started or originated from anywhere, All-That-Is simply exists, and in our terms always was and always will. No words exist in our human vocabulary to fittingly describe All-That-Is, *Seth explained*, or to even understand the reasons why All-That-Is does what "He" does. And as you might have noticed, I myself must use "He" when addressing All-That-Is, as no other word exists in our dictionary to suitably address All-That-Is.

Of course All-That-Is is neither man nor woman, for these extremes merely represent "forms" we Souls adopt here on Earth, so that we could experience all aspects of all that Earth-Life has to offer.

Other systems might very well include asexual beings, or beings that are both man and woman. Keeping in mind our limited lexicon, the following is as best as Seth could describe All-That-Is.

"All-That-Is, is a Gestalt, a conscious intelligent self-aware Gestalt of unimaginable grandiose. In an effort to explore the full range of probabilities, All-That-Is envisioned altering certain portions within (we do not know what percentage of the whole) by changing their 'vibration.' This, out of mere curiosity, or perhaps out of solitude, or possibly because 'exploring' is as natural to All-That-Is as it is to us. All-That-Is experimented with these portions within, for (what Seth calls) 'Eons' in our terms. This continued and still continues today as All-That-Is still continues to experience through us."

"Everything that every individual or being experiences within all physical and non-physical realms, All-That-Is experiences directly! Everything we do; everything anyone does, in every possible dimension or realm of existence is directly connected to and within All-That-Is. Thus everything goes back to All-That-Is."

"Not because All-That-Is is connected to us, but because All-That-Is is us! Nothing therefore exists without—or outside of All-That-Is, for there is no outside! Thus, All-That-Is is aware of everything we do, what every rock, eagle or tree does. All-That-Is is aware of every fish in the sea, every blade of grass bending in the wind, and every sparrow that flies in the sky, for All-That-Is is every blade of grass and every sparrow in the sky!"

"Though grandiose however, even this explanation cannot accurately describe All-That-Is. There are things about All-That-Is we simply have no way of knowing. All-That-Is could have very possibly created a single Universe, or a multitude of Universes, or a larger Universe still—that includes a myriad of Universes within. And although inconceivably big, it could all be but only a 'thought' in All-That-Is' mind!"

And if you are now starting to appreciate the beauty of all this, appreciate and respect all and everything around you, for it was created by All-That-Is. Have reverence and gratitude. Respect yourself first, and then all fellow Humans, all Plants and Animals. Even a rock deserves your respect and admiration, for even that rock is part of All-That-Is!

And so the next time you accidentally step on a seemingly insignificant little ant, say a prayer and thank the ant that gave its life to teach you yet another small lesson, a little more appreciation for the gift of Life.

For what it may seem an inconsequential little ant, may've changed the dynamics of an entire ant colony. Unknown to you some of the ants will go hungry and shed ant-tears today, for the father-ant that went out to find food for its family but never came back.

Thus, have Respect and Reverence for Everything in the Universe, no matter how seemingly small and insignificant. For I am sure you are now starting to appreciate the gift that you are!

All-That-Is did not create you because He had nothing better to do. He created you for a reason! Find that reason! Find your reason!

Love, and appreciate yourself, for when you do, you are honoring All-That-Is' work!

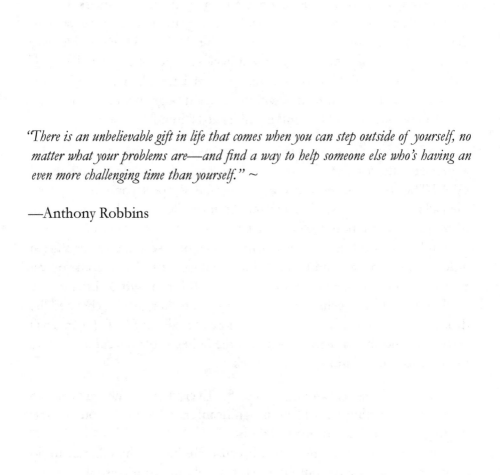

"There is an unbelievable gift in life that comes when you can step outside of yourself, no matter what your problems are—and find a way to help someone else who's having an even more challenging time than yourself." ~

—Anthony Robbins

Chapter 5

The Meeting

I am sure you might've noticed by now how the topics covered in the book, are gradually expanding, becoming more and more in-depth as we go. The first half of the book was so designed, *at the risk of sounding a bit repetitive*, to bring subjects that we were already familiar with, but which we had for whatever reason, swept under the proverbial carpet—back up to the surface. We then went on stimulating our brains a bit further, and touched on subjects, that most folks would normally rather not talk about.

This was in preparation for what's in store in the second half of the book. We can say that the book was so purposefully structured. For as we saw earlier, if you wished to embark on a trip—any trip, you would be wise to first establish your present state of affairs—your present "status quo," from where you are starting your trip. I hope this has helped shed some light and hopefully somewhat clarified not only our present state of affairs, but also the probable scenarios and events throughout history that might have steered us here. Call it "an introduction," call it "laying a foundation," but we have now reached a point in the book where the so-called "veils" need to be removed.

Therefore, the second half of the book will assume that you, the reader, are now ready to explore a much more revealing "truer" version of "The True Nature of Reality." I guarantee you will find several "surprises" along the way, and I forewarn you that some of you may find some of the material difficult to relate to. It really all depends on "where you're at" at present so-to-speak, your personal level of Spiritual Evolution. Some folks who during the book's editing phases read the manuscript, commented that it totally changed them for the better, some said that it was exactly "what they needed or instinctively knew" and related to it very well, some folks said instead that they could only partially understand it, and some folks said that "they did not agreed with it."

But that's my point exactly, for it is "them" who do not "agree" or "relate" to the material, not the material—to them!

Whether you agree or relate to it, has only to do with you—and your personal level of Spiritual growth. The book (any book for that matter) does not change; it stays the same regardless of who reads it! Thus, you should not read this or any book, expecting it to agree with what you already know, and if it does not—decree, "it does not make sense." For you should not judge this or any book based only on how much of it matches your existing level of knowledge, for if that were the case—if that is what you expect of any book, then you would never learn anything new." As Seth once told me, *"It matters not whether you believe, or even understand. The laws of the Universe will still stay the same."* The reason is simple. Too overwhelmed by our usual preconceived perception of our surroundings—what we're accustomed to see, touch and smell, we find it difficult to envision a Universe we call "solid," but that is in fact not solid at all. Not only it is not solid, but that in reality it doesn't even exist.

When years ago Seth first introduced me to this same information, it took me several months before I could even start to think along those lines. But once I was able to put some of the pieces of the puzzle together, it became evident that what Seth was trying to explain was in fact true. More specifically, that this whole "scenario" we are so concerned with here on Earth, is nothing more than a big "movie," a "play" on a grandiose scale, a "simulation" if you like, to which we continuously keep on adding episodes, so that we can keep on experiencing things we couldn't possibly experience in our natural environment, at "Home as Souls."

You might've noticed in the last few years (2010-2017,) the Web and even TV, have become filled with all sorts of documentaries, seemingly all pointing to the very topic we are endeavoring to discuss in this book, suggesting more and more, that this seemingly "solid" Universe of ours, may not actually exist at all. Some researchers call it "Holographic," some a "Simulation," some have even suggested that we all live inside a huge computer of sorts. The truth is that whatever we wish to call it, "movie" and so on—it is still a simulation of sorts, for what is a movie if not a simulation? This, so that Souls can "act-in" and experience——learn what they cannot learn at Home. And I am not leaving out the possibility that this so called movie or simulation may very well be ran by more advanced beings (hint-hint) but even if that were the case, the question still remains, specifically: "who is running their simulation?" In the end, regardless of who is running whose' simulation, we're all inside a larger all-encompassing System, and that's what we call All-That-Is! This will become much clearer as we go along, but please keep this point in mind as you read on.

Now, this next section will touch on my own personal experiences, how this whole adventure of mine unfolded into what it is today. I will describe in detail as many of my personal encounters as I can recall.

These experiences ranged the gamut from Dream Visitations, to O.B.E. (Out of Body Experience) to "UFOs." This is necessary, I *believe*, not only so that you—the reader, can get better acquainted with my personal involvement with the material, but also I hope, that in so doing, some of you may be able to shine some light on your own personal experiences. In the last chapter of the book, I shall endeavor to give the best explanation I know, about the "True Nature of Reality."

As mentioned earlier, at age twelve I was the victim of a serious car accident. February 28, 1972 was a date I shall never forget, but also what turned out to be the starting point of this whole adventure of mine. Many bone fractures and several surgeries later; everything seemed to have returned to relative normality. My teen years had nothing particularly extraordinary to report. Then at age 23, I moved to Canada, and six months later I took ownership of a busy automotive service business. Fully immersed in work, managing a 12-employee shop, nothing of relevance happened for the first couple of years, until one day a customer gave me a book, "Seth Speaks" as a gift.

But as I started reading that book, from the very first pages I felt a very strange but good sensation, which I can only describe as a sort of "I finally found you" kind of feeling. I simply could not put the book down, and when I was finished reading it, I read it again four times. It almost felt as if the book described parts of my life. As if I had somehow participated in writing it, and I later found out why. And from the very beginning, as soon as I started reading the book, my way of thinking changed almost totally. If it makes any sense, I now saw life under a completely new light. And the strangest thing was that just before going to sleep every night, I felt— coupled with a complete sense of relaxation and peace, a notable sense of euphoric excitement coming on. As I went to sleep that first night, I suddenly found myself awake and "floating" a foot or so above my bed.

I felt as if I was in a swimming pool floating flat on my back, only there was no water to hold me afloat. I looked around, the bedroom looked normal. Then I looked down in the semi-darkness and I could see my body under the covers. Frightened and not knowing what to do, my first reaction was to try and push myself down onto the bed again. So I started to mentally push myself down. Finally I slowly started moving down toward the bed, taking me, what I would estimate, a whole of five minutes to reach it. Then, I finally felt myself slowly going through the bed covers. It was a strange sensation, especially when in the semidarkness I could see my legs half in and half out of the blankets, as if sitting in a few inches of water. After much effort I was finally flat on my bed again, I was wide-awake and drenched in cold sweat. I tried moving my fingers and toes, but nothing happened. I was completely petrified, like a statue. "Oh great," I thought; "now I am also paralyzed!"

A few minutes went by, and then I started to slowly feel a strange sensation in my fingers and toes, a tingling of sorts similar to what you feel when a limb falls asleep and then gradually regains sensitivity. A few more minutes later, and I was finally able to move my hands and feet, but nothing more. It took, what I would estimate, another twenty minutes or so, before I was able to regain full control over my body. But I was so overwhelmed with fear that I didn't want to move a single finger until the first light of dawn came peeping through the window.

I laid there, for what I would estimate four hours. As if in a pool of cold sweat, eyes wide open, going over what had just happened. Then at 7 am my alarm clock startled me out of my confusion. I reluctantly got up, took a shower, had breakfast, and went to work. My usual busy workday made me almost forget about the whole thing, but, as I struggled to make sense of it, I couldn't help but wonder what had just happened. While half of me tried very hard to dismiss the whole thing as a dream, the other half knew better. This was no dream!

That evening, I reluctantly went to bed again. I certainly didn't want to go through anything like the previous night. But a sense of curiosity overcame me. While I surely did not want to experience another sleepless night, I was curious to know what it all meant if anything. I instinctively knew that it was somehow connected to the book I had just started reading, but I couldn't put my finger on it. My catholic upbringing at the time, warned me of such things as being "evil" in nature. I was a bit concerned I must admit, as I didn't know what I was dealing with. Somewhat weary I fell asleep. But then I suddenly found myself wide-awake again, floating in a sitting position a few inches over my bed. "Here we go again," I thought. But almost immediately, I felt as if an invisible force spun me around to the side. Still floating, I stood up. I floated into the hallway, then the living room. Suddenly, I had my face only an inch or so from a painting on my living room wall. Still floating and slightly tilted forward, I looked around; I could swear it was my living room. I could see my TV and sofa, but while my real living room had only two paintings, a large one above the sofa and a smaller one on the wall across, this room had four other midsized paintings that I did not recognize.

Still scared out of my wits, I looked around for clues. It was very strange, as if I was able to move toward an object by simply looking at it. I would focus onto something and my body would start floating toward that object on its own. The air in the room had a sort of shiny halo to it, making everything appear a shimmering silvery hue, as if electrified. "I had enough of this," I thought. "Please God, I don't know what's happening, but I want nothing to do with it, please make it stop," I cried as I started to float again toward the bedroom. By now a "floating expert," I was able to steer myself into the bedroom and position myself next to my bed.

To my astonishment I found my bed occupied. My "other self," *my earth body*, sleeping as if nothing happened, while I in the meantime, the "thinking me," was having a difficult time even sitting on the bed, as I couldn't grab onto anything. If I tried, my hands would go through whatever I tried to grab. Similarly to putting your hand through water, you can feel the water, but you cannot grab a hold of it. Eventually, after much mental effort I was able to position myself on the bed. This time I did not need to force myself down, as almost suddenly, I found myself under the blankets, and another sleepless night ensued.

At work the next morning, I couldn't stop thinking about what had happened the last two nights in a row. I needed to know what it meant, and most of all, if it was going to continue. Unable to sleep for two nights now, I was tired, confused and unable to concentrate on my work. Then at 3 pm, exhausted, I asked my shop foreman to lockup for me at closing time and I went home. I couldn't wait to get home and look through the book (*Seth Speaks*), I wanted to find anything that could possibly explain what was happening, some sort of explanation that would give me a clue. But nothing seemed to explain my dilemma.

As you can understand, that night, I was very hesitant to go to sleep, but very tired I fell asleep around midnight. But just as the two previous nights, I once again found myself awake and floating in a sitting position just above the bed. Anticipating the routine, I mentally ordered myself into a standing position—to which my body promptly complied. Then, on its own, my body started to float, but only this time, in the direction of my en-suite bathroom. I had no idea what was happening, but I didn't have to wait very long to find out. As I went through the slightly ajar door expecting to find my usual bathroom, I was very surprised to discover that the bathroom was no longer there. The first thing that came to mind was, "when did I renovate my bathroom?" For what I found instead of the usual sink and shower, was a roughly 25X30 feet checkered floor room. I immediately recognized the setting, as it unmistakably resembled that of a classroom in a school. Surprised out of my mind, I could see a large blackboard on the opposite wall, ten or so student desks, and some other classroom items along the sidewalls.

I had no idea what was happening or what I was doing there, but I did not have to wait very long to find out. An elderly man entered the room from the right. But he did not walk; he instead, while passively looking ahead as if he didn't even know I was there, floated a foot or so from the ground. Then, still floating, he stopped right in front of the blackboard, directly across from me. The man appeared to be about 70 years old, short and chubby. He wore a beige pair of pants and a light colored shirt with red squares in a horizontal and vertical lines pattern. Bald on the top of the head, double chinned round face, he appeared seemingly out of nowhere. Then, while still looking at the blackboard, the man said, "Welcome and I bid you a very good evening Marco, shall we begin?" I was very uneasy and I didn't even want to talk to him. My mind racing, trying to make sense of the whole thing, "begin what," I asked? Or so I thought, because despite speaking the question out loud, to my amazement, no sound came out of my mouth! I tried again, several times, but not a sound came out! I was scared.

I wanted to ask him a thousand questions, "What am I doing here," "Who are you," and most importantly "Why am I floating around?"

But I wasn't able to utter a single syllable. I tried very hard to speak, but to no avail. Then a sudden realization came over me, "was I dead?"

"I must be, why would I otherwise be floating and not walking? Why was I able to see things that couldn't possibly be real." I asked myself? Noticing my uneasiness, the elderly man finally turned toward me and said: "Marco, I have been waiting for you for a long time. We have a lot of material to cover, but I see that you are not yet ready. Go back for now and we shall meet again soon!"

Scared to death, part of me wanted to run, but part of me, *curious to know more*, wanted to stay. I wanted to ask, "Who are you and why were you waiting for me?" A million questions, but an uncontrollable fear overcame me; my breathing became so rapid that I was afraid I was going to have a heart attack. As if he read my mind the man said: "It's all right Marco. Go back for now, we shall meet again soon."

I didn't want to leave, but my body seemed to have a mind of its own, and started floating toward the same door as before. As I went through the door again, this time from the opposite end, I found myself back in my bedroom. Then I almost automatically floated toward the bed, and I once again found myself under the blankets, eyes wide open, unable to move a single finger for at least twenty minutes.

When morning finally came, very confused and having had very little sleep for a third night in a row, I was not in a very good mood. I was afraid something bad was going to happen—a death premonition perhaps? Was I going to die in the near future and I was perhaps seeing "parts of what was to come in the other side?" My religious side was very scared; my thinking side was trying to reason—find a logical explanation. One thing I was sure of, the individual I met there, did not appear to pose any threat, if anything, he instead appeared concerned about my well-being. I spent the whole day thinking about what to do next. He seemed able to read my mind. Should I send him a mental message asking him to meet again I thought, or ask him, *mentally*, to never come back? I am sure you can guess which of the two I did. So I went to sleep that evening, almost hoping I must confess, to meet him again. I needed to know more. I went to bed and closed my eyes. Then I mentally asked to be taken back to that classroom.

I wasn't to be disappointed. I suddenly found myself in the classroom with no idea about how I got there. Reminiscent of my elementary school class, I sat at one of the desks. The elderly man was already there, waiting and floating off the floor, busy writing on the blackboard as usual. He had a wand in his left hand, I assumed to point out information on the blackboard. On the board, I saw a few simple drawings of apparent geometrical nature; a square next to a cube, a circle next to a sphere, and a triangle next to a cone. The first thing that came to mind was some type of relationship between the 2-dimensional versus the 3-dimensional. I also saw numbers on the board; at the time I had no idea what they represented. Two of the sets of numbers stood out, pulsated almost, 2012 and 2072.

(Keep in mind that this took place in the mid-'80s.) As I had prepared myself mentally the whole day, I wasn't nearly as scared as I was the night before. Though a thousand questions raced through my mind, and perhaps out of fear of asking the wrong thing, I did not ask a single thing, I preferred to wait for him to say something first and then ask him.

He stood there quietly for a minute while still writing on the board. Then, he said, "Welcome back Marco, how are you this lovely evening?"

"Good, I guess" I replied, "but," *I continued with a somewhat angry tone,* "before I say anything else, I demand to know who you are, what am I doing here and just what is going on with these 'meetings' that are now taking place every night?"

"Relax Marco," he replied "I will explain everything in due time, and I assure you that you have nothing to worry about." He replied.

However, there was something I needed to know immediately. "Am I dead or soon going to die, I asked?"

"No Marco" he replied, "You're not dead nor going to die anytime soon. You already died once in this life—and returned, do you remember?"

And that's when it all suddenly made sense! "That's what that vague memory I had in my mind all my life was! The floating in midair looking down at the scene of the accident," I suddenly realized.

"Are you referring to the accident I had as a child?" I asked.

"Yes Marco. Do you recall how you found yourself floating up in the air, looking down at your body under the overturned vehicle?" He said.

"How could I ever forget," I replied? "So, what else can you tell me? Who are you, and what do you want of me" I asked?

"I do not have a name, but you can call me Seth if you like Marco. I have been watching and guiding you, unannounced for many of your Earth years. I was waiting for you to be ready, so that you could better relate to the information that will be made available to you." He said.

"Do you mean… are you the same Seth I have been reading about in the new book—and what information?" I asked perplexed.

"Yes, Marco! I am the same Seth from the book your friend Thomas gave you just a few days before he left your plane of existence. Consider it his farewell-parting gift to you. Thomas, as well as yourself, as you will learn later, represented an 'extension'—a 'branch' if you like, from the tree that makes the 'Seth Entity.' But back to us now, we have a lot of important information to cover, but we need to take care of something else first," he replied.

"Wow" I said. "Now it all makes sense. Tom and I were inseparable; we met every day for coffee and talked for hours on end. I considered Tom to be my older brother, is that why Tom and I were so close? Where we part of the same Entity?" I asked. "And what do you exactly want to talk to me about?"

"Yes, Marco, that is why you and Tom were so close, you are both projections from the same "source" the Seth Entity. But before you and I can start working together, there is something I would like you to take care of first." He said. "As you know Marco, you and your only sister haven't spoken in years. This is enriching neither of you. Obviously you love and miss each other, and it is eating you inside. You need to remedy this situation so that you can take this big weight off your mind. Then you'll be able to think a lot clearer," he said.

"How did you know that?" I was going to ask, but then I realized that it was going to be a stupid question.

"Marco, we shall meet again tomorrow," he said.

Then without any warning I suddenly found myself in my bed. Another sleepless wide-open eyes night ensued.

At 7 am I got up to go to work, extremely tired and confused, but strangely, very happy inside. As soon as I got to my office I knew exactly what I needed to do. Because of a disagreement we had a few years earlier, it had been over two years since I had last spoken to my sister., who lived in Italy. I had sponsored her and her husband to move from Italy.

They came to Canada in September, but only two months later the harsh northern winter had the best of them. They went back just before Christmas, despite the fact that I had warned them of the huge life-altering changes, and that they should not make any decision until they had allowed themselves at least two years to adjust to the new lifestyle.

As every emigrant knows, that's how long it takes to get accustomed to the inevitable changes, language barriers, workplace, the cold climate, friends and family that you leave behind. I thought I had made myself clear, but they instead went back only three months later. Aside from the fact that it was a very costly experiment, what bothered me the most was that they never gave it a chance—as they had agreed. Before this incident my sister and I talked on the phone every week. I missed talking to her very much. Seth's suggestion was the push I needed to take the first step toward reconciliation. I called my sister, and it was immediate reconnection.

There was no need for any explanation or apology; simple, genuine brother-sister love, only a brother and sister can understand. Seth was right, it felt as if a huge weight was lifted from my shoulders, I even felt lighter physically, I walked faster and I was happier inside as well as outside. I couldn't wait for that evening to come, I was anxious to talk to Seth again. What other positive suggestions could he give me I wondered?

Going to bed that evening I prepared myself mentally. Before I knew it, I once again found myself sitting behind that same student desk. Seth was already there, and as if wearing a rocket-pack, hovering as usual. He was writing on the blackboard about 15 feet in front of me. I didn't say a thing for a minute or so. I took the opportunity to look around a bit, studying the obvious peculiarity of the room we appeared to be in. The room itself did not appear to be solid. The walls seemed to undulate slowly in and out, as if pulsating gently. Then I directed my attention to the white and black checker floor—that being geometrically accurate, easily gave away the subtle movement, as if shape-shifting. Reminiscent of a suspended bridge in the wind, it seemed to sway from side to side. However, the most peculiar thing was that the room itself appeared to be made of some type of flexible rubber-like material. I could see a door in the far right corner of the room, but I could swear that there couldn't be anything outside. I had the distinct feeling in fact that the room (and everything in it) was all suspended in midair.

Then, a most amazing thing happened. The door to the far right opened on its own. A moment later the room started changing in shape and size considerably. The room, roughly 25X30 feet in size, appeared to stretch to at least three times that size. The room's corners seemed to stretch outwardly, to then retract again by ten feet or so. Then, to my surprise, a figure entered from the door and came hovering in my direction. At first, because of the distance, I wasn't sure what to make of it, but as it came closer, I could now distinguish what appeared to be an early 1900s lady's black dress. I opened my eyes wide to be sure that I was not hallucinating, but the dress was empty, there was no one inside it—and it kept on coming, hovering in my direction. Scared, not knowing what to make of it, "is that a ghost?" I yelled.

"We're all ghosts here Marco, yourself included!" He replied.

"What did I get myself into? I really had enough of these games," I thought. But still hovering, the empty dress was now only ten feet or so from me. Scared, I tried to distance myself from whatever was coming my way; I pushed myself back on the chair as far as I could. Then, I almost had a heart attack when suddenly and out of nowhere, a body materialized inside the dress. A long black haired woman, about 65, short in stature with big dark eyes, suddenly appeared inside the dress. At first the woman did not say anything.

"Seth, who's that?" I asked frightened.

"Marco, please meet my wife Ruburt," he replied.

"Welcome, and nice to meet you Marco," the woman said.

"Nice to meet you too, but you could've entered the room with the dress, instead of almost giving me a heart attack," I said.

"My apologies Marco, but events here do not necessarily follow the same rules you're accustomed to," she said. "I can see that," I replied.

I started thinking about the name Seth had introduced her by; "Ruburt," when I suddenly remembered. Ruburt was the name Seth called Jane in the book I was reading, (Seth Speaks.) Jane was the medium whom Seth channeled information through. In the book Jane was married to her husband Robert Butts, who penned the material on paper, while in a trance Jane spoke on Seth's behalf. Also in the book, Seth instead called her husband Robert "Yusuf." These were names (he explained) he knew them by in other incarnations when they were friends. As Seth would say, the "portion" of the greater Entity, appearing here on Earth as "Jane" died in 1984 from complications arising from a hyperactive thyroid and chronic debilitating arthritis.

As if anticipating my questions, Seth started speaking. "Firstly, you did the right thing calling your sister yesterday. You both feel much better now. Secondly, I am sure you have a lot of questions that I assure you, will all be addressed in due time. For now, I'm just going to give you an introduction of what's to come." He said.

"I am all ears," I said.

"I have been waiting for many of your years Marco, waiting for you to be ready, so that I could make information available to you. I want you to know that you are not the only one I am working with, as a matter of fact I am working with about 2,000 others, right this very instant. As I am speaking to you, I am also speaking to them—simultaneously. These other meetings," he continued, "might not necessarily be taking place under the same set of circumstances as we're in now."

"Similar to you, some take place in classrooms, some in completely different scenarios on your Earth, as well as on other planets or dimensions. Some are taking place in different civilizations, both in the past as well as in the future, as you understand it. When you will be ready, we will visit some of these environments if you like." He said.

"But Seth, why me, and what is the purpose of all of this," I asked?

"Mankind," he continued, "is fast approaching a certain developmental stage, where some ideas now obsolete in your terms need to be replaced by new ones. And by the way, I am not the only one doing so—many other Guides are doing the same at this very moment. We're all an inseparable part of a greater whole, we're simply helping you along through an 'Earth journey' that is also our own. Several thousand 'key people' are being readied for what's to come in your terms. These are individuals who are not afraid to think outside of the box. They are what you would call 'open minded,' the 'Visionaries!' They have what you would describe as 'their heart in the right place.' These individuals will in turn go forth passing the information to the wider masses. Some will make movies, some will speak at seminars, some will write books, some will be—or are already involved in politics. Though instinctively aware, some might not be consciously aware that they are being 'helped' along in their work. Many of your Scientists, Inventors and Artists, as well as some of your Presidents, have all received 'help'—usually in their dreams, or sudden 'eureka' moments. This has been the case all throughout history." He said.

"Are you referring to 'Light Workers?'" I asked?

"They have been given many different names throughout history, I prefer calling them Volunteers," he said.

"Does this mean that I am myself a 'light worker' and do I have any choice in all of this—and is this dangerous?" I asked.

"You always have a choice Marco." He said, "You do not have to do anything you don't want to. You can leave now and never hear from me again, if that's what you wish. To your second question, no harm of the physical type can come to you in any way, you could however experience some degree of discomfort, but as it is always the case, of your own doing".

"What do you mean by "discomfort," I asked concerned?"

"As I will explain in detail later Marco, you are in complete control of any and all of your experiences—at all times, no exception. What this means is that if you believe that a devil is waiting for you around the corner, then a devil will surely be there waiting for you."

"The key word being 'believe' I assume?" I asked.

"Precisely" He replied. "Whether you understand it or not, whether you believe it even, you always manufacture you own reality, moment by moment, based on your belief patterns. You get to decide in fact, what will happen every moment of your life experience. That is so on Earth as well as everywhere else you happen to exist—and take my word for it when I say that you 'exist' in a lot of different places indeed. This is true not only for you Marco, but also for everyone else. If you can remind yourself of this universal truth," he continued "and that you not only create your next moment—but that if you don't like it, you can also change it, then you have nothing to fear".

"What if I panic and forget? And am I going to meet ghosts, bad spirits and so on?" I asked concerned.

"Marco, we are all 'ghosts,' including you! And even when you think of yourself as a 'Human' you are in fact a ghost. We're all simply 'manifesting' physicality to different degrees, depending upon 'where' we happen to be focusing upon at any given time. Think about it, most people are terrified if they see a skeleton, they forget however that inside, they drag one around all day long. And to your second question, 'jokers' are to be found more-or-less on every level of existence, not just on Earth! You will most likely encounter them within any system you might happen to visit. The key is to remember that they cannot do anything that you did not give them permission to—or that your belief system didn't invite them to do." He said.

"Wow, what am I getting into? I am not sure if I want to be part of all this. All I wanted was a peaceful life, now this?" I said.

"A 'peaceful life' you already have Marco," he continued, "and many more types of lives—both past as well as future for that matter. You've been 'guided along,' and you had already volunteered to help your fellow Humans, beforehand. You, Mankind, finds itself in a time of shall we say 'self-enacted need' and you enjoy helping other people Marco, you always have, for a 'helper' is who you are!"

I couldn't agree more, I continuously find myself helping others no matter what city or what career I happen to be in. People seem to come to me for all sorts of "help," Spiritual, financial, even personal issues. It gives me a sense of satisfaction if I can help someone find a solution to a challenge. It has been so for as long as I can remember. Even as a teenager I recall, my friends and even my grown-up relatives often came to me to help them with their personal issues.

Now, these classroom meetings with Seth continued regularly once a week or so, for about seven years. During that time Seth and I covered an enormous amount of information, most of which I am sharing in this book. Seth and I also went on several Out-of-Body excursions. Some of these lessons were fashioned strictly for my own personal growth; helping me address many questions I wouldn't have otherwise been able to on my own. In total Seth and I visited 17 of my "past," or as he called them, "parallel" Earth lives, of which I shall share the ones I consider of greater relevancy. Seth also educated me on a series of techniques on how to experience certain states of self-hypnosis, as well as giving me precise instructions on how to initiate certain processes on my own. Later in the book, I shall also share some of these techniques.

I am very well aware of the fact that most folks reading this, will tend to dismiss it with a simple "they were just dreams" conclusion. Let me assure you that that's what I also thought at first, but as time went on I had no choice but to accept the fact that these couldn't possibly be just dreams. I too have dreams of the regular kind, thus I know what dreams feel like. These were literally "lessons," episodes each picking up where the previous one ended. And I didn't, *as you would in a dream*, just happen to find myself in a session, before getting there, there would always be a sort of preparatory process. One of two things would happen, I would either find myself floating on my bed, then in a classroom, or I would feel a sort of internal rush coming on, as if a flow of powerful accelerating energy, and the next thing I knew I would suddenly find myself in a classroom, or wherever place Seth and I were to meet.

But the clearest indication that these weren't just "dreams," was the fact that while being there, I was not only aware of my surroundings and what was taking place (there) but I was also aware of the fact that back in my bedroom sleeping, I had a body waiting for me to go back to. These things definitely do not happen in normal dreams. Also, if I asked you how many can you recall, out of the tens of thousands of dreams you had, you'd probably reply "one or two" at best. That's perfectly normal, for usually we can't even recall last night's dream for more than a few hours. In my case however, while I cannot recall virtually any of my normal dreams, despite of the fact that they took place way back in the late-'80s and early-'90s, I can clearly recall each and every one of these "sessions" in every detail. How do we explain that? And while on this topic, allow me to just touch on something for now. It turns out that our so-called "regular dreams" are also a much misunderstood phenomena. There is in short, a lot more to dreams than we give them credit for. Later in the book, we shall discuss this and other related topics in more detail.

In no particular order here are some of my personal experiences. *According to Seth, I've had roughly speaking 12,000 lives. Although this surprised even me, he said that this is not unusual. Some Souls have had (depending on a number of factors) 50,000 or more Earth lives he said. And contrary to popular believe, a Soul can have up to a thousand simultaneous "Earth lives." Out of my Earth lives, Seth and I visited 17. Each time Seth and I assumed the role of "observers," or "spectators" from the sidelines, while the other I, the main protagonist in the "scenario," appeared to play the last ten minutes or so of each lifetime in question. In each instance, I would see myself as a different individual and in a different time period. Allow me to share some of them with you.*

—The Crippled Gypsy Beggar. In this scenario I was a crippled gypsy woman begging in the streets of what appeared to be Hungary of a century ago. A small girl, about three years old, my daughter, *I assume,* sat next to me on the curb. Nothing particularly important happened in this scenario other than the fact that this, as well as several other scenarios, had a specific recurring theme in common, "a mobility limitation," mostly with my legs, thing that I am still dealing with, here in my present lifetime.

—The Dutch Fisherman. This scenario took place I would dare to guess, in early 1800s Holland. I saw myself as a white haired elderly tall slender fishermen coming ashore at the end of my fishing day. While standing up on my feet, I lazily rowed my small boat trying to moor it in the shallow water between some of the protruding rocks. But although the water was still as a mirror, I bumped my boat on one of the rocks. Losing my balance I fell, hitting my head on a rock and passing out. Against a beautiful sunset and speechless, I watched myself drown facedown and unconscious, in less than a foot of water. This might be from where I inherited my present fear of open waters.

—The Scottish Hardware Store Owner. In this scenario I was an old stubby hardware store owner somewhere in Scotland of a few centuries ago. For some reason my legs appeared to have been amputated, *here again* *the connection to my present legs issues reappears.* I moved about using wooden crutches. I recall having an obsession of sorts; I was somehow convinced that every customer wanted to steal from me. Therefore, I spent my days sitting on the counter next to the till, so that I could keep a constant eye on my patrons. I knew there was going to be trouble from the very moment these two lads entered the store. I very vividly recall them taking each a hammer from the shelves and coming toward the till and they did not appear to be willing to pay for them. They demanded that I open the cash drawer and give them the money, which I refused to do. I tried to fight them off with my wooden crutches, but they killed me shortly after, bludgeoning me to death, hitting me over the head with the heavy hammers.

—King Tut. *As a premise, let me begin by saying that I know what you must be thinking! "Impossible," you say! And I fully understand, for that's what I said when Seth first shared this particular piece of information, until I looked at it from a different perspective, then I had no choice but to accept the facts at face value. In what is without a doubt the most glamorous of all scenarios, I was one of the most famous Pharaohs in Egyptian history, namely "King Tut." At first, this particular revelation troubled me a great deal. Overwhelmed to say the least, I found it very difficult to accept the enormity of what—historically speaking, this revelation implied. Thus I totally understand if some of you reading this may also have a hard time accepting it. I myself struggled with it for several months; I somehow could not accept the fact that I could have been the world-renowned king. In the end however, I had to examine the facts at hand, and accept a very simple truth. Specifically, if this particular revelation was not true, then everything else Seth had revealed thus far—was also untrue. And because the overwhelming evidence suggested otherwise, I had no choice but to accept the facts. Basically, this was the very point where I had to choose between trusting Seth completely, or not at all. Using my logic, in the end I had to accept a very simple fact, that (as Seth said) whether I liked it or not, someone had to have fulfilled that role. Even today I'm still not sure why I was the one who apparently "volunteered" for that role, but then again, why not? For starters, it explains my lifelong fascination with everything Egyptian. My home is filled with Egyptian artifacts. And on this point, years before this revelation, I happened to be in a shopping mall one day, when showcased in a store window I saw a scaled down reproduction of King Tut's throne. "I have to have it," I said, but I decided to wait and went home. But as soon as I got up the next morning, I just couldn't wait to go back to the store and buy it. I took it home, all the while wondering, why did I have to buy that artifact?*

Now, in this particular scenario, hiding behind long curtains in the royal chamber, Seth and I observed from the sidelines. The chamber, very large and rectangular in shape, had very high ceilings. The young Pharaoh sat on a gold colored throne four steps up on a landing at the end of the room. Two servants stood slightly behind the king, fanning him to keep him cool. From a door on the right, carrying a golden tray and several ampoules, a female servant entered the room. As it appeared to be mid-afternoon, she must've served him what I suppose was a tea-like drink.

But as he started drinking, the king, immediately almost, appeared to fall ill, and then he appeared to pass-out. A little commotion followed as the servants tried to help him. Then the door opened again, and two men walked in the room. But strangely, despite the obvious urgency, they didn't appear alarmed in the least.

Judging from the long tunic he wore, one of the men must've been a religious figure of some kind. The other was definitely a soldier, as he wore a uniform type garment. Then the priest ordered everyone except the soldier out of the room. Once alone, he positioned himself behind and to the left of the king. He appeared to be checking him for signs of life. From our perspective, his head leaning forward, the king appeared to be asleep or passed out. Then to my surprise, the priest reached under his tunic, pulled out a piece of wood and gave it to the soldier.

Roughly two feet long, reddish in color and heavy looking, it resembled a beam you would use in the construction of a house. Then from his pocket the priest extracted what looked like a handkerchief. He folded it three or four times and then placed it on the back of the king's head. My first thought was that he wanted to wipe off sweat from his neck, but to my surprise, the priest looked at the soldier instead and nodded his head.

To my astonishment the soldier proceeded to raise the heavy piece of wood into midair, to then hit the king on the back of the neck. A single hard blow! It would be difficult to say with any degree of accuracy, but from where Seth and I stood it appeared that he was hit at the base of his skull, roughly where the head joins with the neck. I couldn't believe my eyes. Basically we were witnessing a murder. Noticing my uneasiness Seth looked at me, but I could see in his eyes that there was nothing we could do but watch. Then the priest called the servants back in the room.

They brought in a stretcher made of wood and white fabric, on which they carried the king out of the room.

But here is the best part, take a look at the article below which I found just recently in a science magazine.

"More than 3,000 years after the death of the young Pharaoh Tutankhamun, questions are still being asked about how he died. Was it a natural death or was he murdered? The possibility that Tutankhamun did not die of natural causes was first raised 28 years ago when an X-ray analysis of his mummy was made by the anatomy department of the University of Liverpool. It revealed that the King might have died from a blow to the back of his head. The suggestion caused a controversy among Egyptologists and scientists. If he were murdered, who did it? Early this year, a new X-ray analysis cast more light on the subject, suggesting that the King may have been murdered in his sleep. A trauma specialist at Long Island University, in the USA, conducted the examination. 'The blow was to a protected area at the back of the head, which you don't injure in an accident, someone had to sneak up from behind,' said the specialist. X-rays also show a thickening of a bone in the cranium, which could occur only after a buildup of blood. Indicating that the king might have been left bleeding for a long time before he actually died. In short, scientists suggest that the king was most probably hit on the back of his head while asleep and that he lingered, maybe for as long as two months, before he died." (Source: www.touregypt.net.)

—**The Intergalactic Voyage.** This scenario started in the usual fashion. I fell asleep and found myself floating on my bed. Then without any warning I was standing in the middle of a mid-size room I did not know. The walls were completely covered with books from top to bottom, but strangely the room had no ceiling; I could see the starry night sky. I stood there in awe, looking at that beautiful sky. I am not sure where the room was, but I did get the distinct feeling that it was floating in midair. Then seemingly out of nowhere, Seth suddenly appeared. He came hovering down through the open ceiling. Then he said: "Greetings Marco, we will travel to a faraway place tonight, but it won't take us very long, as we will travel faster than light speed."

I looked around expecting to see a rocket or spaceship parked somewhere nearby, but then he extended his hand and he said, "Hold on to my hand." So I did.

We started hovering upwards, slowly at first. "How are we going to get there, a rocket?" I asked.

"No, just hold my hand. We will be flying between the stars, planets, and even galaxies" he replied.

"He must be crazy," I thought, but I did as he asked. So we started flying upwards in the sky, slowly at first, and then faster and faster. Planets, stars and other celestial bodies flew past us at higher and higher speed, until they became a continuous streak of light. Strangely however, while flying at that incredible speed, I could not feel any wind or discomfort.

Then, after a couple of minutes of hypersonic flying, we gradually started to slow down, until we were flying as slow as a helicopter. We landed on what appeared to be an inhabited planet. There were folks in the streets going about their lives, much like us, but dressed in early 1900s clothes. I also saw a dog. One very peculiar thing I recall was the light green colored air we all appeared to be breathing. Instinctively, I looked up to the sky, but there was no sky to look at! No clouds and even no atmosphere. I could see light green as far as my eyes could see.

"We're late for a very important meeting" Seth reminded me, but I had no idea what meeting he was referring to.

We went around a corner, we walked a few steps and then we stopped in front of a very large wooden door. A "doorman," who I assume was waiting for us, opened the door and invited us in. As I stepped inside, to my surprise, I saw about 25 to 30 "people," all sitting in a circle on a series of steps in a circular arrangement around a sunken floor. The best thing I could liken the setting to, would be a "Roman Senate" type arrangement you'd see in a movie, where all the Senators sat in a circle while the speaker would stand in the middle of the floor at the bottom of the steps.

I stood there speechless. I couldn't believe what I was seeing, and I had no idea where I was. Everyone looked different. Some human-like; some, reminiscent of giant crickets, had skinny long bodies and antennae-like protrusions on their heads. One "senator" in particular however, caught my eye, as he very much resembled something out of Star Wars, "Jabba" specifically, minus the tail. A huge cone shaped body resembling an upside-down ice cream cone. What I would estimate 700 lb., basically a one-piece body with the neck-less head being the top portion of the cone. Relative to his body he had very small stubby legs and arms. His voice sounded metallic and high pitched. Strangely they all appeared to speak English.

Surprised, I stood there just inside the large door trying to make sense of what I was seeing; the doorman invited me to take a seat. I looked around to locate Seth, but he was nowhere to be seen. I went down a few steps and sat down, and that's when the whole room said in unison, "Welcome Marco, we've been waiting for you, let's now start our meeting!"

The next thing I knew, I was wide-awake back in my bed. And while this was without a doubt one of the most remarkable excursions Seth and I went on. You'd be wrong to think that this was as strange as this voyage was going to get.

At the beginning of the trip, while holding hands Seth and I became airborne leaving Earth behind, and ventured into the dark night sky. As we approached the outer edge of Earth's atmosphere, I noticed in the distance what appeared to be lumps of white cloudlike shapes. As we got closer and closer however, still traveling relatively slow at this stage, I could make out the shapes more and more. My heart almost stopped, when now in close proximity, I realized that the shapes were actually giant "human heads" and they were all looking at us.

Getting closer, with a welcoming smile some of them moved slightly aside to allow us through. Totally unprepared I asked, "But Seth, these are human heads! Who are they and what are they doing here?" The heads were gigantic in size, each the size of a house, with no neck or body. Some were men, some women, and all of different age. They had hair, eyes, a mouth and a nose, and all the features you'd expect to see in a human face. They appeared to be made of a cloudy-white semi-transparent substance, but as they emitted a semi-fluorescent light, perfectly visible against the dark sky. Seth explained that they were "volunteers," and had been there for as long as our Earth had. They are Earth's—*a volunteer Entity itself according to Seth,* guardians and assistants.

They are responsible for regulating what Seth called the "dynamics" of the planet, everything from weather and wind patterns to earthquakes, hurricanes and water currents. "Wow," I said, "but why have our astronauts and astronomers never mentioned anything about them" I asked? Seth reminded me that we were now occupying a different "frequency," thus a different channel, where different things become visible while others disappear. "It is for the same reason why folks on Earth couldn't see us right now if we stood right in front of their nose," he explained.

"I understand," I replied, "Same radio, different channel?"

"Precisely," he replied.

And here are some of the most significant events that took place during daytime hours.

—The Unsolved Crime, twenty years on and police still baffled! Here is an odd one to say the least. A few months after this whole series of rendezvous with Seth started, one afternoon I was in my office doing paperwork, but oddly I found it very difficult to concentrate. Not only was I unusually tired, I felt as if my mind was wandering away, a strange feeling that totally prevented me from focusing on my work. Then inexplicably, a sudden irresistible urge to get in my truck and go home came over me. But as it was still two hours to closing time, I couldn't understand the reason.

This went on for a few minutes, but then as if I had no control over my body, I literally walked outside to my truck and sat in it, all the while asking myself why I wanted to go home so early! The strange thing was that although I was able to reason with my mind, my body seemed to have a mind of its own. So, against my will and having no idea why, I started the truck and began driving in the direction of my house about ten minutes away, mentally fighting my body all the while, which seemed to function on automatic. This is the strange part, while on one hand I understood perfectly that there was no reason for me to go home so early, I was on the other hand plainly unable to tell my body to stop and go back to my office.

Then, about halfway to my house, I stopped at a red light. And that was probably what I needed. Suddenly I snapped out of that apparent hypnotic state. I was back in full control. So I turned into a Wal-Mart parking lot and shut off the engine. I sat there for a minute trying to make sense of what had just happened, but for the life of me, I couldn't understand where that irresistible urge to go home was coming from. I drove back to my office and sat behind my desk. Not even a minute later my phone rang. It was my (first) wife. She had just got home from work. With a frantic voice she tried to describe what she had found at our house.

"The garage door was wide open, and the side door was kicked in," she said. But the strangest thing was she said that a large number of items, many of value, sat there amassed right in the middle of our driveway. And there was no one in—or outside the house she said. Obviously we had been burglarized. So, I jumped back in my truck, willingly this time, called the police on my cell, and drove to my house as fast as I could. But on my way there, I couldn't help wondering if there was any connection between what had just happened at my house, and the urge I had to go there only ten minutes earlier. But since I had more pressing matters to attend to at the moment, I put that thought on the backburner.

The police got there a minute before me. And with a puzzled look on their face, the very first thing they asked was, "What in the world are all these valuables doing in the driveway in front of the garage?" I was even more puzzled than they were, as I could easily estimate in excess of forty thousand dollars in goods, sitting there on my driveway. Amongst other things we found three expensive TVs, several pro-grade musical instruments, two stereo systems and several collectables of considerable value. But even more amazing—while digging through the items, the police found our jewelry box, with at least twenty thousand dollars' worth of jewelry and gold in it. Then everyone's jaw dropped when a few feet away, one of the police officers found my ex-wife's two thousand dollar gold watch. Speechless, the two officers looked at us in disbelief, then one of them said, "What in the world just happened here? I have never seen anything like this in my life! Why would anyone go through all the trouble of bringing everything outside, to then leave everything here, even the gold watch, which they could have easily put it in a pocket?"

Looking around the house, the police found shoes tracks in the sand belonging to at least two individuals. In the unpaved portion of the driveway they found deep tire marks, consistent with a vehicle taking off in a hurry. The only plausible explanation was that they might have heard a passing siren—and thinking it was coming for them left in a hurry. But even the police admitted that that scenario didn't make much sense. The house was located in a remote rural area well outside of the city. There must've been at least ten different directions they could have taken. It was a wide-open farmland area; they would have heard a siren from at least three kilometers away and seen a flashing light from at least that far. But most puzzling of all, why did they leave everything there, gold watch included?

A couple of years later, I happened to be in a coffee shop one day, when I met one of the two police officers.

Recognizing me, he came close, and asked, "Marco, did you ever find out what happened that day at your house? Because that was one of the strangest cases I have ever seen," he said.

"No" I said. But what I didn't tell him, was that the same night of the incident; Seth had already clarified the whole thing for me.

That evening, after the police had finished taking fingerprints, made a report and left, we reorganized the home the best we could and did an inventory. Absolutely nothing was missing—not even a penny's worth. Then, at around midnight, tired and perplexed we went to sleep.

The usual floating above my bed and then I found myself in the now familiar classroom. Seth was already there waiting.

"Hello Seth. Let me guess," I said, "I bet you have something to say about what just happened today?"

"Indeed Marco," he replied!—And Suddenly, I was projected into what appeared to be a movie scene. Seth was nowhere to be seen.

The scenario started with me arriving home from work, I parked my truck in my driveway and walked toward my garage side door, about twenty feet away. I casually looked up to the sky, and to my surprise it looked different than any other time before. Basically—for lack of a better description, the sky was missing. It was empty, if it makes any sense. I could see all the way through, as far as my eyes could see. Not a single cloud, or even the bluish hue you see when looking up to the sky, total nothingness into infinity. Though very unusual, I didn't think much of it.

Standing in front of my garage side door, I went to insert my key into the lock, but instead, to my amazement the key—together with my hand went through the door, just like putting your hand through water, minus the wetness. Perplexed, I looked down at my feet, and to my surprise they were not on the ground. I was instead hovering a foot from it. I stood there puzzled for a moment, when I heard voices coming from inside my house, but they didn't sound like anyone I knew. That's when I realized that we were being burglarized. Instinctively, I tried to push the door open, but I went through it instead. I was suddenly inside the garage. I had passed through the closed door with no effort whatsoever. Trying to collect my thoughts, I stood there for a second, but when I heard the voices from inside the house again, I couldn't wait; I had to go inside—I was being robbed!

Still hovering, I went toward the door that went from my garage into the laundry room. I did not know what was happening to my body, but I had more urgent matters to worry about at the moment. I grabbed the door handle to go into the laundry room—but again, I instead went through the door. Now in the laundry room, I was still floating a foot from the floor. Piled up on the floor, one of my TVs and several other electronics. Then I heard frantic footsteps coming towards the laundry room. Wearing a balaclava, a man in his early twenties turned the corner. He stood about three feet in front of me.

Instinctively I tried to grab him, but my hands went right through him. "What are you doing in my house, let go of my stuff," I shouted, but he could neither hear nor see me. Again I tried to grab him, nothing. As if I wasn't even there, he put the item down on the floor and went back for more. I didn't know what to do. I tried grabbing a wooden stool from the laundry room, but my hands went right through it. The man returned holding some stereo equipment, which he sat on the floor. Trying to get his attention, I yelled my lungs out, but to no avail. Then, out of nowhere, something materialized in my hands.

About a meter long, the object resembled a piece of heavy water pipe a plumber would use. It appeared to be made of metal, lead or perhaps iron, but I surely did not have the time to worry about the pipe's chemical composition. Trying to hit the burglar with it, I started swinging it right and left. I swung the metal pipe about three or four times—but to my amazement, as if a knife through water, it passed right through the man's body. From the look on his face, it was obvious that he could neither see me nor feel anything.

"Thanks for nothing," I thought, "What is the point of giving me this stupid pipe if I can't do a thing with it?" I had no idea who I was talking to, but then all of a sudden something truly remarkable happened. As I kept swinging the pipe from side to side, raising my arms a bit, I happened to swing the pipe through the man's face. Then while still swinging, raising the pipe a bit more, I saw the pipe literally "slice" through the top portion of the man's head, where, *assuming he had one*, his brain would be. And that is when, to my total amazement, "time" slowed down to almost a standstill. In slow motion, the pipe entered the left side of the man's head, right above his ear, and went through his skull as a hot knife would go through butter. And that's the exact moment when he suddenly saw me!

I will never forget the look in his eyes. The instant the pipe went right through his skull, making—I suppose, "contact" with his nervous system. The contact must've caused him to suddenly see me. I had never seen a man so startled and surprised in my entire life. He jumped backwards in disbelief, and then ran back to the living room where his other brainy friend was. Then I heard him scream, "Ghost! Ghost! There is a ghost in this house, let's get out of here!" He never returned to the laundry room, they must have jumped out of the living room window I assume.

Now, if you asked me to try and explain what took place, I would venture to guess that because I was obviously in a different frequency than his—the man couldn't see me at first. He was in a "physical" frequency, while I was in a "spiritual" one. But slicing through his brain with a seemingly metallic—thus electrically conductive object, must have caused I suppose, a sort of "bridge" between the two frequencies.

I awoke in a pool of sweat. Suddenly it all made sense! I could now explain the unexplainable urge to go home earlier that afternoon, the items left in my driveway, the hurried departure from my house the thieves made. So it would appear that when *that afternoon* I eventually turned the truck around—and returned to my office, a "part" of me, must have instead continued (in Spirit) to my house. The time coincided perfectly. It all made sense now.

And when I asked Seth if that were the case, he smiled, and replied with the now familiar, "Why do you ask that question, when you already know the answer?"

—The Ghost In My Living Room. It was a beautiful sunny Sunday afternoon back in 2005. I was relaxing on the sofa with my feet up on the coffee table. I closed my eyes for a second, but I immediately felt as if someone was watching me. Instinctively, I opened my eyes—and that's when I jumped up at least two feet from the sofa. Someone was watching me—a ghost!

The ghost, (a woman,) stood there in the middle of my living room, a few feet directly in front of me on the other side of the coffee table. Her arms crossed in front of her chest, while smiling, she looked straight into my eyes. An attractive young woman, around thirty years of age I would guess. She wore a black straight cut "Egyptian," *there we go again,* hairstyle. She was dressed in a mid-length sleeveless white summer dress with a large black floral pattern. For what I would estimate three seconds, she stood there smiling, while looking straight into my eyes. Then she simply vanished, but not all at once—but gradually, as if slowly dissipating in the air.

I heard of many ghost stories in the past, but I had never seen one myself. Seeing a ghost appear right in front of you is simply another story. It really changes one's way of thinking.

Because of the material I was working on at the time and the ongoing visits with Seth, I almost expected a visit from a ghost—thus I wasn't overly concerned. On the other hand however, I was starting to think that it might've been time to move to another house. Reasoning through it, I came to the conclusion that the ghost didn't seem to pose any reason for concern, if anything, I felt, *for the short time she was there,* a sort of benign energy coming from her. A few minutes later, wanting to know more, I decided to try a little experiment. Since the "ghost" had just been there I reasoned, could I ask her to reappear? So I did. I sat on the sofa in the same position as before. I leaned back with my eyes closed and said: "I don't know who you are, but I know that you do not mean any harm. If you're still here, can you please reappear so that I can ask you a few questions? But please, try not to startle me this time!"

As if she heard me, *she probably did*, almost immediately I felt the distinct feeling of being watched again. I opened my eyes, and lo and behold, there she was again, in the exact same spot as before. But despite having asked her to reappear—and having readied for it mentally, I couldn't help being startled again! I didn't jump as high as before this time, but I still jumped up and back as far as I could. In that split second, a number of conflicting thoughts flashed into my mind. One telling me that I had no reason to be afraid, another trying to stop myself from jumping, and yet another thought, perhaps the most natural of all, fear—that once again caused me to jump a foot off the sofa. So, for about three seconds or so, the lady-ghost once again stood there exactly as before, smiling and looking directly into my eyes. Then she simply vanished into thin air again.

"Wow," I said, "what in the world was that? What does this mean?" There no longer was any doubt in my mind—I had officially seen a ghost! But I am a human, so I wanted to make sure. "She must still be close by," I thought. I closed my eyes again, and I again asked the ghost to reappear, now for the third time—which amazingly she did immediately. This time she appeared only for about a second or so. If there was one thing I was sure of, it was that I had nothing to fear, and I no longer saw the need to move from that house. What I felt instead was a sense of comfort and protection. It didn't take long for the rest of the story to arrive.

As soon as I fell asleep that evening, I started floating as usual, only this time I immediately found myself in the middle of a large courtyard. The humongous complex resembled an abandoned factory of some type. A number of large red brick buildings surrounded by huge parking lots. I stood in a line, together with another hundred folks or so. I was about 10th place in line. We all walked slowly alongside one of the brick buildings. From around the corner a voice called one person at a time. We all held "papers" of some type in our hands; mine resembled an application, a report or exam of some kind. It was finally my turn.

I turned the corner and sat in the chair in front of a desk. A woman sat behind the desk, head down taking notes. A second later she raised her eyes and said, "Welcome Marco!" *I recognized her immediately—the ghost I had seen in my living room earlier that afternoon.* Surprised out of my mind, "Are you the ghost I saw in my house this afternoon?" I asked. "Who are you and what am I doing here?" I said.

"Do I look like a ghost to you now Marco," she replied smiling? "In any case," she continued, "we do not have a lot of time as I still have to review more than a hundred reports. Can I please see yours?" Not knowing what to do or say, I gave her my "report."

She looked through it for a minute, then she said: "It's all good Marco, you are doing fine and everything is proceeding as it should. I will see you again in a year. If you need help or have any questions, you know what to do. Goodbye now!"

"Thank you," I said. I wanted to ask her a thousand questions but then she said, "Next please".

I stood up. I didn't want to upset the others waiting in line, so I walked away. A few seconds later, I woke up in my bed. In awe, marveling at what had just happened, I began to realize the magnitude and significance. I wanted to both laugh, in happiness, and cry, out of gratitude. I did both.

—I should have died three times, but something saved me. Several oft the businesses I owned required me to drive a lot. There have been at least 3 instances where *there is no doubt in my mind* a higher (divine) intervention prevented me from getting into what could have been a very serious, if not fatal, accident. The first took place when I still lived in Italy.

I was 22 at the time. It was 2 am; I was travelling on a very fast highway from the city of Florence to Pisa. Not only was there no speed limits at the time, but being the middle of the night there were almost no cars on the 5 lane highway. I was driving at about 200 km/h, *normal in a country of Lamborghinis and Ferraris*, it was a perfectly straight stretch of highway and I could see 3-5 km ahead. I was on the far left lane—the so called "fast-lane." In the far distance I could see a car's headlights coming from the opposite direction, but because of the distance and the type of highway I was on, I could never have imagined what was going to happen next.

Sure that the other car was on the opposite side of the highway, I kept on driving without a worry in the world. But as we got closer and closer, at what I estimate still a couple of kilometers away, a voice came out seemingly from my car's speakers. Clear as day, the male voice literally stated, "Change lane!"

"What in the world was that all about" I asked myself surprised, but the strangest thing of all was that my radio was off. Not knowing what to make of it, I wondered if I should just heed the voice for now and then worry about its source and meaning later. So I moved to the middle lane. Keep in mind that this is a very wide highway—5 lanes per side, divided by a metal guardrail. And so while my logic told me that I had nothing to worry about, my gut feeling told me otherwise. So I changed lanes, and that is when I suddenly realized why.

A car, came zooming past me like a jet from the opposite direction, driving on the exact same lane I was just on—at probably 200 km/h or more. "What in the world," I screamed surprised. Could you imagine what would have happened if I had stayed on that same lane? Add my 200 km/h to theirs, and you got a pretty good idea. The next day I called the police.

They said that although rarely, there had been people reporting similar incidents. Apparently, especially at night, some, crazy folks prefer risking their own life to avoid paying the highway toll. Go figure. But still today a question lingers in my mind, where did that voice come from? I asked a car radio expert; he said that he had heard of cases where folks reported hearing voices coming from their car's speakers—even with the radio off.

This is usually due to an amateur's CB-radio operator transmitting in the vicinity, or while driving by a radio station. And this tends to happen more during a thunderstorm for whatever reason. Well in my case, there were certainly no CB operators or radio stations close by—and it was a perfectly clear night sky.

—The second incident happened at about age 40 in Canada. At about 11:30 at night, I was driving home on an 80 km/h rural road. Not a soul in sight and a solid green light ahead, I was driving at about 70 km/h. As I got closer to the 4-way intersection, for no reason whatsoever, something told me to slow down a bit. "Why should I," I asked myself, I got a solid green light ahead, but slow down I did nevertheless—and I immediately found out why. As I approached the intersection, a car went speeding by, crossing only inches in front of me from my left to my right. I slammed on my brakes stopping 30 or so meters on the other side of the intersection. "What in the world, I almost got killed there," I yelled. I did a 180—and while calling the police on my cellphone, I sped up to catch up with the crazy driver. *I know that in retrospect it was not the smartest thing to do, but I almost lost my life there, I wanted to know why.*

The police asked me to describe the car and the direction of travel. Ten minutes or so later they called back saying that they had caught up with the car, and that they would like me to go to the police station the next day to ask me a few questions. The next morning, I went in and a police officer asked me to explain exactly what had happened. My jaw dropped when he said that the driver was an unlicensed 17 years old female, who they were holding under psychiatric observation. It turns out that her boyfriend had just broken up with her and she decided that she was going to steal her mother's car and commit suicide.

"But how," I asked, perplexed?

"She kept on driving through red light after red light at over 100 km/h," the officer said, "until she would have died. You are a very lucky man," the officer said.

He did not know the rest of the story of course, the fact that if it were not for the voice I heard in my head telling me to slow down despite the green light, she would have hit me on the driver side of my car, most likely killing me on the spot.

—The third and last automobile related adventure happened in 2010, also in Canada. Driving eastbound on the Trans-Canada highway two hours West of Winnipeg. It was 1 am and the highway was almost deserted. On a divided 2-lanes per direction stretch of highway, I drove behind a large truck for a while, then tired of looking at its taillights, I decided to pass it. But as soon as I switched to the left lane to pass the transport truck the most amazing thing happened. My steering wheel—as if it had a mind of its own, steered my car back into the right lane and behind the truck. "What in the world was that," I said, but before I could even finish the sentence, a car came zipping by on the lane I was just on, driving on the opposite direction—and get this, their headlights were off! Surprised out of my mind, I immediately called the police. They asked me if I could give them some details.

"All I could see was the color I said, silver, but nothing else, it simply happened too fast."

"Where exactly are you," they asked.

I looked at my GPS and gave them my position.

"We will call you if we need to," they said.

I started thinking about what had just happened. "Who" or "what" steered my car back onto the right lane? Being, *pretty well all throughout my life*, the protagonist of one strange occurrence after the other, I instinctively knew what the answer was, but the other side of me—my "Human" side always doubts and seeks explainable common sense solutions. The police called me back half hour later. The driver of the other car was wasted drunk they said, and upon entering the highway from a right side intersection, they—instead of crossing over onto the other side of the highway, took the first left—our side.

—The Silver Giant. It was the year 2004. At the time, I was the singer and leader of a musical group. We performed until 1 am that Saturday night. By the time we finished taking down the equipment I got home around 3 am. As we performed almost every weekend, the lady I was seeing at the time, was usually asleep by the time I got home, but not this time. Not only was she wide-awake, she was visibly upset and waiting to talk to me. "Why are you still up," I asked?

Visibly shaken and almost in tears, she tried her best to describe what had happened a few hours earlier. She had gone to sleep at around midnight she said, when an hour or so later, she felt as if someone had entered our bedroom. Half asleep and not sure what time it was, she assumed that it was me who had come home. Normally, I would walk around to the other side of the bed, get undressed and go to sleep, this time however, she waited and waited for me to get into bed, but after several minutes—not feeling the bed move at all, she realized something was definitely amiss.

She waited another minute, her eyes still closed, still waiting for me to at the very least sit on the side of the bed or make some noise. Then she finally decided to turn around and open her eyes to see what I was doing. But as she did so, she saw something she will never forget she said. "A being," of some type, a tall human silhouette, silver in color, stood next to my side of the bed. The being (she said) was so tall that his head almost touched the bedroom ceiling.

"He leaned slightly forward toward your side of the bed, and he was moving his hands in a side-sweeping motion, back and forth from left to right, right over the bed covers," she said.

Curious, I asked her to describe the silhouette in more details—and why was she referring to it as a "he."

"It was a simple, undefined 'humanoid' silhouette," she said.

"He had no human features like eyes, mouth or nose. Very difficult to describe, the being was of a glowing silvery color, but it did not emit any light or have a halo around it." She said. And understandably startled and surprised, she felt as if the being wasn't there to cause any harm, on the contrary, she felt a positive benevolent energy emanating from him.

"And I call him a 'he'—by the body shape. Straight up and down body lines, no waistline, or any hint of breasts," she said.

She was so startled by the sudden vision she said, that she immediately jumped out of bed screaming, "who are you?" The being, as if he heard her, turned his faceless head in her direction for an instant—to then vanish into thin air, but not all at once, she said, but gradually.

She could still see the silhouette for several seconds afterwards, becoming less and less visible. Scared out of her wits, she ran downstairs and waited for me to get home. It was almost 4 am by now, and I was extremely tired. I didn't know what to make of it, and since she was the one who actually witnessed the incident, I asked her to explain, in her words, what the being might've been doing there.

She replied that based on what she saw; she could only conclude that the being was there to somehow "cleanse" my side of the bed, perhaps a blessing of some sort. I did not make much of it, not only was I was extremely tired, I was also used to "strange" incidents happening to me almost on a daily basis, that I simply added the "silver friend" to the long list—and went to sleep.

I woke up the next morning feeling like the proverbial million dollars. I felt ten years younger, full of vitality, and positive energy. "Wow, thank you Silver-Man whoever you are," I thought to myself. "I wish you would come and cleanse my bed more often!" I said.

—Did I meet an Angel? It was 2013. I was visiting the beautiful city of Toronto. After a long sleepless night-flight, I walked around in the humid hot weather all day. I was very tired. Strolling around downtown when I somehow ended up in a beautiful park. A blessing I thought, as the heat—and my feet, demanded that I find a spot in the shade and take a break. A bit removed from the main path, I saw a park bench beneath a beautiful tree. That looks inviting I thought, so I took a sip of water at a nearby fountain and sat in the shade. Not even a minute had passed, when a young girl came walking in my direction, looking directly at me.

"She is probably going to ask me for a cigarette," I thought. But to my total surprise—still from some distance away, she called my name and said: "How are you Marco?"

"I am good thank you, but do I know you?" I replied baffled.

"You do not know me Marco, but I do know you—and very well actually!" she replied smiling.

She now stood immediately in front of me, I was still seating down. I took a really good look at her to see if I could remember her from somewhere. She was a very beautiful young girl, twenty or so. Very blonde, tall and slender, she reminded me of a young Brigitte Bardot, but ten times more beautiful. She was dressed in a light fabric floral pattern dress with long dangling sleeves. But the thing that really struck me was her exceptional beauty—something you would only see in a heavily photoshopped magazine cover. But not a sexy provocative type beauty, but a gentle, kind, clean, clear-eyed baby-like beauty. Very hard to explain, her eyes were blue like the sky and sparkled like the stars.

I stood there, in awe almost, trying to remember who she might've been, then she brought me back to reality when she said, "I know you're very tired Marco, and for good reason."

"But how would you know that I am tired?" I asked. "Please tell me who you are, this is driving me crazy?" I said.

"Do not concern yourself more than you have to, Marco. It will all become clear in a minute, I promise," she said. "Can I seat beside you?" She asked.

"Be my guest," I replied. She sat to my right. We both leaned forward at the same time.

Then she said, "Marco, you are doing a tremendous amount of work with your book, and you're working hard in other aspects of your life, your business, your family. You're also constantly helping others, family members, even strangers. And for that we really thank you," she said!

"But who is 'we'—and how do you know me? Please tell me who you are," I asked again.

As if she didn't hear me, she continued, "You feel discouraged, at times overwhelmed, 'why isn't anyone helping me,' you ask. And that's why I am here, to tell you that you are being helped. Even in your loneliest and most discouraging of times you are not alone!" She said.

"Wow," I said, "I think I am starting to understand. You are not from this word are you? Are you an Angel?" I asked.

"Let me ask you Marco, are you from this world? Do you know anyone who is?" She asked. "Take a good look around you, look at those nice folks walking over there," she said pointing in the distance, "are they from this world?" She asked. "You've been told before, and I will say it again," she said.

"I've been told what?" I asked.

"That you have a number of 'helpers'—'Guides' as you call them, always by your side, day and night, they stand ready waiting for you to ask. Ask them for assistance, with anything—'Trouble is," she continued, "you never ask!"

"But how can I ask them for help when I cannot see them," I replied with a hint of frustration in my voice?

"You should know better than that Marco, must I remind you what you wrote in your book just yesterday?"

"What did I write? Refresh my memory," I said.

"There is a lot more out there—a whole lot more in fact, than what our 'physical eyes can see'—you wrote! These are your words exactly!" She said in an admonishing tone, but with a beautiful smile.

"So if you don't take the initiative and ask for help—then we must take the initiative for you—and send help when we think you need it, hence my visit today!" She said.

"Well, I could sure use some help right now, I am exhausted," I said.

"Can you please close your eyes?" She asked.

"Come on now! What are you going to do? I don't even know who you really are," I replied.

"You can keep them open, but it works better if you closed them," she said.

"This reminds me of the time when I met Jane in a dream," I said.

"And so it should, Marco! For you often forget what Jane told you in that dream." she said.

She simply knew too much about me to doubt her. "Ok, you win, I will close my eyes," I said. And so I did. At first, I couldn't feel anything. Then I felt her really close to my right ear.

"Marco, I am now going to cleanse you," she said. I couldn't make out the words, but she whispered something reminiscent of a prayer into my ear. I wanted to open my eyes and ask her what she meant by "cleanse," but she acted before I could speak.

I wish I could fittingly describe what happened next. An incredibly warm feeling came out of her lips and right into my ear, so beautiful, so intense, so loving and gentle. I could feel her breath enter my ear and reach inside my brain. I could hear a warm gentle wind noise inside my head. I wanted to open my eyes—but as if in a trance, I could not. Then it suddenly stopped. I opened my eyes. She was gone. I was alone, sitting in that park bench in awe!

I sat there for a minute wondering what had just happened. Part of me knew exactly, but my other (human) side, the perpetually doubting human side—wondered if it could all have been just a dream. "Had I unknowingly dozed off for a few minutes?" I tried to remember what she had said— that I was very tired, and that help is sent when needed. So I compared how I felt just a few minutes prior, when I almost could no longer walk, and I had to find a place to sit down and rest, but what about now? I stood up, but I stood up as if I were "spring loaded!"

"Wow, what happened to me?" I asked. "I feel terrific, like a million dollars," I thought! I started walking, and I couldn't believe how rested and light I felt, beyond words! But not only physically rested, my mind was clear and sharp, and I knew exactly what I needed to do. A very positive feeling came over me, I felt full of energy. I couldn't wait to get home that night and get to work on my book again. This book.

—The Psychic. Years ago a friend told me that he had visited a psychic and that she was very good. I usually don't go to psychics as there are a lot of charlatans out there, but I do believe that some (very few) are genuinely able to connect to other levels, but I have always trusted my own instinct. I was contemplating a move to another city and changing careers at the time, thus I was curious to see what she had to say in that regard.

Once inside the smoky house, she invited me in the kitchen. We sat at a small table across from each other. "Do not say anything," she said. She pulled out a deck of cards and made a 5 cards spread. "Pick 3 cards," she said. I picked the first, the last and the middle one.

"You're moving West and very soon," she said.

"This woman is a charlatan," I thought, as I had no intention of moving West, instead, if anything, everything pointed to moving East—from the city I was in. "Are you sure I am moving West and not East," I asked her?

"Let's try again," she said. This time she did a 7 cards spread.

"Pick 3 cards," she asked. Again I picked the first, the last, and the middle cards.

"Not only are you moving West—but within a month, and it looks like a very positive move," she said.

"I don't think so," I said.

"I'm positively sure that I'm going East. The company I am employed with is in the process of transferring me to a large city East from here," I replied.

"Trust me Marco, you are going West," she insisted. "And by the way, I don't know if you've noticed, but the 7 of diamonds keeps on showing up in the middle of the spread. This is very good news of course, but just to confirm what I suspect, let me try one more time," she said. And so she laid a 9-card spread on the table this time, and I again picked the first, the last and the middle cards.

"Wow, just as I suspected! You had the seven of diamonds come in the middle of the spread three times in a row, that can only mean one thing," she said.

"What does it mean?" I asked.

"You are going to be incredibly blessed, not just financially but in every sense of the word!" She replied.

"Well that's certainly good news, thank you, but I can assure you that you're wrong about the westward move," I said.

"We shall see Marco, we shall see," she replied.

"I did your cards. What else would you like to know?" She asked.

"Can you tell me about my personal life?" I asked.

"Of course, but for that I will go into a trance," she said.

She sat back in her chair and closed her eyes. She said nothing for about a minute, the room was very quiet and I could hear her very slow rhythmic breathing. Then she opened her eyes, and for a moment she looked as if she was "half here and half there," as if sleeping—but with her eyes open. Then she really startled me when all of a sudden—and without any warning she screamed, "Oh my God!"

"What is it?" I asked surprised.

"Oh my God, please help me, Marco please help me!" She said.

Her eyes started filling up with tears, she sobbed uncontrollably. I was really confused now, I had no idea what was happening or what she was referring to when she said, "please help me," for I was under the impression that I was there for her to help me, not the opposite.

"Why do I keep meeting all the crazy people?" I asked myself.

"Please explain to me what is going on?" I asked.

"OK I will," she said, "but please help me, you don't know what I am seeing right now. Please tell me that you will help me, please!" She said begging almost.

"OK I will help you if you tell me how, but please explain yourself, because I am really confused now," I said.

181

"Please give me your blessing, I don't need any specific help, just your blessing, please Marco," she replied.

"Give you my blessing?" I asked surprised.

"But I'm not a saint you know, I am just a normal guy, why would you want me to bless you?" I asked perplexed.

"Here Marco, please take my hands, and give me your blessing, then I will explain everything, please," she begged again.

So, without having any idea why, or what I was doing, I did as she asked. I just wanted to get the craziness over with. But I nevertheless meant every word when while holding her hands I said, "May God bless you, and may all of your wishes be fulfilled!"

"Thank you Marco, you don't know how much that means to me, now I know that everything is going to be ok with my cancer," she said sobbing.

"You are very welcome, but please explain yourself," I said.

"Marco, let me see. 1, 2, 3, 6, 7, 9, 11, 12… my God, 12!" she said.

"What are you counting exactly?" I asked.

"Twelve, Marco, you have twelve Guides all around you. They are looking at me smiling right now," she replied.

"Twelve Guides all around me?" I asked.

"But why can't I see them and what are they doing there around me?" I asked.

"Marco, they've been with you since you were born. They are there to assist you, help you with your work, mostly your book, they tell me," she replied.

It all made sense now!

"And you cannot see them, unless you go in a trance yourself, as they operate from a slightly altered level than yours," she said.

"This is highly unusual Marco," she continued. "I've met clients occasionally who had one—or sometimes two guides around them, usually their relatives, but you have twelve!

"There is definitely something very special about you—or the work you are doing. You've got some big guns protection around you Marco! You've either been given a very important task, or one will be given to you in the future, of that I am sure!" She concluded.

I did not say a thing, but I instinctively knew what she was referring to. The book I was working on for over twenty years, this book!

When it was time for me to leave, she insisted that I did not pay her, but I still gave her $100 and left.

Not even a week had passed when I got a phone call from the company I worked for. "Change of plans," they said, "we just opened a new store and we would like you to go there."

"Where is it?" I asked, "West" they replied.

And that's when my jaw dropped to the floor. I could not believe it.

The psychic was right after all, and just as she had predicted, I was now in the process of packing up my bags and move westbound!

—The Mysterious Stranger. This last event is not only one of my all-time favorites, but also a recent one, as it happened in July of 2014. It was an ordinary, *or so I thought*, mid-summer afternoon; I was alone in my office finishing some paperwork, when a well-dressed middle-aged man entered my office. Wearing a nice brown suit and very soft-spoken and unusually polite, he appeared to be about forty-five years old.

"Good afternoon, can I help you?" I said.

"Greetings Marco," he said, "but I am actually here to help you," he politely replied.

"Oh no, here we go again," I thought. I hesitated for a second, but since—regardless of first appearances—I must extend to every client the same courtesy and respect, I politely asked, "What do you mean when you say that 'you are here to help me?' What company do you represent," I asked?

"I am here to help you Marco, and I am sent by God!" He calmly replied, while looking straight into my eyes.

I could feel my blood pressure starting to rise. I was really having enough of meeting one crazy person after another. I was a second away from calling a mental institution, but before I could reply, he said, "You don't believe me do you? What can I do to prove it to you?" He asked.

"Oh come on, really? I really don't have time for this," I said.

"You're telling me that God sent you here to help me, could you please get real? I have better things to do," I said angrily.

"Like writing your book?" He surprised me with.

"Perhaps, but how did you know that I am writing a book?" I asked?
The conversation was getting decidedly weirder with every second.

"OK Marco, I can see that you do not believe me. I don't blame you.

Would you allow me to demonstrate to you that I am telling you the truth?" He asked.

I didn't know what to say. I mean, over the years, I've seen and heard all sorts of weird things, and that was perhaps the only reason why I didn't ask him to leave immediately.

"OK, go ahead," I said, "What are you going to show me?" I asked.

"Marco, we have never met before, right?" he asked.

"Correct" I replied.

"So, would you agree that there is no possible way for me to know your most personal of things right?" He asked.

"It depends how personal," I replied, "nowadays you can find out anything about anyone on the Internet," I replied.

"True," he said, "but what about your innermost personal things, can anyone find those on the Internet?"

"Give me an example," I said.

So, he took a small piece of paper and a pen from my desk and wrote something on it, then he crumpled it into a little ball and gave it to me.

"Hold it tight in your hand," he said. "Now what?" I asked.

"Tell me what's your favorite color, you favorite flower and your favorite animal," he said.

"Red is my favorite color, the rose is my favorite flower, and the elephant - no wait, the eagle is my favorite animal," I said.

"Look at the piece of paper in your hand," he calmly said.

I couldn't believe my eyes! On it, he had written three words, "Red," "Rose" and "ElephEagle." "How can this be possible?" I asked. But the incredible thing was not that he had guessed the color and flower, but that he had predicted that I was going to change my mind mid-sentence, from elephant to eagle!

"Are you a magician?" I asked.

"No Marco, this has nothing to do with magic," he replied. "But I can see that you still don't trust me," he said.

"Well, how could I, this is totally crazy," I said. So he took another small piece of paper and again wrote something on it, and again asked me to hold it tight into my hand.

"Marco, what's your favorite number, the day you were born, and the day your wife was born?" He asked. "19, 19, and 27," I replied.

"Please look at the piece of paper," he asked.

So I did, and again my jaw dropped to the floor, as he had correctly guessed all three numbers.

"If you're that good, you should give me the lottery numbers," I said jokingly!

"You have already won the lottery Marco, one way or another—a 'lottery' of some type is coming to you—and soon!" He replied.

"Would you like to try again?" He asked.

I really didn't know what to say at this point, but "why not," I said.

So he went through the same routine. He wrote something on a small piece of paper and asked me to hold it tight into my hand. "What is your favorite precious stone? How many years have you been married, and your favorite jungle animal?" He asked.

"I got him this time," I thought. The first and the third answer were straight forward, but the second answer involved a half a year.

"My favorite rock is the ruby," I said. "I've been married four and a half years, and my favorite jungle animal is the lion," I said, sure that he wasn't going to guess this time.

But once again, to my amazement—guessed he did! He had guessed all three questions perfectly! That's 9 strictly personal correct answers in a row!

"OK, let's get serious now," I said.

"I must say that that's pretty impressive, but what are you really here for?" I asked.

"My apologies, I had to do all that, not for me but for you. You needed reassurance before I could deliver my message, so I hope you now believe me," he said.

"Well, I must admit that what you just did was incredible, but please tell me what message you're referring to," I asked.

"Marco, I am here to deliver a message from God. God sent me here!"

"Let me guess," I interrupted him, "you're going to cleanse me, am I right?" I asked.

"No Marco, I am simply here to tell you to keep going with your book!

Everything is going well—and that once completed, the book is going to be received very positively! You're being helped throughout the whole process, thus do not concern yourself with 'how' or 'who' is going to publish it or even read it. Simply finish the book—then your work is done.

The rest has already been pre-arranged. People whom you do not yet know, will help you get the book published, and 'Angel Investors' will help you finance it!" He said.

"Well, what can I say, thank you I guess, I really needed a little encouragement. I mean it's a really complicated subject to write about. I get discouraged at times, and feel like giving up," I said.

"And that's why I am here. To remind you that you're not alone, you are being helped from the sidelines," he said.

"I must leave now, but before I go I want to give you something." He pulled out a small shiny rock from his pocket and said, "Here, keep this small rock in your pocket. And when you feel discouraged or in a bad mood, simply touch it, and you will immediately feel better," he said.

I took the small rock and put it in my right pocket. But you'd be wrong to think that this was as weird as this episode was going to get.

Another client came in, Sidney the geologist. A well-educated, polite and courteous gentleman I have known for several years. Sidney really surprised me this time, as he behaved in a very uncharacteristic manner.

Every other time Sidney came to see me (which was often), and he found me busy with another client, he would simply take a seat in the waiting area, until I was done. This time however, Sidney acted as if no one else was there with me—and before him. As soon as he came in, he said hello and came straight to the counter—and totally oblivious of the other "client" who stood right there to his immediate left, started talking to me. So much so, that when he put his arms on the desk, as if he wasn't even there, he touched the other man's arm with his elbow!

Puzzled by Sidney's strange behavior, all the while wondering why was he not waiting for me to finish with the other client. I wanted to intervene and ask him to take a seat and wait for his turn.

But before I could say anything, noticing my uneasiness, the other man smiled and said, "That's alright Marco, I was going to leave anyways, just remember what I told you. Good bye and God Bless!" And he left.

I stood there, speechless and confused for a minute. Then I asked Sidney why had he behaved in such an uncharacteristic and impolite manner. Sidney looked at me more perplexed than I was.

"What other client are you referring to Marco? There was no one here with you when I came in," he replied with a puzzled look in his face.

"Do you mean to tell me that you didn't see the gentleman wearing a brown suit, before you—right here at my desk? You were standing right next to him," I said!

"Of course not Marco, you know me, had there been someone else before me I would have taken a seat over there as I always do when you're busy," he replied.

"And you are making me worry now," Sidney continued, "for I don't know what other person you're referring to. I surely did not see anyone here with you," he said!

"Marco, are you sure you are ok?" Sidney asked.

"I really don't know what to think anymore," I said.

"Are you really-really sure that you did not see anyone else here talking to me? You were standing right next to him—and you even touched his arm with your elbow" I asked confused?

"Marco, could he have been a ghost? I mean I believe you when you say that someone else was here, but I can assure you that I did not see anyone else, otherwise I would've waited. You know that I would never dare to interrupt another client," Sidney concluded!

And I totally agreed. Sidney is too polite of a person to interrupt a conversation. "But wait," I said, reaching for my pocket, "here look, he gave me this little rock, here is proof that he was here," I said.

"Marco, I do believe you, but still, I did not see anyone here with you, I swear," Sidney said.

"But in any case, what can I help you with today Sidney?" I asked still perplexed.

"Nothing important, I was just driving by, and I wanted to give you a book.

I think you're going to like it," Sidney replied.

I was still too shaken to even look at the book at the moment; I took it from Sidney, thanked him, and sat the book on my desk. Sidney left.

About an hour later it was closing time, so I started switching my office lights off. On my way out, I grabbed the book from my desk.

I was outside locking my office door when I happened to glance at the front cover of the book—and that's when I, almost fainted.

I had to get back inside and sit down for a minute. I could not believe my eyes. The book title hit me like a ton of bricks. It was a book by Mark Twain. The title,

"The Mysterious Stranger."

Isn't life grand?

"I don't believe that ghosts are 'Spirits of the dead' because I don't believe in death. In the multiverse, once you're possible—you exist! And once you exist, you exist forever—one way or another. Besides, death is the absence of life, and the ghosts I've met are very much alive. What we call ghosts are life forms, just as you and I are." ~

—Paul F. Eno

Chapter 6

We Dream Dreams That Dream of Us

The alarm clock just won't quit blaring in your ear, until you finally open your eyes and turn it off. Somewhat reluctantly you slowly let go of that dream and gradually refocus your attention to "this side." It can take anywhere from a few seconds to a few minutes before you gain full awareness of your surroundings. However, there are mornings when you're so involved with a dream that despite hearing the alarm, you're reluctant to let go of it, and whatever you happen to be doing in it. But the alarm just won't quit, so you must slowly shift—refocus your attention to "this side." Sometimes, while the dream is still very vivid in your mind for several minutes afterwards.

Wow, that was incredible, you think! You get up, have breakfast and go to work. A couple of hours later, the dream flashes back in your mind. "That dream was really something! It seemed so real. Oh well, I'd better forget about it, it was just a dream," you conclude. Or was it?

The "radio" analogy will once again prove useful here, for in reality, "a radio station," simul-casting on a myriad of different channels, is what we are. "A Base Station" is what Seth calls it. And that Base Station is you, the Entity. You the Entity reside at "Home." Home is not a place, it is not Heaven and it is not located on another planet or silvery cloud or even in another point in time. Home is a plane of existence from where you beam out, "impressing"—projecting yourself (the Entity) upon hundreds of Souls that are also you—or better, "extensions" of you (the Entity). These Souls will in turn, via whatever medium best fits each environment "inhabit" a myriad of sub-planes.

Here on Earth that medium or "suit" is a "Human Body,"—body you (Soul,) so proudly drag along all day. A vehicle you wear, so that you could function and move about this specific plane.

Interestingly, and most fitting, we find here the word "in-habit" derived from the Latin word "Abito," which literally translates into exactly that, a "suit" or "dress." And by "sub-plane" I am not implying that it is a plane somehow situated beneath or under the Home plane.

I am also not implying that these sub-planes are in any way of lesser relevance or not as important as the Home level. All Planes are in fact part of a larger system, thus none is more-or-less relevant than the next, for together they form the whole. Just like tree branches are not less important than the trunk, for together, branches and trunk make the whole tree. And since we mentioned a tree, it would be wise to remember that trees have branches both above as well as below ground level, reminiscent, *not by chance I may add*, of our beloved two cones joined at the tips we talked about earlier. This, not by coincidence, but because everything in the Universe— be it a tree or a weather system, always has a "plus" and a "minus," a visible and an invisible side, the "Yin and the Yang"—two opposite but balancing forces, present in everything in the Universe, the Universe itself included.

Now, the Home plane where Entities reside could be likened to a tree trunk, from where a multitude of branches simultaneously spring off in all directions. However, it is important to remember that the Home plane is nothing more than just another branch—of yet another larger "tree," and so on. I realize this can be somewhat confusing, as it surely confused me, when I first started exploring this information. The question is, "Are the Entities at the very top of the pyramid also a 'branch-off' of yet another higher level? Undoubtedly! According to Seth, a total of seven "layers" make the totality of the system. The "All-That-Is."

Now, we should not confuse the "Entity" with the "Soul." As we said earlier, the Entity is parent to the Soul; it is where each Soul is cast and originates from. But the Soul also has its own "Plane" from which it operates from and resides in.*

This level is commonly referred to as "The Astral Plane." A Soul can be recalled "Home" by the parent Entity, or if it so chooses, the Soul can stay either in "an in-between" plane, or in its own plane indefinitely. These "in-between states" are coincidentally where most "ghostly apparitions"— *we see from here*, originate from. Souls and Entities do not need to concern themselves with "time," as it does not apply there. No calendars to watch yourself get old by, or alarm clocks to send you off to work each morning, because work does not apply there either. You can work if you wish, but there, work would most likely consist of painting a marvelous painting or learning a new musical instrument.

Truth is, this physical level of ours, what we call the "Physical Level" is also a Spiritual Level, the only difference being its (slower) frequency, hence it appears more solid than other levels. Hence, <u>All Planes are Spiritual</u>

(See illustration at the end of the book).

(Earth Plane included). For no Plane is at a total standstill! A Plane can be more-or-less accelerated—but never "off." Thus, the more accelerated—the higher the vibration—the closer to Light a Plane is.

Now, suppose that you may be dreaming about visiting another Country, so that you can experience things you couldn't possibly experience in your Country. Suppose for instance that you lived in the great Country of China, but you might be fantasizing about visiting the famous Coliseum in Rome Italy, and while there perhaps, you will no doubt want to experience what a true Italian pizza tastes like.

If you had the means, you could hire a team of architects and workers and have an exact replica of the Coliseum built there in your backyard in China. But similar to the Venetian Casino in Las Vegas, where they replicated parts of the Italian city of Venice, it would look the same, but it would most definitely not feel the same. Likewise, you could Google the best possible recipe to make Italian pizza. You could gather the exact ingredients and follow the recipe down to the minutest of details, but the resulting pizza, although similar in appearance and shape, would never taste the same as the one you could have at the Antico Forno Pizzeria in Rome. And the opposite is also true. If I—an Italian-born—tried to cook a Chinese meal. It would never—despite following the recipe to a "T"—be the same as what I could enjoy in say Shanghai or Hong Kong. For if I truly wished to experience the real thing, I would have no choice but to go there in person, for it is not just the recipe that makes the meal, but the experience as a whole. The red and gold accented plates, the seafood smell in the air, the authentic music, the jade artifacts, and the beautiful mother of pearl art hanging on the bright red walls. Now, that's authentic Chinese! That's the only way to experience a true Chinese meal.

Ask any Italian you know for instance, and they will tell you that nowhere else in the world can you have a pizza as good as you can have in Napoli, Italy. And an espresso coffee just doesn't taste the same unless enjoyed in the traditional white porcelain espresso mini-cup.

But why make these culinary comparisons you ask? I am trying to illustrate a point. At "Home," where we naturally and always reside as Souls, we can think of and simulate any scenario we may wish for.
It will as a matter of fact, instantly materialize right before your eyes. You could say—or better think, "I wish to experience riding a gondola in Venice Italy" and pronto, a gondola, gondolier, waterway and even a portion of

the city of Venice would instantly appear. But it wouldn't be the same! Why wouldn't it be the same you might ask? Because of a minor component that simply cannot be duplicated there—the "Physical component" that is. Being Physical and all that it entails.

Physical attributes you simply cannot experience in a non-physical plane. Should you fall there, you wouldn't feel pain. If you wanted to enjoy that Italian espresso we talked about before, you wouldn't have any taste buds to tell you how delicious it tasted. If you held your lover's hand there, you wouldn't experience that physical touch, that comforting sense of companionship you would experience here on Earth. If you held your newborn baby in your arms, while you would no doubt feel the infinite inner love, you would not experience that warm physical sensation of holding your child in your arms. That warm physical connection we all long for—that all Souls long for! Are you now starting to see why as Souls, despite the challenges, we wouldn't miss the Earth experience for all of the Heaven money in the world?

While watching TV a few years back, I ran into a movie by director Vincent Ward. A movie I highly recommend to anyone who wishes to enjoy a beautiful movie, but also get a very close visual clue about what I am endeavoring to describe here. The title is, "What Dreams May Come" *starring the late Robin Williams.* At the time, I was trying to get answers to some questions. As usual Seth puts answers right in front of me, when I need them. Be it a book at the library that falls off the shelf on its own, or a movie I run into on TV, he always finds a way to send information I need my way—and at the right time. The movie portrays a very authentic interpretation of the Astral Plane. The plane we inhabit as Souls, upon disconnecting from this material realm of ours. I've been fortunate to having been there on three separate occasions, *that I know of,* but of course only as a visitor, this, for my own edification, and to be able I suppose, to report back on the experience in human terms. The movie and its special effects, not only portray a fantastic representation of the—*for the most part,* "self-generated" plane, but more importantly, it gives us a very close representation of the "mechanics" of that system of reality. What the movie proposes is in fact so close to what I actually experienced there, that there's no doubt in my mind that the director must have been there himself.

For pure edification I have extracted some key phrases from the movie that really illustrate the genius behind its production.

Chris (Robin Williams): *"A whole Human life is just a heartbeat here in Heaven, and then we'll all be together forever."*

Chris: (to Albert the Guide): *"So what is the 'me,' my brain I suppose?"*

Albert (the Guide): *"Your brain? Your brain is a body part, like your fingernail or your heart. Why is that the part that is you?"*

Chris: *"Because I have sort of a voice in my head, the part of me that thinks, that feels, that is aware that I exist at all."*

Albert: *"So if you're aware you exist, then you do, that's why you're still here!"*

Albert: *"Thought is real, Physical is the illusion, ironic huh?"*

Marie (Chris' daughter): *"I know they aren't real. I know."*

Albert: *"What's real in our minds, is real, whether some people know it or not. What some folks call impossible is, just stuff they haven't seen yet."*

Chris: *"Where is God in all of this?"*

Albert: *"Oh, He's up there somewhere, shouting down that He loves us, wondering why we can't hear Him!"*

Now, we are addressing subjects of the highest order by merely using human terminology. Humans have agreed en-mass and established a point, when a person could be declared dead. But we placed that gate there, only for our convenience. In reality no such a point exists, it is more of a shift, a change of form. A change of frequency. No particular moment exists when life is inserted or removed from matter. There is no such a thing as "non-living matter" being infused with life at any point. Consciousness is within the smallest of molecules, no matter what that molecule is part of, a living body or a dead corpse, or even a piece of driftwood floating aimlessly in the middle of the sea. Why, you ask? Because everything, living or non-living is all made by one thing only, "Consciousness!"

Everything is therefore Consciousness!

But a question still lingers. "Where did consciousness come from?" And I urge you to pay particular attention to the next few pages; for in them, you will without a doubt find, some of the most revealing information you're ever going to read, possibly in your entire life.

Now, as Humans, we think in terms of "cycles." *"Nothing lasts forever,"* is in fact one of our favorite sayings. Thus, we're accustomed—we even expect that everything must have a "starting point," and an end. That's how we're used to think. Therefore, if someone were to propose that "Life came from a thought" and it is nothing but a "thought," such a statement would not make sense to us. And yet, in the next few pages I shall endeavor to demonstrate precisely that.

In larger terms, "Time" does not exist, but for the sake of the argument, in human terms there was a "time" when pure consciousness imagined permeating into matter, which is also made of that same consciousness—but decelerated. Thus, matter was inherently conscious. But the transformation did not take place say "gradually" over a period of time, but all at once, in an "Illumination," a "flash" if you like.

And behold, I hereby present to you the "Flash" our scientists like to call "the Big Bang!"

Now, just as an ocean touches all of its shores at once, Light also is everywhere at once. Thus, the "Flash of Consciousness" permeated all levels, all the way from Spiritual to so called "Material," all-at-once! Consciousness flashed everywhere at once, but not as an "after-effect" of that flash, but because the flash itself was consciousness! Hence, Consciousness became the only medium for all that exists! And at that precise (hypothetical) point, all possibilities, Past, Present and Future, Including all Life, became possible. Seth calls it,

"An Illumination happening everywhere simultaneously and hence every point became aware of itself and of its possibilities."

But not gradually, but all at once! And from that point on, in those Planes where "Time" was to be a factor, "Time" started ticking!

Still today, all species, all forms of life, all of existence in-fact; be it an ant, a Human or a tree, still possess an awareness of being part of a Common Larger Source. It is thus fitting to say that while we are the product of our environment, our environment is also the product of us! Now to the million dollars question that has been the topic of a million debates:

"Is there a design and a designer in all of this?"

Of course there is, but both the design and the designer are so inter-combined, that they're actually one and the same!

The Creation is therefore within the Creator, the Creator within the Creation. The whole still continues to create, as we speak!

So, when trying to pinpoint the beginning of the Universe, we're only referring but to that small visible portion (of the Universe) we see from our perspective. "Consciousness" is then within us, as well as in the whole. Thus, an invisible-conscious side of the Universe exists—from which the Physical-visible Universe emanates. Then, our Universe did not begin at any given point, or by any "primordial explosion," but it was instead "thought into existence"—everywhere, forward and back, and in all directions, Spiritual, Physical—all at once!

Now, the inner intent of the invisible-creative side of the Universe vibrates at such intensity that it literally—*vibrationally speaking,* "permeates" the entire physical system—simultaneously. Thus, our Physical Universe exists as an "idea!" If that weren't the case, ask yourself why does, when examined under an atomic microscope, your seemingly solid kitchen table show its true intimate composition, "Pure Energy?"

The Universe was not "created" at some point to be left abandoned to fend for itself. The Universe is continuously being created, even now! And in that grandiose process, every single moment of our time also exists, for "Time" is also part of the original Creation!

And unlike what Sir Darwin would like us to believe, species did not "evolve" from other species. All species, each and every one (past as well as future) was meant to represent itself—and only itself! Each species possesses its own identity; it existed and exists just as it was intended. Hence, contrary to what we think, dinosaurs did not evolve into modern animals. Dinosaurs were intended to be just that—dinosaurs! The so-called "prehistoric Mammoth" did not evolve into today's elephant. The Mammoth was intended to be just that—and the same goes for the elephant. The true and only reason why some species appear so fascinatingly similar, and all species appear to exhibit common traits and characteristics is simply this: "They're all being thought by the same Thinker!" Thus, just as any artist paints or sculpts in his own recognizable style, All-That-Is also creates in a certain style—His style. Therefore, all manifestations within, all possible species, formations and features of all types, all levels of physicality, all dimensions in fact, all originated from the same "thought."

From a human perspective, we could envision this process taking many millennia, but from a Creator's perspective "time" was not a factor by which to create, but a factor stemming only within certain portions of the whole (Creation). Therefore Creation happened all at once—and it is still happening now. The Creator did not use any calendars or clocks—we created those. No point existed when consciousness decided to vitalize matter, for matter is consciousness, and consciousness is matter. "Aware" is not an "added feature," or a "switch" that the Creator had to flip at some point, to make everything become aware. "Aware" is a "natural state." In Seth's own words,

"Aware, is the only way everything comes!"

From a human perspective, we find this concept difficult to accept, but that's only because we normally think of consciousness as something we come in-and-out of. Someone falls and bangs their head, "they lose consciousness," we declare. But that's not the case. Even if the individual ends up dying as a result of the fall and the Soul departs from that body, the atoms and molecules that form that body remain conscious and aware. Atoms are inherently aware of their own identity and what their "task" is—at all times.

Now, from a Creation standpoint, if we for instance were to think of the Universe as a painting, the Artist would not have first painted the sky as a background, then all the foreground objects, trees and so on, to then introduce the first forms of life, starting with microorganisms, evolving later, into more and more complex life-forms. The Artist would've instead started —not with a blank canvas, but with a panel of pure (aware) light. The (aware) light being the under-painting on which all of the other components—living and not, were already intended, already included, but not in detail, but just as ideas or rough outlines. Then, as the painting and the Artist were one and the same, the painting itself, in a creativity that came from within, began transforming from within, in ever increasingly richer colors, defined patterns and detailed outlines. Thus, the Universe or Universes, became aware and alive within the painting, simply because they were themselves made of awareness—and within a painting that was also aware of itself.

Now, I urge the reader, to pay special attention to this next piece of information, for when I finally grasped its full meaning, it caused the biggest mystery science has ever been faced with, to—at least for me, instantly evaporate.

As we saw earlier, in materialistic terms, no matter what the "source" maybe, you need a "space" in which to create. Science is therefore at a total loss in pinpointing "where" that "Source" that caused the *so called* Big Bang was—before space itself existed. The answer is,

"The Artist painted within, not without!" The painting, the canvas and the Artist, are therefore one and the same! Hence, the energy and vitality of the Universe came from within. And though at that point still invisible, the moment the Creator conceived it, the Universe became alive. Thus, no actual "place" or "space" exists nor is needed, for the Universe to materialize, grow or expand into. The Universe only exists "in a thought state," more precisely "A Spiritual Realm in the Creator's mind!"

This is almost impossible to explain in human terms, much less recognize, for we observe what appears to be a physical Universe. We measure it, we touch it, and therefore it appears to be "real." But I ask you to define "real." Which would you say is real, the kitchen table you can touch, or your feelings you cannot touch? The water in the ocean you can immerse your hand into, or the sky you cannot touch? Are the solid mountains real, or is your intangible imagination real instead? What is real, a human brain we can operate upon and dissect, or thoughts, which we can neither see nor touch? What about love, a love that we can neither touch measure or see. Is love real?

We seek to find "a beginning," again, because that's how we're accustomed to think. "Everything—the Universe included, must have begun from somewhere—sometime," we conclude. We spend untold resources and effort trying to explain its origins, and the creation of life, for that is how we see things here in our material plane, thus that is the only train of thought that makes sense to us. We go forth seeking to understand divine questions by merely using human made instruments.

But, could a drop of water comprehend the greatness of the ocean?

We seek to know the "Origin of the Universe." But we fail to understand that this seemingly "physical" Universe of ours is in fact an extension of a Universe that originates from within. Not as a cast-out duplicate, or mirror image, but instead as a continuum. We fail to realize that the "Physical" part of the Universe is to the Universe what your skin is to you—but not "you the body," but "you the Soul." That skin, which you can touch and call yours, simply could not exist without its inner counterparts, life's essence—you the Soul. But each layer is not separate or independent from the next, but instead each a component of the whole, together forming the whole. We find this concept difficult to relate to, because we routinely ignore what we classify as "invisible realms." "If we can't see it and touch it, then it doesn't exist," we conclude. And generally speaking the scientific community supports that incredibly erroneous assumption. Thus we forget, hence devalue the Universe within, rendering it inconsequential. We feel, we think, we dream, we love, but we do not believe these "mental states" actually exist. We know they exist, but not "actually exist" thus missing the larger part of the whole, for most of it, is in fact invisible. This, because; the "All-That-Is" System is for the most part Spiritual!

We focus upon and fool ourselves into believing that the thin layer of ice on the ocean we walk upon is the whole ocean, thus missing the enormous amount of water under the thin ice—water without which, the ice we walk upon couldn't possibly exist. We therefore concentrate on but a miniscule portion of the whole, sure that that's all that is real. Then we are unable to explain why when examined under the microscope, does that seemingly physical side we call "solid," also proves to be made of invisible energy. If we truly wished to know the origins of the physical Universe, we must be willing to look where we don't normally look. Do I need to again remind you, about what all Prophets throughout history have tried to tell us, when asked "where" was the Creator to be found?

"Seek to know thy Creator not outward, but inward instead!"

Using that same beloved kitchen table of ours as an example, Seth said that despite the fact that we only see one single "copy" of the table, many less visible copies (layers) of that table co-exist immediately within it. To begin, let's remind ourselves that what we "see" is strictly dictated by our eyes limited visual range, but not distance-wise but frequency-wise. The same goes for our hearing. As you know, different animals (humans included) can only hear within a certain frequency range. A dog can hear a siren minutes before its master can. This is not because the dog can hear farther, but because the dog's hearing can perceive frequencies in a range unperceivable to its master.

Similarly, our friend the kitchen table is made of many less and less visible copies (layers) of itself, immediately next to the copy we can see and touch, all the way to invisibility—then pure energy. But not each layer beside the next, but within and without. Just like the orange peel is not next to the orange, but external to it—still part of the whole, so does a table, *and everything else for that matter,* have its many layers spawning from the visible tangible copy, inwardly, all the way to invisibility.

What is the purpose of these other layers you may ask? What is the purpose of this layer—the one that we can see and touch here, I ask? "So that we can use it here," you may remind me. But so are all of the other layers, for these less and less visible layers are there for the exact same reason, to adorn our less-and-less visible kitchens, in less-and-less physical layers. Whether you are aware of it, or not, or whether you believe it, or not, the fact is that you simultaneously exist in all these other less visible layers. And it turns out that the "you" in those other layers—also need kitchens and tables. The truth is,

"A poet can describe the Universe in a short poem much more accurately than the astrophysicist who compiles a ten year, ten thousand page report."

"A child can describe a butterfly more accurately than the biologist who spends ten years and ten million dollars researching it."

From a higher perspective, the Universe has no beginning and no end. Thus, from that higher perspective there are no contradictions. All-That-Is is aware of all possible realms, visible as well as invisible. We, on the other hand, can seek a beginning and an end for as long as we wish—and in human terms that seeking would make sense to us, but from a higher perspective—from All-That-Is' perspective, it is all one and the same, it makes no difference whatsoever. It would be equivalent to looking for water while inside the ocean. Simply put, All-That-Is is aware that a cluster of beloved Humans, in a remote corner—within (Himself,) keep themselves busy trying to understand their immediate perceived surroundings. And they do so using science, technology, and instruments that they have made—and only they understand!

Then, in some other remote little speck of reality (still within Himself) some other cluster of beloved life-forms, try to do the same using sciences and instruments familiar only to them. From All-That-Is' perspective, it is really that simple!

Picture if you will, a colony of microscopic bacteria spending a lifetime on a single eyelash. To them, that eyelash is as big as the Universe is to us. And because of the enormous distance (from their perspective) they will never be able to visit the next eyelash. Thus, as far as they are concerned, that single eyelash—is the whole Universe.

Now, we exist in the mind of All-That-Is! Not only are we in one of His "thoughts"—we are the thought! "But then, if it is all but a thought, why do we perceive our surroundings as real," you might ask?

Allow me to address this point from a different perspective. Think of a dream you had—any dream. Were you (in that dream) aware of being in a dream? Did the "you" in the dream know that you were being dreamt by the "you" here? What do you suppose happens when the "you" in the dream goes to sleep there at night? Could it be possible that the "you" there—dreams of the "you" here perhaps? On this point, let me tell you about a very revealing dream I had a while ago.

In the dream, a good friend of mine and I were traveling somewhere in California. It was early afternoon; we stopped for lunch at a large country-style restaurant. It was a very noisy place, with a noisy wooden planked floor, and a very loud TV on the wall. We got our food, but as soon as we started eating I heard—what sounded, like a low rumbling noise lasting a couple of seconds. Not sure what it was I didn't say anything. But a minute later I heard the noise again, this time a bit louder. And I also felt a light tremor through the floor and the chair I was sitting in. I asked my friend if he had felt anything. "No I did not, it must be the loud TV and the noisy floor," he said. We continued eating.

Then a couple of minutes later, a strong tremor shook the floor, but so violently that some of the chairs tipped over—and the TV came off the wall crashing down on the floor. Folks started running in every direction. "Earthquake" everyone screamed. My friend and I ran outside to the parking lot, where dozens of people had gathered. More and more folks came out in the open from every direction. We could see smoke in the far distance. Then we heard one siren, two sirens—many sirens in a concert of sorts. Confused, we started walking in the direction of our car parked twenty meters or so away, when I heard a phone ringing. But too preoccupied with the earthquake, I did not bother to answer it. I kept on walking, but the phone kept on ringing. I was going to answer the cellphone in my back pocket, but when I reached for it, I realized that the ringing was not coming from my cellphone, but instead, from a different "reality."

And so, I intentionally unfocused from that shaky earthquake channel, and focused my attention here to this reality. Don't ask me "how" but that's what I did. I awoke to my ringing cellphone on the night table, the dream still so very vivid in my mind that I could still hear the people screaming all around me.

Once done with the short phone call, I put my head down on the pillow for a few minutes, going over the dream still very vivid in my mind. I could still hear the frantic voices; I could still see the dust rising from the busy parking lot, cars driving away in a hurry. Then a sudden eureka moment. It suddenly dawned on me! The answer I had long been seeking to something Seth had said years earlier, something of paramount importance.

"We exist only in the mind of God!" He said. Now I knew!

Allow me to explain. While in the dream, the "me" living in that dream surely had no idea that he was being "dreamt" by the "me here." The "me there," running scared from the earthquake, felt very much in danger—and in that scenario, it all felt very real indeed. I wasn't thinking, "oh well, I shouldn't worry about it as it is all just a dream," as from there, it surely did not feel like a dream at all. I was instead very scared, and as aware of my surroundings there—as I am aware of my surroundings here now.

Thus, from the "here" perspective, we call those events "dreams," but we only do so because they do not take place "here" on this level. "They are not real," we reason upon waking up in the morning. But they are surely nothing to joke about when you're there running for dear life. And you sure are as alive and fully aware of your surroundings there, as you are here. If someone there harmed you, it would surely hurt—there. And suppose that you were having a sexual escapade there, the "you" there would surely enjoy it, wouldn't you agree?

So, if that's the case, "what are dreams then," you may ask?

As mentioned earlier, dreams are simply other levels of reality! But just as real as this level is, and most importantly just as valid! In essence, it is another "concurrent life." But what happens to that "life" there, upon awaking here? Exactly what happened to me in the middle of that earthquake—it continues! It continues with whatever scenario you left it at—when you switched focus back onto this life-reality. Does a movie on TV stop just because you switch channels?

Now, do we always focus on the same level every night when we sleep? According to Seth, no! We in fact simultaneously inhabit hundreds of levels. And each of these levels continues, each with their own given "programming." Just like listening to a radio, where you can only tune into a specific channel at a time—thus forgetting that many other channels still exist. But forgetting them does not cause their broadcasting to stop. But why do we exist on so many levels simultaneously, you may ask?

The short answer is "why not?" But according to Seth, the real reason is, "So that we the Entity—and by extension All-That-Is, can experience as many different—simultaneous scenarios as possible." It is really that simple! Seth explained.

Each level, independent and free to alter its own programming (hence "Free-Will") but all connected on a larger scale. Why have only one experience at a time, when you can have many? Suppose you're facing a challenge here, another channel—getting a hint from the "collective" will come to the rescue, giving you a different perspective on the matter. A different scenario, helping you to see that same issue under a different light, helps you to choose the best course of action here. It goes without saying of course that we do the same for our "fellow other-selves" living on those other levels.

Allow me to share another short personal case in point, which illustrates this process perfectly.

A decade or so ago my parents went through a messy divorce. I hoped they would have taken the amicable route, but once lawyers get involved, that rarely turns out to be the case.

And so things took an ugly side. My Mother asked me to help her with the process, thus understandably, things between my Father and I cooled off a bit. I tried my best, but our divergence of opinions made it impossible for my Father and I to arrive at a mutually satisfactory middle ground. We still communicated to a point, but we both knew that things between us were not the same as they were before. He didn't like the fact that I took my Mother's side. But since—as a result of a mid-life crisis he was experiencing, he was the one seeking the divorce in the first place, I felt compelled to side with my Mother.

After it was all said and done, my Father and I barely talked for almost two years. Then we started talking sporadically, but the pink elephant in the room grew bigger every day. We both knew that we had to do something, but neither of us took the initiative.

The interesting thing was that almost as immediately as our divergence of opinions started, I began having a series of dreams, which upon later examination, allowed me to experience firsthand how different levels of reality can—and do influence one another and how they can come to the aid and assist in the resolution of challenges, either directly, or by offering a different perspective on a given matter.

Simply put, the dreams were a series of continuing "episodes," the next picking up where the previous had left off—all sharing the same theme in common. In all of the fifty or so dreams, my Father and I were "soldiers," left behind by our platoon somehow. In trying to escape and regroup with our platoon, we fought in streets of cities, in a war, and against endless waves of enemy soldiers I did not know. It felt so real that when I woke up each morning, I would be shaken for several hours afterword, as if I had really been in a war. The constant fear of being killed, the whistling noise of the bullets flying all around us, the frantic running, trying to hide behind anything we could find, a park bench, a tree, a parked car. This went on for months.

Then I decided to ask Seth for his input.

He explained what the dreams were trying to suggest. Basically, what it came down to in the end was that no matter what the personal disagreement, faced with an external threat, my Father and I would face that threat together side-by-side. Essentially we were still family after all, no matter what the issue was, we had to stand united. There couldn't be any other way. And so I decided to have a heart-to-heart talk with my Father. We both realized that we were basically interpreting the same issue from different perspectives, thus neither of us were completely wrong, but half-right instead. We certainly didn't want our relationship to suffer over mostly material issues; family always comes first. We found a common ground and the issues became easily resolvable. Needless to say, the war dreams stopped that very same night, never to be had again!

Now, from a human perspective, most dreams do not seem to make sense. "We do very strange things," we *from here* think, Cities, even our homes, can appear different than what we are so used to. "If I don't have my 55 inch TV in my living room there—it is not real," we think.

But that's only because we compare there with here—and the things we have here. My good friend Joe, for instance, who because of three consecutive strokes is 70% paralyzed here, walked perfectly there in the dream. As humorous as this may sound, can you see how the two "Joes" were actually helping one another?

Now, have you ever wondered why we "need" to sleep every night? It is certainly not because "our mind," or we the Soul, need the rest. Just as we park our cars in our garage every night, our physical body, also a "vehicle" needs to rest, "recharge its batteries" so-to-speak. So, what is the Soul—the real you, to do, while its Earth vehicle recharges? You switch focus onto another level, onto another, *running*, "Vehicle."

Now, this channel and that (dream) channel might be situated immediately next to each other. However, this does not mean that they are physically beside each other, but instead, in a slightly different frequency. Just like the many layers in an onion make the onion—our many layers form the Entity. Hence, these layers would be "next" to each other—but not physically, but frequency wise.

If we wished to use a radio for comparison sake, we would compare it to say channels 87.7, 87.8, and 87.9, on the dial and so on. That might explain why we seem to switch back and forth from one layer to the next with such ease. However, this does not mean that we do not switch to channels farther away; actually we do so every night. This is easier to understand when you look at the whole from the Entity's perspective. From there, it is easy to see how you actually exist on all channels simultaneously, and no single layer is more or less important that the next.

To further stimulate your thinking, if you agree that while in a dream you're seemingly unaware that it is a dream, can you see how it could be possible that this channel—this "here-now" could also be a dream? And just as you would in any dream, from within, you are unaware of that fact? From this perspective, we label this channel as "the real one" and all others "dreams," but you sure don't call them dreams while being there, right? Isn't it true that while in a dream you think of that life as being real? Why would you otherwise run from danger? What if when we go to sleep there—we dreamed about this, *here,* channel? What if, these, as well as all other channels, all of the "different lives" we seemingly live, were actually taking place in All-That-Is' mind? What if it was just one of All-That-Is' dreams?

But why are we seemingly unable to see other channels, if they all belong, *in a wider sense*, to us the Entity? We do in fact. Despite not being consciously aware of it from here, not only do we (the Entity) interact with all channels, we are actually in all of the channels simultaneously. For the Entity is in all channels at once. And you—not your body, but you the "Reasoning Mind" are the Entity!

In setting in motion such a grandiose Divine design, a mechanism of sorts was put in place, and Seth himself had a difficult time explaining Divine subjects in human terms. Our language simply does not include the lexicon needed to accurately describe these subjects. We never needed to, we thus never developed the suitable terminology. Keeping these limitations in mind Seth explained the system as follows.

"If we liken the Entity to a radio station, simultaneously emitting on a number of channels, hence these channels can be said to represent 'projections' of the Entity. And through these projected-selves the Entity broadcasts, again so that it can experience as much 'variety' as possible—a number of different scenarios-programs, simultaneously. Some scenarios might take place here on Earth, some on other systems, but not necessarily on other planets within this (Earth) level, but on different existential planes. Some even in different eras."

"So, much like an actual radio or station, where the parent station broadcasts simultaneously on a number of channels, but where each channel is independent of the other," I asked?

"That's an excellent analogy indeed Marco! Each channel, while being aware of the larger 'parent station,' each—independently broadcasts their own programming. And in order to avoid direct interactions between these channels," Seth continued, "a type of 'filter' was set in place. This is achieved by allocating to each channel a different frequency. However, each channel is instinctively aware of the larger all-encompassing Entity."

"Envision a mechanism functioning much like a one-way mirror. The 'mirror,' somewhere halfway between the Entity and each projected channel," Seth continued, "allows the Entity to always 'see' all channels, while from the opposite end, the channels, while still aware of being part of something greater, are prevented from looking back homebound in the direction of the Entity.

Thus, the source (the Entity) can see and interact with all channels simultaneously, while allotting to each channel a certain degree of independence, a semi-disconnect if you like. Each channel however, is instinctively and always aware that though invisible, an underlying overall-guidance still exists—and this is precisely the reason 'why you seek to know' and have a natural pull toward the source. You look up, but you don't really know why you look in that direction. You yearn to validate that inner feeling, that inner knowledge that conveys an inner truth, suggesting that you are part of something much greater. Some folks, disillusioned and tired of looking, give up and declare that 'God does not exist.' However, deep inside even the Atheist and the Agnostic know that they are not alone, that they are part of something greater."

Now, the mirror example is only used, *Seth explained*, so that we could better relate to the actual process. In reality no actual mirror exists, but instead a type of "fog" or more precisely "electromagnetic plasma." The plasma serves as a dividing curtain if you like, from a given channel to the Home Base. Some folks have actually not only seen the fog, but have ventured in—and even past it. While looking homebound, they've actually experienced the immensely loving light that exists on the other side of the fog. Those for instance, who like myself, have temporarily "died" and come back, know exactly what I am referring to. This is the very reason perhaps for the existence of those "filters" in the first place. Think about it, if we were able to freely see homebound, how many of us would choose to stay here?

Now, our doctors seem unable to determine conclusively where to draw the line, between what we call "a Comatose State" and "Death." The reality is, that while a body is in a coma, the Soul is simply deciding whether they should return here—or disconnect altogether from this channel. And, since "time" does not apply there, they may or may not be aware that a year might have passed here on Earth. Hence, a coma can, *from our standpoint*, last from a couple of weeks up to—in some cases—several years. The body is basically left at idle, to exist on its own. The sans-Soul body is kept from disintegrating, as we discussed earlier, by its atoms' in-built self-awareness. The following comparison may sound somewhat amusing, but we could liken this process to an appliance, once its electrical cord is unplugged from the wall, switching to backup battery power. The atoms, *batteries in this case*, possess a built-in awareness, energy that basically keeps the body in an "idle" state, while the true life force, *the Soul*, decides what course of action to take.

Now, a coma is usually caused by severe trauma, like for instance an accident. The Soul exits the body an instant before the accident itself. And depending upon the severity and the damage suffered by the body, the Soul finds itself in a sort of "limbo," from where it can see—and is aware of both its human side, as well as its Spiritual source. The "attraction" that exists from Source, is simply too strong and beautiful to give up easily. For the Soul is at that point finally aware of the full meaningfulness of its existence, and is very tempted to simply abandon an earth existence of apparent tribulation, and simply return Home—to Source!

And that is mainly why, Guides will be made available at that very crucial stage. Counseling is given to help in the decision-making. That individual's life achievements are reviewed, so that the individual can carefully evaluate their options, as they are faced with choosing between returning to a perhaps limited lifestyle, lack of mobility, loss of limb or ability to communicate, versus leaving their loved ones behind, and an Earth life they cherished.

From a medical-physical standpoint, it may appear as if that individual's consciousness might've been away for months, sometimes years, but ask any doctor, "away where exactly?" And no doctor will be able to tell you. But from the Soul's standpoint they were away for only a few moments, for again, "time" no longer applies once outside of this channel.

A comatose state however, is very different from actual "death." Deathimplies a total disconnect, "a cutting of the cord" on the part of the Soul from the body. Coma is instead a partial disconnect from the body, sort of having a foot here and a foot there.

However, invariably those who do decide to return here, will have a broader—more spiritual understanding of the experience we call "Life."

Some other folks, unable to make sense of it, but mainly for fear of ridicule, prefer to sweep the whole experience under the carpet and keep quiet, while many others will go on talking about their extraordinary life-changing experience.

Some will go on to write books, make movies etc., but all—after such an experience, will invariably never be the same.

"All Human beings are also dream beings. Dreaming ties all of mankind together." ~

—Jack Kerouac

Chapter 7

The Greater Design

The so-called "five-senses-reality" is heralded as, "What life is all about." However, the truth is that the life we perceive as real is just that—a perception, or better yet, a sum of perceptions. Everything we observe, is "Energy-Manifesting," but only when we consciously observe it. Our scientists will in fact tell you, that atoms are nothing more than "Energy," but atoms that—*much like chameleons*, behave and can group and re-group, to assume any form they need to. Thus Energy cannot be destroyed, but it instead changes form continuously.

We're conditioned to think that the Universe around us has a definite material reality. Hence we build our lives around that assumption. However, in the last few decades our scientists are starting to realize more and more that this concept amounts to nothing more than a mere perception. All information we have about the external world is conveyed to us via our five senses, "Sight, Hearing, Smell, Touch, and Taste." Hence, the world around us consists of nothing more than the sum total of what our eyes see, our ears hear, our nose smells, our hands touch, and our tongue tastes.

Totally dependent on those five senses since birth, we believe in an external world, oblivious to the fact that it all amounts to nothing more than what we—via those five senses, perceive as external. However, scientific research is revealing more and more that the "matter" making up the external world, is in fact a continuously changing mass of energy, constantly re-arranging, "mold" as needed, based on our individual as well as our collective perception.

Let's for instance take a look at one of our five senses, "Sight."

"Seeing," *we're told*, is a progressive process that starts with light, or more precisely photons travelling from a given object to the eye. Once there, it passes through the eye lenses, and is then reflected and finally focused on the retina, located at the back of the eye. Keep in mind here that all that we have up until this point is "light." Then, once in the retina, these same rays of light are transformed into electrical signals, electrical signals, that via neurons are in turn transmitted to the center of vision located at the back of our brain.

Called, "Primary Visual Cortex," and located in the occipital lobe at the back of the brain, it is a thin sheet of tissue, less than 2.5 mm thick and about 30 mm wide. Thus, here in this area, is where "seeing" actually happens—not in the eye, as we normally think. So, everything you see throughout your entire life is actually seen here in this tiny place at the back of your head. However, let's pause for a second, as it is imperative we understand a very important point made at the beginning of this paragraph. The "image"—which is not an image, but a mix of light signals, is not seen by the eye, but instead "received" by the eye. Thus, the process of seeing does not start from the eye, but from the object itself, object that emanates photons, photons—that travelling in all directions, are picked up by whatever eyes care to receive them.

We could liken this process to a camera. The camera does not seek to see objects, the camera simply picks up through its lenses, light (photons) emitted by a given object. Hence through a microchip, the camera processes that light, converting it into a digital-electrical signal. Then through connections, this signal is sent to a "visual processor," which in turn displays that original light onto a video monitor as an image. So whether you are watching a movie on TV, or you're up on a mountain admiring a beautiful landscape hundreds of kilometers wide, you are actually seeing all of this, through much that same process—and all of it ends up in this tiny little space of only a few centimeters, at the back of your brain. So when you say, "I am seeing a given object, person or landscape," what you are actually seeing is the image that is being generated through the process just described above, inside that little space in the back of your brain. You think you are seeing something with your eyes, but in reality what you are seeing instead, is the end product of all that "transmitting and translating." Let's make an example to illustrate this concept better.

Suppose you were a sea researcher and you wanted to explore the ocean floor. From your ship on the surface, you send a remotely guided camera in the water. The camera is tethered to a monitor on the ship, from which you can see everything the underwater camera sees. The only problem was that you forgot to remove that magnifying yellow filter from the camera lenses. Hence, everything you are going to see on the monitor is going to appear not only larger than it really is, but also yellowish in hue. From the surface, you assume that what you see on the screen is what the floor of the ocean looks like—and you write a detailed report about it.

So, going back to our "human camera," when you say "I see something," what you are actually doing is interpreting electrical signals in your brain, being received by what is happening in the back of your brain. Furthermore, we mustn't forget that our brain is completely enclosed and sealed to light by our bony skull, thus, it, and by extension "you," cannot "directly" see an object. Therefore, what you think you see out there, is nothing more than the end product of a series of "translations, interpretations, filtering, electrical transmissions, stimuli, and projections," all of the time. Your brain—hence you, always rely on electrical signals, as they are being transmitted and translated inside your head, well past the point of what you are actually seeing out there.

As a case in point, "Daltonism," most commonly referred to as "color blindness" or "color vision deficiency," is the inability—or decreased ability to see colors. This is mainly due to an underdevelopment of certain light receptors within the retina. But the individual having the disorder, does not know they have a disorder until they are told so, which brings forth an interesting question. Consider the following. What would happen if the entire world's population had the so-called "condition?"

For starters, it would no longer be classified as a "condition" but instead perfectly normal. But in addition, we would simply never know, as there wouldn't be anyone to tell us otherwise! We would all carry on with our lives despite not being able for instance to ever buy a red or a green car—and we would never know the difference. But what about animals that only see a limited number of colors or no color at all? Did you know for instance that while folks cheering at the Spanish Corrida (bull fight) assume that the bull is busy chasing a red cape, the bull does not see a red cape at all? It sees it gray! What if our eyes were only able to see in shades of gray or black and white? But the million dollars question is, "If our eyes could only see shades of gray, would colors out there still exist?" And I am sure you're wondering, "What exactly am I trying to suggest here?" You will understand in a minute.

We just touched on how the process of "seeing" works. In reality that same process of "external interpretation" processing and end-product equally applies to all our senses. Everything you smell, touch, taste, or hear, is similarly picked up by your external sensors, then *via bio-wiring*, sent to your brain and interpreted. You thus believe that what you end up with in your brain, *the sum-total of all that your five senses perceive, then transmit, filter and re-interpret along the way in a multitude of internal processing*, is in fact "what is going on out there." You are thus fooled into assuming that what you're experiencing, inside your brain, is actually "out there." When in fact, surprise, surprise, it is only inside your brain! So the totality of the external world, all of it as a matter of fact, exists only inside your brain.

This brings forth an undisputable conclusion. Specifically, "Everything we think is out there externally, everything we perceive as "material," including the environment around us, the sky, galaxies, even the Universe, all amounts to nothing more than a series of electrical signals, all inside our brain." So when you look up at the night sky and you see the moon, that moon is not actually there in the sky, but only inside your brain! Then, from your brain, your senses make the moon appear to you as if it were some 380,000 Km up in the sky. But that's only because of the way your senses "see" it. But let me ask you a most revealing question.

What do you think would happen to the moon, if someone would hypothetically clip off the wiring between your brain and your eyes?

The logical answer would be of course, "Well, the moon would no longer be there for me—but it would still be there for everyone else whose wiring is still intact." Of course it would, but I am sure you can already anticipate what the next question is. "What would happen if we clipped off everyone's wiring?" And yet we're far from done! Let's take it one step further; for we can still work our way around it by arguing that despite no one being able to see it, the moon would still be there. For you would be sure that a totally blind Humanity could theoretically still program a rocket to take us there, and land on it, right? Not so fast!

What if—in addition to the sense of "sight," we were also to clip-off the sense of "touch" from our brain? Then, what would we be landing on exactly? And for as "strange" as this may sound, this is just the start, for it gets much, much weirder than that.

The truth is that you are not looking-feeling-tasting-touching-smelling an object that is out there—to then via your sensors and bio-wiring interpret it and see in your brain, but instead, the exact opposite!

What this means, is that when you look up at the moon—and see it at 380,000 Km from you, what you are really doing is that—that moon is actually inside your brain's center of vision, being projected outwardly by you, the Soul, from your physical brain—via your physical eyes.

So lo-and-behold your eyes are no longer viewing devices or cameras as we just saw, but instead "projectors." That (camera explanation) was a necessary interim-step I had to take, to put things into perspective. What we must do instead, is—take that explanation and totally reverse it. For it turns out that our eyes are not "cameras" recording what's out there—to then send what they see to our brain, but instead the exact opposite. In essence, our eyes are "projectors," sending out there—what we, the Soul, manufacture inside our brain.

But let's for the sake of the argument, use a more down to earth example, as I totally agree if you think that these are way-out-there suggestions. To illustrate the concept more clearly I needed to choose an object, which would make use of all of our five senses, "Sight, Touch, Smell, Hearing, and Taste." At first, I wanted to use an orange, but unless you banged it against your ear—possibly injuring yourself, you wouldn't get any sound to come out of it. So I happened to, *accidentally as usual*, look in the direction of my kitchen, and there I see a nice big coconut sitting on the counter. So, our dear coconut will serve as our guinea pig. Let's start.

Suppose you're looking at a coconut while you're holding it in your hand. You can also smell that coconut, and if you opened it you could taste it, and if you shook it you would hear the liquid splashing inside. Thus the coconut causes you to use all of your five senses. Now suppose that we are going to hypothetically clip-off one of your five senses at a time. We start with the sense of "Smell." So, you bring that coconut in front of your nose and you can no longer smell it.

Next we are going to clip off your sense of "Hearing." You bring the coconut next to your ear, but if you shook it, you could no longer hear the liquid squishing inside.

Let's now clip-off your sense of "Sight." And suddenly you can no longer see the coconut.

You're still holding it tightly in your hand, thus, "No problem" you say, for "I can still feel the coconut in my hand. I could even break it into pieces and put a piece in my mouth and I would still know that it is a coconut," you declare!

Of course you would! But let's now clip-off your sense of "Taste." Would you now know whether you'd be holding a piece of coconut, a piece of wood, or even a rock? "Of course I would," you reply, "for through my sense of touch I can feel the difference in consistency." And you would be right, but I am sure you can already anticipate where this is heading.

What do you suppose will happen once we clipped off that last of your five senses, "Touch" that is? What are you now holding in your hand? "I can no longer smell, taste, see, hear, nor touch the coconut in my hand, but it would still be there for everyone else to see," you argue.

Do you truly believe so? For I am sure you already know where we are going next. "What would happen to the coconut—if no-one on the planet had any of the five senses? Why would anything "exist" physically, if there wouldn't be anyone out there to see, taste, touch, smell, or hear it? Think about it!

But it does not end here—for this is only the beginning. In case it hadn't yet occurred to you, by the time you had disconnected all of the five so-called "physical" senses, not only the coconut, but your entire physical body would have also ceased to exist!

And so, we assume that what we see in our brain is actually out there, external from us the observer. But this is only because we take it for granted that everything begins from the physical, to then travel inward. Hence, we assume that the physical world out there is what's there first, then our body—and lastly our "mind," there only to process all that, *again*, physical data. That couldn't be farther from the truth, <u>for the exact opposite is actually true</u>. It goes something like this.

You the Soul wish to experience holding a coconut in your hand. In expressing that wish, through your brain and then your body's five senses—*body that is also a projection*, manifest that coconut into physical existence. Think about what comes first, does the coconut jump in your hand by its own initiative—and then you realize what just happened, or do you first "think" about holding, buying, stealing a coconut, and you make it so—physically? And by the way, you in fact do so continuously, every moment of the day. You wish, you think—then project outwardly everything around you. This includes the home or building you're in now, even your body. <u>It all exists in your brain</u>, and then via the combined effort of your five senses you project outwardly. This is so that you—the Soul, can have a "less-Spiritual"—what we call "Physical existence," physical existence, which you couldn't otherwise experience in the Soul's Spiritual world.

"But I bought the coconut at the store. It did not materialize on my kitchen countertop," you would argue. And you would be right, but that's all part of the larger-collective illusion. We all agreed en-mass, to experience certain processes; we've setup and use for our convenience, cities, cars, and homes, grocery stores included. But if you really want to go crazy now, the physical brain is itself also nothing more than a mere sum of perceptions! Two very important questions come to mind.

—A) If external physicality amounts to nothing more than a mere projection—projected by us the observer, then, how can we really be sure that the world we can see and touch out there, really exists?

—B) For what purpose does this grandiose mechanism exist?

These are both very good questions, especially the latter. The answer to the first question is that (as our scientists are becoming more aware every day) we cannot be sure whether or not the external world actually exists physically. Actually, let me correct that—

I personally know for a fact, that it <u>does not</u> exist!

But until such time as science gets up to speed, or until those of you reading this—if you haven't already, get up to speed, it would be unfair of me to ask you to simply take my word for it. For each of you, as I have, will have to arrive to your own conclusion, <u>at your own pace</u>. Truth be told, the real question should not be "whether or not the physical world out there does exist," but rather: "<u>Are you ready to accept the fact that it does not</u>?" For if you were ready you would automatically know the answer.

The answer to the second question is a derivative from the same concept, only taken a step further. It has to do with "who" is in control of the brain in the first place. This computer of ours we like to call "our brain" makes all outward manifestation possible, but for what purpose, and most importantly on whose behalf? What is indisputable is that in the last decade or so, the concept of a "Holographic Universe" is becoming more and more the center of attention of just about every scientific study. Scientists observe a Universe that appears to be made of Matter, but which upon deeper examination, reveals its true fabric. What they find is Energy!

Many theories have been formulated on Matter's relationship to Energy. Matter vs. Anti-matter as we commonly label it, is what's really driving scientists crazy, for they are so close, but yet so distant. As what they erroneously label, "Two opposing forces," is in fact one, each a projection of the other. Aware Energy projects itself outwardly as Matter, no exception! That includes you! Thus, your skin is nothing more than your outermost inner expression of you the Soul. Your skin is in essence your Soul's counterpart, the outermost layer of YOU, the whole, all the way from Spiritual (Energy) to Physical (Matter).

Now, many argue that the brain is "where the buck stops at." Many others argue that it all comes down to a series of chemical reactions, again taking place, inside the brain. We shall endeavor to address this question, *and it is no small task,* with the following little experiment.

For the sake of our discussion, let's suppose that a brain surgeon were able to perform surgery on his own brain. So the nice doctor saws his own skull open. Then with his brain still wired to his body, takes his brain and places it on the operating table. So, hypothetically speaking, he can see the brain on the table with his eyes, and he can touch the brain with his hands. But how does he know this is so, if not from that same brain on the table?

"This is my brain," he reasons. "If I can look at my brain with my eyes, then it is no longer 'me' but part of the outside environment. But isn't my brain where I should be seeing everything outside of me from? But how could my own brain simultaneously be outside of itself—and look at itself? How could my brain reason that it sees itself on the table, when all of that reasoning should supposedly be happening 'inside' the brain itself?"

But the question is, "if the brain sees itself, then who is doing the thinking?" The answer is "It is the Soul who's doing all of the thinking, regardless of whether your brain is in your skull or on the operating table." The Soul is where you "project" that externally perceived world from. A world, which is not external at all, but only, imagined as being external, and through your five senses, "projected" outwardly. And I wish to pause here for a moment to clarify this point.

The "projector" example is the best thing I can liken the process to. For the not so faint of heart however, the truth is that, you are not actually seeing—or even projecting anything at all! All, and I mean all, which you perceive as being outside of you, takes place inside of you instead, period! Including what you call "outside"—externality itself! I wish I could put it into more digestible terms, but, you do not actually exist—you're only imagining that you do! And these two excellent articles from the "New Scientist" website may help us better understand the process.

—"**Man with tiny brain shocks doctors.** *A man with an unusually tiny brain manages to live an entirely normal life despite his condition, which was caused by a fluid build-up in his skull. Scans of the 44-year-old man's brain showed that a huge fluid-filled chamber called a ventricle took up most of the room in his skull, leaving little more than a thin sheet of actual brain tissue.*"

"It is hard for me [to say] exactly the percentage of reduction of the brain, since we did not use software to measure its volume. But visually, it is more than a 50 to 75 per cent reduction," says Lionel Feuillet, a neurologist at the Mediterranean University in Marseille, France. Feuillet and his colleagues describe the case of this patient in "The Lancet." He is a married father of two children, and works as a civil servant."

"Massive enlargement"— "The man went to a hospital after he had mild weakness in his left leg. When Feuillet's staff took his medical history, they learned that, as an infant, he had had a shunt inserted into his head to drain away hydrocephalus— water on the brain. The shunt was removed when he was 14. But the researchers decided to check the condition of his brain using computed tomography (CT) scanning technology and another type of scan called magnetic resonance imaging (MRI). They were astonished to see "massive enlargement" of the lateral ventricles—usually tiny chambers that hold the cerebrospinal fluid that cushions the brain."

"Intelligence tests showed the man had an IQ of 75, below the average score of 100 but not considered mentally retarded or disabled. The whole brain was reduced—frontal,

parietal, temporal and occipital lobes—on both left and right sides. These regions control motion, sensibility, language, vision, audition, and emotional and cognitive functions,' Feuillet told New Scientist."

"Brain adaptation"—"The findings reveal 'the brain is very plastic and can adapt to some brain damage occurring in the pre—and postnatal period when treated appropriately,' he says." "'What I find amazing to this day is how the brain can deal with something which you think should not be compatible with life,' comments Max Muenke, a paediatric brain defect specialist at the National Human Genome Research Institute in Bethesda, Maryland, US." "'If something happens very slowly over quite some time, maybe over decades, the different parts of the brain take up functions that would normally be done by the part that is pushed to the side,' adds Muenke, who was not involved in the case." (Source: www.newscientist.com-Daily News-20 July 2007)

—**"Woman of 24 found to have no cerebellum in her brain."** *"A hole at the back where the cerebellum should be" (By Helen Thomson)—"DON'T mind the gap. A woman has reached the age of 24 without anyone realizing she was missing a large part of her brain. The case highlights just how adaptable the organ is."*

"The discovery was made when the woman was admitted to the Chinese PLA General Hospital of Jinan Military Area Command in Shandong Province complaining of dizziness and nausea. She told doctors she'd had problems walking steadily for most of her life, and her mother reported that she hadn't walked until she was 7 and that her speech only became intelligible at the age of 6."

"Doctors did a CAT scan and immediately identified the source of the problem— her entire cerebellum was missing. The space where it should be was empty of tissue. Instead it was filled with cerebrospinal fluid, which cushions the brain and provides defense against disease."

"The cerebellum—sometimes known as the 'little brain'—is located underneath the two hemispheres. It looks different from the rest of the brain because it consists of much smaller and more compact folds of tissue. It represents about 10 per cent of the brain's total volume but contains 50 per cent of its neurons. Although it is not unheard of to <u>have part of your brain missing</u>, either congenitally or from surgery, the woman joins an elite club of just nine people who are known to have lived without their entire cerebellum. A detailed description of how the disorder affects a living adult is almost non-existent, say doctors from the Chinese hospital, because most people with the condition die at a young age and the problem is only discovered on autopsy (<u>Brain, doi.org/vh7</u>).

"<u>Comparison with a normal brain</u>"—"The cerebellum's main job is to control voluntary movements and balance, and it is also thought to be involved in our ability to learn specific motor actions and speak. Problems in the cerebellum can lead to severe mental impairment, movement disorders, epilepsy or a potentially fatal build-up of fluid in the brain. However, in this woman, the missing cerebellum resulted in only mild to moderate motor deficiency and mild speech problems such as slightly slurred pronunciation. Her doctors describe these effects as 'less than would be expected', and say her case highlights the remarkable plasticity of the brain."

"These rare cases are interesting to understand how the brain circuitry works and compensates for missing parts,' says Mario Manto, who researches cerebellar disorders

at the Free University of Brussels in Belgium. The patient's doctors suggest that normal cerebellar function may have been taken over by the cortex—brain scans should reveal the answer." (Source: www.newscientist.com-This Week-10 September 2014)

Reading incredible stories such as the two above, forces us to re-think what we know and have accepted as factual about the brain and its purpose. Of course the first and most natural explanation is to attribute it (as the scientists in the articles seem to suggest) to "brain plasticity"—in other words, the brain's ability to mold and adapt—re-adjust itself as needed. To me instead, this points out something altogether different, and that is, that the brain is simply an "organ"—a "computer" and nothing more. Not the source of consciousness, or where consciousness resides, but instead an "interface," again a "computer" through which the Soul—hence Consciousness directs the body—regardless of its (the brain) size, structure or shape.

It all comes down to this. It is an inconceivably difficult concept to grasp—until such time as we are able to, but above all willing to "switch places" and think as a Soul would, from the Soul's perspective and not from the body's perspective. Only then, will we be able to comprehend the relationship between the Spiritual and the Physical! It would in fact benefit us immensely, if we "reversed" how "we Souls" relate to the external world.

Six or so years ago, circa 2010, was when I was finally able to achieve this "switching of perspective," and doing so really changed everything for me. Likewise, instead of seeing yourself as a physical body inwardly feeding external physical data to your Soul, try to see yourself as a Soul instead, wishing to experience the physical. For what you really are, is not a body with, possibly, a Soul somewhere in it, but instead a Soul, wanting to experience less Spiritual realms!

A Soul envisions a number of more-or-less physical existential scenarios. Thus, *since Energy is the only thing it has to work with,* it modulates Energy, modulated Energy that will become the "tools and the mechanisms," the "clay" which to mold a given scenario with. In this (Earth) scenario our "Five Senses" are such tools and mechanisms. And I am with you when you think that this is not easy pill to swallow.

The difficulty arises mainly from the millennia of reversed indoctrination—where humanity has brainwashed itself into seeing itself into nothing more than a bunch of unworthy "cast-out bodies," that may or may not include some form of intelligence therein. And "the powers that be" did not mind that at all, instead they reinforced that misconception, for this produces more controllable-gullible masses. For the "Truth" will empower you! For if you were to find out about "Who you really represented," find out about the true power that lies within you—power you've inherited from your Creator, chances are we wouldn't have the enormous social inequalities we have today. Except that, "that is the 'growth path we chose." It is thus a reverse learning process that we are experiencing. We are learning "from the outside-in" so-to-speak. From the rough, ugly, painful, decelerated side of life, all with one goal in mind, finding our Id-<u>Entity</u>, reconnecting with Source.

It comes down to this. You the Soul "imagine scenarios," including the environment you're in right now. Hence, while the projectionist in the movie theater gets to decide what to project in his theater, you get to decide what to project in your own personal "Earth Theater." The only difference being that while the theater projector actually sends images out and onto the movie screen, you instead <u>manufacture the whole scene inside of you</u>. Theater, chair, the air around you, and last but not least, even your own body. Your "movie" takes place inside of you! And your personal experience is not only intertwined with—but it also influences everyone else's experience, the whole constituting the "en-mass" experience. The fascinating thing is that there exists enough power to give each a personal—unique experience, "a personal Universe" if you like, within the wider en-mass experience.

Not long ago, I was watching a four-part TV documentary about the latest findings on the nature of the Universe. According to the documentary, very recent findings seem to point not to a Universe, but instead to Multi-Verses. Our physicists are starting to take seriously the idea, *first proposed about a century or so ago*, that not only does the Universe exist "in our imagination only," thus being "created" moment-by-moment based on what we think the next moment should be, both at a personal as well as an en-mass level, but that it may also coexists next, beside, or together, a multitude of other (we do not know how many) simultaneous Universes, all more-or-less symbiotically interacting with one another.

Our scientists are truly close, for what they are now starting to perceive, are nothing more than the different levels, channels of the System we discussed earlier. However, these are not—as they are normally referred to, "separate individual Universes existing inside something greater," but many concurrent levels of existence, all within one larger System. Each level, complete with all that it needs, based upon the scenarios we wished to experience there. Thus, from the perspective of someone living within a given level, everything would appear as "real" there, as everything in that level would specifically and naturally match in frequency. And once again, our beloved onion example makes perfect sense here. Think of each onion layer as being one level of existence, the combined layers making the whole onion. In this case, the combined levels make the System.

Now, you are presently here now, as well as 500 years ago—and 500 years in the future. From a human standpoint Time appears to flow linearly, but from a universal standpoint, only "Now" exists. Thus, from that perspective, all scenarios, all moments in "time" simultaneously exist, now! If we once again use the radio as an analogy, all channels broadcast simultaneously, but each independent from the next—and each has their own programming. But interestingly, each channel is only consciously aware of their own programing, thus each channel assumes not only that theirs is the only real one, but that all others are nothing more than pure fantasy, dream channels at best. And isn't that precisely what we do here in this channel I ask?

As mentioned, this Human channel of ours has been engineered in such a way that events appear to happen in a linear moment-after-moment fashion. Each moment appears to follow the one before, immediately followed by yet another moment. This is the very mechanism that gives birth to the illusion of Time. But why was such a mechanism introduced into the channel's blueprint you may ask?

Seth explained that it has nothing to do with choice but instead with "location." The "area"—not geographically speaking but frequency-wise, where this channel is located within the system, brings about certain characteristics that cause a number of "distortions" of sorts, resulting in a number of given "illusions," one of which is "Time." And then we proceeded to build "devices" to keep track of it.

Now, inspired by All-That-Is, the Entity decides the scenario it wishes to experience, in each diverse and more-or-less physical environment. Though difficult to fathom and most of all accept this truth, there is really no need to dissect the process more than it needs to. But if it helps, this seemingly impossible scenario becomes clearer if you saw it not from a human perspective, but instead from the Entity's perspective, again, by switching viewpoints. Simply put, from that perspective, the Entity sees its projected selves operating each by a different set of rules; rules that may or may not include specific measurement systems, such as "Time" for instance.

But "what is Time exactly?" It would be preposterous to suppose, that one could explain in a page or two, something that has taken some of our best luminaries most of their careers to even begin to understand. But once again, allow me to remind you "who" is doing the explaining here. When Seth first attempted to explain to me the true nature of time, he used terminology that I could easily relate to. Then, with that in mind, I endeavored to conceptualize my own "mental picture" of Seth's explanation, in what he called "human terms," so that I could begin to relate to the extremely difficult concept (of Time.) The following are the two approaches I used.

—**Example 1**. Suppose that you're in an empty room. An infinite number of small boxes lay on the floor. Each box contains a moment of your Earth life. <u>The boxes are all here now</u>—and <u>the Entity can see the totality of them.</u> However, because of specific rules and limitations that exist here (Physical Earth), the "Physical you" is unable to see all of the boxes at once, as you the Entity would. <u>You, the physical you, can instead only open one box at a time</u>. Hence, these limitations forced us to devise a system by which we could somehow "measure" and keep track of this "opening" of each *box*moment-after-*box*moment.

Hence, we invented devices such as watches and calendars, thus establishing a system we call "passage of time." We are so immersed in, so accustomed to this system, that we see "time" not for what it really is "a measuring system," but a normalcy, a factor to live our lives by. Then we wreck our brains trying to understand what "Time" is. In essence, time-measuring devices keep track not of time itself but of each boxmoment we open. Basically, it all has to do with how the human brain is wired. The difficulty arises from the fact that <u>our brain can only perceive the process of opening each boxmoment "linearly" instead of simultaneously as the Entity would</u>. Seth explained that the biggest obstacle preventing us from appreciating the process is that we do not fully comprehend the magnitude of—and power "we, the Entity" have at our disposal.

—**Example 2.** For this example you will need to get a blank sheet of paper from your desktop printer, a pen or pencil and a pair of scissors.

Using your scissors, cut the page up in small squares, so that you end up with about 100 or so squares. Write on each square a number, from 1 to 100. *(Conversely you could write the numbers first and then cut them out.)* Now, on your desk in front of you, place all of the pieces of paper in numerical order. Each square representing one of your earth years, you are of course able to see all of the pieces of paper, thus your entire life, at once. And that is how <u>You-the-Entity sees your Earth-Life—all at once</u>. As such, it can freely roam both forward (future) as well as back (past). However, now starting from 1, count the pieces of paper, 1, 2, 3, and so on. <u>And that is how your Physical-Self (you the Human) sees and lives your Earth-Life</u>.

Now, throughout this book, *especially in this chapter*, I have suggested that you should practice "switching places," switching perspective from the usual way of observing the world around you, the human way that is—to the Soul's perspective. I have practiced doing this for so long that it now comes as natural to me. I no longer think of myself as a "human body" that may or may not have a Soul, *which is incidentally how most folks see themselves*, but I instead think of myself as a Soul energizing a human body, a body that is also "me," an extension of me—the Soul! This helps me immensely in being able to relate to scenarios that proved impossible to understand from my usual human perspective, but became totally clear once I switched places. Adopting such a mindset is in fact very helpful, as it allows me to disassociate from the usual narrow-minded human interpretation, to a higher, wider, more encompassing viewpoint. This affords me a much broader sense of awareness, instead of the usual "bottom-up" human viewpoint, that not only has limited data to work with, but can only process, as we just saw, one moment at a time.

Imagine if you will, you-the-Soul concurrently living a hundred Earth lives. As we just mentioned above (in the time examples) as a Soul you are able to see the wider picture, thus, things which do not make sense to you the human, make perfect sense when you can see the wider reasons behind what you do as well as everything that "happens" to you, here. If anything, you will begin to appreciate the sacred you, and the sacredness of your Earth life. Things, events that before you perhaps "blamed" others for, will suddenly become clear, you will be able to appreciate that these were not "things done to you," but instead "things done for you." And that truly changes one's perspective on life. Take for instance the terrible accident I had as a child. While me the human fails—or refuses to understand and accept, why should a child have to go through such trauma and suffering, me the Entity, not only understands and accepts it, but also blesses it. For as I said earlier, that event—although extremely traumatic, made me what I am today. And most importantly gave birth—opened the door to what was going to become "my life mission." The irrefutable truth is that without that accident, this very book would have never existed.

Switching gears now. I am sure that as it surprised me, the following information will surprise many, but according to Seth, the seven billion people populating the planet consist of only Nine Groups of Souls, or as Seth likes to call them, "Families of Consciousness." Basically, these groups volunteered to populate the planet, thus all of its seven-plus billion inhabitants. When Seth first introduced me to this idea I found it difficult to accept it at the time. But once he explained it in more detail, it actually made sense. Old folklore tales talk about each of us having on the planet, "seven doubles." Well, it turns out that it may not be folklore after all, and that we might have a lot more than just seven! The many simultaneous "projections" all exist independent from the next—but still connected to a greater Source, the Entity. And although not an absolute rule, just as a flock of birds pirouetting harmoniously in the sky, and a perfectly synchronized school of fish, are all but a single entity, you and every member of your family are likely all different projections of one and the same Entity. And more interesting, your worst enemy may also be cast by that same Entity.

So in essence, your worst enemy is also you! This, so that you can experience all possible and opposing sides, positive as well as negative, so that you can learn and grow in all and every aspect. Thus, you and your worst enemy are both learning from, as well as teaching one another.

And, not only are you and your Mother almost certainly cast by the same Entity, but you perhaps are, *notice I didn't say "were,"* your Mother's mother in yet another scenario. And in yet another scenario your Grandfather might very well be your daughter, and so on. But allow me to stimulate your thinking a bit further by asking you, "Do you believe that the fact that most family members look alike, behave and share similar traits, is only due to DNA? Or do you think it could have something to do with being all children to the same Entity?" Do you think the old saying, "Coming from the same stock" is just that—a saying—or could there be more to it?"

What "stock"—if not the Soul—are we referring to exactly?

Now, these "scenarios" may be played out in a number of geographical areas, eras, and circumstances. A total of nine "Groups" volunteered to populate the scenarios, perhaps for the simple pleasures of the experience, both at the individual as well as at the en-mass level. For let's not forget that what the Human (body) experiences—the Soul experiences, what the Soul experiences—the Entity experiences, what the Entity experiences— All-That-Is experiences!

So, while the nine Groups all have common characteristics, they each exhibit specific traits of their own. Be it by chance or by design, in the wider picture, this allows us to experience an infinite variety of probabilities. An individual waking up somewhere in New York one morning looks outside the window and thinks; *"Another beautiful day, I can't wait to get to work and make a ton of money!"*

While just across the street, another individual, looks outside the window and thinks; *"It looks terrible out there. It's going to be another of those days, not a single customer."*

Interestingly, the two individuals interpret the exact same scenario each their own way. We are not going to get into details for now, but as we will see later in the book, very valid reasons exist for this.

Now, the nine Families of Consciousness populate this plane. And it would appear that each family' characteristics is what most likely gave birth to the idea of "Astrology." So, "who you are" has nothing to do with your horoscope. Astrology is in fact nothing more than another system of measurement, whose purpose is to catalogue each group's different characteristics. And Families of Consciousness should not be mistaken with Earth-Families. As I said, you and your Mother (same Earth family) may both very well be a projection from the same Entity, but you may've taken on characteristics, each from a different Family-Group. That's because immediately after "Learning," "Variety" is objective number two! Here according to Seth, are the names of the nine Families of Consciousness and their main characteristics.

—1)-Borledim. The "Caregivers." Family being their numero-uno preoccupation in life, they not only love nurturing their own families but can also be found working or volunteering their time in retirement homes, hospitals, third world countries, war zones, etc. They are the "worrying— caring bunch" of our society.

—2)-Sumafi. This particular family is mostly interested in the art of teaching and knowledge in general. Many schoolteachers and public speakers belong to this group.

—3)-Gramada. This group specializes in organizing. They are the founders of large corporations or large organizations. They can also be found in politics. These individuals tend to exhibit a sense of urgency in everything they do. They can be aggressive at times.

—4)-Ilda. The Multi-Culturals. These folks are mostly concerned with the exchange of costumes and ideas between ethnic groups. They travel to other nations sharing ideologies and social concepts, mixing cultural and political views in an effort to better each side's condition.

—5)-Sumari. *(Not to be confused with The Sumerians.)* The performers and the innovators. The bold, impatient, playful types! You will find them mostly in the arts, movie actors and singers. They fill any position that places them in the "public eye." Fascinated by scientific matters, but bored by its "dryness." They are the "Entertainers" of the World.

—6)-Milumet. This family's main interest lays in the exploration of Nature. Naturalists, vegetarians and explorers belong to this group. These individuals tend to be somewhat introverts and of a timid nature.

—7)-Vold. Activists by nature, most of these folks are "reformers," the leaders and the initiators of revolutions. Their main drive and purpose is "changing" the status quo of just about anything they get involved with.

—8)-Zuli. These folks are mostly concerned with "appearance." These are the body builders. Fitness fanatics, aestheticians, and fashion designers also belong to this group. Architects and graphic designers are also part of this group. They are obsessed with perfection and details.

—9)-Tumold. These are the "Healers." They are the Doctors, Nurses, but also people in so called unconventional medicine. Spiritual as well as physical healers of all discipline belong to this group. Religious figures, Shamans, Psychologists and social workers also belong here.

I asked Seth how would one know the Group they belonged to. He replied that each of us is instinctively aware of the family they belong to. Seth said that I have represented each and every Group several times over.

In this lifetime I am a "Sumari."

Now, your many "talents" as well as "personal character traits" represent instead "hints" from other lives, (please note I did not write "past lives"). It would seem that each life you live will have one chief purpose and many secondary ones. In another life, you could be a president, a doctor, a musician, or even a pope. Each role fulfills a specific purpose, "learning" mainly, but also anything that you could not have experienced as an Entity. In other instances, your main purpose could have been that of serving as a "teacher," or to inspire someone else, a group of people or even a whole nation. And Light-Workers such as Mother Theresa, Nelson Mandela, Martin Luther King and Gandhi were such teachers. Many even sacrifice themselves, so that others can benefit—and start new social movements. In all cases, the purpose is always one and the same, that of "Learning," or "Teaching," which of course also results in learning.

Now, the Entity casts—projects "portions" of itself onto different existential states. These portions are what we call "Souls." Then Souls—based on the Entity's larger directive, will in turn vitalize more-or-less physical counterparts. However, this whole process from Entity to physical counterpart, does not take place one-step at a time, but all at once. And no actual point exists when the projection or vitalization takes place, for as I mentioned earlier, at the Spiritual Level, Time does not apply. Thus in human terms, these "connections" have long come and gone, but from the Entity's standpoint, all personalities, past, present and future, and all locations as well as all frequencies, exist all at once! And whether or not a given projection experiences the (illusion of) passage of time, depends solely upon the specific environment that particular projection resides in; our Earth environment being one. And as we said earlier, each channel may or may not include specific "rules," hence, each level will each result in a totally different experience. As we said, our Earth channel—together with a multitude of other rules and because of the "address" it happens to occupy within the system, amongst many other (rules) also includes a specific rule we like to call "Time." Hence, this rule creates the illusion that events here take place in a linear fashion (Past-Present-Future) instead than—as the Entity would instead see it, simultaneously.

Now, the Entity chooses the Earth eras, the Earth areas and the Earth

Families it wishes to experience. And usually, the Entity prefers to stay, *but not always*, within environments and families it is already familiar with and loves. At times, mainly for the sake of the experience, a single Soul can choose to "vitalize" (incarnate) into two or more "bodies," in the same (Earth) family. We call this process "Twins."

What we refer to as "Soul Mates," is instead a somewhat different process to that in the case of twins. Soul Mates are also a single Soul who, *like twins*, incarnates into two separate bodies, only that in the case of soul mates, the two bodies will instead each be part of two different Earth families, sometime a Continent apart. And similarly to twins, should soul mates happen to meet, the two will instinctively be aware that each is a part of the other. Thus, Twins, as well as Soul Mates, will feel an immediate natural sense of belonging with one another. They know and understand each other so well that they read each other's mind. That should come as no surprise, as they are each other's mind. Thus together they feel safe and at home. But contrary to what most love and relationship experts would like us to believe, in the long run, marrying your soul mate is not necessarily a good thing. For what would be the point in spending a lifetime with someone who agrees with everything you say and likes everything you like? Contrast, a bit of disagreement even, when constructive, can be very beneficial in a relationship. So, while it's true that we all long to find a compatible partner, they shouldn't be a mirror image of ourselves.

A relationship is called a relationship, because it represents the combining of two individuals and how they relate to one another, each contributing to their knowledge, experiences, likes and dislikes, each helping each other's growth process. A relationship with a soul mate, though cozy and comforting at first, will inevitably develop into a predictable, unchallenging and repetitive relationship. Not the most ideal ingredients if a long lasting relationship is what you want.

Now, what our doctors label as "Multiple Personality Disorders," are in fact no disorders at all. These are simply the result of several Soul-Fragments, *hence multiple*, into one single body. Normally, a Soul will inhabit a single body or, *as in the case of twins*, two or more. However, on occasion a group of Souls can elect to allocate to a single body each their own "input," hence the "multiple personality" designation. However, one of the fragments is always in charge of the group. This is so that it—the "Soul Fragment in Chief" can experience the resulting life with all of its advantages and disadvantages.

But when examined by a doctor the individual will appear to exhibit other—extra personalities. But these, *extra,* personalities are not, *as we refer to them,* "imaginary" at all. To the individual they're as real as any other. The individual will in most cases enjoy a normal life, except that they're constantly aware of the other personalities, having an input in just about everything they do and say. In some cases, the individual can become overwhelmed by the enormous and at times conflicting amount of information. The many ideas and feelings they're forced to deal with on a continuous basis can make them appear to exhibit several types of disturbed behavior—when in reality, it is just the many Soul fragments wanting to have each their own say. That's sure to make an interesting life experience no Entity would want to miss. But remember, no actual brain malformation exists in any of these cases. The "problem," *if that's what we wish to call it,* is merely at the psychological level. Or should we say "Spiritual level?"

In some cases the opposite can instead be true. Personalities might choose to experience a lifetime plagued by mental or motor difficulties, or a combination of. This is also done, *as it is always the case,* for the sole purpose of learning, overcoming the resulting challenges.

Autism, Alzheimer's disease, and Tourette syndrome amongst other similar conditions, are instead the result of actual physical brain malformation and/or damage, due mainly to one or more of several factors. Ranging for instance, from birth defects, to accidents, to infections.

Think about it, no "Autistic" Soul could possibly exist. No Soul could have Tourette syndrome. The Soul is always whole, integral. Thus the Soul always sends a clear signal to the brain—brain that is in turn responsible for translating psychic-input into physical-output. Hence, a perfectly clear psychic signal will cause a "wrongly wired brain" to misfire so-to-speak.

Picture a wrongly wired double-throw light switch if you will. You flip switch number 1, but light number 2 turns on instead. The same applies in this case, the Soul tells the brain to move the right arm, but instead the left arm moves. You get the idea.

I feel for our doctors in fact, for they couldn't possibly be aware of nor detect these relatively simple truths. Again, the problem originates from being given the wrong set of rules and tools. Thus, doctors constantly find themselves having to choose between a Darwinian interpretation, which is erroneous at its very core, and a religious interpretation, semi-magical and grossly misinterpreted at best. Thus, they are left with no choice but to disregard anything that doesn't fall within "the physical category." Anything intangible, anything non-physical, is considered nonexistent, even spooky.

Thus, they couldn't possibly be aware of the "sick" individual's mental state. For no amount of X-rays or CAT-scanning could possibly show an individual's mind, an individual's Soul. And it goes without saying that all such scenarios are always—and deliberately chosen by the Entity, again, so that it could experience each resulting personality, together with the associated challenges. Unaware of these truths and himself a victim of a misguided system, the poor doctor has no other recourse, but to prescribe antidepressants.

Now, as we said earlier, each channel includes a specific set of rules, resulting each in a different experience. Close proximity channels share a degree of similarity, but this is not always the rule. As we saw earlier, what we call "dreams" for instance, are not—as we normally think "just in our head," but instead channels that closely resemble this Earth channel.

As you know some dreams can exhibit very strange scenarios, but "strange" only when judged from this channel's perspective. Again, when you're there, everything is perfectly normal—there. The "you" in that channel in fact, does not see what happens there as "strange" in the least. And interestingly, while there, you may not only dream of this channel, but you may in fact think of it (this channel) as strange. *"Why are folks on that Earth channel unable to fly,"* you may be wondering from there?

And each channel has its own version of a "Universe." A canvas, a backdrop if you like, a "movie set" where the movie script is played out.

Each channel will have an Earth, a Sun, a Moon, myriad of stars, celestial bodies, and so on. However, the difference is that while, *in this channel*, we chose to inhabit planet Earth, on other channels, our counterparts might've instead chosen to inhabit the Moon, or some other planet.

Ours is therefore an "Earth-In-Chief-Channel," featuring an inhabited Earth and a multitude of bare planets like Mars and the Moon. Another channel could instead be a "Mars-in-Chief" channel. There, our counterparts would inhabit Mars, surrounded by a bare Earth and other bare planets. And in yet another channel, our counterparts could instead inhabit the Moon. Thus, their sky will include a bare Earth, Mars and so on. And these "Channels" are what our scientists are starting to perceive and call "Parallel Universes." And surprise-surprise, while Seth talked of this truth back in 1993, look what I found today in an online article.

(November 26, 2016) "There ARE parallel universes: Physicists state multiverses are INTER-ACTING" "PARALLEL universes DO exist and they influence each other, according to a revolutionary theory from a group of physicists."

"Academics are challenging the status quo of the single universe theory by claiming many different universes coexist and they all affect each other.

"Professor Howard Wiseman and Dr Michael Hall from Griffith University's Centre for Quantum Dynamics, and Dr Dirk-Andre Deckert from the University of California claim parallel universes are a reality and influence one another through quantum mechanics.

"In the well-known 'Many-Worlds Interpretation', each universe branches into a bunch of new universes every time a quantum measurement is made.

"All possibilities are therefore realized—in some universes the dinosaur-killing asteroid missed Earth. In others, Australia was colonized by the Portuguese."

(Source: "There are parallel universes: Physicists state multiverses are INTERACTING," by Sean Martin, Daily Express).

The interesting thing is, that the inhabitants of these other—what Seth called, "Channels," but our scientists call "Universes," are most likely training their telescopes toward <u>their</u> bare planet Earth as we speak, wondering why no one lives here!

And this brings us to a whole new and fascinating subject.

The U.F.O. Paradox.

"The universe is a pretty big place. If it's just us, seems like an awful waste of space." ~

—Carl Sagan

Chapter 8

The UFO Paradox. Are We Stardust or Monkey Business?

As I am sure you'd agree, a book of this genre wouldn't be complete without touching on one of the most fascinating riddles we—as a species, have ever ventured to unravel, namely the UFO phenomena. And since this is as good a place in the book, as any other, let's endeavor to shed some light on this very elusive but, *according to Seth*, totally misunderstood phenomena.

How many books have been written on the subject of UFOs? How many investigations, how many documentaries have been produced on the subject? Yet, despite all the smoke and mirrors, despite all the propping and embellishments the movie industry likes to strut on the subject, according to Seth it comes down to two simple facts.

—A) Throughout our civilization, to date (Seth said this in 1995) no actual "nuts-and-bolts" flying saucer has landed here on Earth—period! Visitations have occurred, but none of the "Physical" kind.

—B) Here in this channel, besides us, no other beings exist "anywhere near" our Solar System!

Let's look at this fascinating phenomenon in more detail. But let's first take another look at the two points just made above, as they carry far more "information" than meets the eye.

What we have is a multitude of channels, each more-or-less technologically advanced. Eventually, as inhabitants of a given channel become aware of the existence of other channels—and their probable inhabitants, their natural inner explorer's instinct, invariably pushes them to try to find ways to meet their neighbors. And may I remind you that we are doing the exact same thing? On the surface, it is really that simple. We want to know what—and who's around us, why else would we spend billions every year, wanting to explore planets that we can already see that they're uninhabited—from here? But it has to do with a lot more than just mere curiosity, the truth is, we are lonely! We need to know, we long to find our place, in an unfathomably large Universe.

"There surely must be others out there, it's just a matter of time until we get to meet them," we reason. We go on exploring; hoping to stumble onto some exotic life form. Naturally, just as we long to connect with them—they long to connect with us. Exploring is in our blood; for exploring is just another word for "Learning," the true and only reason why we all exist in the first place. We all—regardless of what channel or even Universe we occupy, share a common source of origin we should not forget. Thus, we all have a natural longing to find one another, but all for a single specific purpose, finding our Source, hence for our Source to find It-Self. For Source to know It-Self.

Now, compare today's technology with that of fifty years ago. Then try to envision technologies of say fifty years from now, especially when factoring-in the so-called "Moore's law," which in layman's terms, suggests that by the year 2050 your average home computer will be roughly speaking, a million times faster than today's average computer. And that's in only a mere 33 years. The decades ahead will bring unimaginable new ways of transportation. Cars, even air travel, will all be sans-pilot. We'll be able to travel to the Moon in a matter of seconds. "Teleportation" will become ubiquitous. Today, we may think of all this as being science fiction, but let's not forget that so were cellphones, and going to the Moon as recently as a century ago.

When it comes to meeting our "Alien" friends however, the real challenge lays not in transporting an individual from one planet to the next—for that only entails finding faster means of transportation, but instead in "transposing" that individual, from one "Channel" to the next—an altogether different frequency. Suppose that the inhabitants of a close proximity channel, were technologically speaking, a thousand years ahead of us. Further suppose that they had found ways to travel from point A to point B within their system, in a blink of an eye. However, what they really long to do, is to be able to travel to another system, which they're actually trying to do on a daily basis it seems.

That said, according to Seth, no actual physical intersystem (from one system to another) visitation will take place until sometime between 2030 and 2040. In the meantime, many attempts are constantly being made with more-or-less success. However, Seth said that sometimes between the year 2015 and 2025, most likely 2017-2020, is when an official "Disclosure" will take place. Although not physically, a visual, or more precisely, "Holographic" official contact, will finally be made.

Now, here is where the difficulty lies when physically attempting to travel between channels. The biggest obstacle is not "distance" per se, but instead as we said before, the different rules and laws (of physics) in place, or lack of, in each different system. Thus, each system, may or may not include different rules specific to that system. Take "Gravity" for example, but not "gravity" as it relates to mass, but instead its "ratio"—ratio that could or could not be the same as ours. Thus, some systems might have no Gravity at all, while some other systems might have ten times our Gravity. If that were the case, if an astronaut weighing 200 lbs. here, was to somehow materialize there; they would—the moment they materialized there, weigh 2,000 lbs. and crashed under their own weight, die instantly. As I'm sure you'd agree, not something to look forward to. But it goes much further than just Gravity; it actually gets much more exotic.

The greatest obstacle any given species would need to overcome prior to attempting any sort of intersystem travel, would be that of "Molecular Arrangement," or more precisely "Re-Arrangement," and the laws governing that process. For instance, if in system 100 you have an airplane, when transposed onto say system 101, what started as an airplane, in that new system, would perhaps reassemble itself as a car, a park bench, or even as a semi-transparent one mile tall tree. There is no telling what it will change into. An airplane looks like an airplane here, simply because its blueprints, together with the materials and tools utilized to build it, are also from here. Thus, every component and every stage of construction, all follow the same rules and laws of physics. Think what would happen to the crew on board once their vessel crossed over onto another system, and the molecules that made them would also have no choice but to reassemble.

Nothing too exciting to look forward to.

So as you can see, the challenges anyone attempting inter-system travel must first overcome, are numerous, regardless what system they hail from. But despite the enormous difficulties, some instances of momentary or partial penetration have indeed occurred, and continue to do so, on a daily basis. Many accounts exist, of folks reporting seeing a variety of "shape-shifting—cigar-shaped" objects throughout the planet. And these elongated-shimmering shape-shifting apparitions illustrate the problem described above perfectly. They can only exist here for no more than a few seconds at a time. They've been unsuccessful, *until now*, in assembling into an actual solid "object" that could exist here for any appreciable length of time, hence they shape-shift for a few seconds and then disappear. And because of the un-natural non-native environment they find themselves in, an enormous amount of energy is used in each attempt, which accounts for their very short stay. They've been observed to shift in shape and size from a few meters, to as long as a football field. They've been observed to shape-shift from something resembling a long cigar to a sphere, to a square or even a triangle. They usually appear a silvery color, at times semi-transparent, but not because silver is the color extraterrestrials like to paint their vessels in, but because that is how something "neutral" and undefined appears to us. And whether intentionally or not, they may appear to us as an undefined cloaked shape, sometimes resembling a cloud or something similar.

These shape-shifting objects that we do see, might or might not be occupied by a crew, but if I had to guess I would say that they're not, for as we saw before, together with the vessel, the crew would also be subjected to a most painful transformation. I believe these to be unmanned "drones," either remotely guided from their channel of origin, or pre-programmed to perform specific tasks. Their purpose may be to scout ahead of an eventual visitation.

Whatever the case may be, one way or another, they're surely trying to talk to us. Crop Circles, *minus the many fakes*, are one such example, one that screams to be heard, but that instead keeps on falling on deaf ears.

Now, while it is true that we cannot (yet) transpose a solid object onto another system, what can be instead easily transposed is "Light." For light-is-light, no matter what its source—or what system it manifests in. Light-is-always-light, period! And when we say "Light," we must also include "Holographic Light," AKA "Holograms." Hence, "light" or "lights," are the only, *real*, UFOs countless people continue to see all over the planet time and time again. And as a matter of fact, several years ago, while driving in the Canadian Boreal Forest, a friend and I were unwilling witnesses to such an appearance. I suspect these lights are most probably "probes," and are most likely remotely guided or pre-programmed. Their purpose may be to take, *their version of*, photos or video, or whatever type of "media" they use there. And perhaps, soil, air, and water samples are also taken. This is necessary information our neighbors need, if they wished to learn what we breathe, eat, and drink, so that they can prepare.

The more they learn about us, the faster they will be able to extrapolate a method to—though briefly at first, appear here physically. Wouldn't you do a little pre-planning and research about a place you were planning to visit?

And these "lights" many folks see, do not come here for the sole purpose of collecting samples, but to somehow try and establish some type of communication. Again, Crop Circles are such an example, but because some incredibly wise folks have nothing better to do, and like to spend their nights making fakery, we are left with having to discern between the few real ones and a sea of fakes. And granted that the vast majority of them might very well be fake, the fact remains that some genuine ones also exist, basically screaming at us, *"Hey you! What in the world do we have to do, to show you that we also exist?* The intricacy, the precision and the meaningfulness of the messages some of the circles display, is simply impossible for any human to make—no matter how much time and how many tools and computers they used. Such lights make the "genuine Circles." The lights are somehow pre-programmed to deliver these pictorial messages. In much the same process as a desktop printer prints an image on a sheet of paper, these lights follow their internal programming—"engraving" the message on our fields.

At first, this may appear to be a fairly simple task, but it is a whole different story once we factored in the equation the "different frequencies" issue mentioned earlier. In addition, as you might know, we Earthlings have adopted a computer language we commonly refer to as "Binary Code," AKA "Ones and Zeros." In simpler terms, when you for instance press the letter "A" on your keyboard, what your computer sees instead is: "01100001" a binary string representing a combination of "switches," "0" being "off" while "1" being "on," all so that the letter "A" can be displayed on your monitor. For the sake of this argument however let's keep it simple and let's think of these "switches" as only "numbers."

But in another system that exact same combination (01100001) which produces an "A" here, could very well produce a completely different result, hence the difficulty. They would not only have to first program the lights with the intended message they wished to communicate in their language, but they would also have to extrapolate what once it reached us—that message would translate into in our language. Thus they must be totally familiar with our binary code and know exactly how we—once translated, would read each message. That said however, there is nothing stopping them from using, intentionally or otherwise, a system similar or identical to ours. I wouldn't be surprised if they did, but I am not suggesting that they, like us—also use computers, but then again why not? I am only trying to point out the obstacles each channel faces when trying to communicate with other channels, no matter what system they adopt. But just for the fun of it, suppose you were somehow able to telephone someone living in another system. You may say "Hello, how are you, we would like to come and visit you!" but they would instead hear "I hate you; I'm coming to kill you!" Surely not be the best way to start a friendship.

Now, time and again folks see flying lights in the sky. These are the probes we mentioned earlier. But strangely, when reporting the event to the authorities, they instead swear that they saw "a flying saucer—surrounded by lights." But how could this happen, you may ask? The reason is complex but fascinatingly simple. For starters, let's clarify one basic fact once and for all, and that is—that if these were real nuts and bolts flying saucers, they would not need any navigation lights! Our planes do—but not UFOs!

But it comes down to a simple fact, our brain works by virtue of "photographic association." When you look at an object (any object) your brain instantly scans its memory banks for something similar already stored there, something it had already seen before, and "saved" into memory. Each and every object you've observed in the past is in fact stored inside your brain's memory banks. This "process of association" happens so fast and seamlessly that we're normally not aware of it, but that's how we recognize things nevertheless—no exceptions. But what do you suppose happens when we see something, which we had never seen before, and the brain cannot find any match for it in its memory banks?

"Plan-B" is what happens, in other words "the next best thing!" Thus, the brain will either pull something similar from its memory banks, or even artificially fill in the blanks or a combination of the two. And it does so, so that it can make sense of what we're looking at, all of the time. But why would the brain take on the liberty of artificially filling the missing imagery, you may ask?

The simple answer is, because it has no other choice, or we would have an incomplete image with blank spots in it. How many times have you told someone that you saw them somewhere, but they said it wasn't them? How many times you thought you saw something from a distance, only to realize that it was not what you thought it was, once you got closer? A perfect example would be what just happened to me the other day.

I drove a friend to the airport. Since I was going to be there only a few minutes, I parked in the "short-term" parking lot, which according to a sign posted there has always been free for the first half hour. And after dropping my friend off, on my way to the tollbooths, I read the huge green sign, which said just that, "first 30 minutes free." That is why I was very surprised when the woman at the tollbooth said that I needed to pay a little over 3 dollars.

"But isn't the first half hour supposed be free of charge" I asked?

"Yes, but that changed on the first of this month," she replied.

"I have no issue paying the 3 dollars, but it would be a good idea to change the sign right behind me," I said.

"But we did change the sign," she replied surprised.

"Impossible. I just read it and it still says 'free'," I replied.

"No Sir, you must have misread the sign, for it sure shows the new pricing," she insisted.

I could not believe my ears; I had just read the word "free" on that sign. So unconvinced, I paid the fee, parked my car on the side, and so that I could prove her wrong, walked back a few feet. But surprise-surprise, she was right. The sign clearly displayed the new pricing, and nowhere in it said "free." I was amazed out of my mind, for I clearly recalled actually reading that specific word "free." I would have bet my life on it, but I would have lost the bet. So, getting back in my car, I recognized what had just happened. Having seen that sign a million times before, my brain—despite driving a few feet from it, simply took a shortcut, and pulled from its memory banks, information already stored there. When this artificial-filling takes place, *which unknown to us happens continuously*, we're no longer able to discern between what's actually there, and what's been filled-in by the brain. The brain can in fact go as far as artificially manufacturing, or even filling-in a given image, so that it can show us a whole picture.

We—seeing a "complete picture," are satisfied—without ever knowing what just took place. Thus, since common sense tells us that lights couldn't possibly fly on their own, we automatically associate the lights, *we do see*, with a plausible supporting "frame" of some kind—frame that is not actually there, but allows us to make sense of the whole so-to-speak.

We need in other words, something physical we can attach the lights to so that it makes sense in physical-human terms. For in a material world where we are conditioned to think that everything must be physical—or it can't exist, everything we see must therefore fit into that category.

We thus fill the empty spaces between the flying lights, with an imaginary sort of, *flying*, object, which is not actually there, but that we see nevertheless—if only inside our brain. So, if we happen to see three lights flying in a triangular formation, *reasoning that lights cannot fly on their own*, we will report a "triangular object" with a light at each tip. If we see ten lights flying in a linear formation, we will report a football sized flying saucer with ten illuminated portals on its side. The interesting thing is, that some folks have even reported seeing aliens inside the portals. But I am sure you now know the reason why.

Now, there is no doubt that our next-channel neighbors have been trying to contact us, perhaps for millennia. Many examples of *what they appear to be* unexplained lights in the sky are in fact depicted in many centuries old art and cave drawings—all over the planet. However, unlike us they, *most probably*, no longer concern themselves with political or religious dogmas. They no longer need to worry about being "politically correct," nor are they scandalized when someone there, suggests the possibility that they might not be alone in the Universe. Think about it, we have no issue believing that out of a zillion planets—only one planet is inhabited, but we're scandalized at the thought that another of these planets could also be inhabited. Unlike us, they instead not only know, but also welcome that fact and long for the day when they will actually get to meet us.

Perhaps, they too went through a period of growth and self-discovery, a period when they too—misguided by their own respective leaders, like us, had to progress the hard way, wars and so on. But just like our thinking will eventually evolve, theirs already has, perhaps ages ago. They're aware that no matter what system we happen to inhabit, we're all part of one and the same Source. However, unlike us, they most likely no longer fool themselves with presumptions and arrogance, or self-describe themselves as "the only special or chosen ones." But times are surely changing, even for us. Interestingly, here is an article I found in the Scientific American Magazine back in 2008.

"Fr. José Funes (Vatican Chief Astronomer) says it's OK to believe in aliens." (Article by Ariel David.) "Believing that the Universe may contain alien life does not contradict a faith in God," the Vatican's chief astronomer said in an interview published Tuesday. Rev. Jose Gabriel Funes, the Jesuit director of the Vatican Observatory, was quoted as saying "The vastness of the Universe means it is possible there could be other forms of life outside Earth, even intelligent ones. How can we rule out that life may have developed elsewhere? Just as

we consider earthly creatures as 'a brother,' and 'sister,' why should we not talk about an 'extraterrestrial brother'? It would still be part of creation." In the interview by the Vatican newspaper L'Osservatore Romano, Funes said that "Such a notion does not contradict our faith, because aliens would still be God's creatures. Ruling out the existence of aliens would be like putting limits on God's creative freedom," he said in the interview, headlined "The extraterrestrial is my brother," covering a variety of topics including the relationship between the Roman Catholic Church, Science, and the theological implications of the existence of alien life. Science, especially astronomy, does not contradict Religion." (Source: Scientific American Magazine).

Note: As recently as 20 years ago the Vatican categorically dismissed the possibility that other beings could exist, and if they did they said, they would amount to nothing more than evil spirits trying to infiltrate our planet. As recently as 15 years ago, the Vatican openly declared that the Internet was the new tool the devil would use to gain control over people's minds. Today the Vatican has one of the biggest and most elaborate websites network on that same Internet, over one hundred sites in total. Things are surely changing!

Now, as you may recall, at the beginning of this "UFO" chapter, two points were made by Seth. The first point means exactly what it implies, that "To date no actual physical visitation has taken place." However, "key" to our argument, that first point also states something else, and that is: "within our civilization." And we will discuss this point in some detail in a moment. It is however the second point that for now deserves most of our attention, just in case you missed it, here it is:

"Here in this channel, besides us, no other beings exist "anywhere near" our Solar System!"

Note: It didn't say "No other beings exist in this channel," but instead, "No other beings exist anywhere near our Solar System." This is very important!

Now, I am aware of the fact that information such as what follows has the potential to cause some folks to question their personal belief system. Initially, I had decided not to include it in the book, and upon further soul searching I decided that if I didn't, was I not only withholding information—which is not mine to withhold, but also that I would be doing the reader a disservice. In the end I decided to include it in the book. Be forewarned however, that this particular piece of information is not only very difficult to explain but even more so to relate to. When Seth first introduced me to it, not only did I have a difficult time wrapping my brain around it, but also at first, I couldn't accept it as factual. Seth explained at the time, that our physical brain is simply not, yet, equipped to allow for this type of thinking, we are thus pushing the proverbial "envelope."

Similarly to what we discussed earlier, it would be like trying to measure 1,000 degrees temperature with a thermometer that can only reach as high as 100, if you know what I mean. Nonetheless I asked Seth to elaborate. Here is how I interpreted his explanation. I shall endeavor to simplify this intrinsically complex subject as much as possible.

Most folks are familiar with the mechanics of the 3-Dimensional environment we, *physically speaking,* live in. These are commonly referred to as; "Height," "Width," and "Depth." In simpler terms: Up-Down, Across, and Front-to-Back. As early as 1916, with the introduction of the so-called "Theory of General Relativity" Einstein proposed the existence of a 4th Dimension. The "Theory of General Relativity" is a theory in physics that describes "Gravity" in a geometrical fashion rather than as a "force." This new approach totally changed Newton's concept of "motion," which reigned unrivaled until then. Basically, General Relativity proposes that "Time" is not a "uniform constant" as Newton had proposed, but rather "Relative to Motion." Without making this point more complex than it ought to be, it basically means that "Time" is relative to the "velocity" the observer himself is travelling at. In even simpler terms, this means that the faster you travel, the slower your Time, *whilst appearing unchanged to you,* will appear to a stationary observer. The following example, one that our scientists have used many times, would be a simpler example yet.

Suppose we took two identically accurate atomic watches and gave one to an astronaut to wear, and keep the other on the ground with us. Now suppose that we placed our astronaut on a rocket capable of travelling at 90% the speed of light, *keep in mind that the two watches are perfectly accurate and in absolute sync.* The astronaut and his spacecraft take off, with instructions to return to Earth in precisely one year. Thus, the astronaut—using his wristwatch as a reference, lands back at our space station in what he's sure is exactly 12 months later. But when comparing his watch with the one left on the ground, we see that not 12—but instead almost 28 months have passed. We call this phenomena "Time Dilation." Wikipedia explains it as follows: *"An accurate clock at rest with respect to one observer may be measured to tick at a different rate when compared to a second observer's own equally accurate clock. This effect arises neither from technical aspects of the clocks nor from the fact that signals need time to propagate, but from the nature of 'Space-Time' itself."* (Source- *Wikipedia).*

Again, in simpler terms, this has to do with Einstein's correct observation, that "Time and Space have a curvature."

Now, this much-simplified explanation of the mechanics of the 4th Dimension was necessary to make—as a stepping-stone of sorts, to the intended target, namely the "5th Dimension." According to Seth, our scientists will be very busy researching the now, almost, deciphered 4th Dimension for a while, *coincidentally dismissed as fiction only a couple of decades ago.* However, an even bigger surprise awaits us just around the corner. Pointless to discuss at any length at this point, a "5th Dimension" will amongst other things, allow us to travel incredibly large distances in mere moments. Allow me to explain.

Until now, we've kept busy building faster and faster space-vehicles, but always thinking of distances in a linear-forward fashion. Conventional wisdom tells us that if we travelled to the Moon, a roughly 385,000 Km trip—at say 10,000 km/h, it would take us almost two days to get there. It doesn't take Pythagoras to extrapolate that if we were to double that speed, we could cut that time in half. At first examination that makes perfect sense, but the moment we try and apply that same principle to much greater distances, we soon realize that it is the drawing board where we instead need to go back to. Not only is there no simple way to develop a propulsion system that could last the length of that trip, but also it wouldn't make any sense to do so in the first place. For provided it were even feasible, who in their right mind would want to embark on a thousand or even a one hundred years trip? According to Seth, a much-much faster and safer way exists.

"Instead of linear-forward travel, envision 'Sideways Travel,'" he explained. So again, when we think of "distances" we refer only to "linear" or forward travel, that principle, whether you travel to the next city or the next galaxy remains unchanged. However, that approach can literally only take us so far. "Sideways Travel" instead implies and recognizes that "all locations are here now." Then the difference between say this channel and the next, would no longer be a matter of how many kilometers, but instead "what frequency." Thus, it all comes down to finding ways to travel from channel-to-channel, not linearly-forward but sideways, just as your radio does, which coincidentally is exactly what our so called Alien neighbors are trying to do on a daily basis. And let's not forget that to them, <u>we are the aliens</u>!

Now, we have talked about Inter-dimensional (from another dimension) beings, but what about Intra-dimensional being? Are there any other intelligent beings within our own dimension or channel?

The answer is a definite yes! But here is the challenge. At first look, meeting our same-dimensional friends would appear to be a simple matter of linear point A to point B travel. Seth explained however, that the biggest challenge lays in our very limited view of the Universe. "You simply haven't even begun to understand how large the Universe is," he said. According to him, what we think of as an immeasurably large, *our*, Solar System, amounts to nothing more than the proverbial drop of water, but not in the bucket but in the ocean. What that means is that our same-dimensional friends reside at such far away distances that we couldn't even hope to come close to, not even if we travelled for a million years. And this is not merely metaphorical, Seth pointed out that the distance between us and our closest intra-dimensional neighbors is in fact so great, that if we wanted to write it on paper, we would have to use so many zeros that the numbers would no longer make any sense, and instead formulas would have to be used. It is therefore pointless to keep on spending time and money on technologies that we already know are literally going nowhere, Seth said.

"We would be much better off" he said, "if we instead concentrated our efforts in understanding the true 'fabric' of the Universe, and researched methods of 'sideways travel'." For as impossible as it may seem, we stand a much better chance of developing ways to travel inter-dimensionally, *sideways*, than to travel impossible intra-dimensional linear distances, *within our system*. "The day will come," he explained, "when we will be able to travel to this and that system in a mere moment." "This," Seth said, "as we would no longer travel forward, but much like a radio, by merely switching frequencies." And according to Seth, our rudimentary understanding of "Worm-Holes," is indeed the path we should be pursuing.

Many folks have asked "If in my opinion, other beings in this or other Universes (Channels) would be of a benevolent nature or otherwise." Should we in other words, be concerned about the day when we will finally meet them? I sincerely do not know the definite answer to that question, but judging by our own history—and the changes that have taken place within our own species, I must deduce that these neighbors of ours will indeed come in peace. Unlike what most folks might think, we've come a long way; from a rudimentary, violent and misguided beginning, to the technologically advanced, united Spiritual society we are now starting to see on the horizon immediately ahead of us. We still aren't out of the proverbial woods, as you and I know, we still fight senseless ongoing wars, but we are slowly but surely getting there. I say this with confidence as in my opinion wars are without exception due to two distinct but synergetic factors, a limited mentality from a Human standpoint, and from a Spiritual standpoint, a necessary stepping stone in our *Spiritual*, growth process.

From a Human standpoint, we are, *from the surface*, experiencing what is the result of a limited mentality that sees our planet as having limited resources, resources we all must compete and fight for. We will still have to endure I estimate, anywhere from ten to twenty years of a similar status quo, as things will stay for the most part unchanged until around 2025-2030, then things will quickly start to change for the better, and in all facets of life. And not to stray off-topic, but as an example in point allow me to share a personal story of what a limited mentality can do.

For as much as I loved my Grandfather, to whom I will be eternally grateful for sharing with me a great deal of wisdom, looking back at his mannerism and how he interacted with us children, allowed me to better understand how we as humans evolve with each subsequent generation, both on a personal as well as on a societal level. My Grandfather was without a doubt the most loving and well-meaning person I have ever met. By merely being in the same room with him made you feel immersed in immense wisdom and compassion. Not much of a talker however, he knew what he knew from his own life experiences. He was the epitome of a self-made man.

Born in the island of Sicily in 1918, he was called to arms in the Second World War. *"Whom am I supposed to fight against,"* he asked the recruiting officer? *"The Germans,"* the guard replied. *"But they never did anything to me, why would I fight them,"* my Grandfather replied? *"Because Mussolini and Hitler are no longer allied,"* the guard said. *"Well, if Mussolini and Hitler have a problem, tell them to resolve it with a one-to-one boxing match,"* my Grandfather replied.

By then, Germany had already taken Poland, France and a few other Northern European countries. Initially Italy—with Mussolini at the helm, was allied with Germany. In the meantime, my Grandfather, being totally against the war, for fear of being arrested for desertion, spent the first two years of the war hiding from place to place. But being liberated—*or depends who you ask "invaded,"* by the Americans from the South, Italy had no other choice but to switch sides and turn against the Germans. Thus, together with countless others, my Grandfather was taken prisoner by the retreating Germans and ended up in a German concentration camp, where he spent the longest and most painful two years of his entire life.

As a child, I recall how my Grandfather loved to sit by our kitchen window. And I remember how angry he would get when we children turned up our young noses to certain foods. *"I would have killed a German soldier (metaphorically speaking),"* he said, *"for that piece of bread when I was prisoner there."* My Grandfather, a man of medium stature whose normal weight was 75 kilograms, while a prisoner, got down to only 35 Kilograms (about 75 lbs.). Basically a walking skeleton, he recounted how the guards would come around every morning with mule-pulled carts to gather the bodies of those who had died of starvation and cold overnight.

One piece of stale bread and a cup of water was all they were given each day. On Sundays each barrack of about fifty, would get a large pot full of dirty water and some spices. That was their "chicken soup." They tried everything to add flavor to that dirty water, even pieces of leather they would cut from their already disintegrating shoes, so that they could dream of a flavor they had long forgotten, meat. While preparing a large pot of soup one Sunday, a large rat fell from a beam in the ceiling straight into the pot of boiling water. I feel like crying when I think of this, for I cannot fathom being in that situation, and I feel ashamed for these guards who felt that they had the right to bring Human life—a sacred gift from the Creator, to such a despicably low level. However, to my Grandfather and his fellow prisoners, that was the best meal they'd had in months.

While walking in a single line in the camp one morning, in a pile of garbage outside a kitchen hut, they saw some potato peels. Well aware of the danger but unable to resist the hunger, four prisoners broke the lines and launched themselves on that pile of garbage; my Grandfather was one of them. They managed to eat some of that garbage, but the soldiers saw them almost immediately. Two of them got shot to death right on that pile of garbage. My Grandfather was hit on the back of the head with a rifle butt, passing out. He awoke in the barrack with an incredible headache. His friends told him that after passing out one of the cooks came out of the barrack and hit him repeatedly over the head with an iron frying pan.

Months later, with the Russians at the gates, wanting to save their own skin, the escaping guards abandoned the concentration camps—and the prisoners to their own devices. My Grandfather and a friend walked all the way from Germany to the Italian southernmost region of Sicily where their families lived, over a two thousand kilometer long walk that took them over three months. Unsure if the war had ended they kept clear of inhabited centers, walking from one bush to the next. They survived by eating anything they could find along the way, mushrooms; a fruit here and there, even dried animal excrement. Once home with their families—their digestive system no longer accustomed to process normal amounts of food, my Grandfather told his friend to only eat a light meal. He somehow had a natural wisdom that guided him throughout his entire life.

As a first meal, my Grandfather had only a piece of bread, a tomato and some black olives, olives he had dreamed about for over two years. His friend instead, sat at the table, his wife happy to finally prepare a real meal for her beloved husband, filled the table with all sorts of delicacies, pasta, deli meats, homemade bread and so on. He ate what would be a normal meal, but, no longer used to process that quantity of food, his digestive system went in a sort of shock. A few hours later he died.

What happened back then, should have served us all as a lesson—and it certainly has. But I am sure you may be wondering what is the point or connection I'm trying to make between my Grandfather's story and the topic at hand. His story is certainly not unique; many of our grandparents endured similar experiences or even worse. Today's Germany is an exemplary and industrious nation, but it goes to show how misguided any nation can become under the wrong leadership. And at the same time, from a Spiritual standpoint, this is but one small example of how despicably low the processes of learning we have chosen to experience can get. That's the point!

So, for better or worse, from a Human standpoint this is our present state of affairs. So the next time you hear about another war being started, you will know the reason. Thus, from a Spiritual standpoint everything is going as it should. All of the wars, strife and struggle going on are a reflection of a changing of the guard, a way for us to really decide what direction to take. We are forcing ourselves to face the monstrosities and atrocities of war, and we are doing so in a big way, all at once—so that we can really "disgust" ourselves, for the lack of a better word, and hopefully wake up—grow from these experiences. But that's not all. An even bigger "scenario" is at play here. From a Society-Human standpoint an external changing of the guard is indeed taking place, but that's certainly not the full story. A second (almost) unknown—"behind the scene" scenario is unraveling, which we will discuss in the next few pages.

However, before shifting gears and, *as this is not information you will read about in the daily newspaper*, to recap our UFO discussion, earlier in the book we talked about how other life-forms exist within our dimension—but reside at too great a physical distance to establish any practical form of communication. We also talked about how other beings from other dimensions are indeed trying, *like us*, within the limits of their technology, to communicate with us one way or another. However, they are aware that the only way to do so, is to find ways to travel—not in a linear, but instead in a sideway fashion, "switch channels" inter-dimensionally so-to-speak. In our case the biggest obstacle stopping us from seeing the bigger picture is mere arrogance it seems! Arrogance that not only fools us into believing that "we're the only ones" in an incomprehensibly large Universe, but also fools us into believing that we were "the first ones—ever!" Most folks believe in fact that not only are we the only and first, but also the last. And as if that weren't enough, that we're also "the chosen ones!"

But Spiritual growth aside, what in the world would possess our Human side to think that we're alone in such an unfathomably large Universe? Does the fact that our rudimentary telescopes are unable to reach the farthest depths of the Universe, where other beings may be, give us the right to declare ourselves "The Universe's only inhabitants?"

The truth is that we're just one of many! And many civilizations have existed on this very planet before us, and many will exist after us! Friends, it is time to wake up and smell the coffee—espresso in my case! And if you cannot accept this fact, then you are greatly limiting yourself, together with the information that could be available to you. But let's now endevour to address a second vastly more elusive scenario.

However, let me start by reminding you about a "warning" of sorts you may've read at the very beginning (page 2) of the book. As you may recall, I had inserted an "Author's Note" there, making the reader aware that some of the information in this book may not necessarily go hand to hand with their own personal belief system. As I am sure you can understand, I have no way of knowing what each reader's background or level of Spiritual advancement is, therefore, information that may resonate with some readers, might not resonate with others. And most importantly, keep in mind that the vast majority of this information cometh from Seth, I am simply putting it into terms we can all relate to. And as Seth himself put it, "It matters not whether or not we believe in something—the Universe is-what-it-is, regardless of whether we believe it or not!"

That said, since "nothing happens by chance," and by virtue of the fact that you're reading a book of this genre, it would be safe to assume that not only must you be an open minded individual, but more importantly a "seeking" individual. You are seeking to know, find any and all possible clues you can add to your own personal search. And this is what this book represents—another stepping-stone, on whatever you consider "your own personal growth-path" to be. And for much the same reasons, I assume that most of you are familiar with a book author by the name of Zecharia Sitchin. A brilliant author and researcher, Sitchin wrote a series of very interesting books, an enormously complex lifelong task, focusing mainly on two subjects: "How" and "Why" Humans were created. According to Sitchin a civilization called "the Anunnaki" created man, basically in a laboratory.

I read most of Sitchin's books and I found them very interesting, but when I asked Seth to further clarify the subject, he replied that "Sitchin was right on the mark for the most part, except for one (major) discrepancy he seemed to have somehow missed," Seth said. Specifically, contrary to what Sitchin repeatedly wrote, the Anunnaki did not come to Earth from another planet and created us. Instead, the Anunnaki were already here long before us, and that they "created" us, prior to departing—but not departing from this planet physically, but instead departing from this planet in "frequency," "spiritually," or more precisely, onto a more elevated dimension. In simpler terms—they've "switched channels." For it would appear that when a, *any*, civilization completes a given "learning cycle," it will "ascend" to a higher dimension. We are now, as a matter of fact, in the midst of doing so ourselves. We will discuss this process later in the book.

Now, what really puzzles me is how archeologists can spend decades researching the Pyramids, or for instance the hieroglyphics adorning their inner walls, or even the famous Inca Lines, then categorically conclude that, "we were not the ones who made them,"—but still refuse to accept that *someone else must've made them.*" I don't know if you'd agree, but to me it comes down to a simple process of elimination; if we didn't make them—and chances are that the artifacts did not spontaneously hatch out of the ground, wouldn't you agree that someone else must've made them? So the question is, "Why are we refusing to accept the fact that other beings must have made them?" Because, it would change everything we know as factual, that is why! And as we know, we Humans do not like changes. Therefore, we much prefer fostering a lie or a fantasy, or even a totally fabricated fable, as long as we don't have to change. That is the sad but true reason!

Back in the eighties a well-known Asian car manufacturer, whose name I will not mention, sat out to put an end, once and for all, to the question, "how were the pyramids built?" They sent a large team of engineers and workers to the Egyptian desert, and after months of preliminary planning they began construction of a half scale pyramid. However, after three months trying, they realized that they had taken on a task of much greater scope than they had anticipated. So in an effort to save time, they instead opted to build a much smaller pyramid, 1/10 the scale. And in an effort to keep the experience as faithful to the original as possible, they started by using methods and tools described in the history books.

But as months went by, they soon realized that they had no choice—but to go back to the drawing board. And so they hired a fleet of excavators, bulldozers, and all sorts of lifts and cranes. But despite doing so at a mere 1/10 the original size, they were still unable to build anything that even remotely resembled a pyramid. Unwilling to concede defeat, they brought in the big guns, computers and all sorts of measuring and plotting equipment. Six months later however, still unable to decipher the layout of the original pyramid and its functions, they finally conceded defeat.

Conventional thinking does not allow for any type of out of the box thinking. But in adopting such a mindset, other truths can—and do escape us unnoticed. But why does our way of thinking allow us only one option, I ask? "We built it" and in some rare cases two options at best, "we built it" or "extraterrestrials built it." Think about it, what if other Civilizations were here before us? What if they were the ones who built the many unexplained monuments and the many artifacts scattered around the globe? The Anunnaki Sitchin wrote so extensively about were in fact one such a previous civilization, one of many as a matter of fact. And the Atlanteans were also another such a civilization and so were the Lemurians. Atlantis was, *according to Seth*, a large continent in the Atlantic Ocean, *hence the name*, situated just south and to the east of the southern tip of Florida, and it stretched as far as the middle of the Atlantic Ocean, and as far North as where Greenland is today. *Today's Caribbean's are what's left of Atlantis. The Hawaiian Islands are instead what's left of Lemuria.*

But the question should be, why are we so immediately scandalized at the thought that other civilizations could have existed before us?

As a civilization, the Anunnaki reached a very elevated level of technological and spiritual advancement. And similarly to us—where we use "electricity" as our primary "tool" to do just about everything, "Sound," or the mastery-of sound, was instead the Anunnaki's primary means of building—as well as destroying I might add, just about everything. We seem to have retained a faint memory of that long lost knowledge, we're aware to a degree of the constructive, as well as the destructive properties of sound, but we don't appear to be interested in using it as a "tool," we instead think of it as music.

Now, just as it is the case today, there were plants and animals on Earth at the time of the, *original,* Anunnaki. Eventually however, the Anunnaki became so technologically and spiritually advanced, that they "graduated"— for lack of a better word, progressing onto a higher frequency.

With Spiritual and scientific advancement, their bodies also evolved, so in a way the switch was more natural, "automatic" if you like, than it might have been intentional. I am sure some of you know exactly what I am referring to, when I say that with a heightened spiritual awareness, certain foods, certain noises, even certain everyday household chemicals— that we considered perfectly "normal" before, become an irritation, even poisonous. Something as basic and ubiquitous as faucet water for instance, or sugar, flour (gluten) or even salt, which you'd been using all your life, suddenly no longer agrees with your body.

That's not far from what happened to the original Anunnaki, but in a much larger scale. They overgrew, *this,* Earth. And perhaps without the vast majority of them realizing it, they switched to a higher frequency. But here is the fascinating part and indeed a very important point. The Anunnaki didn't actually board a fleet of spaceships and left for another planet—like say the Moon or Mars or even "Planet X" as many like to think, the Anunnaki are still on Earth, but on a different more elevated, *version of,* Earth. More elevated frequency-wise!

And I totally realize that this may sound very strange to, *some of,* you, for you are perhaps not accustomed to think in this fashion, but you'd be wrong to think that only one Earth exists. It is true that only one Earth exists <u>here in this frequency</u>, the thing is that <u>there are an infinite number of frequencies, hence an infinite number of Earths</u>. Do you recall that multilayered kitchen table we mentioned earlier in the book? Do you recall the onion we used as an example on several occasions throughout the book? Well, it is not just tables and onions that have "layers" or frequencies, everything has layers and frequencies, and by "everything" I mean everything, with no exceptions! And it goes without saying that an infinite number of "you" also exist. "Infinite" is the keyword to remember here.

Thus, the Anunnaki didn't actually leave "physically," for chances are they didn't even realized, *or maybe they did*, what was happening, for the so called "switch" is more of a "flow" than it is a switch—thus it does not happen all at once, but gradually, a slow seamless, *Spiritual,* switch.

This in fact, happens continuously. Every moment of your life, you are mutating spiritually—hence you are constantly changing levels (frequencies.) And even now in this very moment, as you are reading these pages, you are switching to another "you"—and another—and another! Constantly elevating onto the next frequency.

Allow me to emphasize once again that I fully realize how "strange"— even crazy all this must sound, but can you come up with a better explanation? And in my place, what would you have done? How else could I have written this book? Should I've written it at face-value unchanged, or should I've sugar-coated it, or pick and choose from the material Seth delivered—so that I wouldn't scandalize anyone?

We live in a constant never ending flux. It is a fluid Universe, made of an infinite number of Universes. You are constantly shifting frequencies every moment of your life. Everything around you also shifts. Your surroundings, your friends and family, your car, even the air you breathe. And once in a while, *I am not entirely sure what the determining factors are,* we "graduate" so-to-speak to a higher frequency. Similarly to going to school as a child, you started with kindergarten, and then you graduated to elementary school—and then high school and so on. In that case you graduated intellectually, while in this case you graduate, "Spiritually." So that is what happened to the Anunnaki. They progressed and progressed to then graduate onto an altogether higher dimension.

I'm sure you have heard of the so-called "Rapture," an event where a number of folks, *we're told*, are supposedly "lifted onto Heaven." But while theologians interpret this phenomena the best way they know how, Rapture is nothing more than a graduation—not to Heaven, but onto a higher level. And also keep in mind that a Rapture unfolds in much the same way from either perspective, that of those who leave, as well as those who stay, for both sides would in essence experience much the same event. Those who stay would see many "instantly vanish," but so would those who leave, as they also would see others vanish from their perspective.

Now, the Bible you know, and take for granted, talks of an "Elohim Creating Adam and Eve" hence "Man." The only problem is, that's not what the passage actually means, that's what we are told it means! But not in the sense that the Bible is inaccurate or misleading, but whether purposely or not, it has been grossly misinterpreted. The Bible in fact, couldn't be any more specific; it tells us exactly what took place, the problem is, we translate it, amend it and re-interpret it, based on what we need or want it to mean, at any given point throughout history.

Sitchin wrote, *and many agree*, that for some unclear reason, at the time the Anunnaki needed to mine large quantities of gold. But not out of sheer greediness, or because of its intrinsic monetary value, but because of its chemical and electromagnetic properties. Gold is the "eternal metal," it never tarnishes or changes in any way, even for millennia. For electrical conductivity gold is third in line after silver and copper, but unlike silver and copper it will never corrode in any environment. And as far as our topic at hand is concerned, it really matters not whether the purpose was to mine gold or to simply pick potatoes from their fields, whatever the reason, at first they most likely, *much like us*, used different types of machines or robots; then in an effort to perhaps increase yields, they endeavored to engineer a "smarter worker." And I don't think it would be too farfetched to assume, that seeing the underutilized potential of some of the existing primates, they might've started experimenting with them. Physically strong and easily trainable, they were natural candidates to further improve upon. If they could've only made them a bit "smarter" that is, so that they could follow orders, then they had a winner. And so, they must've started by experimenting with different types of primates, perhaps modifying their DNA. Then someone must've had the bright idea to inject some of their own DNA into the primate's.

And lo and behold, we just found the elusive "Missing Link!"

And this is, by the way, precisely the reason why Sir Darwin failed to find it (the missing link) in the first place. For common sense would suggest that if, *as he wrote*, "Humans evolved from apes" then today, we shouldn't have any apes left on the planet! But let it be perfectly clear however, that this does not mean that we did not "come" from the ape—for we actually did. What it does mean is that we did not "linearly or naturally evolve" from the ape! Simply put, we were instead "derived—branched-off" from it. It wouldn't be too farfetched to think that what we in fact are, is "modified-upgraded apes." The Anunnaki scientists, who in appearance looked much like us today, except larger in stature, extracted some of their own DNA and "injected" it into several types of existing primates. This caused the (injected) primates to "morph" into a half ape—half Anunnaki hybrid.

And behold, the "Adam" or "First Man" was born!

Thus, when you read in the Bible, *"The Elohim made man in His image,"* it means just that! More specifically, when in *Genesis-1:26* you read: *"Let us make mankind in our image, in our likeness..."*—it means exactly that! There is no point to, (so that we obtain the translation we want), propose that "At the time, 'us' meant 'me' in the singular"—alluding to a single "creator." "Us" meant—and still means just that, "Us"—in the plural! In this case, "us, the Anunnaki creators"—no more no less! We should not misconstrue it and try to read into it something that's not there!

As, contrary to what most religious scholars and Sitchin himself proposed, the word "Elohim," does not mean "God," or as Sitchin wrote, *"Those who from the sky came,"* but simply "Gods" in the plural form. In the Judeo-Christian Bible, the words "El" and "Eloah" both translate into "God," while "Elohim" translates into "Gods." This is something you can easily verify yourself. I don't have any idea where Sitchin got his translation from, but what I do know for sure is that it does not translate into, *"Those who from the sky came,"* as he wrote, or "a single creator". And that is a verifiable fact.

Now, after many trials and errors, it would appear that they were finally able to produce a suitable "worker." And I do not fool myself into thinking that they created us out of love. It would've perhaps made us feel a little better, but it most likely had everything to do with "productivity." Or better yet, let's just stop walking on eggshells and simply call it for what it is, "Technological Advancement." They simply didn't want to do the hard work themselves (does it sound familiar?). And that's what we did day in and day out; we worked and worked, mining the gold for our "masters-creators." Have you ever asked yourself why do we—still today, have such a fascination and attachment with gold? Why do we consider gold to be the most desirable and most precious thing to give as a gift? Because it cost us blood sweat and tears, that's why! Now you know!

Eventually the time came for the Anunnaki to "switch channels," but again, not by boarding a number of spaceships and travel to another point in space, but "frequency-wise." Call it "A Rapture" if you like, for here again all of the terminology and symbolism we find in ancient texts, were all accurate. It is "we" who misinterpret—question and change things along the way as it best suits us. But surprise-surprise, not all Anunnaki switched frequencies! Many stayed behind on the same old Earth they knew, some intentionally perhaps, but mostly simply because they weren't "ready." Their "frequency" didn't yet match that of the level the others switched to, as simple as that!

Compared to us "workers," little more than "slightly smarter apes"— but apes nevertheless, (to us) the remaining Anunnaki must've appeared as super-beings. Try comparing yourself to a chimpanzee—even the smartest chimp on the planet; do you get the idea? Thus, it doesn't take Sigmund Freud to see how we, *at that level of advancement,* must've seen them as "gods" creators-gods to be exact.

And as it is the case with most parents, these parents must've also developed a certain liking for a "select few" amongst their children. They "helped" some along, while perhaps heartlessly destroying others—by the thousands it would appear. And the Bible describes just that!

That is by the way, the exact same process we are experiencing as we speak; we're gradually but surely "elevating" to the next higher vibration. So when you read *"...and the Lord killed every inhabitant of Sodom and Gomorrah, and the surrounding plains, by brimstone and fire out of heaven..." (Genesis 19:24)* do not reinterpret it, for that is exactly what it means! They had weapons and flying machines of course.* They had technology that to us, armed with just rocks and wooden sticks, must've looked like weaponry only gods could have; lasers, beams of light, columns of fire, nuclear or similar weapons. The Bible describes just that!

And if you really want to clear all doubts once and for all, all you have to do is read a specific passage from the Bible, which I am sure you've seen many times before, but it never "registered," as you perhaps never realized or wondered what its real meaning was. For the Bible tells us—no more no less—the way the story went, it is we who choose not to see, or altogether

---

(If you care to know what these flying machines looked like, do a Google image search for: "Egyptian Hieroglyphs" or take a look at the picture at the end of this book).

change what we don't like or what we find too difficult to accept.

Do yourself a favor, read and understand "Genesis-6.1" and I promise that everything will suddenly make sense. Here it is.

"When men began to multiply on the face of the earth, and daughters were born to them, the sons of the Gods (some bibles say "sons of God") saw that they were fair; (some bibles say 'beautiful') and they took wives for themselves of all that they chose. Then the sons of the Gods went in to the daughters of humans, who bore children to them. These were the heroes that were of old, warriors of renown."

Does the above need any translating?

Now, at the time, *from our perspective*, we must have seen the Anunnaki, *the ones who stayed behind*, as our "creators." They could therefore do or undo us anyway they wished, for as you might recall, the only reason for making us, was to do work they did not want to do themselves.

But, *as the above Bible passage proposes*, as the remaining Anunnaki continued to intermix with the "lab-made hybrids" over time, off-springs became increasingly indistinguishable from themselves.

I do not wish to imply that illustrations of primitive cavemen should be taken as factual, as those are just that—illustrations, but if you have ever seen photographs of actual prehistoric human skeleton remains dug out by archeologists, it is plainly visible how "ape-like," *the skull especially*, we looked back then. And as stated earlier, if you Google, "Pyramids Hieroglyphs," together with some of their flying machines, you would also plainly see Anunnaki "kings" or "lords" as they liked to be called, being idolized, served and showered with gifts every chance we got. For simply put—to us, they were just that, "Gods!"

And for as much sense as the above appears to make, you must be wondering what proof do I have. Simply put, none! It comes down to my own personal conclusion—as I have eyes to see, and a mind to reason. And combined with over twenty years of research, a lot of help from Seth. But it wouldn't be fair of me to ask you to simply take my word for it, for this book was never intended to force-feed information, but instead to stimulate your thinking. Thus I invite you to read the next few pages—then draw your own conclusions. For the next part is where it gets really interesting.

While doctors can easily trace the origins of all types of Rh-Positive blood, they are at a loss trying to trace the origins of Rh-Negative blood. For Rh-Negative blood does not appear to be linked to its positive counterpart in any way shape or form. This is especially the case with Rh-Negative blood of the "0" type, also known as "Universal Blood." This particular blood type (Rh-0-Negative) in fact really baffles the medical community, as it appears to be a totally unclassifiable type of blood, whose origins' no one seems able to determine. But what does it all mean? What exactly is the difference between Rh-Negative and Rh-Positive, you may ask? Without making it more complex than it ought to, if you have Rh-Positive (Rh+) blood, it means that you have the "Rhesus-Monkey Protein" (surprise-surprise!) in your blood cells. While if you have Rh-Negative (Rh-) blood, it means that you lack—you do not have the Rhesus-Monkey Protein in your blood. So, what does it mean in even plainer English?

Well for starters medically speaking this is extremely important. Those with any type of Rh- (negative) blood for instance cannot take a transfusion from any type of Rh+ (positive) blood. The difference is so extreme in fact, that when a woman who is Rh- becomes pregnant with an Rh+ baby, she will naturally produce antibodies that seek to destroy that baby, as her body interprets it as a "foreign object." Researchers were caught totally by surprise in fact, when they finished deciphering the Human Genome. As instead of the anticipated 100,000 to 140,000 genes, the Human Genome was instead found to contain roughly 20,000. Not even double that of the common fly's 13,601. Quite a different outcome than what one would expect from a "species" sitting on the "Pinnacle of the Tree of Life."

And not only did the Human gene lack anything special or found to be "unique" in any way, but they were found to be virtually identical to 99% to that of the chimpanzee. Take a look at this article from the August 2014 online edition of Scientific American:

"In 1871 Charles Darwin surmised that Humans were evolutionarily closer to the African apes than to any other species alive. The recent sequencing of the gorilla, chimpanzee and bonobo genomes confirms that supposition and provides a clearer view of how we are connected: chimps and bonobos in particular take pride of place as our nearest living relatives, sharing approximately 99% of our DNA, with gorillas trailing at 98%. Furthermore, Human genes were found to be identical in every way to those of other vertebrates as well as invertebrates such as plants and even fungi."

This very telling discovery confirmed that all life on Earth had to have originated from only one source of DNA, but it also allowed scientists to back-trace the evolutionary process and extrapolate how "complex organisms" evolved genetically all the way from basic life forms to the "Homo Sapiens." However, the enigma our scientists had the most difficulty with—and were in the end unable to answer, was that there didn't appear to be any plausible explanation for the seemingly sudden—sideways shortcut Human genes took. What they found was that the vertical scaling of the evolutionary tree seemed to progress predictably as one would expect it to, all the way from the basic organism, to the monkey—incrementally. But then took a sudden unexplainable "side-turn" from the monkey to the Human.

And although not exact, for the sake of simplicity, the sequence of numbers below should help us shed some light on this mystery.

As you can see the number of genes increases predictably, roughly doubling, up to the ape, but not so from the ape to the Human.

1 - 625 - 1,250 - 2,500 - 5,000 - 10,000 - 20,000(Ape,) **- 20,223**(Human).

As you can see, Humans have only 20,223 genes, not the anticipated 40,000. But stranger yet is the fact that while all genes *up to the ape* could be said to be an "upgraded-doubled-version" of the previous, all of a sudden—and for seemingly no reason whatsoever, Humans, who came immediately after the ape, acquired not an exponential number of genes, as one would have predicted, but only an extra 223. And the next paragraph is the telltale of all telltales. Here is what the baffled scientists had to say:

"These extra genes are totally foreign—and have absolutely no correlation or provenance, in any shape or form, with that of the apes or any other prior life form. These extra 223 genes are in fact completely missing from all prior phases of evolution up to and including the ape, to then mysteriously appear in the Human! A rather recent horizontal transfer! Specifically, it would appear that Humans acquired at a relatively recent time in evolution, an extra 223 genes, not through the predicted gradual—vertical evolution on the Tree-of-Life, but sideways, an unexplained sideways insertion of genetic material." ("Insertion" being the keyword).

So now that you have read the above information, which you can easily verify on your own, I invite you to draw your own conclusions!

And so to recap, as we saw, the Bible talks of Elohim (Gods) who said: *"Let us fashion the 'Adam'* (which literally translates into "The First Man,") *in our image and after our likeness."* Thus, it doesn't take Machiavelli to see what the Anunnaki did. They simply took existing vertically evolved primates, and "upgraded them" genetically if you like, by "injecting" them with some of their own DNA. Hence, that is what *"Let us fashion the Adam in our image and after our likeness,"* means!

But where did the name "Anunnaki" originate from, you may ask?

The name "Anunnaki," as well as the much simplified course of events described above is not something which I—or even Seth, simply dreamed up or pulled out of the blue, but are found literally inscribed and cast in stone, over and over again, in numerous ancient texts as well as illustrations and carvings. And there are far too many of them to be coincidences.

Now, if you happen to belong to the Rh-0- (Negative) blood type in particular, you may be interested to know that not only is your blood the oldest blood type known, but that you are also a direct descendant of the Anunnaki. A direct descendant of those left behind Anunnaki that is! If your blood type is instead any other type of "Negative," A, B and so on, your blood is only partly "Anunnaki." Simply put, Rh-Negative blood represents the very first "batch" (for lack of a better definition) of blood, we inherited from our "makers" and that blood type—(Negative) being the "original blood" will never change. And that is also why RH-0-Negative blood is commonly referred to as "The Universal blood," for all other blood types resulted from subsequent human inter-combining. And it may not be by coincidence alone that Negative type blood is commonly referred to as "Blue-Blood" or "Royal-Blood." And although I have not fully verified this information, it would also appear that 0-Negative blood people in particular are immune to all sorts of viruses, including Ebola, and even HIV-AIDS. And although I am not 100% sure, this may very well explain why my Hepatitis-C disappeared on its own. For in case you are wondering, my blood is in fact of the 0-(Negative) type.

And when I did some research, which you can easily verify for yourself, I was surprised to learn that pretty well all of the world's royals, as well as most folks in any positions of relevance, be it political, entertainment, corporate, industry, etc., all belong to that same type of blood group!

But here is the million dollars question. "If we were created by the Anunnaki, then what is All-That-Is' role in all of this?"

Everything! Suppose that a little goldfish in the ocean spent its life believing that it was created by the ocean, and then suddenly discovers that it was not the ocean that created it, but instead the shark.

Well, if there were no ocean in the first place, no fish would exist, including the shark! But here is the part preventing us from seeing the miracle of Creation for what it is. Be it intentionally or genetically, we are programmed to envision a "Creator" apart from "Creation" itself!

As I said before, what is the first thing we do when referring to God?

We automatically look upwards to the sky, as if God's abode were up there on a cloud somewhere. But "up-there" where exactly I ask? Inside or outside the Universe? We only do so because "in human terms" this is how we're accustomed to think—we customarily make and build everything externally and apart from us. Hence, we envision a Creator, acting in much that same fashion. A Creator who one day decided to "create" the Universe "out there" somewhere (hence the Big Bang paradox) and then made people appear on that paradox. Thus the many problems our scientists and religious scholars alike face in deciphering the Miracle of Creation. The reality is that the "Creator" and the "Created" are one-and-the-same! The Creator created, and still creates within—not without.

Therefore, it matters not if the Anunnaki—or even some other civilization created us in the lab or in the womb, and it matters not what we ourself will in turn "create," be it humans, robots or hybrids, for create we will! What matters, is that it all unfolds <u>within</u> the Creator. Thus, the Creator is not only inherently responsible for His own "direct-creations" but also for everything that His creations will in turn "create!"

But what about the "Soul" you may ask? If we were not "made spiritually" but instead physically by another pre-existing Earth civilization, where does the Soul fit into all of this?

Simply put, Souls seek "vehicles," or ways to exist physically, in any way, shape, or form. Granted that from our perspective it can be disappointing to discover that we weren't—and still aren't the "chosen and only ones," but a Soul's only objective is to experience the physical, thus try and think from the Soul's perspective if you can. It is "we" who for whatever reason, think we're special, to a Soul we're just another "car" parked in a parking lot full of cars from which to choose. It matters not that the red car thinks it is the best (car) of the lot. A Soul couldn't care less if it experienced the physical in a Human or an Anunnaki vehicle. Truth be told, from a Soul's perspective, the more the merrier, as each "vehicle" will result in a different experience.

Once again, the problem lays in the fact that we interpret the whole issue from a flawed perspective—thus we stand virtually no chance to see it for its true grandiose. Most folks simply do not fully appreciate the miracle of "Creation" and what it truly represents. So, still today, the most widely accepted interpretation goes something like this:

"For reasons we are not supposed to know, God made us and us alone, in an inexplicably large Universe. Then someone sinned, we were hence thrown here abandoned, to pay the price for someone else's sins, while we wait for Jesus to return and save us. Therefore repent!"

But repent for what? For something, *namely the apple incident,* none of us had anything to do with?

But let's stop and ponder this last point a bit further, for this is indeed a very important and revealing point. We scoff at the idea that another civilization could have "created" us. "We aren't as special as we assumed, we're a mere lab experiment" we conclude disappointed. But isn't that exactly what we are doing right now, I ask? Aren't we continuously building better and better robots—trying to make them as human-like as we possibly can? Have you watched the excellent 2015 movie titled "Ex Machina?" And isn't just a matter of time, until we start "inserting" our own human DNA into these lifelike robots, or even other species? Or are we perhaps (hint-hint) already doing so? And let's take this a step (or several) further and let's try and envision where we might (technologically speaking) be, say a hundred years in the future.

By then, robots will be so indistinguishably human, that we will no longer be able to tell them apart from us. Robot-Human hybrids will be ubiquitous and responsible for doing just about everything there is to do. And if you do not think that to be the case, then I suggest you pull your head out of the sand! Robots will eventually be so advanced, so intelligent in fact, that they themselves could become a "species," a society of their own. But this is not where it will stop of course, for progress cannot be stopped. We will eventually have "robots" made completely from lab-made human organs. This progress is not a mere probability this is a fact! As you know, we're already manufacturing human skin, ears, heart valves, etc.; soon we will be able to make every human body component including veins, the smallest of capillaries and soon after, even a brain. So the question is, "What would the difference be between a womb-made and a lab-made human?"

The only thing that comes to mind is that, the first is with-Soul, while the latter would be sans-Soul! Or would it? Can you think of a single valid reason preventing a Soul from deciding to "energize" *inhabit* a "lab-made" (human) body? And even further, if the lab-made body were so flawlessly human that it could also reproduce, then what would prevent a Soul from entering those robot-made future babies? Think about it.

On the other hand we might go the Anunnaki route and experiment with other animals, *thing that as you know we've been doing for decades*, or a combination of animals and robots. And as previously said, we could of course always use our own DNA to further enhance—"humanize" them. Whatever the direction we chose, it isn't hard to see how after centuries of experimenting and "creating," we could start to become "attached" to our "lab-made-children." And whether we will eventually switch frequencies ourselves, *and switch we will*, or simply leave the planet physically in search of a better more suitable home, it isn't hard to imagine how we could perhaps elect to—instead of exterminating them with a global flood or something similar—let our "lab-children" fend for themselves, choose their own path so-to-speak. And isn't that what was done unto us, I ask?

So, the "wheel" keeps on turning, we do unto others that which was done unto us. And our "lab-children," they too will one day perhaps do the same unto their own "lab-children," but not because we're all caught-up in some crazy Frankensteinian play, but because we're all part of a larger experience. All-That-Is is, simply put, "experimenting," exploring the full range of (His) probabilities. Being part of, and within that experiment, we have no other choice but to go along with the larger plan. Here is the problem—but also the solution! <u>We truly ought to stop thinking that we are "special," because we ain't</u>!

It is not that some "special" beings made other beings, "less-special," who will in turn build "even-less-special" robots<u>; it is all special</u>! Everything, everyone, every tree, every bird, every mountain, every star, every cloud, every blade of grass, every extraterrestrial and every Anunnaki and even every robot is special, and every one of the thousands of screws, bolts and nuts that hold that robot together is, believe it or not, also special! This because everything is <u>within</u> All-That-Is, thus everything <u>is</u> All-That-Is!

The Source, the only "ingredient" available is inherently "Special" thus you couldn't possibly build or create something "non-special." The only ingredient, the Source of everything is only one, All-That-Is!

Simply put, how could you possibly make an unsweetened sugarless cake, if the sugar is already in the flour?

Now, if you've read the Bible before, for much the same reasons we saw earlier, your brain translated each and every passage in a fashion, which you could relate to at that time. Believe it or not, *and I will prove this in a second*, unknown to you, your brain deliberately missed not one, but many-many passages, as if they weren't even there. When you read something, anything, while your eyes read each and every line, your brain sees instead the "bigger picture," thus it extracts only that content, that meaning, which makes the most sense at that specific time. When it encounters something for which you had no prior correlation, your brain simply causes these (foreign) paragraphs not to "register." Thus, it causes you to either skip these paragraphs, or despite reading them, to have no effect on you whatsoever, as if you didn't even see them. Here is how I will prove this to you.

Once you've finished reading this book, armed with a little more information, *I hope*, or at the very least a different perspective, read the Bible or any other "spiritual" book you've read before, once again. I positively guarantee you that you will find things in them, which will make your jaw hit the floor. You will even question, *as a friend of mine did*, if someone secretly switched your book just for the fun of it. In it, you will suddenly see passages, which you'd swear weren't there before. You will thus see that Bible, or any other book, under a totally new light. And while I won't venture to go as far as to presumptuously suggest that it will make "more sense" to you, I guarantee that it will at the very least "flow" much smoother than it did before.

What we need to remember is simply this; the Bible (the original unchanged version that is) as any other "Master-Book," has in it much more information than any reader could ever fathom. For when you read a book, any book, you don't just read the ink printed on its pages, but instead "its meaning" the insight, the emotions that ink provokes in you—in direct correlation to where you're at on that specific subject.

Thus a book will have a totally different meaning to you, than it has to your Grandmother. If Leonardo DaVinci read the Bible for instance, chances are that in it he would've found a hidden coded message on how to build the first helicopter. But if Leonardo Di Caprio read it instead, he would have most likely missed that coded message altogether and he would've perhaps seen a quote in there, inspiring him to become an even better actor than he already was. But when my dear cousin Nella reads the Bible, all that she sees in it are "devils, fire and brimstone, and of course punishment"—for that is what she expects, almost hopes to find. For books—any book that is, can only complement each reader's predefined mindset—and reinforce it. No more no less.

Of course this book is no exception. As it was the case with the select few who read, *mainly for editing purposes,* the pre-release "beta" manuscript of this book. Some found it inspirational, some even life changing, and some "total-bull." And that's how it should be! If you, plain and simple—do not believe that Spirit Guides exist in the first place, then what is the point in reading a book about one? To you such a book would amount to nothing more than total nonsense. For we humans do not like changes, we grow comfortable with what we know and have accepted as true, and when we read something, which doesn't agree with what we already know, we readily label it accordingly.

And when it comes to you, you might've perhaps been looking for a word of encouragement, and this book may've inspired you positively in some way. Or you might've been feeling disillusioned with your belief system, and this book might have perhaps helped you clarify certain aspects of it. Or you may be of the mindset that life amounts to nothing more than a bunch of "philosophic bull," and the book of course would have further reinforced that sentiment. I too went through much that same experience, back in the eighties, when I first read the Bible. Then after years of interactions with Seth I read it again and I couldn't believe how much of it I had missed the first time. That is why you always understand a movie better the second time you watch it!

Now, keeping in mind the grandiose "play" we're all acting and participating in, which we intentionally set forth—all by choice and common agreement I may add—play or not, there still exist a "Human-Physical side" we all must navigate through so-to-speak, on our way to enlightenment. Again, all for the sole purpose of "learning," we assembled—we set forth a playground of sorts if you like, so that we could experiment—experience what we could not possibly experience at the Soul level. But movie or not, playground or otherwise, this physical level of ours, this beloved Earth-Level we so cherish, has "rules" we all must play by. Rules that we also implemented. And it goes without saying that rules or not, you will still get to "graduate" sooner or later, regardless. But why not try and make our stay, our sojourn here a bit easier, a bit more comfortable—a bit more enjoyable? Try to at the very least recognize these so called "rules" and become aware of them?

But if it is a "movie" or "play" that we are acting in, then why is the

Internet flooded with a new conspiracy theory every other hour it seems? Everything from "UFOs," to "The government is out to get you," to "The lizard people are coming," to "I know what happened to flight number so-and-so." Why are we being kept (seemingly,) in a constant state of fear and confusion, bombarded with an enormous amount of misinformation, on every side? What's really going on here? Who is conspiring against us, you may ask?

Well, truth be told, at the "Earth-Movie-Level," some folks are in fact conspiring against you. The thing is, that's information you may not want to know, but then again, it is not by chance that you are reading this particular book—thus "you are ready to know." And should you not be (ready) then despite reading it—your brain would simply not register the information anyways. However, I urge you to read the next few pages with a so-called "grain of salt," keeping in mind that you (the Soul) the real you, be it for your own edification or for the edification of others, has chosen to partake in the movie. You are here, *on Earth*, to learn, or to teach something.

Thus, you shouldn't take whatever (Earth) situation you may be involved in, (be it good or bad,) too seriously, for "it matters not" in the larger picture, or more precisely, accept, recognize the fact that despite the (Earthly) appearance, good as well as bad—in the end, it all translates into learning, and learning is always a positive thing. Thus, as I said before, try to see things from the Soul's perspective, and see for yourself how it will all suddenly make sense. With that in mind, let's therefore backpedal a bit.

As we said, a number of Anunnaki were, *for whatever reason*, "left behind," they "didn't make the band" so-to-speak. This, not as a form of punishment or anything similar, and neither does it imply that—they did not progress to the next channel, because of their ill intentions. What it does imply is that they simply were not at the same level the others were, those who instead did "make the band."

We mustn't forget that whatever traits we have—they have. Not because they copy us, but because we inherited these traits, from them. Thus, just as we experience feelings of love, compassion, hate, etc., they could also—only in a more amplified fashion. Thus, those amongst us who, *for no decision of our own*, happen to be the direct descendants of the Anunnaki, find ourselves, *effortlessly almost*, gravitating toward positions of relevance. And it shouldn't be difficult to understand why. It comes down to this; each individual on the planet today belongs to one of three groups;

—1) A descendant of the original leaders.

—2) A descendant of the original workers.

—3) A combination, *to any degree*, of the two.

However, it is the first two groups we are going to discuss, for the third, *the combined group*, falls somewhere in the middle. Thus we have "leaders" and we have "workers," but as we know, not all leaders (or all workers) think alike. Some, *from either group*, are going to be more-or-less well intentioned than others. Thus, those who—from the so called "leaders group," like to think of themselves as "superior," *for in effect they are*, choose to exploit that fact—and take the "greedy-route." These are the so-called "bad guys" in the movie. We will henceforth call this bunch "Group-G" for "Greedy." Those who instead choose to take the "compassionate"—"these are my children" route, will use that same power, *they know they have*, for the benefit of others. These represent what we call "the good guys" in the movie. We shall henceforth call this bunch "Group-C" for "Compassionate."

The greedy bunch chose that route for a number of reasons, simple boredom, or perhaps personal discontent, or perhaps for the same old reason we do everything, "learning." But it's not the reason that's important here, I am simply trying to demystify the subject and make those who wish to understand—understand! For once again, it is up to each of us to decide the life we want.

And furthermore, do you recall when back in 1987, *speaking at a United Nations meeting,* then President Reagan said: *"...And yet I ask you: Is not an alien force already among us?"* Could he have alluded to the "left-behind" Anunnaki? Just a suggestion.

Now, the folks from "Group-C" the compassionate bunch—and there are many, constantly provide you with the information, the tools you need to better yourself! My dear friend, you are in fact holding one such tool in your hands right now!

The positive books are there for you to buy, the informative documentaries are on TV and the Internet for you to watch—free for the taking. Then do take them! Educate yourself, become the very best you can become!

There is a "pie" on the table, a huge pie, and contrary to what you hear on TV, it is a never-ending-limitless pie. You read right, "limitless!" Those from Group-G and Group-C are fully aware of this. They know that if one took a piece of that pie, it would instantaneously get replenished—but not from just the planet, but instead from the whole Universe. For it is all "Energy," the whole Universe is Energy, so you could take and take—and take some more, but there would never be an end to that pie. This being a Universal truth!

But what about the nice folks from "Team-Compassionate" you may ask? These are the folks (most likely from the Rh-Negative blood group) who are indeed eager to help you any way they can. They want to share what they know, with their fellow Humans. And there is no shortage of them. And they are the true future Leaders! They, (just like "Group-Greedy") have been around as long as time itself. And it wouldn't be too farfetched to say that without them, whose mission is to keep tabs on the Greedy bunch, whose only intent seems to be that of "taking"—but to never contribute, there wouldn't be anyone left on the planet, most likely not even the planet itself. For obvious reasons I will not mention names, but if you look, if you open yourself to receiving, nice sincere folks are everywhere!

Trust your Higher Guidance, open your mind and above all your heart, and you will automatically find all the help you need on your personal spiritual growth process. For when you're open and ready to receive, you will receive! For you will always attract to yourself "what you focus upon"—no exceptions!

Again, we must realize that a greater force is at play here!

A "Sacred Universal Play" and it knows exactly what each is "ready to receive" at any given time. How could it know what we each are ready to receive, you ask? Because it is you and I—it is all of us! But here is the caveat, do not underestimate your own powers! Do not forget that you are a Co-Creator also! You are in fact at the very "Leading-Edge" of Creation. As such, you have a huge input—first-say in fact, on what you receive—all of the time, no exception! Thus, you cannot meet nice folks, if you believe that "no one can be trusted!" You cannot achieve financial freedom, if you believe that "you were destined to a life of struggle and lack," or if you believe that wealth makes people greedy. You cannot be healthy, if you think that "sickness is everywhere." You cannot win at anything in life, if you believe that "only lucky folks are destined to win." Do you understand

how important your mindset is—in what happens to you?
Fortunately however, a (any) mindset can be changed, even instantly if you wish. All you need to do is, decide so!

Now, earlier we talked about how the vast majority of the Anunnaki switched frequencies, while some did not. And since we are ourselves going through—experiencing a similar process, let's clarify this point a bit further. As we said earlier, we evolve constantly. We evolve at a personal level, we evolve as a society and we evolve as a planet. The Universe itself is in an ever-changing flux, and evolves constantly! Everything evolves— and that's non-negotiable, we do not have any choice in the matter. Do the clothes in the clothes dryer have any choice about which direction they are going to spin?

As I said many times, a lot of information in this book is unconventional to say the least and not an easy pill to swallow. However, I trust that if you made it thus far in the book, chances are that you now have a pretty good idea of the magnitude of the subject at hand. Again, I do not have any way to prove any of this to any of you, nor to demonstrate any of these processes or ideas "scientifically" in any appreciable fashion, but when you really think about it, if you can at the very least accept the fact that it is all "Intelligent Energy" at play here—and that this Energy has infinite power, then you may just be able to see that the word "limit" no longer applies.

I promise this will make much more sense later in the book, for I shall endeavor to demonstrate—if only ideologically, how incredibly fantastic, yet incredibly simple All-That-Is really is.

And allow me to remind you once again, that Information—any information that is, only comes to those who are ready and willing to receive it. Thus, it is not I who deserves the merit for bringing this information to you, but instead you! You are the one who was seeking. You are the one who took the initiative, and decided to read this book. Be it because you were ready, or be it because you simply needed a different perspective, the fact remains that you attracted this book to yourself—thus, all praises to you!

Now, a bit earlier, we talked about how societies gradually evolve and every so often "graduate" so-to-speak, switching onto the next channel. For the sake of simplicity we used the school example, where kids attend kindergarten for a given number of years, then elementary school, then high school and so on. Well, we go through much the same process—as a society. Only our graduations lack an actual paper diploma, for ours is instead a "Spiritual Graduation."

As you know we just went past the year 2012, and although a number of Hollywood movies and doomsayers alike all foretold of an imminent end of the world, 2012 came and went—and we're all still here, unchanged!

Or "unchanged" only on the surface?

2012 was in fact one such a "Graduation!" And the next is due on or about 2072! But what exactly happened in 2012 you may ask?

As I said before, it is not a "physical change" that takes place, you are not going to grow a larger brain or antennae on your head—it is instead a "Spiritual Upgrade" that you experience. And although 2012 was the pivotal point—the "switching point" if you like, it does not happen at say exactly midnight of a specific day, but gradually, a process that started long before the year 2012, and will continue long after. 2012 represented the top of the hill, "the hump," the Thursday of the process if you like. Seth said in fact that the actual process (the switch) started as far back as the mid-seventies. And when you really think about it, thinking back, he may just be right. For if you recall, we went from the so-called "post-war" era, to an era we liked to call "The start of a new era of peace and reconciliation." Why did we use those labels? Because we intuitively knew it had started, even if only ideologically, we could feel it.

Now, again, the idea of an infinite number of Universes is strange to say the least, but I am telling you what I was told, and what our scientists are increasingly suspecting, and are sure to discover in the next couple of decades. If anything (as I do) you should consider yourself fortunate to have come across this information twenty years before it becomes common knowledge. Simply stated, Seth said this: *"Categorically speaking, nothing could possibly be even imagined, unless it already existed, somewhere—somehow!"*

Thus, the Universe we will switch to, *when the time comes for us to graduate,* is already here and everywhere. But since everything is Energy, we cannot possibly see it physically, but only "sense it Spiritually."

Suppose you're an actor in a movie, *which in fact you are,* and that the movie starts with you driving down the highway. Unknown to you the cities and people you drive past by are of an increasingly less "physical," and of an increasingly more "spiritual" mindset. But that's not all; further suppose that you and your car are also experiencing that same gradual transformation. Thus as you drive past each city, you and your car match each and every new frequency—but ever so gradually, that you do not notice the change. You keep on driving, and things around you, the buildings, the people and their mindset, you and your mindset, all "evolve" ever so gradually—but in harmony. Ideas you held at the beginning of the journey no longer apply—no longer make sense to you. You therefore amend, adjust to, you gradually "grow" spiritually and in every sense of the word.

"But that's just a movie" you may argue. Yes, but isn't that exactly what takes place in so-called "real life?" Dig out some old family photos. Look at you and your parents and try to remember how you and your folks thought—the things you believed to be factual and took for granted back then. Then tell me if you, *and them*, have not changed gradually. Do you recall when TV personalities used to smoke live on TV, and your family doctor used to smoke in his office, while assessing your cough? "But that's progress" you may argue. No, that's "Spiritual Growth!" For what is "progress" if not "Spiritual growth?" You are gradually growing spiritually, leaving the "old you" behind, moment by moment, constantly! We gradually grow throughout a so-called "era" once in while however we reach a new milestone. We turn the page so-to-speak and when that happens, a New-Era begins. A Graduation!

Are you now starting to see why the year 2012 had so many folks worried that the world was going to end? So many, sold everything they owned and left for the hills, some spent fortunes buying underground shelters for themselves, while so many others waited in absolute peace?

So, what happens exactly when we do "switch frequencies?"

We could liken the process to that of our physical body, where the totality of our cells is—*unknown and unseen to us,* completely replaced every seven years. Thus, from our (human) perspective, nothing at all happens. For it is a "fluid" switching that we experience, but from a Spiritual perspective it is a totally different story, for we now inhabit a totally "New-Earth." We switched from a dying old tired negatively dominated Earth, to a New-Baby-Earth, and a new era of Spiritual Cooperation. If you agree that is!

Let's now switch gears once again. Conventional wisdom teaches us that a Human being can only be either "Man" or "Woman." What if in the near future we were to discover that no such a thing as "man" or "woman" actually exists? Truth is, you are neither—and yet, you are both at the same time. Confused? Allow me to explain. And I am very well aware that, at first look, this topic and the last may appear totally unrelated, when in reality they are just another angle by which we confront the apparent "ugliness of life on Earth, again for the same purpose of learning and spiritual growth.

Still today, a lot of well-meaning folks suffer and have been suffering throughout history at the hands of so-called "normal rulers and lawmakers." But not because they committed a crime of some type, but simply because of the leaders' ignorance about what it means, "to be Human," and all that the definition stands for. Therefore, they waste no time in condemning any person or ideology that does not fit <u>their</u> definition of what is "normal." For their definition of "normal" translates in nothing more than "like them." Did you know for instance that in 1994 an estimated one million people got slaughtered in Rwanda, mainly because their nose (yes you read right) were different in shape—than that of the governing bunch at the time?

Thus, *"Not-normal! A menace to the continuum and wellbeing of our species"* they quickly declare. However, the truth is that they for the most part see it as a threat to themselves. This only uncovers of course, their inability to deal with their own inner-phobias. You'd be surprised how quickly their stance changes, the moment one of their own children comes out of the proverbial closet, and openly declares for instance, that they are gay. Suddenly, as if by magic, the lawmaker goes live on TV and announces that *"It is okay... to be whatever their child happens to be!"* So, what is this big misunderstanding all about, you may ask?

As Spirit you are genderless! Neither Man nor Woman, you simply are, period! The Entity, via a number of Souls, can vitalize hundreds of physical bodies and choose whatever gender, or any combination of.

This does not mean that in their environment, *if it so wished,* a Soul couldn't be a man or a woman. A Soul can in fact think itself into being anything it wished, physical appearances included. The only difference is, that that environment is, *obviously,* devoid of physical attributes. There, things like touch, etc. can only be simulated. But do not confuse "simulated" with "fake," for all that this really means is that each environment allows for certain things, while rendering others impossible. So, there, you may not be able to do everything you do here and vice-versa. In simpler terms, there, in its natural environment, if it so chooses, a Soul can assume the appearance of a man or a woman. If it so wished, it can be 30 years of age for an eternity. And by the way, around 30 is the age most Souls prefer to stay at, there.

But do not mistakenly assume that this and that environments are "separate" independent localities, similar to say "this and that city," but instead an extension of each—a projection if you prefer. And this—our so-called "physical environment," being the outermost level, is the leading edge (of that projection) if you like. The tip of the sword.

Now, a Soul can simulate everything we would experience on Earth, except that again, it would all amount to just that—a "simulated experience." Much like, *for those of you who are familiar with Star Trek,* a "Holodeck experience," the only difference being, that while computers are what power Star Trek's Holodeck, "Divinity" is what powers the Soul's environment—and in fact all other environments. No exception.

If a Soul wished to experience a "Real Earth experience," it must do so—not by leaving their environment, but by projecting onto the (Earth) environment instead. And it goes without saying that if it wished to experience something other than Human, then it must project onto whatever channels that given experience can take place.

However, I am not implying that a Soul's own environment is not real, on the contrary, that level, being closer to Source, is in reality more real than Earth level will ever be. The only reason why a Soul would want to experience Earth is simply that each and every level has characteristics specific to only that reality. This, so that inhabiting each different level could result each into a different scenario. Thus, no level is more-or-less real than the next—but instead a continuum. This because despite each level being different in context, they are each an equal part of the whole. So when we humans customarily like to label "Spiritual" realms "less real," the truth is, that the farther from Source you are, the less "real" you become, regardless of how strongly our human common sense suggests otherwise.

From the Entity's standpoint, it is all one-and-the-same—it is all "Real." And, for what it's worth, this Earth level is in fact as far from "real" as it could possibly get. For starters, we must use a "shell" to move about, a shell we like to call a "body." Source is Spirit, thus the closer to Spirit you are—the more real you are. So, whether we like it or not, ghosts are more real than us. But again, this does not imply that the human physical side isn't real, or not as important, on the contrary, it is all one and the same. They are different facets of the same diamond.

And once again, our beloved onion will prove itself useful in illustrating this concept. Which "layer" of the onion would you say is more real, the inner core or its outer skin? It is of course all one and the same! Not only does each layer make the whole, but also each layer is inherently and interdependently symbiotic to the next. But wouldn't you agree that the onion's essence—its seed, emanates from its inner core outwardly, all the way to its outermost layer? And isn't it true that the closer to the core, the more transparent—pure if you will, the onion becomes, while the closer to the outer shell, the tougher and more "physical" it become? Coincidence? But isn't that true for anything?

The notion of what is real and what is not is subjective, for it all depends from where you're doing the judging. If you compared any of the Spiritual levels to the Earth level, you are going to assume that "here"—the ground you're standing on, is real—while there, is not. But switch places for a second and instead look at the Earth level from a Spirit's perspective. Where would you say is real now? Especially when you can see that Earth is nothing more than one of a million other levels. Millions of vacation destinations, or better, "learning destinations."

Now, try to envision a reality where all levels including the Home level exist at once, simultaneously. There are no switches that Spirit must throw to turn a given level on or off. The Entity, together with the Home level and all probable levels, sub-levels and so on, simply exist all at once! No part is more or less important than the next, for the parts make the whole, (remember the onion?) "Time" is simply put, a "component" a by-product of a given scenario's location within the system. However, as our Earth level travels through that system, "time" adjusts itself accordingly, and by this I do not mean "time-zones," but acceleration-wise, slowing down or accelerating to match each new address accordingly, and always in relation to Source. But what about outside of this level you may ask? Does Time exist on other channels?

It may or it may not, or it may exist in different formats. Spirit "projects"—beams itself onto each specific level, be it Earth or any other reality. Each beamed portion must then wear the appropriate "costume" to exist in that specific scenario. Just like an astronaut must wear the appropriate spacesuit to walk on the Moon, so must a Spirit wear the appropriate suit—to function on each specific level. And specific adjustments must also be made. These adjustments may or may not include "time" to different degrees.

But back to the Man vs. Woman topic, as we said, conventional wisdom would like us to believe that only two sides of the coin exist. However, this is only so because conventional wisdom advocates are—to put it bluntly, afraid of what they perceive as "different" from them. These nice folks can only envision a God, who's only able to create what they see as "perfection." It does not occur to them that All-That-Is created them—as well as everyone else, regardless of race, gender, religion and sexual preference. However, this self-serving, self-defined "perfection" is only but an artificial label, which they established, but one that they expect everyone else accepted and lived by nevertheless.

All-That-Is simply "creates," period! He does not love a person born without legs any less. In All-That-Is' eyes, we're all His children, for All-That-Is created the person with legs, as well as the person without legs. All-That-Is does not make "mistakes," for He only creates Entities. Entities then in turn create Souls, Souls who in turn inhabit physical forms. And it is only at this stage that physical attributes do appear.

So, it is the Soul who ultimately chooses the type of experience they wished to have, be it no legs, one leg or two; All-That-Is is simply the "Source," the "vitality" the fuel if you like, behind the whole (system) so that all possible scenarios can be experienced.

All-That-Is is the "electricity" that powers the system—and yet All-That-Is is also the system! Thus, not only must we realize that what is abnormal to some, may be perfectly normal to others, but it shouldn't be too difficult to see how one's notion of "imperfection" can only spawn not from a "Creation" standpoint, but from one's own personal or social inner phobias, pushing them to sub-consciously and automatically see—hence label, anyone who they perceive as "different," a threat to their own continuum. I do not need to remind you of the injustices so called "different folks" had to endure throughout history at the hands of those who called themselves "perfect." Must I remind you of the old saying: *"Who would be the handicapped, if 99% of us were in wheelchairs?"* But let me once again remind you, that despite the labels we attribute, "racism," discrimination" and so on, they too are a necessary step on our road to enlightenment. For the "hard-way" is how we learn, and how we grow!

So, Spirit projects life-force into beings, that are also made of Energy. Beings manifest here and on every other reality by choice. And by choice they choose the Country, the City, even Family and friends. By choice, Spirit chooses all challenges, victories and setbacks they wished to experience, through that specific child's eyes. And they choose not "what gender" that child will grow up to be, but to what "degree" between the two extremes will that life be experienced as. Extremes we like to call "Man" or "Woman."

However, nothing is cast in stone; these are only roughly laid-out plans, approximate traits and characteristics Spirit wished to experience. And researchers have clearly proven that whether "Man" or "Woman" in appearance, each of us carries within, a certain degree of the "opposite sex's" building blocks. In simpler terms, we're all inherently predisposed, we in-fact all have the necessary building blocks to be both man as well as woman. And depending upon the experiences we decide to have in a given lifetime, Spirit will then "activate" more-or-less of the gender specific "building blocks" as needed, so that the intended life experience is obtained. It can in-fact be said that a man's sexual organs are nothing more than a woman's sexual organs inside-out. Try to envision if you could, a "State of Being," an existence where there are neither men nor women. Just Human Beings!

Now, once a gender is chosen, the degree—or predominance of that gender is also decided upon, again, based upon the experiences that Soul wished to have. Based upon specific scenarios, challenges and other factors a Soul may choose to experience, an either markedly "masculine" or a markedly "feminine" body will be projected. The first will predominately take on masculine physiognomies such as a marked aggressiveness, a hairier—more muscular body and so on, while on the other hand, the latter will assume a more "feminine" projection together with all of the related—accompanying factors. Hence, constantly re-molded as needed, the projected-body will adjust, "morph" accordingly. And it goes without saying of course that that same process of adjustment also applies to any degree therein. To better understand this concept, try to envision a "scale" of sorts. For simplicity sake, the scale would range from left to right, the left representing "Masculinity," the right "Femininity." This is however not to be confused with the so-called "Man-Scale" devised over a century ago. *That particular scale is not only still highly controversial, but it only endeavors to measure one's level of "masculinity" based upon specific so-called "manhood tests."*

Now, in our imaginary scale, if you fell anywhere near the left-most extreme, you would be of a markedly masculine nature. If you instead fell anywhere near the opposite (right) end, you would be of a markedly feminine nature. We are all more-or-less a combination of the two. Most folks fall in fact neither all the way to the left nor all the way to the right, with the vast majority falling somewhere in between the two extremes. Keep in mind however, that even if you totally fell to either extreme-end of the scale, you would still have in you 10% of the opposite gender, for it is well agreed in the annals of medicine that no entirely man or woman individual exists. The next time you happen to be in a shopping mall food-court where a lot of folks gather, observe people as they walk by. You will notice that the vast majority fall within a somewhat neutral range. Seldom will you see an individual of a marked masculine or feminine demeanor. And should one happen to walk by, they would be exceedingly easy to spot. The ones who like to strut their gold chains adorned hairy chest through an unbuttoned shirt, and walk with a sideways gorilla-like swing. But have you ever wondered what all that exhibitionism is about? I am sure many will disagree, but believe it or not the two extremes are rarely the norm.

If "0" is the left and "10" the right, normal would be somewhere between 3 and 8. That is in fact where ninety percent of us fall. But what do you suppose happens when an individual falls at either extreme-end of the scale—meaning from 0 to 3 or from 8 to 10? This can in fact result in a most challenging life; as while your body would be screaming total masculinity, *or femininity*, your psyche would still entertain ideas from the opposite sex. The psyche therefore receives conflicting signals, which the individual can perceive as abnormalities—but that unknown to them are actually perfectly normal. Thus the insecure individual, feeling the need to compensate, ends up overdoing it. So together with marked exhibitionism, bragging, and advertising, in an effort to leave no doubt—and mainly for self-reassurance, they are constantly on the prowl looking to score as many sexual partners of the opposite sex as possible.

Now, said "scale of probabilities," *if that is what we wished to call it,* should help us understand the probable reasons why we're having such a difficult time accepting that there is no such a thing as a 100% man or woman. Of course, no actual "scale" with numbers actually exists, we're using this example to simplify the idea, but a sort of Gender-Level selection process does take place. Before birth, a choice is made from a range of probabilities—and even this is not final. A Soul can choose to enter a life at any given point on that imaginary scale, to then later in life change in either direction. Once a gender or a degree thereof, a Family, a City, a Country and so on, is decided upon, a baby is born to parents whom, for reasons of their own, had also agreed to parent that particular baby. And on this point, a number of folks have asked if, during the course of the pregnancy, a specific point exists when a Soul actually enters the baby in the womb.

It can vary considerably. However, every woman who has experienced pregnancy has no doubt recognized a specific point, *usually late in the pregnancy*, when the baby—though still in her womb, seemed to have suddenly assumed a life of their own; a sort of disconnect or independence from the mother, if you will.

This assuming of Id-Entity usually takes place anywhere from about 7 to 9 months in the course of the pregnancy. However, many times the Soul prefers delaying entering the baby until just seconds before, or even immediately after birth. It is fascinating however, how—prior to the baby assuming that independence, the mother feels in absolute unity with the baby in her womb. As during and up to that point the baby is not only physically attached to—and inside the mother's body, but in essence an extension of the mother, thus—up to that point, the baby is being "energized" so to speak, by the mother's Soul.

However, the mother will always be aware of the exact moment the Soul enters her baby and takes over, for it is at that precise point that "separation" takes place, for what was her baby a moment earlier, suddenly becomes a person with a mind, *a Soul actually*, of their own. And when that assumption of Id-Entity takes place, while still in the womb, an interaction of sorts begins between the mother and her baby, as the mother is now completely aware that though still in her womb, the baby has now reached a state of self-awareness. Thus, she instinctively initiates a form of two-way relationship, talking with the baby as if it were another person—this despite being still in her womb.

A "miscarriage" instead, is usually the result of an actual physical cause such as a fall or a car accident. But miscarriages always happen prior to the Soul entering the baby. Thus, although a lot of folks may disagree with this point, a miscarriage or an abortion should not be seen as a destruction of life. According to Seth, the baby is not a "Person-with-Soul" yet. Therefore, for the sake of the argument, we could liken a miscarriage with the mother losing a limb, but not a loss of "life."

"Stillbirths" are on the other hand an altogether different story. There are instances when a Soul simply "changes its mind"—and decides that they no longer wish to experience a given lifetime after all. A million reasons can exist for that decision. In many cases it is instead the mother who was perhaps unprepared or unwilling to assume that role. Many women, *especially when young*, may wish to experience pregnancy, but are not ready to, and do not wish to experience being a mother.

"Sudden Death Syndrome" has instead baffled our doctors for many decades. For no apparent reason, a perfectly healthy baby will suddenly die—usually in their sleep. This can happen at any time during the first three years of a baby's life. Doctors are completely helpless in being able to pinpoint the cause, for again, they are used to look for a physical explanation, when the reason is a purely Spiritual one. The cause can, for the most part, be similar to that in the case of stillbirth babies. The Soul can decide that they do not wish to proceed with a given life experience after all—again, many reasons can exist for that decision. However, from a medical standpoint, amid many other possible causes, it will appear as if the baby suffocated in its sleep, when in reality it was instead the Soul who decided to depart.

Now, when we die, a relatively seamless transition of sorts takes place. In the case of accidental death for instance, which in the larger picture is no accident at all, Spirit automatically exits the body, *as in my childhood accident*, a moment before that body suffers irreparable damage. Thus, as it is often the case, a Soul can find itself outside of the body disoriented, without realizing what just took place—and since this is exactly what I experienced as a child, allow me to clarify this point a bit further.

A Soul's primary purpose is to "energize" a body. The Soul is to the body what electricity is to a robot. Hence, the Soul may or may not be readily aware of the larger plan the Entity has set in motion. It all starts from a "Higher Place," All-That-Is if you like. Then Entities—in line with the larger directive, project portions of themselves onto a multitude of environments—portions that will then become Souls. These Souls will in turn energize more-or-less physical end-projections, the Human Body being one. Therefore, while the Entity is aware of the larger directive, Souls may not necessarily—hence the disorientation. But most fascinatingly of all, while this all starts from the "Top-Down" or from "All-That-Is down, it all still takes place within All-That-Is!

Now, as incredible as this may sound, "birth" on the other hand, can be much more of a trauma than death. As a baby you're removed from the comfort and warmth of your mother's womb. Then, strangled through a tight birth canal into a cold noisy environment—and you only have a few moments to learn how to breathe. Then, to make matters worse, a doctor has the bright idea to spank your behind. Welcome to the Human race!

Adults might not necessarily realize that from a baby's perspective this world of ours must appear very intimidating. Babies—who see us as giants to begin with, are often bounced around as if they were toys. We grab them from the floor and bring them up to what is a comfortable height to us, but what must feel like 30 feet high to them. Merely hanging from our hands, we swing them back and forth as if they were dolls. We plant our gigantic faces right in front of theirs, and with our loud voices we scare the living daylights out of them. We even shake them, and we toss them up in the air. I wonder how we would like it, if a giant were to grab us and tossed us up in the air. We may see it as funny, but I'm not too sure how funny it is to the baby.

Now, babies know a lot more than we give them credit for. They arrive on this Earth as "Spiritual Beings," as pure—and in fact, as close to Spirit as a Human being will ever be.

However, it is fashionable of course, to fool ourselves into believing that we are going to "raise" them and teach them everything we know. So, if a child grows up being what we classify as "successful," we will pat ourselves on the shoulder for a job well done, if on the other hand the child grows up being what, *again*, we perceive as "different," "antisocial," or not as successful as we would have liked, we then blame ourselves accordingly. We go on torturing our minds for decades, asking, "Where did we go wrong?" Not realizing of course that children have their own life path and blueprint to follow, regardless of their parents. Thus, a baby whose blueprint calls for a life of success will become a successful adult, even when born into the most underprivileged and challenging of circumstances.

We nonetheless try to educate them about what we're sure are "the proper ways of life," when in reality, with each passing day, with each new "life-lesson," we instead get them farther and farther from their innate and instinctive inner Spiritual knowledge.

Oblivious to this Spiritual truth, we gradually strip them—force them to unlearn their oneness with inner knowledge, divesting them of their God's-given-Sacredness. We gradually replace that purity of heart with our corrupt—misinformed ideas. We teach them what we think, or what we were told, life should be. But again, in the end, none of that matters! For those children, whose chosen path is that of a life of challenges will conform regardless of how aristocratic their upbringing will be. While those children, whose chosen path was instead one of success, will attain it—regardless of their upbringing. Many, who were born in the plushiest of environments without having to work a single day in their life, a life of total luxury and splurging, will end up a homeless penniless adult. While many who were instead born in the most challenging of circumstances, perhaps in a German concentration camp, only minutes away from being sent to a gas chamber, having nothing to eat but a piece of bread a day, will become a business mogul. It is therefore not the Country, City, Family or upbringing that makes the adult; but instead, the child's own life blueprint.

At birth, children are always accompanied by one or more "Volunteer Guides." Their task is to aid the child during the initial time of adjustment in the most challenging of levels—the Human level. They usually stay with the child anywhere from 3 to 6 years, and depending on circumstances, in some cases (i.e. cases of child abuse) the Guides may never leave. The child is perfectly aware of their presence. To the child, they are as real as his mother and father are, thus they cannot understand why mom and dad can't see them. Oblivious to this truth, the parents will waste no time in labeling the Guides, "imaginary friends." However, they're only imaginary to the parents, for—having changed frequencies, their eyes are no longer attuned to see them. To the child, the Guides are just as real as you and the house cat.

Thus a child spends the first few years of his life on Earth in a slightly altered frequency, "a frequency in between," or better yet superseding two frequencies. And unknown to us, the child is at this stage a fully-fledged "psychic medium." For we can say that it has a foot here and a foot there, which is coincidentally what a, *real,* adult psychic medium is, hence their ability to see or communicate with Spirit. As that is what a (genuine) adult psychic is essentially, some who for one reason or another "never grew up"—hence they live their life with one foot here and one foot on the next frequency.

With each passing day, children will (in most cases,) disconnect from their sacred source more and more, and instead, gradually adopt the physical as "real," eventually ending up switching channels altogether. This might very well be the reason why very few adults are able to recall the first two or three years of their life, as a switch in focus from a reality to another takes place. Hence the first few years of a child's life takes place in a slightly altered frequency, and the more the new (Earth) frequency sets in, the fainter the memory of the former frequency will become. Seth refers to the two levels as "Framework-1" and "Framework-2." And just as the names imply, these are two areas of existence where all the "work" gets done, closely tied with—and symbiotic, each an extension of the other—in both directions.

Now, Framework-1 is our so-called "Physical Level," the external layer of the onion, where everything is, or better yet "appears to be" physical, but that is in reality "the least Spiritual" of all levels.

Framework-2 is instead where we, *and everything else,* exist in a "probable" state. Thus, everything that manifests here in Framework-1 is already there in Framework-2 in a non-physical state. Framework-2 could be likened to a store's "backroom," if you like, a warehouse where everything is available in all possible variations and—as an idea is set forth from Framework-1 (the storefront) if maintained long enough and depending upon its intensity, that idea becomes "credible" hence valid. Thus, Framework-2 will then—and only then, provide the energy necessary to make that specific wish materialize here, from there. We call this process "The Law of Attraction."

Now, being totally natural to them, children are inherently aware of and accept this mechanism without questioning it. This is mainly because they themselves have just arrived from Framework-2. Up to about age six in fact, they continue taking full advantage of that bounty. Then, with each passing day—as they gradually become more and more like us, they grow up and unlearn the truths they knew as children. They forget more and more of the connection they once had with Source, but most importantly the innate Sacredness they themselves represent.

Therefore, infants are, *unlike most adults,* perfectly aware of the cooperation that exists between the two systems. They often use and take advantage of this double bounty. As—having just arrived from a place of bounty, it is perfectly natural to them. They constantly experiment with the two systems, being aware that they can bring forth whatever they desire here—from there. Their parents in the meanwhile, can't wait to teach them that nothing comes easy in life. Everything is earned by the sweat of their brow. And in an effort to "teach them the proper ways," they make sure they take their children to their favorite place of worship every week, which is coincidentally where most of the damage is done, the gradual divesting of their All-That-Is' given powers.

Now, children experiment constantly. They purposely create events and circumstances to test how Framework-1 and Framework-2 interact and relate one to the other. They're fascinated by what they can achieve here by simply using their thoughts. Sadly, by the time they become teenagers, surrounded by a sea of negativity, and a belief that everything results from sweat and sacrifice, they totally forget about their All-That-Is' given creativity they had as children. Hence, immersed in an objective Universe, bombarded by negative information from all sides, they soon become convinced that they too are at the mercy of an endless chain of negative experiences, and they inevitably end up buying a ticket on the "survival of the fittest" bandwagon. They buy into the idea that they are powerless and have no control over what happens to them and their environment.

Growing up, having nothing to show for but one disappointment after another, they end up convinced that any memory of inner creativity and the power of the mind are nothing more than mere delusional fantasies. Unfortunately, the very process of becoming adults and everything that it entails, only adds to the contradiction. Those of us, who are fortunate enough to still be able to awaken the child within, are instinctively aware that a deeper power exists within. For the inner-child still remembers a sense of long-gone creative power, an inner dimension from where we were once able to literally manifest our dreams into life. As children we were naturally aware that everything here comes from another source.

Unknown to the adult in fact, children experiment constantly; they wish to know to what degree they can affect others by simply using their thoughts. For children know very well the importance and power of "make believe" the power of "pretending," for they instinctively know and can see the results first hand—especially when the pretending is persistent.

Children are also aware of the fact that Framework-1 (here) being a denser-heavier channel is not as responsive or as "precise" as Framework-2, which they're very familiar with. That is the reason why they not only persist in their pretending, but they also always overdo it. For what we call "pretending" can—and in fact has the same effects as actually doing something.

"Persistence" and "Expectation" are in truth the two main keys to everything that manifests here in Framework-1. In simpler terms, the child instinctively knows that if he wants two cookies, he should ask for four. The mother will then give him three.

Children rely on their inner senses, their natural instincts, and their yet uncompromised judgment. Uncompromised by misinformation they will invariably be fed throughout their entire adult life. We can safely say that as a child, you were as close to "Spiritual" in fact—as close to All-That-Is, as you're ever going to be. And as you grow older, you actually unlearn, you grow ever farther apart from your inner source, that pure All-That-Is' given knowledge. Thus, with each passing day, you become ever more engulfed in a life full of mistruths, misconceptions, and fabrications.

That is the very reason why, you would be wise to think and behave like a child, as often as you can!

"If there is anything that we wish to change in the child, we should first examine it and see whether it is not something that could better be changed in ourselves." ~

— C.G. Jung

Chapter 9

Thoughts Are Objects

W̶e are now fast approaching the final phases of the book. I say this with joy, as over twenty years have passed since I started writing it, and I cannot believe the final stretch is now in sight. In this final phase of the book we will endeavor to "tie-it-all-together" so-to-speak. And in the next few pages, for the benefit of anyone wishing to experiment with alternate realities, a number of "exercises" will be explained in detail. These are exercises I often use myself and are sure to give you results. And a couple of very (exceptionally in fact) important points will also be revealed later in the last chapter, which I am sure will not only amaze but also surprise most of you.

Now, a "shift of consciousness" is indeed taking place in this—what we call our "Earth-in-Chief-Level." Call this shift the "New Age," "Age of Aquarius," or whatever the label, the shift is real! As it has been the case many times before, we have reached a point in history where old information needs to be replaced with new. Remember the highway milestones we talked about earlier in the book? For our Human history is nothing more than a voyage along the Universal highway. A voyage where events take place based upon each address reached, and as we saw, that's coincidentally what produces the illusion of time.

I've always been fascinated with ancient Mayan history. Back in 2010 I asked Seth to clarify the so-called "End-Times Mayan Calendar," in particular the "2012 End-Times Prophecy," everyone was so concerned with. Seth explained that December 21, 2012, was indeed a landmark in time, when an invisible "shift" was to take place. Then, in June of 2012 archeologists in Guatemala discovered never seen before thirteen centuries old rock carvings, depicting the second known reference to the famous "Mayan Calendar of the End-Times." Heralded as one of the biggest archeological discoveries of modern times, the discovery clearly points to December 21, 2012—but not as the apocalyptic "End of the World" many doomsayers and Hollywood alike wanted us to believe, but instead, much as Seth had described, "a start of a New Cycle." Some could argue—and argue they do, that the start of a new cycle always follows the end of a previous one—and I agree to a point, but why must we always insist on calling the glass half-empty instead of half-full, I ask?

Now, a "shift" is in fact an invisible "marker" in our continuum. We have now reached a new milestone, and undetectable from the surface, people everywhere are now gradually adopting a new type of ideology, this again, as a result of a new milestone in our universal travels. At first, the change may not be readily noticeable, but those who do pay attention—or know what to look for, will know the signs. The introduction of—and the increasing acceptance of new philosophies that in reality are not new at all!

Concurrently, old outdated ideologies are becoming obsolete, or morph to accommodate newer more era appropriate information. And coupled with the inevitable changing of the guard that is taking place in virtually every area of society, it will all translate into a major turning point indeed, a new era—what Seth calls "a graduation." However, the speed at which these events are taking place and how readily we are embracing and adjusting to the new information is what is taking many by surprise. Institutions, governments, and dictators alike, laws that have been in place for centuries and supposed untouchable before, will fall or be replaced in a matter of not years, but days. This new "awakening" will help a great deal. We will go forth with a new mindset—a mindset that will allow us to see more clearly, understand, and realize what it all really means. As Seth puts it, "Great things are coming!"

I asked Seth if that was the "final" stage of awakening for us, would there be—in other words, other major turning points, or as he calls them "Graduations." He laughed.

"Do you really think that yours will be Earth's last civilization? Do you have any idea, contrary to what your scientists believe, how many civilizations were there before you and how many there will be after you? Many a so-called 'Shift in Awareness' has taken place in the past; many more will take place in the future. The so-called 'highway' is many millions of times longer than you can possibly envision—endless in fact," he said.

"But then, when will the next shift take place for us?" I asked him.

"2072 is when the next major shift is due. And the 2012 shift should not be seen as a de-facto shift in consciousness, but the beginning of a stage, or better yet a transition, the 'Thursday' between two major phases of an era of gradual awakening lasting 60 years. The next major phase will start around the year 2072," he said.

As I am sure many of you might be wondering, I too wanted to know what the year 2072 would actually bring for us. So I asked him.

"It would not make sense to even talk about that future phase," Seth replied, "as at that stage, technology, Spiritual awakening, and common knowledge, will be so alien to you today, that you would have a difficult time relating to it." But I still wanted to know, give me an example I asked.

"If I told you that in your near future every home will have a type of computer able to provide you with wonderful recipes, as well as the complete ready-to-eat meal without having to put any ingredients in it, would you believe me?"

"If I told you that in your near future people will be able to travel, almost instantaneously, from one place to another and later even from planet to planet, carried by a 'Beam of Light,' would you believe me?"

"If I told you that in less than 50 years (he said this in 1987), scientific advancements will be made that will not only slow your aging—but also reverse it. In essence people will be able to decide whether or not they wished to get old, would you believe me?"

"If I told you that in only a few decades you will be able to rent an apartment, in a living complex, or go on vacation on the Moon, would you believe me?"

"So, can you give me an example of what life on Earth will be like, say 150 years from today?" I asked.

"Truth is Marco that you—as well as those who like you use their imagination, already have that information. However, for the sake of this exercise, let's just say that 150 years from now, Humans—if we could still call you that—will pretty well be in control of just about every aspect of life. And unlike what your apocalyptical friends would like you to believe, it will be a pretty good life indeed! It is true that you still have a few hard lessons to learn, this mainly for refusing to heed to the many warnings the planet—and its Guardians had been giving you.

The result will be some rather impressive weather related devastation. Let's just say that you're so-called "leaders" not only allowed it to happen, but aided the process, as they wished to test nature's full destructive powers and their war-tech toys. As you write in your book Marco, this has mainly to do with mis-information on their part, and the ghosts of experiences past. But as you would call it, a "necessary evil," for that's how you learn.

However, as more and more new blood will be elected, *replacing the old,* this sad but necessary state of affairs will slowly but surely be forgotten in the annals of history. People everywhere will gradually realize that they have a lot more to gain from cooperating, instead than bombing the living daylights out of one another. As I said, your future looks very good indeed." He said.

"The shortsighted among you may envision a boring utopian future," (he continued), "where no one has to work unless they wished to, but who really does enjoy work I ask? Some may consider work an enjoyable activity, even honorable, but that's only because for centuries, they've been brainwashed to think that way. However, what they don't realize is that those who promote those lofty ideas, are the same folks who employ them. Truth be told, if managed fairly, there is enough wealth on the planet to make every single person on Earth—wealthy now!"

"In the next (21st) century, *(he said this back in 1990 or so,)* the average citizen will spend the majority of their time in a virtual reality environment. Technological advancements will allow anyone to experience firsthand the God-given creative abilities each and everyone inherited. Just about everything you will do, will be done in a virtual world. This will be just as valid, as what you now do in what you call the 'real world,' for in the near future, you will realize that you already do live in a virtual world!" He said.

"In your future, you will be able to access vast amounts of information at will," he continued. "Today's Internet will become a powerful— enormous—yet invisible web of information, but not separate from you, and accessible only via a computer as you do today, but instead integrated, as a part of everything, you as well as your environment. Everything, from your food, to your clothes, to your windows and walls, to your transportation, to your medical facilities, will be integrated with everything else. So, the moment you sneeze, for instance, your doctor will know you sneezed. When you merely think of calling a cab to the airport, a cab will be dispatched and a seat on the airplane will be automatically reserved for you. Today's Internet will evolve into what will essentially be 'a Global Mind'—an invisible mind embedded in everything, from transportation to government, to food and clothing, to your home climate, to the pillow you sleep on. Every component will be inherently aware, and in communication with the whole".

"You could still work if you so wished, but it would only amount to more of a 'learning' or 'entertainment' type work. The notion of 'earning a living' will be a thing of the past, and no form of currency will exist in the not too far future. In addition, factories, and every form of production will all be highly automated. Human intervention would not only be unnecessary but unfavorable, as it would only slow down the process. By then, the Human body itself will have become a hybrid, a technological marvel, only remotely resembling today's human body. What you call 'Nano Technology' will be further dissected yet a million folds—and then another million. The Human body of the future will be filled in fact with Nano Robots". "They will not only be pre-programmed to automatically repair anything that needs to—but they will also respond to remote inputs, so that any issue can be resolved remotely without the need for hands-on surgery. Your doctors will know of a patient impending heart attack days in advance—and from their office, instruct the Nano-Bots in that patient to perform the necessary repairs, all remotely"!

"You will be able to decide the color and length of the hair you wish to wear each morning, and your wife what color makeup she wishes to wear every day. Inbuilt technology will make the required adjustments for color, style and length—at will. What you will call 'wearable technology' in your near future, will gradually be replaced with 'implanted technology.' Sub-epidermal microchips will store information about you, ranging from everything your doctors need to know about your health, to your location at all times, your bank accounts and your passport information amongst many other things. So-called 'Super Humans' will follow soon after, at first in the military, then in sports and industry, and then everywhere else. You will label them 'Augmented Humans.' Deafness, blindness, amongst many other conditions will be a thing of the past. And soon after, even the brain itself will be easily repaired and/or replaced partially or entirely—with an artificial one. You will make more and more 'human-like' robots, and you will make more and more robot-like Humans. The two sides will eventually merge, until there will no longer be any discernible difference." *(Seth said the above in 1987.)*

"But why would a Soul wish to incarnate—or project into a robot, or even a 'part robot'?" I asked.

"Marco, can you think of a single reason why it would not?" He replied. "Again, you must stop thinking of yourself as the only special thing that ever happened to the Universe. To a Soul, a vehicle—any vehicle, is just that—a 'form of transportation'—hence, the more the merrier. The more diverse the 'vehicle,' the more interesting the experience," Seth surprised me with. "You make it sound as if we were just a bunch of cars in a parking lot, waiting for a Soul to come and 'buy' us," I said disappointed.

"A good analogy indeed Marco, then why not be the shiny red Ferrari instead than the old beat down Pinto?"

"OK I get it. What about 'sharing, cooperation' and so on?" I asked.

"Everything will be shared in the future. Internet sharing communities that are labeled 'pirate websites' by the (for profit) web giants today will become the distribution hubs of the future. Imagine if you will a world where—provided they do not infringe on other people's rights, everyone will have everything they need or desire, produced instantaneously and within their own home. People will be encouraged to upload their own personal knowledge and ideas onto the web for the benefit of everyone else. It will indeed be an, 'information is wealth,' based society."

"Wow Seth, I don't know if I can process all that information" I said.

"Isn't that what I had warned you about Marco?" Seth replied.

"And what about wars?" I asked. To which he replied.

"There will be no wars in the future, especially after 2072. A type of 'World Court' will be in place banning wars altogether. This is not to be confused with the various so-called 'World's Courts,' or 'United Nations' in place today, for these were not established for—nor being used as they were intended. Wars, bar-none, are always the result of misinformation and limited mentality. When man accepts the idea that they inhabit a limited Universe, then they believe that they must compete for a limited amount of resources. That will soon change, for that couldn't be farther from the truth, for it is instead a limitless Universe that you inhabit. In addition, 'non-weapons' will be created in your near future."

What in the world is a "non-weapon?" I asked.

"Non-weapons are a technology that makes conventional warfare obsolete. A 'Sound' or 'Frequency' undetectable to the human ear can induce temporary paralysis or sleep upon thousands, simultaneously. In addition, other types of 'electronic-waves' will be developed, that can put any computer or command center out of commission at the throw of a switch. As these technologies will be available to all sides, starting any wars would be pointless," he replied.

Then I asked him; "Seth, is what you describe, what we've been calling 'Paradise' for so long?"

"More-or-less. And it will indeed last about a millennia of your time," He said.

"Seth, on a totally different topic, last night my friend Daniel and I were discussing the so-called, 'Second Coming of Jesus.' What can you tell me on that subject?" I asked

"Marco," (Seth replied), "I was there with you and your good friend Daniel last night, in Spirit of course, and may I say that I very much enjoyed the exchange. Let's just say that neither of you were right. Daniel however, is not really speaking for himself; he's simply reciting what he's told at the religion classes he attends on Sundays. I don't believe he totally understands the words he speaks, for the *Jesus will return as a thief in the night* idea he speaks of, is at best a really humorous interpretation, if I may say so. However, when it comes to the so-called 'Second Coming,' it does not imply a literal-physical return to Earth. The projected fragment you call Jesus—who was by the way only but one portion of the whole 'Christ-Entity," simply put—had a message to deliver, hence the title 'Messenger.'

The message was delivered, and He therefore fulfilled his mission. Thus the so-called 'Second Coming,' does not refer to another actual physical return, but instead the understanding of the original message itself! That's what Jesus as well as all other Prophets and Masters wanted to convey. The timing and the locale might have been different, but the message was always one and the same. When mankind finally understands what Jesus as well as all other Prophets actually meant when they said: 'Search for God not outwardly but inwardly instead'—is when mankind will finally accept the fact that we're all part of the same Sacred Consciousness, and "That's when the Second Coming would have taken place!"

"Seth, what did you just mean when you said that 'Jesus was only but 'a portion' of the Christ-Entity'?" I asked.

"What you call 'The Christ' is but a symbolical representation of how mankind envisions God. Your idea of 'God the father' forced you to envision a God you could understand in human terms. There were in fact three individuals, who together made-up the Christ-Entity. They are historically known as "Jesus," "John the Baptist," and the third, "Saul," *(Paul)*. The three individuals were born on Earth and they each had their own separate 'mission' to fulfill, but contrary to what your historians report, none *(of them)* were crucified, not even Jesus. A highly symbolic drama was played-out indeed, but no actual (Jesus) crucifixion took place. The crucifixion idea, was more a psychic event than it was a physical event".

"Now, while it is true that the Christ personality was mainly composed by these three individuals, the other Apostles—twelve in total, were also part of that same Christ-Entity. They each existed physically, and they each had their own personal life to live and mission to fulfill, but the source— the Energy behind them, all came from one Entity, the Christ-Entity. This, so that it could manifest-in and experience all possible aspects, all possible 'traits'—characteristic of the Human experience."

"As we said, the historical Christ was never crucified—nor did He have any intention of dying on a cross. And Pontius Pilatus, who had become well aware of Jesus' higher wisdom, did not want Him to die. But because of a popular prophecy circulating in the area at the time—that needed fulfilling, a crucifixion was necessary—but again, Jesus did not partake in it. And so that all sides could be satisfied, it was in fact Pontius Pilatus who suggested (to Jesus) a conspiracy of sorts. The Judas personality was to play the role of the betrayer, but Jesus was well aware of it and went along with Pilatus—the main architect of the entire play. As in the eyes of the people and the local (Judean) authorities, someone had to be made a martyr. And so someone bearing a close resemblance to Jesus was chosen and he himself volunteered to be crucified in Jesus' place. Heavily drugged, the man had a difficult time carrying the cross, and that is why he had to be helped. Mary and the group that attended the crucifixion came mainly out of compassion for the man who had volunteered to die in Jesus' place, but also so that no-one suspected anything."

"However, symbolically the crucifixion idea was a necessary evil, for it greatly influenced the human psyche from that point onward. And so the crucifixion became—symbolically speaking, of far greater importance than the actual event in itself. And the Christ-Entity, well aware of the ensuing drama and historic value this event would impress on many generations to come—basically not only allowed it to happen, but helped in the process."

"But if Jesus did not die on the cross, how and when did He die?" I asked.

"It goes without saying, that after the (fake) crucifixion, the real Jesus had to be moved away from the area," he said. "Mainly at night, under the cover of darkness, He and a few close trusted friends travelled first to Egypt, then to Turkey, and onward to Europe. Jesus was especially fond of the French countryside and He spent a great deal of time there, but He travelled as far North as Scotland."

"Wow, that is incredible," I said. "Why is this hidden from us?" I asked.

"For obvious reasons, but mainly because it does not agree with the 'agenda' being enacted at the moment on your planet," he replied.

"So, how did Jesus eventually die?" I asked.

"After spending many years in several European Countries, unable to reveal who He really was, He lived in anonymity for decades. Eventually Jesus felt the need to re-connect with His inner-self—spiritually. He travelled to India, where He spent many years as an unknown man. Then in His later years, He travelled to what you call Tibet. That is where He spent the last ten or so years of His life. He died at age 87, peacefully and surrounded by friends."

"And what about Mary Magdalene, was she His wife—and what became of her?" I asked.

"Mary Magdalene was Jesus' beloved partner, but never His wife. She went everywhere He went, and stayed by His side until the end of her days," he replied.

"By the end of 'her' days? Are you suggesting that she died before Jesus did?" I asked.

"Long before," Seth replied. "She died very young in fact, in her late thirties, in southern France," Seth concluded.

"Wow, I am dumbfounded by all this, thank you Seth," I said.

"You are very welcome," he replied.*

Coming back to Earth now. We are discussing very difficult material indeed. As you can imagine, this has not been an easy book to write. And time and time again I noticed something interesting happening every time I started working on the book. As I started writing, I usually went back a few pages and made some adjustments. This helped me to get into the right frame of mind. Then after a few minutes, I experienced a sort of awareness shift, as if daydreaming, or a "semi-trance" I suppose. As if becoming slightly detached from my surroundings—and that's when the information would start flowing.

Sometimes the phone rang, and when that happened, despite it being right next to me on my desk, it felt almost as if I had to step down a "mental step," so that I could rejoin with my surroundings, and only then

---

(Thinking back, one thing I do regret is that it never occurred to me to ask Seth if Jesus had any children. It just never came up in the conversation).

would I be able to answer it. At times it would take as many as four or five rings before I was able to answer it. Stranger yet, the first few rings sounded *to me* as if coming from some remote faraway place. I do not know if we can call this "automatic writing," as I do not know what it is supposed to feel like. But what I do know is, that when I looked at what I had written, the next day, sometimes I could not believe my eyes, for it was definitely not the way I would normally speak or write. And, because of the fact that I would usually be in my office *when working on the book*, being a business phone, I could not switch it off. And in all honesty, I almost needed it to keep me grounded, prevent me from flying-off too far.

Now, Framework-1, the so-called "Physical Level" and its counterpart, Framework-2, are not beside—or one beneath the other, but are instead one and the same, *(remember the onion?)* Or more precisely, Framework-2 is the level where the Psychic Universe exists.

Framework-1 represents its outer material layer instead—where psychic energy flows out onto, morphing into physical matter, matter which appears solid—physical to the outside touch, but only because it is touched by physical hands. In reality, as our scientists can easily prove, what we call "the physical level" is also made of Energy—Energy that exhibits psychological properties, *no surprise there*, even if material in appearance. In simpler terms, Framework-1 is to Framework-2 what ice is to water. And again our beloved onion will once again prove itself useful here, for as we saw earlier, the onion's essence emanates outwardly from the inner core all the way to the outermost (peel) layer. This does not make the inner core more-or-less important than the outer peel is, for without any of the layers, the onion simply could not exist. Our scientists are in fact becoming more and more aware of the interdependence that exists between each dimension.

However, they are still far from discovering how the two Frameworks relate to each other. In the meantime, they have no other choice but to use labels such as "Matter vs. Antimatter."

Now, in March 2012, I read on the web that for the first time in history a Canadian scientists had been able to "measure" a unit of "Antimatter." For science, this is a hugely important milestone, as it finally proves the existence of what scientists' call "Antimatter"—antimatter that they have long suspected existed, but had been unable to prove for several decades.

"Scientists at the Large Hadron Collider in Cern seem to have finally been able to prove the existence of what they refer to as 'The God Particle'." "This," they say, "could explain why all matter has mass, and it opens the door to a whole new realm of sub-atomic science."

However, had they read some of the Seth books back in the seventies, they would've already known that information three decades earlier. Here is what the great mind of Stephen Hawking had to say about this latest discovery; *"This is an important result. But it is a pity in a way, because the great advances in physics have come from experiments that gave results we didn't expect."* Dr. Hawking actually confessed on the Internet that he had just lost a 100 dollar bet he had made with a fellow scientist, betting that the so-called "God Particle" would never be discovered because, *he thought*, it didn't exist. Keep in mind this is Dr. Hawking we are talking about, one of my personal heroes and widely considered the greatest scientific mind since Albert Einstein.

But upon reading of these "new" findings on the Internet, my twenty-year-old son said; "But Dad, didn't I already read that information in your book?" "Yes," I replied, and by the way that information has been in the book since 1997. The real question should instead be, "Why does such a gap exist?"

The answer is that unfortunately conventional science has long ago decided to flatly disregard any and all information that cannot be materially proven—an approach that not only causes decades of progress and billions of taxpayers' dollars to go to waste, but also forces researchers to approach the proverbial dog "by the tail." For the unmovable opinion that "only things of a material nature can exist" has basically forced our scientists to start looking—start their research, from the outside inward. The "Physical"—Matter, *being the first thing they see and touch*, is where the research starts from, then realizing that Matter exhibits what they call "strange psychic behavior," they—in an attempt to understand it's true source, what in other words "makes it tick," endeavor to scrutinize the inner workings of that Matter, inevitably ending up with what they erroneously call "Antimatter."

Why erroneously? Because "Anti" implies an "opposite," when instead, it is not an opposing or competing force they should be seeking, but a "continuum" of one and the same force. The problem is further complicated, *and for reasons that escape me*, the solution further pushed aside, when scientists label "Psychic-Sacred-Energy" "an illusion," or a mere by-product of Matter itself. They give-in to the idea that "physical" is all there is, when in fact, Energy is not only at the heart of all that is physical, but also what makes everything physical. Eventually, Energy's true nature will surely be understood, for as the saying goes "All roads lead to Rome." Only that in this case, all roads will lead to All-That-Is! However, it promises to be a long and arduous journey, that's because our scientists are unfortunately on the verge of making yet another miscalculation of enormous implications. Here is why.

Increasingly, researchers seem to be of the opinion that: (if it exists at all they say,) Antimatter is nothing more than Matter's counterpart—sure that "one is the mirror image of the other." Hence, they still consider Matter, *the physical side that is*, to be the only real part of the two. But that couldn't be farther from the truth. In reality, neither of the two parts is more "real" than the other, but if we wanted to stubbornly designate one as "more real" or "more important"—then, the opposite would actually be much closer to the truth. For our beloved onion does not start from the outer peel growing inwards, but always from the inside, from a seed to be exact—outwardly all the way to the outer peel.

However, an even deeper question remains, namely, "What is the invisible force that makes that seed grow and develop into an onion, a fruit, a tree, or even a Human being, in the first place?" What is, in other words, that invisible force driving everything and everyone on the planet, and indeed the Universe itself? That is what our discussion should really be about, not the peel—or the core or even the seed, but instead the unseen force, the intelligent Sacred Spirituality that encompassing the whole, causes everything to bloom, explode from an inner-invisible Source onto the outer material Universe. The two sides are not a mirror image of—or opposite sides of the other. The two sides are instead one and the same, all the way—and throughout the complete gamut from Spiritual to Physical. Matter is not the "real" side of the two, but only the "outer portion" of the whole, that is, the most decelerated thus "solidified" portion of the whole. Therefore, Matter is nothing more than the decelerated-physical-end-product of a Psychic Source. Once again, Matter is to Energy, what your skin is to you—the Soul! Your outermost expression!

Researchers make what they call "tangible rational observations," yet they are well aware that tangibility and rationality alone cannot explain, much less give birth to the Universe. So they limit themselves in examining only but a small portion of the whole—the physical portion. They look for "Physical" in a Universe that is 0.01%, *if any at all*, Physical, and 99.99% Spiritual. When analyzing a human brain, physical analysis alone will never show the power that fuels our thoughts, dreams, and imagination. Therefore, as a whole, *from Spirit to body*, what percentage of a Human, would you say the physical <u>brain</u> amounts to? Everywhere physical we look, its greater spiritual side is visibly apparent. You couldn't possibly explain, much less understand an onion by only studying its outer peel. Similarly, you couldn't possibly explain—much less understand a Human Being, by simply studying his material brain.

Who could have guessed that a simple little onion could describe the Universe better than billions worth of scientific instruments could?

For everything in our world, be it a cloud or a tree, a child, or a bee, clearly hints, it screams actually, that its source and vitality comes not from their outer tangible material side, but instead from their inner intangible psychic side! But for those who still need proof, here is a little experiment that clearly illustrates this point.

Get in front of a mirror and take a good look at yourself. Now ask yourself this question, "<u>Who am I</u>? Am I the physical body that I can see in the mirror and I can touch, or am I the incredibly Sacred Being who's doing all of the thinking right now?"

You are of course both your body as well as you—"the thinking side." But what percentage, what importance of the whole-you, would you attribute to your physical body, and what percentage would you attribute to your thinking—Spiritual side? Of the two extremes, which would you say is in control of the whole? Is it your body—or that part of you doing all of the reasoning? Answer that question and in so doing you will know the answer!

Now, using detailed techniques, described by Seth, I was able to deliberately travel to the Spiritual Level not once, but on three separate occasions. But allow me to first and foremost emphasize that whether you're aware of it or not—you're already "travelling" back and forth from the Spiritual Level(s) daily. You are actually there, now and always, for that is where your "True Essence" emanates from—and projects a portion of yourself here. As you should know by now, we are all connected to the "whole," all of the time, and the only difference being "where" we focus upon at any given one time. Our Earth based focus, is so overwhelming, we're so busy processing seemingly "material" data, that we forget and shut ourselves off from anything non-material.

Now, some folks have asked about the possible dangers associated with "astral travel." Let me restate categorically that you are already there. You the "Source," you the "thinking part" are always there and you have therefore nothing to fear. However, some unexpected results can—and have occurred. The "danger," *if that's what we wish to call it,* can come from the fact that you would be doing so (travel there) intentionally, hence "aware." And as the old saying goes, "what you don't know can't hurt you."

Truth be told you already do travel there on a daily basis, but you do so unknowingly, while in this case you would be consciously initiating the trip—and "being aware" is exactly what could result in some self-manufactured dangers. Not because these dangers actually exist, but because you would expect these dangers to—thus they would be there waiting for you. This is because, regardless of whether you accept this or not, you are in fact the creator of your own reality, at every level, no exceptions! Thus, these "dangers" would have no choice but to actually "obey" your expectations— hence materialize, just as you expected. These erroneous pre-assumptions are in fact what would constitute the real danger. To clarify this point, here is a more down to earth example.

Suppose a friend whom you trust asked you to wear a black eye-mask, and while blindfolded, took your hand, and unknown to you, walked you to the very edge of a cliff. Chances are that not being aware (of the cliff)—you wouldn't be afraid. You trust your friend who assures you that you're instead standing in the middle of a parking lot. But now imagine the exact same scenario, except that once on the edge of the cliff your friend removes your blindfold—and behold, you open your eyes and you're standing less than a foot from assured demise. Startled you instinctively jump backwards, and in so doing possibly injuring yourself, hence the danger. Similarly, danger could arise from (willingly) venturing onto another level of existence—but equipped with a mind full of fear and misconceptions. For we are brainwashed to be scared of anything to do with what we call "the other side." Thousands of so-called horror movies and books further reinforce that programming. "Ghosts, devils, zombies, and all sorts of bad spirits await you there," they assure you. Thus that is what constitutes the biggest "block" we need to overcome before attempting any such conscious voyage.

I highly recommend that before trying such an excursion, you gained a level of working knowledge and understanding of these processes. In the end, as we said before, it would be the same as saying, "I am scared of skeletons," while carrying one inside 24-7. It is imperative that we understood and accept the fact that we create everything with our thoughts, for if you think that bad devils are what you'll find there, you will most likely find them there. They would not be real of course, for surprise-surprise, nothing is real, but unknowingly brought into that reality by your own believes and most importantly your expectation. Thus, for as long as you are in that frequency, to you they would be real. Always remember that you create your surroundings based upon your thought patterns, regardless of what level of existence you happen to focus upon, at all times. And it goes without saying, that a similar process takes place when we die and cross over. If you believe that a dearly departed old friend, your Grandmother, a devil, or even Mother Teresa will be there waiting for you, you can bet on it, they will be there waiting for you! "Believe," is the key word.

Now, when experiencing an O.B.E. (Out of Body Experience) you of course do not do so with your physical body; but you instead travel there "psychically." However, do not wrongly assume that the psychic you, is not "real," for you simply could not be any more real than when in Spirit. You would in fact be more real there than you are here. For a "Psychic Being," wearing a physical body is what you really are.

When you Astro-Travel, it would appear to you that you left your human costume behind, while the real you travelled there, when in reality, no one went anywhere. It is instead a shift of focus that takes place, you the Soul, focus onto that level. Just as in the radio example, (as that is a very suitable comparison indeed,) you simply change frequency—and tune onto that level. Hence, while there, and for as long as you stay "tuned" (focused) into that frequency, the alignment of frequencies causes that specific level to appear "real" to you. Allow me however, to reemphasize once again, that you never leave that, or this plane, you are in all planes at once, only the focus changes. Here is how you can easily try this yourself.

The next time you're home alone, lie down comfortably on your sofa and relax. And then relax some more. Now relax your breathing. After a minute or so, your mind will start to wander. In reality, it is not your mind doing the wandering, for you are your mind, but instead "where you focus."

You will notice your thoughts seamlessly shifting from one scenario to another. One moment you're thinking about what you did yesterday, the next moment you're vacationing somewhere in the Caribbean's. You can even hear the people's voices. You effortlessly "float"—switching from one reality to another. What happens is, that you un-focus from this channel, scan for—and tune onto other nearby channels. Choose one. Focus on any one "scenario" and just "jump-in" so-to-speak. *And this is by the way exactly what happens when you are under so-called "hypnosis."* Fully involve yourself with that scenario whatever it happens to be. You will feel as if you were actually there, so do stay there for a few minutes. Walk around, do whatever comes natural (there). Then, whenever you feel like it, refocus back onto this channel. You will see the other scenario slowly melting away, right before your very eyes, your "mind's eye" to be precise. And for a few minutes, you will (though ever so faintly,) still see these scenarios.

Once fully refocused back here, it will feel as if you were daydreaming. And "daydreaming" was exactly what you were doing! For that's what daydreaming is, a drifting, a shift of focus between channels. Otherwise, where would you daydream to—if not onto another channel, the moon?

Now, time and time again I've been asked, if while focusing somewhere else, especially while you sleep at night, another Spirit could take possession of your "idle" body. The answer is both "yes and no." But the best way I can clarify this, is by instead asking you a question. What would your answer be if I asked you: "Could a visiting guest—while you went for groceries, take possession of your home?" You must remember that you "own" your body, and that you're not only always "attached" to it, but one with it, no matter what frequency you happen to be focusing upon. So, in an effort to demystify—and at the same time, "lighten-up" the subject, let's use a somewhat humorous example. This is a scenario which is never going to happen, but suppose that while sleeping—hence focusing onto another channel, Joe the joker-spirit, no longer energizing a *human* body, having nothing better to do, tries to and does enter your idle body. Joe could be someone who perhaps passed away recently—and not yet prepared to completely leave the Earth plane, in an effort to re-enter the human plane without having to go through another reincarnation cycle, he could try a shortcut and take partial possession of your unattended idle body.

So, suppose that upon refocusing back onto your body you found it occupied by Joe the Spirit. All you need to do is, *just as you would with your house,* affirm ownership of your body, by simply asking Joe the guest Spirit to leave. Polite at first, but should he persist, you would simply order him to exit at once. Do not forget who the landlord and who the tenant is. Can they refuse to comply? No, they cannot, because again, that Spirit is to your body, what a guest is to your home. It lacks the link—the title to your home, so-to-speak. Therefore, just like a houseguest wouldn't have the title to your house, similarly the guest Spirit wouldn't have the title to your body—you do! Simply put, the guest Spirit must leave when you so decide.

But are we referring to the types of possessions usually portrayed in movies such as "The Exorcist" here? Yes, in a way we are, but it goes without saying that movies greatly exaggerate the matter. Let's for instance take Joe's (the spirit) case a step further.

As you do every night, you shift your focus onto one of many probable levels, thus you leave your body in self-sustaining idle mode. So another Spirit—again Joe the former used cars salesman, longing to relive a few minutes of an Earth life it once cherished, may seize the opportunity and, in your absence, enter your (idle) body. Thus, upon refocusing back on your body, you find that another Spirit occupied it. Not knowing what to do and scared by what you remember from the movies, you become disoriented and confused. And feeding on that disorientation, the uninvited guest further seizes the moment and somehow manages to con you into a sort of "shared accommodation" arrangement. The whole exchange of course, all taking place at the psychic level.

Now, Joe the Spirit, once vitalized a used car salesman body from back in the 1970s when they would sell you a Chevette while instead making you believe it were a Cadillac. Hence, unprepared, you allow the arrangement. You agree to co-exist with the salesman's Spirit, in a body that is in fact yours. That Spirit—having found a "shortcut" of sorts, wanting to re-enter the human level minus the normal steps of reincarnation—birth and so on, is not only literally enjoying the free ride, but also tries to steer you—the rightful owner, into an Earth existence he longs to relive. And so for no apparent reason you start behaving strangely. You eat at fast food joints every day. You take-on smoking, and you even start looking for employment at used car dealerships. Your friends and family also notice the sudden changes. You change demeanor, assume a different tone of voice and even your accent. So sure that you're possessed by a devil, your loving Grandmother calls your neighborhood preacher and has you exorcised.

It is of course not a devil who "co-possesses" your body, but a stubborn

Spirit who cannot be convinced to leave. But keep in mind that forcible expulsion (exorcism) is only necessary when the rightful owner, *you in this case*, unaware of his God's given powers and rightful ownership, allows the other Spirit to do as it wishes. A similar scenario actually happened to a close relative of mine. Years ago, at age twenty or so, my cousin's Cathy' demeanor suddenly changed. Her voice sounded like that of a man, a foreign accent, and an extremely erratic, almost crazy behavior. Being very religious, my Aunt—thinking her daughter was being possessed by a devil, called a priest to exorcise her. After a couple of hours, the unwanted guest Spirit finally agreed to leave my cousin Cathy, and as soon as it did, the Cathy we were all accustomed to came back, having no idea about what had just happened. I was there and witnessed the whole incident with my own eyes from start to finish. Her two brothers, her brother in law and father held her down on the bed while the priest performed the exorcisms.

Let me emphasize however that this is an extremely rare occurrence, thus nothing to be concerned with. It would amount to saying "I will never fly in an airplane because it could crash." As whether you're aware of it or not, and regardless of whether you believe it or not, you do in fact focus away from your body every single night, thus how many times have you awaken in the morning and found an unwanted guest in your body? Chances are never; chances are it will never happen!

—**My First O.B.E. Voyage.** Using techniques described by Seth,* I willingly ventured onto other channels on three separate occasions. It started with intentionally focusing outside of this reality. However, in this instance, *to my surprise,* I found myself in a totally pitch black environment, so dark in fact that I could not see anything. I could not tell whether I was standing in a small room or in an infinite open space. Nor could I feel anything under my feet if it makes any sense. The only thing I could see was an unimaginably long, somewhat wavy "string" originating seemingly from my solar plexus area, extending straight up to infinity. I do not know what that string's precise purpose was, but if I had to guess, I would say that it was some type of "connection," a symbolic safety harness, the knowledge that you're attached to something greater. The string was in fact my only point of reference. Had the string not been there, I would have probably felt completely lost, and I would've most likely panicked. The string appeared to be made of a silver color. It extended upwards to

---

*(For anyone wishing to use them, I shall later describe this and other techniques in detail).

infinity, as far as the eye could see. Naturally, if I wanted to go anywhere from there, there was only one place for me to go—the direction from where the string seemed to originate.

I looked up and I made a mental request. "I wish to go in that direction," I thought, *while looking in the direction where the silver string seemingly originated from.* Slowly, I started to float upwards. It truly felt as if I was immersed in an infinite ocean of nothingness, but for some reason I was not scared; the silver string gave me assurance, a sense of belonging. Strangely, I didn't feel alone, as if although invisible, a million benevolent eyes watched over me. I moved upwards for a few seconds, then, suddenly and inexplicably, I found myself walking on what resembled a road of some type. And let me tell you, what a place! What a vision! If there were a single word I could use to describe my surroundings, it would have to be the colors! Not that what I saw there, appeared much different than what we have here, but the colors were of an unparalleled beauty, as if here on Earth colors were hiding behind an opaque film of some kind, preventing them from showing their (no pun intended) "true colors." Green is green and red is red I agree, but colors there, were just so much more intense, vibrant and deep. I just stood there in awe.

The road I found myself on looked like a dirt road, but very neat and well maintained. Two hundred meters ahead was what appeared to be a small village. Fields of tall incredibly green grass on either side, gigantic flowers each as tall as a tree, graced both sides of the road. The incredibly beautiful flowers appeared to sway ever so softly in a gentle breeze that I could not feel. The giant flowers appeared to be made of a rubbery gel-like substance. They looked aware, and as if acknowledging my presence, they slowly turned in my direction, undulating gently as if welcoming me. I walked a few steps down that road. Homes seemed to spontaneously materialize on either side. I had the distinct feeling that they were being created as I walked, for my personal visual enjoyment, or, that I was perhaps the one "creating" them, as I walked. Wondering where all the people were, my mind must've caused both the homes as well as the people to materialize. However, despite this, I had the distinct feeling that behind it all, a greater power was at play. An unseen "orchestra director."

In awe I walked down that road, I looked up to the sky but there was no sky to see. No blue hue of any sort, plain and simple emptiness, but a shiny luminous emptiness. Some folks stood outside their very colorful exceptionally manicured homes. Everything there appeared as if just freshly painted. Some of the people were enjoying what was a calm afternoon, some lazily watering the gigantic rubbery flowers in their garden. Judging by the way they all greeted me, it felt as if they knew me from before, the same feeling you get when you walk down your street and your neighbors greet you as you walk by.

I kept walking for about five minutes or so, and that's when it suddenly hit me. I remembered what Seth had mentioned, that "Time" did not apply there. Judging from their demeanor, folks there didn't seem to give a care about "what time of the day it was." I mean—I don't even know if it ever got dark there, or even if they slept. They all seemed to simply "exist," without a single care in the world, about what time, what day, or even what century it was. But coming from a place where everything is done according to "Time"—if only from my perspective, it felt as if some type of "time" did indeed pass. "Time" I reasoned, must somehow pass while I walk from point A to point B. But the question was, "just for me, or also for everyone else?" And so I decided to find out.

Getting closer to one of the people there I asked, "Excuse me Sir," I said. "What time is it?" They all started giggling. I knew the answer.

So I kept on walking; the road became wider now, while the homes on either side became fewer and fewer. Huge luscious green fields were now visible; one especially large field appeared to have been prepared for a large construction project of some sort. As I got closer, I could see several people in blue work overalls and yellow hard hats. But what I found very peculiar was that once again everything appeared to be so perfectly clean. Even the construction crew clothes were off-the-shelf brand new, not a speck of dust on anyone or anything. At some distance away from the rest of the workers, two men stood on the side of the road to my left. What I suppose were two engineers or architects, wearing white smocks similar to what a doctor would wear, and hard hats, studied what appeared to be construction blueprints. One held the blueprints open in front of them, while standing to his immediate right, the other moved his arms in a sideway motion, as if indicating where the structure would be positioned.

Curious, I stopped some thirty feet behind them. But to my astonishment and without any warning, as if coming out of thin air, a huge building complex started to materialize in the middle of the empty field, right before my eyes. First I saw the reddish brown metal framing coming together. Then suddenly and from nothing, the walls appeared. Then the windows and doors appeared into place, and then the roof. Finally out of nowhere, the landscaping, grass trees and all. I couldn't believe my eyes. The building simply grew out of nothing, directed seemingly by the architect's arms motion. Just as an orchestra director would direct his musicians, these architects directed the building into existence. Incredibly, the whole "construction" did not take more than a minute to complete.

A beautifully finished building, reminiscent of a school or a university complex complete with beautifully manicured lawns, freshly asphalted driveways, trees, flowers and all, simply came out of the ground, or better yet, out of thin air. There it was, ready to be used. "I wish we had that kind of technology on Earth," I thought to myself.

In awe, I walked another half a kilometer or so. The small town now well behind me, I reached what seemed to be the end of that road. There, I found a circularly shaped stone paved opening, but again, very clean and perfectly constructed. About 100 feet in diameter, the circular space overlooked a ravine. A stonewall about three feet in height surrounded the space—to protect I assume, visitors from falling in the ravine. In the middle of the stone paved space, about 30 to 40 feet in diameter and about 25 feet tall, a holy structure of some type. The structure had a domed top and surrounded by tall columns. It resembled a small Baptistery or perhaps a small Mosque. But despite the obvious holiness of the structure, no type of religious affiliation or symbolism was displayed anywhere on or near the structure. Looking for an entrance, I walked past the outer columns. I saw three shallow circular steps immediately inside the columns, then another row of smaller columns topped by arched openings.

Walking inside, I found myself in the middle of a smaller circular space about 15 feet in diameter. Then, without any warning, all of the columns and arches instantly vanished, to be replaced by a series of white doors. I did not count them, but I would estimate seven or eight. All closed, the doors appeared to be made of a wood-like material, painted in a very smooth bright white seemingly fluorescent finish. In accord with the shape of the structure, the doors stood in a circular arrangement. Each door was about a foot or so from the next. The wall between each door appeared to be made of a white marble. Trying to understand what it all meant and why was I there, I stood in the middle of the circular floor looking at the doors for a minute. The only thing that came to mind was the non-denomination of the structure, suggesting equality, or neutrality. Not a single Soul, *appropriately so*, or noise anywhere, only complete silence and an incredible sense of peace.

I needed to decide what to do next. I instinctively knew that I was somehow being tested; I certainly didn't want to open the wrong door. The doors were all identical, so I did what I suppose most people would have done in a similar situation. I opened the door directly across from me. But as I reached for the door handle, the whole floor—the whole building actually, instantly vanished, to be replaced by an incredibly beautiful white light. I stood totally immersed in that incredibly beautiful sea of soft white light. Totally engulfed in pure love, I was immersed in incredible peace and wholeness. In that moment, I truly felt in—and one with All-That-Is! A feeling so beautiful that it would be impossible to describe in human terms. No matter how much emphasis I would place on the word "Love," it would still not suffice to describe what I felt while engulfed in that Sacred Light.

The next day I asked Seth to explain the meaning of that experience. He looked at me and smiled. "What is there to explain?" He said.

—My Second O.B.E. Voyage. My second *deliberate* O.B.E. voyage was a brief one. This time I used a method, *(described later in the book,)* I like to call "The Helicopter." After initial "take-off and landing" I found myself in the middle of a courtyard. The initial first impression was that of being in a Roman-era movie set. Several temples of different sizes, large marble columns and structures stood all around me. At first, I couldn't see anyone, but I could hear voices coming from nearby. I walked a few steps when a young boy came zipping out from around the corner. About seven, the boy appeared to know me.

"Welcome back Marco," he said. "The Teachers are waiting for you. Let me take you to them," the boy said in a calm gentle voice.

I didn't have a clue about what he was referring to, but unable to come up with a better option I followed him. We walked around two or three temples. Then we arrived in an open square, paved in large white stones, surrounded by several temple-like structures. Several folks dressed in Roman-era garments walked about their business.

"Look, there they are," said the boy pointing to a row of steps in front of a large door.

Three elderly men sitting on the stone steps, clothed in long white robes, each 80 or so years of age I would dare to guess. As we approached, the elders appeared engaged in a discussion of sorts, one of the three men held a gigantic open book. The humongous book, centuries old in appearance, had parchment like pages and a discolored ivory leather cover. But what struck me the most was the fact that while the book must've weighed at least 50 Kilos—something any young person would have struggled with, the elderly man seemed to instead have no issue at all handling the book.

At first they didn't seem to notice me. 'Hello," I said, wondering who they were—and what did the boy mean when he said that they were waiting for me. The three Elders raised their eyes and greeted me with a very welcoming warm smile, but a greeting so enthusiastic that it felt as if I was returning home from a long far away trip. It felt as if we were somehow related. Then they invited me to sit with them; in the meantime the boy had found a wooden stool, which he positioned right behind me. One of the elderly men then thanked the little boy and invited him to go play. The boy happily complied.

The elder holding the large book started talking.

"Welcome home Marco, we were expecting you," he said.

"Thank you, but who are you?" I asked.

"We do not have a name here, but if you find it easier, you can call me Ezekiel, he, *pointing to his right*, is Matthew, and he, *pointing to his left*, is Luke. We're all related to you, we belong to the same family of consciousness. This is the reason why we are talking to you now."

I didn't feel intimidated or in danger in any way. Nor did I feel the need to run away or be alarmed. It really felt as if I was talking to family. Being the only logical thing I could've asked, "What is this meeting about?" I said.

"A review of what you've learned thus far," the Elder replied. "We're here to assist you and answer any questions you might have. Also, to advise you about what lays ahead for you in your Earth future," he explained.

I didn't know what to say. A million questions came to mind, but the answers seemed to flash into my mind even before I could finish thinking the question, as if from within. And although I intuitively knew the answer, I asked what was probably the most obvious of questions. "Are you the historic Ezekiel, Matthew, and Luke, we hear about on planet Earth?" I asked.

"That and much more Marco, that and much more," the elderly man replied. Then I suddenly found myself awake in my bed.

—My Third O.B.E. Voyage. The third intentional excursion was in response to a question I had asked Seth earlier. The question was regarding "Ethereal Levels," specifically, "if relationships of the amorous type existed there." But instead of giving me a direct answer Seth replied that it would be best if I experienced it firsthand.

"If I tried to answer by merely using human terminology alone, I would be far from adequately conveying the meaning. Why don't you go there and find out on your own?" He said. So I did.

The following Sunday morning, *which is coincidentally my favorite time to experiment with O.B.E.*, I took off, using yet another technique (details later in the book). Upon landing there, I found myself inside a large department store. It resembled something like Sears or The Bay. "Wow, these guys have really expanded their territory," I thought. I started walking inside the store; I could only see a few "customers" here and there. Walking through the isles trying to find an exit, I happened to walk by the ladies' clothing section. A woman stood there looking at some clothes, but as she was looking away from me, I could only see her from behind. As I got closer however, she happened to turn around—and I could not begin to tell you how surprised she was to see me. I could now see her face, a face that I could not put a name to if my life depended on it.

"Hello Marco, how are you, it's so nice to see you again!" She said while walking toward me. And then she gave me a big hug.

And I am going to try my very best to describe what took place next, but I am not really sure where to start. I remembered what Seth had warned me about *"...no human terminology can adequately describe..."* but I will try nevertheless. But believe me when I say that whatever image comes to your mind, you must multiply it a million folds. When you hug someone here on Earth, you feel your body against the other person's body, in a mutual embrace. However, this was a totally different feeling. Instead of our bodies stopping one against the other, it felt instead, as if we each "entered" one another. (I warned you that this wasn't going to be easy to explain.) Basically, our bodies became one. No longer were we two separate individuals, but each inside the other, similar to pouring water into water, if it makes any sense. And I have to assume that she must have felt the same as I felt.

I stood there in awe. As her body was smaller than mine, I could feel her inside me, whole. As if two Russian Matryoshka dolls, where each doll fits perfectly inside the next, I could perfectly discern her body inside me. An indescribable sensation! The conscious feeling of melting—merging, blending with—and into one. But that was not all. Although an incredibly fantastic feeling, that was only the beginning. I stood there amazed and in awe. Then within a few seconds, an incredibly sweet, deep-to-the-core vibration, started pulsating from within—and if I said that what it felt like was like having a thousand simultaneous orgasms—all exploding into the sweetest and deepest of feelings you could ever imagine, you would perhaps get a glimpse of it, but that wouldn't suffice still. But not to be confused with an external "sexual corporeal type orgasm" I am sure we're all familiar with, but at an inner level, at a core level, at a Soul level.

The incredibly sweet sensation seemed to originate from a point somewhere in the back of my neck. Then like a warm reverberating wave, propagating throughout every molecule in my body. It flooded my entire being, making me reverberate internally, externally, and at every level. Each atom in my body filled with an indescribable feeling of love, compassion, hope, bliss, wisdom, belonging and oneness, while an indescribably intense inner pleasure reverberated throughout my whole being. No human words could accurately describe what I felt.

The intensity of that experience was such, that although only for a moment, it brought me to a sudden realization.

"Ironically, it is instead here on Earth that we're dead" I realized.

Slowly coming back to my human senses, I wallowed in bliss as if cradled within a soft gigantic cotton ball made of love and light. Now I knew what Seth had tried to tell me so many times!

We are going to open this section with a quote from Napoleon Hill. In one of his books, he stated:

"Truly, thoughts are things—and powerful things at that!"

And if there were one single piece of information I wished you retained from this entire book, it would be this,

Thoughts are objects!

Do yourself a favor, write the above sentence *(Napoleon Hill's)* down on a piece of paper and put it somewhere you can see often. Put it in your wallet or pin it to the wall next to your desk. Do this, because next to awakening to the realization of All-That-Is' true grandeur, no single message is more important, in this or any other book. No single message is more relevant, brings forth more implications, or influences this Earth life of ours more. For even if we began to understand the meaning, we would not only be much better off personally, but the whole of mankind would also greatly benefit.

I am however fully aware of the fact, that this is also a preconceived "component" of the "movie" we're all partaking in. And that this Earth Plane of ours was so designed, so that the full extent of this "rule" or "law," the so-called "Law of Attraction" to be exact, could be fully appreciated and experimented with.

Now, "Learning" is what drives us—our very reason for existing in fact. And in fact, the predominant factor, the main focus of our so-called "New Age of Awakening" will be precisely that—"Learning!"

You've probably heard it a thousand times, *"You are what you think,"* *"Garbage in—garbage out,"* *"Be careful what you wish for,"* and so on, but do we really understand, that not only is this <u>a fact</u>, but most importantly <u>the only rule </u>responsible for driving the totality of our existence?

Many books, documentaries, and websites exist, trying to drive that very point home. I myself have watched the excellent documentary, "The Secret," a dozen times, which is coincidentally a documentary I would highly recommend to anyone, as nothing other than an improved and more fruitful and rewarding mind-set could result from it.

However, all of the information I have come across over the years (The Secret Included), falls far short from explaining the "Sacred Mechanics," the "how" this so-called "Secret," or "Law of Attraction," actually works, or better, "why does it work," in the first place.

It goes without saying that it is extremely beneficial to read or watch any positive material. "Think positive, you'll get positive results," "Believe in something and it'll eventually become reality," you hear often.

That's very valuable information indeed, of which I suggest you ingested as much as possible. And besides anything from Anthony Robbins and Ester Hicks, *I listen to Ester on YouTube every morning*, some of the books I highly recommend are: "As a man Thinketh;" and "Think and Grow

Rich." These titles should in fact be an integral part of every school's curriculum; for they would undoubtedly help our young become better—more compassionate successful adults.

But despite the thousands of books and documentaries available on this topic, the main reason, *I believe*, why most folks are unable to grasp how monumentally important and all-encompassing the concept is—is simply because they do not realize that it is not by "magic," by mistake or even by some abstract coincidence that "wishes do become reality."

Some folks will in fact call this "nothing more than pure fantasy." However, what they do not realize is that it has nothing to do with fantasy. Simply put, "fantasy"—hence "Thought" is the very and only mechanism responsible for driving the Universe. It is an integral part of existence. Thought is to the Universe what fuel is to your car. <u>It is</u> the fuel that energizes the Universe.

"Why" you ask? Because <u>a Thought</u> in the Mind of All-That-Is is what gave birth to the Universe—all the way from the Spiritual to the Physical. Hence "<u>Thought</u>" is the very driving force—the "Sacred Fuel" that still does (and forever will) continue to manifest our Universe, in all of its aspects.

<u>Thought is the only process at work here</u>. No other process exists—period! "Thought" is the very ingredient All-That-Is chose to use, or perhaps the only ingredient He could've used, as He thought, *literally*, this Universe into existence.

And science is very much in the dark when it comes to deciphering what "thoughts" really are. Where do they originate from, or where they reside—and last but not least, why do they exist in the first place?

Many theories have been proposed over the years. Conventional wisdom tells us that thoughts are nothing more than "The by-product of chemical reactions in the brain," or that as our synapses fire (some propose), thoughts are made and stored—giving credit once again to the physical, and not the Spiritual. But then a surgeon dissects the brain and surprise—no thoughts are anywhere to be found anywhere in it. But what tells the synapses in your brain to fire in the first place you may ask? Could you amount to nothing more than a lifeless body that "thought" itself into being, to then wonder if it may or may not have a Spirit? Or are you instead a Sacred Spirit, thinking—extending into—and steering your earthly body through a physical life? Or as Seth egregiously explained, "The Soul is not something that you may—or may not have. <u>The Soul is what you are!</u>"

If Sir Darwin had his way, we would have a thoughtless materially driven Universe, where everything happens by chance. In such a scenario, no explanation would be necessary for "what" or "who" caused this so-called "chance" to occur in the first place. We would have a Big Bang that happened to be there by chance, that exploded by chance, and that by chance—became the Universe we know today. All planets including Earth would also have formed by chance. The seas also formed by chance, and bacteria formed in the water by chance, from chemicals that happened to be part of that primordial soup, you guessed it—by chance. Then by chance those bacteria developed an "instinctive" drive for survival. Then still by chance they "realized" that if they wanted to survive, they needed to find nourishment. But that's not all, as still by chance they also "reasoned" that if they "wished" to preserve their kind, they should find ways to procreate and multiply. Then purely by chance those bacteria "decided" to venture onto dry land. And lo-and-behold, still entirely by chance, they went on to evolve into every "thinking" living being on planet Earth! And yes, that "instinctive" drive for procreation and survival, and most importantly the "awareness" that drove them throughout the whole process, flashed into the bacteria's "mind" somehow—also by chance!

But I thought they were not supposed to have a "mind?!" Go figure!

Darwin went on proposing that in such a scenario, where "chance" reigns as king, we've all equally arrived here, of course by chance. Our "superior mental prowess" he declared, being the only feature distinguishing us humans from every other "animal" out there. "Mental prowess?" <u>Where did that come from</u>?

Now, as fascinating and amusing as Sir Darwin's theories are, they remain just that "theories," best guesses at best, for the exact opposite is in fact true. For it is not "Matter" that creates "Thought" or "mental prowess" but instead the opposite! You could always ask me to prove it of course, but the truth is that if you really paused for a second, and without having to look very far, you examined "your own thoughts"—"within" that is, you would instinctively agree that <u>you are really your thoughts</u> before you are your body. For it is not your thoughts that obey your body, it is instead your body that does everything you—the "thinking Soul" tells it to do!

I don't know about you, and correct me if I am wrong, but the last time I built something, went somewhere, bought something, ate some food or put gas in my car, I had to first think about it—and then do it. Think of the last time you filled-up your car. Did your body drive your car to the gas station, filled your car's gas tank, and then you suddenly realized what just happened, or did you first decide to drive there and then filled your gas thank? Ask yourself this question. Does your leg take a step on its own to then inform you about it, or do you first decide to take that step, and then send a signal to your leg to move?

So, where does that "decision" come from? If not from You-the Soul?

Now, the Universe is not a "fixed-finite thought," but instead a thought in constant development. It is not a "passing thought" All-That-Is had once—and then forgot all about it. It is an ongoing—still developing thought, for if it was not, you and I would instantly vanish as if a pierced birthday balloon. The thought is in fact "expanding," hence, what our beloved scientists call the "Expanding Universe" is in fact an "Expanding Thought" in the mind of All-That-Is!"

I am telling you so because underpowering you is the very and only purpose of this book. And the only way I can do so is to give you the tools you need, and hopefully realize that "thoughts" are not something abstract that come and go from your mind. Thoughts are in essence "All-That-Is," and therefore "all-there-is!"

As you know, nothing can exist if it didn't first originate from a thought. Not only you first think about what you'll have for dinner tonight or what you'll do this weekend, but you also constantly think moment-after-moment, what you will be doing the very next moment. The process takes place so seamlessly and so incredibly fast, that you are not actually aware of doing so—*that you are constantly thinking your next moment into existence.* Do not ask me "why" it is so; I am only writing about it. Only the Creator (of the system) knows why He so chose. But let's take it one step further, and let me tell you that not only is each of us—each creating each moment as we go, but that we are each creating "our very own next moment" as we go. We are in fact each creating our very own personal—independent, *but symbiotic,* Universe—and each (personal) Universe seamlessly interconnects and coexists with everyone else's. Together we form the whole Universe! That's how powerful All-That-Is is.

Now, in a movie reel, frames come into focus at such a high speed that the gaps in between each frame (what Seth calls "off moments") go unnoticed. Thus, a series of still images or in our case "on moments" become a "live" scene—hence "the movie." At any given time for instance, two friends standing next to each other at a bus stop, can each experience an entirely different Universe. One thinks the weather is cold, the other hot. One believes that people are inherently good; the other thinks no one can be trusted. One thinks the economy is sinking and that there are no jobs, the other thinks it is the best it has been in a while and sees "hiring" signage everywhere. One thinks life stinks; the other thinks life is a beautiful thing.

But what's really fascinating, is that unbeknownst to them, their personal thought patterns create each their own personal experience, hence their own "Personal Universe!" And even more fascinatingly, each Universe will then "adjust," conform to each main protagonist's <u>expectations,</u> and supply them with a steady stream of experiences, each mirroring what each demi-creator thinks—therefore "expects" the next moment to be.

Then the Universe, while delivering to each individual actor what they expect, also gives to each their own personalized version of the Universe. And the truly marvelous thing is, that not only is the Universe capable of accomplishing this enormous task, but to also make all of these innumerable "personal" Universes, all coexist simultaneously! All melding and interacting together within the larger Gestalt, all seamlessly! "How could that be possible, how could the Universe be so incredibly powerful" you may ask?

A child's play once we remind ourselves "Who" the Architect is!

And there is more still. For at the end of the book, I shall endeavor to illustrate how the actual process works. As for as incredibly grandiose and powerful all of this may seem, it is at the same time, incredibly simple. I promise you, the answer will amaze you.

Case in point. Several years ago a well-publicized experiment took place in a scientific lab. Two researchers simultaneously examining a single molecule under a double eyepiece atomic microscope, suddenly and unexpectedly came across an extraordinary observation. One of the two scientists said, *"Look, it is moving to the left!"* But with a surprised voice, the other replied, *"No, it is moving to the right!"* Perplexed, they looked at each other pondering the point for a moment. And then, it hit them like a bolt of lightning. They were both right! The single molecule was in fact doing what each scientists "<u>thought</u> it was doing"—simultaneously. To their astonishment, they were both correct at the same time, in essence, each "making" their own personal Universe as they went along, by the simple virtue of "thinking"—what the molecule should do. That's how powerful the Universe is.

By its own right, this very point alone should give us a hint or two, about how unimaginably powerful the "Universe" can be—but there is more! Not only is the Universe so powerful that it <u>can manifest for each demi-creator a personal Universe</u> all seamlessly interconnected within a larger system, but it also <u>gives each of our individual thoughts their own Personal Universe!</u> And I fully realize that this is no easy thing to wrap our brain around to, but let's try and explain this point a bit further nevertheless.

Basically, the Universe is a series of more-or-less "Psychic Planes" all the way from pure Psychic to Physical and back, all symbiotically interconnected to each other, all feeding into—and from each other. From a human standpoint, we may tend to believe that the Universe does indeed "start" from here, our Physical Earth that is, to then dissipate into less and less material planes. "We're the center of it all!" "We're the only thing out there!" "We're the chosen ones!" "Everything else revolves around us," we foolishly and egotistically proclaim.

However, when we will finally wake up and smell the proverbial coffee, *make mine a cappuccino*, that's when we will begin to realize that that's not the case at all—not even remotely so.

Each and every single plane <u>is the starting point</u>—for <u>those on that level</u>, but only for them, whatever the degree of physicality they may happen to be in. To them, that is where it all starts! Thus it is not always beneficial for us to think of ourselves as "the only important thing" in the Universe—because we are definitely not. It might be fashionable and self-lifting to think so, but definitely not beneficial.

It is of course easy to fall for that illusion. "We can see and touch here; we have tangible proof that this level does in fact exist," "this must therefore be the main plane," we end up convincing ourselves. But so do the beings living in their own plane, wherever—whatever frequency that might be. To them, we are nothing more than a probable distant cousin that may or may not exist. To them we are the "aliens" and the ghosts that may or may not exist! Think how funny it would be if they too had television documentaries where their experts called us aliens and ghosts—and argued about whether or not we existed.

What we need to understand first and foremost is the fact that All-That-Is is truly indescribably powerful. This is perhaps something we humans might not be equipped to fully appreciate. And of course I am not saying this in an attempt to belittle ourselves, but it would be much like a drop of water trying to understand the full might of the ocean. Though being made of the same components as the ocean, the drop of water simply cannot comprehend the full magnitude and "power" the ocean has at its disposal. For even if you were able to somehow sum-up all of the droplets of water that make-up the ocean, something would still be missing. For once whole and complete, the ocean assumes an altogether new set of powers, unfathomable, unattainable to the single droplet of water. As Seth eloquently explained: "If you were to assemble all of the parts that make the entire All-That-Is, you would still not have the full magnitude of the whole. For the whole is more still. Simply put, All-That-Is is more than the sum of its parts!"

We should not be surprised then if the driving force behind and within this Universe of ours, is able to express into existence an innumerable number of "Personal Universes" all within a larger one—effortlessly.

And I do not believe that I need to stimulate your mind further hinting perhaps that even this larger Universe might in fact be but only one of many more, inside a larger one still, for I think it would be safe to assume that the thought may've already crossed your mind. For let me remind you that no single thought could in fact exist, unless its seed were already somewhere out there. You would simply not be able to think a thought— any thought, unless that thought's energy didn't already reside somewhere in the vastness of All-That-Is. This is true for any and all thoughts.

In trying to rationalize this notion, we must once again keep in mind, the fact that from All-That-Is' perspective, "Time" does not exist. Time, as we saw before, only exists within those levels where it was deemed a "necessary component," or was included, in order for specific scenarios and enactments to work. The Universe, the larger Universe that is, includes all of the possible "movies" and enactments, levels and probabilities that could ever exist. It also contains all of the thoughts anyone in all levels could possibly ever think. Thus, every single time you think about something, you are "fishing" so-to-speak, that thought from an enormous pool of probabilities.

And continuing on this train of thought, "Time" does not exist as far as the "whole" is concerned. However, time does, *obviously,* exist in our Physical Universe. As a result, another equally fascinating phenomenon takes place every single time we formulate a thought in our mind. In essence, the reverse result of what we saw earlier. Allow me to explain this fascinating point.

Picture this; relaxing on your living room sofa, you daydream about your upcoming summer vacation. While waiting for ticket prices to fall, you are still undecided about where to go, Mexico, France or England? You have friends in each of these places; thus you would be equally satisfied with any of the three destinations. In the meantime, you imagine yourself sun-tanning on a Mexican beach while sipping a margarita with your friend Maria. Then you let your thoughts wander all the way to France where you see yourself and your Parisian friend Jen, admiring the Eiffel tower. And then you let your thoughts wander to London England, where you see yourself doing the night pub run with your mate David. It feels as if you were actually there! You hear the loud voices in the pub, while you're having a good time with your British lads. And if only for an instant, you'd swear you could taste that dark Guinness. Then you switch your attention to Mexico and you can feel the breeze from the ocean. Then suddenly your cellphone rings, and you're abruptly brought back into your living room. The images in your mind instantly vaporized like an exploding birthday balloon.

Absorbed talking to your coworker on the phone, you totally forget about what you were daydreaming about only a few minutes earlier. But what you might not realize is that from a Universal standpoint everything starts from a thought, this being an unchangeable law.

Thus, if only as thoughts in your mind, the very moment you allowed the different scenarios to exist—unknown to you—you gave birth to a process of conversion from non-physical to physical, a process of materialization, Creation if you like. You seeded the three probable scenarios—"seeding" that is all that the Universe needs to initiate the process of transmutation from Energy into Matter. And if held in mind a bit longer, would have eventually manifested (physically,) here in the physical realm. For all possible scenarios—and I mean all—already exist in "thought-form" in the non-physical Framework-2.

Our physical Universe is not detached from the non-physical, but instead "an extension-of"—a continuum (remember the onion?). It is therefore not from our Physical Universe that our plane of existence "originates"—backwards to its source, but instead from Source, the non-physical, manifesting, extending outwardly here onto the Physical.

As we saw earlier, the physical Universe is nothing more than your store's showroom, manifesting outwardly, while the non-physical—its "warehouse," where everything is stored, ready to replenish the shelves here in the visible, physical, tangible storefront.

However, the three probable destinations you were daydreaming about can only reach a level of materialization matching the point at which you last stopped that thought. Thus, they only exist as "probable realities"—but realities nevertheless, suspended somewhere between the physical and the nonphysical, in whatever channel happened to match that (non-materialized) thought's frequency.

And these probable scenarios, which you had initiated—but had only partially materialized, will not simply stop-and-die-off, or somehow disappear, simply because you halted the process. Unknown to you they will continue to exist and form each their own personal Universe, in whatever level of materialization you abandoned them at, independently from you here, but still connected to you in a wider sense.

And there in their level—magnetized by your thoughts, these probable scenarios, depending upon the intensity and desire—the level of engagement you imparted on them, initiated their own quest to (physical) materialization. In simpler terms, these equally valid probable scenarios, became increasingly more physical. The more vividly you visualized them, the more "real" they felt in your mind—the closer to physical they each became.

For simplicity sake, let's call them probable destinations "London," "Paris," and "Mexico," and suppose that in the end you decided to go to London, and abandoned the other two destinations at a level of physicality somewhere between Framework-2 and Framework-1. Having made your choice, you continued to mentally prepare for your trip to London, hence bringing forth what was once only a probable trip, all the way from "probable"—to here (Framework-1) the physical level. But the other two choices will not simply cease to exist and "puff" disappear. Again, although abandoned, unknown to you, they will each form their own continuum—whatever that might be. And your friends in those probable destinations also exist there as "probable-selves." Chances are that they too fantasized about your upcoming visit, unaware that though from several thousand miles away, their "fantasizing" also helped stimulate you into choosing the actual final destination.

The instant you decided on London, you started to mentally (ironically) prepare for that trip. You imagined the airport, the flight, the arrival, meeting your friends. The more you focused, the more defined and real the experience became. When the time finally came to take that trip, you knew (no wonder) the whole trip by heart. Barr a few minor diversions, which you had also allowed for, you had preconceived the whole experience in your mind, and it all went almost exactly as you had imagined it.

In the book, "Think and grow rich," written in the 1930's, the great Napoleon Hill eloquently stated:

> *"This little planet (Earth) floats, in a form of energy moving at an inconceivably high rate of vibration, and that ether is filled with a form of universal power which adapts itself to the nature of the thoughts we hold in our minds; and influences us in natural ways, to transmute our thoughts into their physical equivalent!"*

O.B.E. Exercises

As we are fast approaching the end of the book, as promised, I shall endeavor to describe two techniques for those of you who wish to achieve a spontaneous O.B.E.. I have personally used these techniques many times, and although they both work equally well, the first is my favorite. Use them at your own discretion.

—O.B.E. Technique 1 - The Helicopter. Be it because (to me) it feels the most natural, or be it because of my fascination with everything aviation, this is by far my favorite technique. "Natural" because whether you realize it or not, you go through that same process of taking-off and landing every single night and morning. And I know many of you are having a eureka moment right now. *"Is that what that loud buzzing hissing sound in my ears was the other night as I was falling asleep, or the other morning as I was waking up?"* Yes indeed! That's precisely what it was. You the Soul switching frequencies, un-focusing from or refocusing back onto the physical.

What we call a "buzzing" or "hissing" sound is in actuality the change in speed of the vibration as it accelerates or decelerates accordingly. This allows you the Soul to travel and focus onto other channels. As you should know by now, this Universe of ours is made of an infinite number of different vibrational channels, that just like in a radio, they each exist within their own frequency. Therefore, the higher the frequency or pitch, the farther from the Physical—and the closer to pure Energy, pure Light they are. Conversely, the lower the frequency, the more Physical they are. It goes without saying that this physical level of ours, that we are so fascinated with, resides in a very low frequency, and that's precisely what gives it its physicality. But let's not forget however, that "Physical" is not opposite—or counterpart to "Spiritual," but instead a decelerated—denser part of Spiritual, but still Spiritual nevertheless!

Now, I have specifically instructed my body to awake each morning ten minutes before my alarm goes off. This allows me a smooth transition from whatever frequency I happen to be in—to this.

But if you are like most people, you are likely startled awake by the alarm, and because of the sudden shift, you simply do not notice the gradual transition from the nonphysical to the physical, which takes place every time you return and refocus here on this channel.

Some mornings however, *in my case Sundays*, you awake more gradually than usual. It's your day off perhaps; so you did not set the alarm. Thus, you slowly drift, gradually transition back here onto the physical. Announcing the beautiful day outside, a sunray peeps in through the blinds. Still deep asleep, your ears are gradually starting to register the far away noises from the slowly awakening city. Your eyes still welded shut, with each passing moment you become more and more aware of your surroundings. Your body still half paralyzed, as if floating on a warm sunbathed cloud, you're not yet quite ready to open your eyes, for it is a pleasant state you're in. Half awake, half asleep, your mind is still wandering in and out of sleep. You know where you are, and you can choose to either slow down your breathing a little—and again drift away into deep sleep, or shift your thoughts to the day ahead and gradually become more and more alert.

Then, seemingly out of nowhere, you hear a somewhat pleasant "buzzing sound" seemingly originating not from outside, but inside your head. Some have likened it to an electrical buzz, some a car engine buzz, whatever the name—it is a "buzz" of some type. Every individual can of course interpret it differently, and in my case the buzz can last anywhere from a few seconds to a few minutes. There were times when, while in the process of waking up, I would become aware of the sound. The high pitch would gradually decelerate, until it would become a low—slow "flapping-like" sound, reminiscent of a helicopter sitting idle on the tarmac, hence the name. In my case this process started to happen uninvited.

Seth said that the noise is caused by nothing more than the shifting between planes. The Soul accelerating or decelerating in frequency to match that of the next plane. "Not only does this occur naturally and several times daily, but that we can learn to use this process, *should we wish to consciously visit other planes*, pretty much anytime." He said.

As mentioned, I find Sunday mornings to be the best time for me, as there is less of a chance of being unexpectedly interrupted. Choose whatever day and time works best for you, and in case you're wondering, there is nothing you need to be concerned about, should you—*while in the process*, be suddenly interrupted. Your alarm clock is already doing so every single morning. It would only make sense however to choose a time when there is less of a chance of being prematurely interrupted. Here is the technique explained in detail.

Sunday morning, *in my case*, as I gradually become awake, knowing that it is my day off, I deliberately choose to remain in that "in between state" for a while longer. I basically keep my eyes closed and avoid focusing on anything. Then, should I wish to "travel," I visualize a "helicopter" waiting for me idling on the tarmac. You can choose the type and color of course, but since you don't have to pay for it, go ahead and splurge, pick a top notch Sikorsky, or whatever else tickles your fancy. As you walk toward the idling chopper, you will hear the loud flapping sound made by the blades slicing through the air. Get into the pilot's seat. Seat belts are optional.

Now shift your attention to the engine sound, or more precisely to that familiar "flap-flap" sound the blades make. You're at the controls; the helicopter is waiting idle, for you to decide what to do. Visualize a "knob" on the dashboard, that you turn clockwise to gradually increase the sound frequency. And as you turn that knob, you hear the (flapping) noise rise in pitch accordingly. You can hear and "feel" the flapping sound inside you. Focus on the sound more and more, until now in perfect sync, you become one with the sound. Slowly, mentally continue turning that knob, until you can feel the helicopter starting to lift from the tarmac. Do not forget that you are in total control—then nothing bad can happen. Do this until the helicopter—with you in it, starts to hover a couple of feet off the ground. Maintain that level for a few seconds, it should stay there effortlessly. Focus on the feeling of weightlessness as you and the helicopter hover in mid-air. Then, whenever you feel ready, slowly turn the knob a bit further, feel and hear the rotor blades spin faster and faster, making an even higher pitched sound. Do this gradually, more and more, until the flapping sound becomes a continuous high-pitched hissing sound. You are now hovering at several meters off the ground.

At this point one of two things will happen. You are either going to stay there experimenting with the knob, raising your helicopter up and down off the tarmac, or the pitch—now so high, will have reached a threshold where you automatically "switch." And when that happens, you will suddenly find yourself onto another level. Congratulations, you have switched frequencies!

However, you needn't worry—for it is not a sudden "falling" or entering into another level that you will experience, but an effortless spontaneous "manifesting" into the new level. And neither need you worry about losing your connection with your physical body. For that simply can't happen. As, should you—while there on that new level, intentionally or otherwise happen to "think" of your body—even for an instant, you'd instantaneously and automatically find yourself refocused here into your physical body, with your eyes wide open, likely wondering what the heck just happened. This "mechanism" can also serve as a "safety valve" of sorts. Though you have absolutely nothing to worry about, it is a nice feeling to know that you can immediately put an end to any experience, at any time. All you need to do is to simply think of your body, your bedroom, or even what you are going to do tomorrow, and much like a "home button" on your web browser, you will instantly return back here into the physical. As we said earlier, you already do—and experience this whole process every single night, as you fall asleep and upon waking up every single morning. The only difference being, that in that case you do so naturally, while in this case you do so intentionally.

However, allow me to give you a word of advice, especially if you're new at these types of experiences. For the first few times, limit your experimentations to simply "lifting" on-and-off the tarmac—get a feel if you like, for the new helicopter you just bought. Then, as you gradually become more and more acquainted and proficient with the "controls," venture a bit higher every time, until you're comfortable enough to go all the way up and onto the next frequency. As far as the destination is concerned, you can either (as you already do every night) leave the decision to your Higher-Self, or you can make a mental pre-flight request. Simply tell yourself mentally, "I wish to go visit my Aunt Gilberta, who lives in Gillenbeuren, Germany." And so you shall!

I have personally done so dozens of times. Sometimes I like to visit my Mother, *who still lives in Italy.* Sometime she could be in the kitchen preparing foods and totally oblivious of me, and I would be sitting up on her fridge, or at the kitchen table with her. This is a process however, only those of us who are familiar with by-location or Astral Travel can achieve.

At first glance the described method above may appear to be a somewhat difficult and lengthy procedure, but that's only because, *for the benefit of those who haven't had much experience in this area,* I meticulously described every single step in detail. In reality, once you become familiar with the method, you can get up and running in less than two minutes.

Here is a recap of that same procedure in "expert mode."

—1) Make a mental request of the destination.

—2) Close your eyes and get to a point of deep relaxation.

—3) Mentally visualize the helicopter on the tarmac, and the idling flapping engine noise. Walk to it and get onboard.

—4) Mentally increase the sound pitch, and simultaneously visualize yourself becoming lighter and lighter while rising upward.

That is really all that it takes. I normally go through this whole process in about a minute.

—O.B.E. Technique 2 - The Dot on the Ceiling. This method is one of the simplest I know of. The basic idea is to have a point of reference to focus upon. That point will then become "your door"—your gateway into the next frequency.

Start by painting or placing a dot of some type on your bedroom's ceiling, directly above you. It could be anything, a dot, a little star, a butterfly, any type of sticker you like. It should be placed so that when lying down on your bed, the dot should naturally and effortlessly align with your line of sight. This is important, so that you don't have to distract yourself trying to find the dot.

Find a quiet time, so that you are not going to be interrupted. You might also want to turn off your phone. If you have a noisy wall clock in your bedroom it would be best if you temporarily removed it from the room. While resting comfortably on your back, relax and make a mental request of the destination you wish to visit. Alternatively, leave the decision to your higher self. Relax your eyelids and allow them to close, and then focus your attention on your breathing. You will notice that after a few seconds your breathing will take-on a sort of predictable pattern. Listen to the sound of your breathing, as you inhale and exhale through your nose. Hear and feel your breathing becoming ever louder and slower. Now switch your mental focus to your heart.

Mentally find and listen to your heartbeat for several seconds. Mentally ask your heartbeat to slow down to about 60 Bpm. Now mentally ask your body to relax even further, until you feel totally relaxed. Your breathing should have become very slow by now.

Now find the dot on the ceiling, but not with your eyes (as they should be closed) but instead with your "mind's eye" located in the middle of your physical eyes. Although not looking at the dot with your physical eyes, the dot will still appear as clear as day.

Think from your Soul's perspective. Don't be your body—but instead "feel" your body, and how heavy it has become, as if sinking into the bed. Then feel how light you-the-Soul are—and feel yourself starting to move upward, while gradually separating from your body. Focus on that gradual "separation" but choose to be the Soul, not your body, <u>for you are the Soul!</u>

As you feel yourself slowly rising upward, visualize leaving your heavy body behind, at rest on the bed. Using the dot on the ceiling as your focus point, while you slowly ascend in its direction, mentally ask the dot to assist you. Feel yourself floating in midair, a few feet from the bed. Do not hesitate or question it, simply trust yourself and the process. Remember, that unknown to you—you do this every night, and it is therefore totally normal.

Continue focusing—and (with your third eye) continue looking at the dot on the ceiling, and as if it were a magnet, allow it to pull you up and toward it.

Now imagine getting closer and closer to the dot. You see the dot becoming bigger and bigger, as big as a door in fact. And as if it were a door, enter it—and emerge on the opposite side. You have now switched frequencies.

Congratulations, you have now arrived at the destination of your choice!

The Universe is very, very big. It also loves a paradox. For example, it has some extremely strict rules.

Rule number one: Nothing lasts forever. Not you or your family or your house or your planet or the sun. It is an absolute rule. Therefore when someone says that their love will never die, it means that their love is not real, for everything that is real dies.

Rule number two: Everything lasts forever." ~

—Craig Ferguson

Chapter 10

All That Is' Dilemma

Now, I couldn't possibly cover in this book everything that I wanted to cover, or everything I experienced during the seven year long adventure of mine with Seth, plus the more than two decades of research since. Because of space limitations, I had to choose from a large amount of information, and a lot of the material Seth and I covered goes well beyond the scope of this book, some being strictly personal. And although of a personal nature—there is one experience in particular, that because of its peculiarity and because it could potentially be of benefit to others who might have had similar experiences, I would like to share nevertheless.

Many folks have written about certain unusual experiences. Some for instance, could swear feeling as if someone tapped them on the shoulder. Some had the distinct feeling of someone else being in the room with them. Some swear that they distinctly felt as if "someone invisible" were resting in bed with them. Some even said that the invisible being pushed against them—and that they had to push back. I have personally experienced these and many other things. Let me remind you that ghosts are basically disembodied people—but people nevertheless. The only difference being, that while we are Spirits still energizing a body, they are Spirits no longer energizing one. Thus, we shouldn't be surprised if—and when these encounters do occur. And intentionally or otherwise, at times, a Spirit may—if only momentarily, stumble onto this plane of existence. This happens more often than we think. However, let's not forget that to them, we are the ghosts.

Human beings, or better yet, all beings—whether Earthlings, Spirits or Extraterrestrials, possess an innate and natural yearning to belong. We long to be together, we long to communicate, share, coexist, and cooperate with one another, any way we can. It is the natural "pull," springing from the innate sense of oneness we each instinctively know we are all part of. But it goes much further than that, and it has to do with the very reason why All-That-Is created us in the first place.

Although impossible to adequately describe in human terms, All-That-Is could have perhaps experienced a sense of loneliness. Think about it, before creating us, regardless of the indescribable wisdom, in essence,

All-That-Is was alone. Thus out of pure loneliness, or perhaps a longing to know Himself, or out of simple curiosity, He could have imagined of Universes within, to then experience and experiment with.

We should not be surprised then if a Spirit seeks to connect—in their place we would do the same, actually that's exactly what we do every moment of our lives, for if you remember, we established earlier that the only reason for existing is to "Learn," but learn what exactly? For what is learning if not "getting to know ourselves—thus our Source?" Why do you think is everyone walking around with their eyes glued onto their cellphone's screens these days? Why do you think social networks such as Facebook and Twitter are so incredibly popular? What are folks really seeking there? To connect! Talk about themselves, what they do, what they wear, or what they eat. They compete trying to get as many "friends" and "likes" as possible, for again, the more friends you have—the more liked you feel. We yearn for acknowledgement; we want others to know that we exist!

Ultimately, just as All-That-Is wants to know that He is not alone - we want to know that we are not alone. For where do you suppose our quest for self-discovery originates from, if not from All-That-Is' original quest for self-discovery?

For what would be the point of possessing an infinite amount of knowledge, love, wisdom, and compassion, if you could not share it with anyone? Isn't that the very reason why you and I exist in the first place? Isn't that the very reason why you are reading this book? You too seek to know yourself. You too long to belong. You too seek to know what your reason for being is—and what your place in the larger picture is. It's all part of the Wider Purpose. Although in much smaller scale, you also inherited that same "Original Purpose." In essence, you are contributing, helping All-That-Is to know Himself.

Now, at times, some Spirits can—and do, push the envelope, but so do people, and just like people, *for people is what they are*, there are times when—for whatever reason, a Spirit could attempt to invade your personal space. But allow me to place this point into proper perspective. Interestingly, Seth revealed that there is never a moment in our life when at least ten or more other "people" are in the same room with us, this being totally normal. The ether around us is in fact always filled with other entities going about their own business, in their own plane of existence. Seth refers to this as "same location—different frequency." But there are instances, *more the norm than the rarity,* when different frequencies interact with—transpire, bleed into each other so-to-speak. This can happen by intent or pure accident. Thus, for every ghost that you see or sense, a thousand walked by unnoticed. We must accept this fact and learn to live with it, for it is not only natural but also the only way it could be. However, there is no need to be concerned in any way. Don't be fooled by the many scary movies out there that with their special effects exploit and capitalize on people's fear of the unknown. Spirits are "people" just like you and me, going about their own business in whatever astral plane they happen to reside in.

However, it would be unfair of me, if I said that there are no clowns or jokesters on other planes. But isn't that also normal I ask? Don't we have clowns here too? But mainly because of misinformation, you would likely fear more a ghost-joker, than you would a human-joker. The truth is that a human-joker can cause you a lot more trouble than a ghost-joker ever could. A ghost-joker has as much power over you—as you let them. "Fear" is in most cases, *as we saw earlier,* your worst enemy. A Spirit who wished to have some fun, or one who has nothing better to do and wants to scare the bejeebers out of you, could actually take advantage of your own fear, and pour—as the saying goes, "more gasoline on the fire."

Suppose that, *as I have many times,* out of the corner of your eye, you saw a shadow going by in the corridor. You could approach this in a couple of ways. You could—recalling the many scary movies you've watched—scream, "Oh my god, a ghost," and overtaken by fear, you run, falling and hurting yourself in the process. Or, remembering what we just discussed, you could remind yourself that ghosts are nothing more than other folks, and chances are, that poor ghost had no intention of scaring you in the first place, as they most likely appeared by accident. And seeing you, most likely scared the living daylights out of them. Thus, if you can manage to stay calm, simply talk to the ghost as if you were talking to one of your friends. Invite them to go toward the light and wish them love and good fortune.

Remind yourself that it is a benign Universe we live in, at all levels. A Universe of love, for love is the only thing you will ever need, in any and all circumstances. Send love to any Spirit, Ghost, or Entity—but also Human you happen to come into contact with, and even the most callous will feel disarmed and powerless when faced with such true and ultimate power.

Remind yourself what their real reason for appearing here is. It is to be acknowledged, to belong, and to be loved.

Have you ever heard of the so-called "3-A's Rule?" Attention, Affection, and Appreciation! Termed: "The rule that will make any marriages endure forever," truth be told, isn't that what—married or not, we all seek, regardless of the plane of existence we happen to reside in? I am sure that you are starting to see the only and real reason why this wonderful Universe of ours was created in the first place.

Now, over the years, I had many interactions with Spirits of many forms and of many intentions. Spirits who's only intention was to help me along this at times challenging but wonderful journey of mine, and Spirits who tried to take advantage of my "augmented perception" wanting to interact with me in ways which I neither invited nor wished for. Beside Seth, the other type of Spirit I interacted with the most is what I jokingly call, "the bed type." I am a loud snorer, so because of that—and comfort, I like to sleep alone. Many a times I would be awaken in the middle of the night by a distinct presence in my bed, as if someone were in bed with me. Sometimes, it felt as if "whatever it was" was trying to push me off the bed.

Taken by surprise at first, but then remembering what Seth said in this regard, I would state my position of authority—both verbally as well as physically, and almost immediately the Spirit would leave. However, there have been times when I distinctly felt as if someone actually touched or caressed my face.

A few times a weak force of some type—definitely hands, but not physical hands, "energy hands" around my neck, as if jokingly trying to strangle me. I am not sure if the real intent was to scare me—or just play with me. The grip, from the invisible hands, was never strong enough to disrupt my breathing in any way, just the uncomfortable sensation of having someone's hands around my neck, nothing more. A sensation I would still feel on my neck several minutes after the Spirit left. I am sure many of you reading this, also had similar experiences and that's why I am writing about it.

One night for instance, I had to literally push-off whatever was on me, by forcibly pushing with my elbow (whatever it was) away from me, while yelling "leave now!" No need to be concerned however; as this happens with such a rarity that in over thirty years I've only heard of two other similar experiences. This happens so rarely in fact, that it is not even worth mentioning it. The only reason I did mention it, is because if someone reading this has had a similar experience, they can find comfort in the knowledge that they are not going crazy. And as far as danger is concerned, no real harm can come from these encounters. Just remember who the rightful owner of your body is. You have both Spirit as well as Physical force on your side. The Spirit only has Spirit force; thus they must comply and leave.

The second reason why I am mentioning it, is because it was one such encounter that prompted me to find the time to get back to work on this very book and complete it. As I mentioned earlier, I started writing this book back in 1993. But after about five years of on-and-off writing spurts I stopped for several years. At the time, my sessions with Seth were still ongoing, thus my understanding of the subject evolved and expanded almost on a daily basis. This forced me to start over from the beginning each time. Thus I had decided to wait until I had a more complete understanding. Eventually however, I had to resign to the fact that this is a subject, which one can never hope to fully comprehend.

One early morning in June 2010, I was startled out of my sleep by a definite presence in my bed. I was lying on my back when suddenly it felt as if "someone" was lying flat on top of me. This is hard to explain, but whatever it was—felt not like a "physical body"—but a much lighter non-physical presence. I could feel some type of weight pushing down on me, but an invisible-intangible type of weight if it makes sense. Still half asleep, I tried pushing "it" off of me, unsuccessfully. Then, realizing that it was a spirit, unable to free myself from that uncomfortable sensation, I pushed it away, while verbally ordering it to leave at once. And this is when the most incredible thing happened.

By now wide awake, I saw a transparent silhouette, a humanoid shape of some type—literally "jump" from on top of me—onto the night table to my right. I truly wish there was a better way to describe it, but that's the closest I can come. Basically, some type of transparent human silhouette jumped literally, from my bed—onto my night table—to then vanish. And that's precisely when my cellphone, charging on that same night table, started to ring. Keep in mind that the whole incident, from feeling the initial pressure over my body—to my cell phone ringing, all happened in less than five seconds.

With my eyes wide open and now fully awake, I could distinctively hear the ringing cellphone, but it wasn't the usual ring I was accustomed to, but instead a different type of ring, one I had never heard before. A fast repetitive pulsating type ring, something like, "ring-ring-ring-ring!"

Somewhat annoyed about the entire incident, I sat on the side of the bed looking at the ringing phone on the night table. I noticed that in addition to the incessant ringing, in sync with each ring, the phone's screen flashed off and on very brightly. I had never seen my phone doing anything similar before; it is true that the screen would normally light up when the phone rang, but in this case, it lit up as bright as a neon bulb. I grabbed the phone and flipped it open.

"This is not a normal phone call; someone must be trying to text me," I thought. What I found on the screen was neither a call nor a text message, but instead a "countdown." Perplexed, I read it. Below is a verbatim copy of what I found on my phone's screen,

Countdown Name: New Age
Time: 11.14 pm
Date: 12-21-2012
Time Remaining: 805 Days, 13 Hours, 25 Minutes, XX Seconds.
(The "seconds" value changing rapidly with each passing second).

Trying to make sense of it, I looked at the screen perplexed. "What could this mean—did I put it there?" I asked myself. I tried very hard to remember if I had somehow programmed that countdown into my phone and forgot all about it, but I was sure I had not. I sat on the side of my bed for several minutes; I could not recall doing so at all. What could have the reason been, for me to program such a countdown into my phone in the first place? I could swear that I had never programmed anything into any of my phones—countdowns or anything else for that matter.

Later, during breakfast, the incident still fresh in my mind, I tried to reason my way through it, in an attempt to arrive to a logical explanation. Using a process of elimination, I was 100% certain that I had not programmed that countdown into my phone, but let's for argument's sake, suppose that I had somehow—and that I had forgotten all about it. Here are the questions, which simply put, did not add up.

—A) Why would a countdown alarm go off some 805 days before it was supposed to?

—B) Why would it go off at the exact same instant when the entity (for lack of a better word) jumped from my bed—onto the night table?

There is more. Like all modern phones, my phone has a dozen or so ring-tones you can choose from, but when I tried each and every one of them, none came even close to the ring I heard earlier that morning. How can I explain that?

Reluctantly, I had to accept the facts at hand, and conclude that "someone" was trying to tell me "something." And that's what I did for pretty much the rest of the day; try to determine what that something could have been. One thing, which I was sure about, was that there was no doubt that the phone incident had to be linked with the entity in my bed. And because I seldom believe in coincidences, I had to accept the fact that it was indeed the entity that caused my phone's alarm to go off. I mean, what else could I have concluded? What would you have done in my place? In the end, I had to accept the fact that the entity or whatever it was, was somehow trying to tell me or remind me about something. And based on what I found on the phone's screen, I couldn't think of any other possible explanation, than to remind me that December 2012 was fast approaching.

Why was that particular date so important you ask? It was important because as Seth had already explained long before, that date did not signify the "end-times scenario" Armageddon-mongers would have liked us to believe, but instead the ushering of a New-Era. Thus, I had no other choice but to conclude, that the *phone* incident had to represent a "reminder" of some type. That it was time to go back working on my book again, this book.. What other explanation could there have been?

And so, after a couple years' break, I started writing again. And here I am, after many years of hard work, researching every single bit of information I could put my hands on, recalling as much detail from every encounter with Seth. I can now finally take a well-deserved breath of relief in the knowledge that I have completed the task I was given. For contrary to what I thought when I first started, writing this book was not to become just another hobby, or a side-project of some kind, but clearly and without a doubt, the single most important project of my entire life. My humble contribution to mankind if you like.

I would have liked to write more, but a book cannot go on forever. I sincerely hope this book has served its intended purpose. I hope someone—somewhere found within it, that little piece of the puzzle they needed, to help them along on their own personal Spiritual growth. As I said earlier, the purpose of this book was not to try and change anyone's mind, the scope was simply to share my story with whoever cared to read about it, share information I was fortunate to receive, allowing me a much better understanding and appreciation for life itself, my reason for being here—my existence.

As Seth once said, "It matters not whether folks believe in God or not, Creation, the power of Love and Reincarnation, for God will still exist, He will still Create, He will still Love them, and they will still reincarnate, regardless!"

Now, my sessions with Seth ended mid-1997. He said at the time that based on our present level of evolution, that was as much information as he could possibly give me. He reiterated the fact that we were then entering an altogether new phase—a new philosophy and a whole new set of beliefs. This new era, which he said started in the mid '70s, was to coincide with the often-mentioned 2012 date. But not the apocalyptic-end-of-days we often hear in the movies about, but what he instead called, "A New Spiritual Era."

As I mentioned, Seth reiterated that this transitional phase would only last about sixty years. And circa 2072 would be when another major turning point in our spiritual evolution would be introduced. He went on saying that the so-called 2012 shift—we were all so concerned with, contrary to what it was heralded as, was a "precursor," a transition, a gradual easing, into an altogether "New Philosophy," to be fully established by the time 2072 comes along.

His work here was done he said, and that he would move onto other planes where his contribution was needed most. And despite his disconnecting with this Plane for a while, I, *and others*, would be able to "connect," or communicate with him, just by asking.

Other than very recently, (June 2016) *when he appeared briefly to answer an important question I had asked*, true to form, I have never had any more sessions with Seth, since 1997. As far as his "presence" goes however, it is a whole different story. I can feel his presence next to me, slightly above my right shoulder, all of the time. And before he left, Seth and I made an agreement of sorts. "How will I know that you will still hear me?" I asked.

"Simple," he said, "every time you ask a question, pay attention to the very first set of numbers you see in front of you. If you happen to be driving, your car clock, the license plate on the car in front of you, a billboard and so on. Or if you are home, your TV, or the time on your microwave and so on. Even, or sequential numbers," he continued, "imply a positive response, while what you call 'odd' numbers imply a negative response."

"Can you be more specific?" I asked.

"Sets of numbers like 1-2-3, or 5-5-5 for instance, they imply a 'yes.' Conversely sets of unrelated numbers like 8-5-7, 1-7-0, etc., all mean 'no'! And the more similar or sequential the numbers are, the more favorable the response," he said.

"Give me an example?" I asked.

"3:33, or 11:11, for instance is a definite—very strong Yes! Or you are on the right track. While combinations such as 1-2-3, 7-8-9, 2-4-6 or 10-20-30, are more a 'maybe' than a 'yes,'" he said.

"Ok. I get it," I said.

True to form, almost daily, I ask Seth a mental question, perhaps while driving my car, I look at the radio dial, and it would display "11:11" or "09:09." A license plate would read "something-222," or "456-something." And the main reason why I wanted to mention this, is because many have asked me about this very topic, specifically, *"Does it mean anything, when you have a question in your mind—and the first thing you see is your digital clock displaying a strangely sequential or matching time?"*

Yes it does! Again, no coincidences exist! That is simply your personal Guide, your higher-self if you like, trying to interact with you, guide you along. Believe it, welcome it, and above all, thank them.

Just a few days ago the strangest thing happened. I logged into my bank's website and opened a new account, and in it I deposited exactly $10,000.19 *(Ten thousand dollars and nineteen cents.)* Why 19 cents you might ask? For good omen, the 19th is my birth date; hence I have always considered the number 19 to be my "lucky number," no other reason.

As I opened the account at the end of the month, on the first day of the following month, the bank calculates whatever the interest happens to be, and deposits it into the account.

The next morning, not even thinking about the interest component, I logged back into the account to make sure it was properly setup. Only a minute earlier however, I had mentally asked Seth a question on a personal matter, completely unrelated to the bank account. I had just put an offer on a new home, and I asked him if it would be accepted. I could not believe my eyes when I looked at the new account balance, which had changed from the original amount of $10,000.19 to $10,019.00 after interest. Well, I now live in that home.

Now, this *indirect connection with Seth point,* brings to mind a somewhat humorous incident, which took place about ten years ago. I received a call from a psychologist one day. He said that from a friend we had in common, he had learnt about what he called, "an unusual conversation I was having with an unusual being." And that, as he was writing a paper on a similar subject he said, he wanted to ask me a few questions. So he asked me if I would be willing to meet him at his studio. But from the phone call alone I could already tell that the polite but somewhat sarcastic sounding voice was that of a diehard skeptic. I instinctively knew that his only intention was to reinforce his personal believe that only material-physical things could exist, but I still accepted to meet him, and a few days later I went to his studio.

We sat across from each other. I felt immediately at ease, he on the other hand appeared somewhat nervous. After a minute of idle talk he finally posed the much-anticipated question. "So, what can you tell me about this so-called Spirit you're supposedly communicating with?" He asked.

Having learned that when in an awkward situation—you should always answer a question with another question, "What would you like me to tell you?" I replied.

"Well, I must confess that I am somewhat skeptic about these things. I am a scientist you know, I hold a doctorate in psychology, it is my duty almost—to question anything that cannot be proven physically in a lab, but I am curious to know regardless," he said.

"I totally understand," I said, "but I can feel Seth has something to say before we begin."

"What does he want to tell me?" He asked with a smirk on his face.

"I will speak for him," I said, "but I must forewarn you that I have no control over what he may or may not say. Is that ok with you?" I said.

"Well sure, go ahead," he somewhat nervously replied.

I started talking. "Seth says that you're in the process of packing up your bags and moving to Toronto in less than a week. The official reason for the move is to find better opportunities there, while the real reason— that only you would know, is to get as far as you can from your mother, who according to you, is driving you insane."

With his eyes wide open, and totally skipping the part about his mother, "But how did you know that I am moving to Toronto?" He asked.

"I didn't, Seth did," I replied. "And by the way," I continued, "Seth would also like to point out, that it would be best if you called-off your upcoming wedding, as the homosexual orientation you're trying so hard to hide, will totally come out of the closet within a year. Marrying a woman will not change who you are. And if you do marry, she will divorce you soon after," I said.

(I felt extremely embarrassed saying this, but I couldn't hold it in. I could actually sense a certain amount of frustration coming from Seth himself, something that I had never experienced before).

His face white as a ghost—the psychologist asked, "But what do you mean?" Then after a moment of hesitation, realizing that he could hide nothing from Seth, he said, "Thank you Marco, really thank you for this information. And please thank Seth for me too. This information will spare me from a lot of headaches, but could you please keep it confidential?"

"Of course," I said. *(And writing about this episode here does not mean that I did not keep my promise, for I never mentioned his name.)* I got the distinct impression that much like me, Seth was simply annoyed with the nice psychologist whose sole purpose for inviting me to his office was to make a fool out of me—and by extension, Seth. I think we both learned a very valuable lesson that day, but especially him. I don't believe he will ever again call anyone over to essentially ridicule them. But the thing that I found most peculiar was that as he himself said, "He only believed in tangible things"—while his work *supposedly* consisted of helping folks deal with their "psychological issues." But since when I ask, did "psychological issues" become tangible?

Now, over time, I have become accustomed to this whole "Seth adventure." I am no longer surprised at anything; it has become a way of life for me. Premonitions, knowing in advance who's coming to visit or who's about to call me, it now happens on a daily basis. Just the other day for instance (July 15th 2016) out of the blue, I started thinking about a very good friend of mine who lived in another city, but so intensely that I had a hard time concentrating on my work—and for no apparent reason. When we lived in the same city, my friend Gino and I were very close. And when I moved several years ago, we kept in touch talking on the phone about once a week. This was a strange sensation I felt however, we had just talked two days prior and everything seemed normal. But somehow, it just did not feel right, it kept bothering me all day, until that evening when I got home, something told me to check the obituaries for the city where my dear friend Gino lived. And my heart sank when Gino's obituary was right there at the very top. He had just passed the day before, unexpectedly. *Rest in peace my dear friend.*

And so I walk this beautiful life, mindful of an experience most would call "special" but that I know is available to everyone. Something I wish everyone would get the opportunity to experience, for I know that just as I have—everyone else would also greatly benefit from. But why do most folks seem unable to have similar experiences you ask?

The only answer I can give you is that most people's "door" or more precisely their heart and mind, is unfortunately closed. I wish we would all realize that by so doing we are shutting ourselves out from infinite knowledge, wisdom and compassion, all there, available to us for the taking. All we need to do is simply believe that we can, and then ask for it. When you shut yourself out, you are not doing yourself any favors.

And I am not suggesting that you take this book as the golden truth and adopt it as your new way of life, for as you may recall from the very beginning of the book, that was the exact opposite of what I—and Seth intended. This book's purpose, and, *I believe*, Seth's through it, was to share information, the rest—as always, is up to you. And if reading this book has helped you, even if just a little, then it has done what it was intended to. The "true message" of the book—its essence, was simply to allow you to realize—that whether rich, poor, healthy, sick, black, white, blue or yellow, gay, straight, wheelchair bound, one leg, two legs, or three, you are in fact a great-great deal more <u>Important</u>, <u>Essential</u>, and most of all, <u>Sacred</u> than you might think—or have been led to believe. That was the intended message! One more time—and in bold letters.

You are a great deal more Important, Essential, and Sacred than you give yourself credit for!

Thus, do not let anyone tell you otherwise, for they truly do not know of what they speak about. Some folks, convinced that they must pay for a sin they never had anything to do with, condemn themselves to spend their entire lives in a self-imposed prison of sorts—and choose to live their lives with their head in the sand, sure that they're under the constant watch of an unforgiving, merciless, revengeful, uncaring god, who—they believe, spends his days pen and paper in hand, keeping track of who he's going to reward and who he's going to zap every day.

That's their god, not yours!

Your God, All-That-Is, <u>is in you, within you, He is you</u>! Let me remind you once again of the two droplets of water in the ocean who wanted to know "where" exactly the ocean (their creator) was. They looked and looked but the ocean was nowhere to be found. Then one day, the two droplets of water suddenly realized, that not only were they inside and totally immersed in that ocean, but that the ocean was also inside them, thus they themselves were part of that ocean.

Busy looking outwardly, we fail to recognize that—had we searched within instead, we would've discovered that not only are we made of the same building blocks, but that we in fact <u>are</u> within the Creator. However, the incredible Sacredness in all of this is, that despite the fact that we reside within our Creator—despite the fact that our Creator <u>is</u> in each single atom that makes us—thus <u>is</u> every single atom that makes us, we still retain our unique individuality and freedom of thinking. And much like the droplet of water in the ocean who longs to find its creator-the-ocean in all of the wrong places, we too look for our Creator in all of the wrong places.

"Omnipresent! God is in everything, He is everything, and He is everywhere," we are told. But in that same breath we are also told, that "He is somewhere up there—but not down here." Then to complicate things further, we're constantly reminded that despite the fact that He is everywhere and He is everything, He couldn't possibly be "us." Do you see anything wrong with this picture?

At first examination, everything! But not once you remind yourself of the grandiose "play" we have all agreed to participate in. So, the next time you hear of atrocities on TV, wars and so on, simply remind yourself that "that is how we chose to learn and grow as a society," and send them love. And you have done your part!

Now, earlier in the book, we briefly touched on the so-called "Law of Attraction." In the last few years, mostly on the Internet, a new wave of information is starting to emerge, addressing the "new ideology." So much so that it has become fashionable to include the intriguing modality in just about everything we do.

Well, for starters, this so-called "new law or idea" is not new at all. Secondly, when misunderstood, it can do you more harm than good.

It is not new because it has existed as long as mankind itself, more precisely as long as Creation itself. This is in fact the very thing I have been hinting to—many times in this book. It is the power, which you know you have—but you don't believe you have! The power you inherited from Source, hence you inherently possess. You are not apart from, but instead part of Creation, thus the Creator. In effect (allow me to repeat this one more time) just like the droplet of water is part of the ocean it resides in, you are part of the Creator - you reside in!

But why have we been so busy looking for our Creator in all of the wrong places?

The simple-short answer is that we've all been subject to centuries of misinformation that, for obvious reasons, tried very hard to convince us of our externality—to, instead of our internality—to our Creator. Over time, this has caused us to lose touch so-to-speak, forget our innate Sacred Powers we've always and inherently possessed. Powers, we once used as a normal fact of life.

Thus, this wrong indoctrination can be said to be the main reason why, misunderstanding—thus misusing the "law of attraction" can do you more harm than good. Much like you can't lose the fifteen pounds you gained over the last fifteen years—by dieting for 15 days, you simply cannot undo centuries of misguidance, by simply watching a documentary or two on the so-called "Law of Attraction." It takes years of practice, research, and most importantly, understanding, applying, putting the principle to use as it were intended to, or you'll end up more disappointed and discouraged than when you started. In the end however, where the many books and documentaries on the topic all fall short, is that while they all do an excellent job describing the principle and its mechanics, they all fail in giving power where power is due—you the individual!

In all fairness, it also takes considerable effort on the part of the individual, for as the saying goes *"You can lead a horse to water, but you can't make it drink."*

It would be preposterous to think that one could undo centuries of damage with just one book. We cannot expect someone who's been subject to centuries of negative indoctrination—to read one single book and suddenly scream "eureka," much less accept the fact that they are solely responsible and in total control—"creators" in fact, of their own life experience, when they for so long have been told and believed the exact opposite. *"A bunch of worthless sinners, totally and constantly at the mercy of a devil,"* is what they've been told they are.

"You are constantly being watched, rewarded, or punished as needed," they've been relentlessly reminded—and that they should be grateful for it too. But that's only because that is what the "Play-Script" calls for!

Therefore, watching a documentary promising you that: "There exists a Universe ready to fulfill any and all of your wishes just for the asking—in an Aladdin's magic lamp fashion," can in fact only produce the exact opposite effect of that which was intended. For such an idea will only reinforce the very problem it was intended to remove, as it implies that there exists a Universe, external—separated and apart from you— ready to deliver upon your every wish—"but only if you ask the right way" they caution you.

Hence, the ill-prepared individual has no other choice than to envision a "warehouse" of sorts, filled with all sorts of goods, from sports cars to homes, to mountains of cash, to yachts and big screen TVs, all in a semi-materialized state—there waiting to be delivered to them (provided they asked in the proper fashion,) UPS style, over onto this side." But the question remains, who's in charge of that ginormous warehouse?

Hence, a warehouse manager, a middleman, or some type of Genie of sorts, must be brought into the equation, ready to deliver the goods to you for the asking. *"All you have to do is ask,"* you are told, but the catch is, "you must formulate the question in a certain way." Hence, when the goods are not delivered, you are promptly blamed, for you must have not formulated the question properly.

What you instead need to understand is that no magical warehouse exists anywhere ready to ship goods to those lucky individuals who manage to discover the elusive secret. And more importantly, what you need to realize, once and for all, is that <u>it is you</u> the individual who has not only the key to—but also the whole warehouse itself—within! The warehouse is not somewhere in the sky or some other exotic place, but instead <u>in your own mind</u>! But why is it in your own mind you may ask? Because as you may recall from earlier in the book,

<u>In your mind</u>, is where everything is!

A few pages back however, we talked about a store backroom of sorts called "Framework-2." Its purpose was to bring forth you may recall, whatever you wished here in "Framework-1" and I agree that in light of what we just discussed here, this may sound like a contradiction of sorts, that I may have given the wrong impression by suggesting that "a sort of warehouse exists somewhere." But that was only half of the story, for I too had no choice but to gradually introduce you to the concept of how the mechanics of creating your own experience work. However, as you may recall I never hinted or implied that there existed a middleman, a warehouse manager, or genie, anywhere between you and the goods. Thus, here is the other half of the story that completes the picture:

You are the "<u>Asker</u>," the "<u>Creator</u> of," the <u>Warehouse</u>, and the <u>Goods</u>. And last but not least, you are also your own <u>Genie</u> or <u>UPS man</u>!

Throughout this book, I've stated time and time again that you are not "apart" from Creation—but instead a-part-of! You are not someone who was created, to then be cast abandoned to live a life of suffering, as punishment for sins you never had anything to do with." Instead, what you are is,

"A Spark of Sacred Energy!" An individual Spark of Sacred Energy, living in an infinite sea of Sacred Energy, All-That-Is the Creator! All-That-Is did not create you externally—for there isn't anywhere "external" to be in. All-That-Is created you within. For how could there be an outside to All-That-Is?

So, it is not that you "ask or wish" for something, a new car, a home, a job or even a spouse—to then get it delivered from some semi-transparent warehouse located on some semi-transparent level. <u>What you seek and desire is already here.</u> Your future partner or red Ferrari, is not being built in an "ethereal warehouse," to be delivered to you at a later date. They are already here! What is "being built" instead, are the "events" and circumstances. The events and circumstances that will bring you to the object of your desires are in a constant state of flux, the "energy" being constantly remolded, changed, as it tries to match your constantly shifting expectations and desires. And it goes without saying that;

You're the one who's doing all of the molding!

For the simple act of formulating a thought—any thought, good or bad—if maintained, sends out an increasingly stronger, specific magnetic pattern, a signal that will seek and find that resonating—in-kind matching frequency. Thus, said object, person or experience you seek, will maneuver their ways, until their paths intersects with yours—and yours with theirs. Hence, stop being a "moving target"—constantly re-thinking what you want.

Instead, set a Goal, focus on it, and stay the course!

In an article on Entrepreneur.com by Grant Cardone, here is what he said, *"You can never get truly wealthy by diversifying your investments. Wall Street has done a great job of selling the public on this idea of diversifying because it benefits Wall Street. Mark Cuban says, 'Diversification is for idiots.' Andrew Carnegie said, 'Put all your eggs in one basket—and then watch that basket. If you want to create real wealth learn everything you can about a space—and go all in.'"* (Source: www.entrepreneur.com)

In other words, follow your heart, decide what you want—and stay the course. <u>And the events and circumstances will find you instead!</u>

And now my dear friends, you have the other half of the story!

And this mechanism works equally well in any situation, regardless of how positive or negative, constructive or destructive the original thought was. Your higher self then simply steers you and the object or situation you seek—to a common intersecting point. But this not by some type of "magic game" the Universe plays with you; this is simply "how" the Universe works! But how does the notion that you create your own experience actually work?

I shall endeavor to explain this fascinating process as plainly as I can. Basically, I am going to describe the very process that I myself used to eventually grasp the concept. This allowed me to gradually overcome the many mental blocks I too had been programmed with and had accepted as reality. However, allow me to start by giving you a few words of advice that could drastically change your life for the better.

Suppose that you found yourself in a difficult situation, perhaps a job that is making your life miserable. You can't seem to be able to get out of the so-called "rat-race." Or suppose that you do not seem to be able to find the right life-partner. Or you don't feel in control of your financial situation, or any other situation for that matter. The question is, "what is causing that 'blockage,' what is hindering the normal and plentiful flow of the Universe to come through to you?"

As much as I dislike telling you, and for as much as you are going to dislike hearing it,

You are your own "blockage!"

But you mustn't be too harsh on yourself and take all of the blame, for as we saw a page or two earlier, you are the result of centuries of negative conditioning. Thus over time, this constant influx of misinformation has made you into your own worst enemy. You are the bottleneck to the infinite wealth and wellbeing that is yours by birthright. You may be wondering why you seem unable to tap into that divine abundance that is supposedly there for the taking—so that you too can enjoy an accomplished happy life. You may be struggling to make ends meet perhaps—and then you turn on the TV and see folks who seem to have anything they wish for. Some have so much wealth in fact, that they don't even know how to spend it.

Well, if you asked me to try and explain this whole "injustice" in just a couple of sentences, I would have to say that first and foremost you must understand and accept this very simple but golden rule.

"Thoughts are objects waiting to materialize!"

And secondly, you must find the direction your own personal "current" flows in. Then stop swimming against it—and instead start swimming with it. Search your heart and understand once and for all:

What your "Life's Calling" is!

You switch jobs every few years, even every few months, but you cannot seem to be able to find what you should do. You search but you cannot find. What is the right job, business or profession for you? The answer is a lot simpler than you think—and it has been right there in front of you, all of your entire life,

Do for a living whatever it is that you do as a hobby!

"What?" You may say. "How could I possibly turn my fishing hobby into a business? How could I turn my passion for soccer, my passion for writing, my passion for fixing computers, or my passion for music into a business? Where would I get the funds? And how in the world would I pay my bills and feed my family in the meantime?"

Well I am sure that you must have heard of other folks having done just that! You must know of someone who—tired of being yelled at by their boss, decided to get their act in gear one day and took the responsibility and their own life into their own hands. I am sure you must know of someone who has opened a fishing store, a computer shop, a sporting goods store, became a successful writer or even a successful musician.

"But they would surely have had to receive some type of help from someone, or maybe they were just plain lucky," you convince yourself.

Plainly put, these are the excuses folks make to justify why they are not doing as well as they would like. They simply put, refuse to assume responsibility for their own life. Most folks simply cannot see through the fog and realize that not only must they be willing to assume full responsibility for their own life, but most importantly recognize and accept,

The Sacred Power that inherently resides within them.

So, instead of making excuses about why you cannot assume responsibility for yourself, <u>understand your inner power</u> instead—get off your comfy derriere and do something about it!

Start paying attention to the things in your life that seem to "flow" effortlessly and make you happy effortlessly. And even if they promise to make you a ton of money, steer away from those ventures or activities that seem to go "against your grain" and make you miserable.

What you enjoy, <u>what you have a passion for</u>—whatever that may happen to be, is always your "natural flow," your life's calling, with no exceptions—no matter what it happens to be! The things that you enjoy and come "natural" to you, are always the "right path," while the things you do not enjoy, or feel "wrong" are always the wrong path. That's simply your Higher-Self's guiding you. So why fight it? Simply allow it!

This is the very reason by the way, why many who inherit a successful business from their father, will—within a few years, fail. This is because that was their father's dream and passion. Not theirs!

The universal laws at play here, as always, act in a neutral fashion; they don't favor one person over the next. When you say, "that person is lucky," you're doing yourself more harm than you could possibly imagine. For starters, what is "luck?" Is it something you buy at Wal-Mart? Is it something some folk's find hidden in a treasure chest? Remember what we said before? If you consider yourself "unlucky," you are calling for

Framework-2 (your Higher Self) to respond in-kind—and keep you in that state. Your Higher-Self must assume that "unlucky" is the experience you are seeking to have. Thus it will give you just that! This couldn't be any easier to understand!

Why you ask? This is because the Universe—since it does not concern itself with "time," only operates from the "now" perspective. Therefore, it does not recognize the idea of "wanting" or "wishing," for that only implies something that is not yet here. Thus, when you think of yourself as "being unlucky"—and perhaps think that some other "lucky folks" don't deserve such bounty, and you are perhaps a little jealous, then your Higher-Self—hearing you, has to match, thus gives you exactly that. It will keep you in that unlucky state and all that it entails—jealousy and all. It will keep you in that state of wishing and wanting!

For, as long as you want or wish for something, you plainly "<u>do not have it</u>." Thus, "not having it" <u>is what you get</u>!

Simply stated, your Higher-Self does not and cannot discriminate! It must respond equally, *it has no choice*, to all that its physical counterpart wishes to experience, regardless of whether they end up liking the outcome or not! For in creating the Universe, All-That-Is set forth a Divine Creative Force. This is not something, which some folks can opt out of, we all have it, whether we like it or not. You are a part of, inside of Creation, hence yourself a "creator," thus you automatically inherited that creative force. The ocean couldn't possibly produce a single droplet of water—which did not possess the same properties and chemical composition as itself. Therefore, when you analyze a droplet of water, you are in fact analyzing the ocean.

All beings, regardless of what or where they are, regardless of what they believe or what they've been led to believe, carry within, not only a divine spark from the Creator, but they are themselves "immersed" in Creation—hence the Creator! We can say that a droplet of water represents the ocean, but it is not the ocean. Likewise you represent the Creator, but you're not the Creator! The Creator is instead in you! And just like a droplet of water is inherently connected to every other droplet of water in the ocean—you too possess the inherent ability to tap into that infinite Creative Source, and draw from it, and from it "create" your own personal experience.

But you must know—and above all accept, the rules!

—**Rule 1)** You must assume the right mindset, <u>for your "mindset" is to your life, what your car's steering wheel is to your car</u>. This does not mean that you must go to a place of worship once a week or give money to every charity out there; these are choices you make that have nothing to do with what you receive from Framework-2 (your Higher-Self.) And to really drive the point home, it matters not, as far as Framework-2 is concerned, whether your intentions are good or bad. <u>You decide the experience</u> and your Higher-Self simply delivers! As we said earlier, Framework-2 is that portion that is also you, through which you get the energy you need to materialize whatever experience you wish to have here.

—**Rule 2)** Accept once and for all that you and only you, are responsible for everything that happens to you, and by "everything" I mean everything—good, and not so good! Therefore, think with your own brain! You and only you are who decides what you are going to get and experience in life. As a co-creator, you create your own experience. You therefore also create your own rewards as well as chastisements. It is true that All-That-Is creates everyone and everything—but it is also true that He gave everyone and everything "Free Will." It is therefore entirely your decision what you are going to do with your life, whether or not you are going to put it to good use or otherwise. The laws of manifestation are still the same; they're not there to "judge," but instead manifest—hence manifest is what they do.

So, stop cursing at—and envying or blaming wealthy or what you consider lucky people, if that's what you're doing. The only thing they're guilty of is "knowing what the rules of the game are," and most of all, doing the work necessary to achieve their objectives! They have a clearly defined goal in life. But most of all they have the unwavering belief and most importantly the expectation, that they can achieve that goal—no matter what the obstacles! They are more than willing to do the necessary legwork, the necessary research. They educate themselves not only about the "goal" itself, business venture or profession they wish to get into, but also on how the rules of the Universe work. They don't simply give up at the first obstacle, citing "lack of luck!" What you call "lucky folks" never waver. They never lose focus of the goal—and spend as much time and energy as it takes to achieve it—no matter what. For as we said before, the "clay" is being constantly molded, thus, if you change your mind every other day, it will never amount to a finished sculpture.

Do you know what the only difference between a successful and an unsuccessful individual is? <u>The first does not quit!</u> But do you know what the most amazing part of all of this is? All the information you need is available on the web—and free of charge! And for as sad as this is, when it comes to achieving your goals, friends and family can sometimes be—believe it or not, your worst enemies. "Get a real job," or "this is not going to work," they warn you. But successful people do not accept any negative input from anyone, not even their own mother. For as much as we love them, perhaps out of pure protection instinct, they are usually the first to discourage you from what they see as "taking risks." Successful folks never doubt or second-guess themselves; they steadfastly pursue their goals, never losing faith in their ability to accomplish them.

And just for the fun of it, let me tell you a very short but true story. In his younger years, my uncle Sal was a semi-pro motorcycle racer. But every time he raced, his Mother (my Granny) went to see him off at the starting line and yelled: "Please don't go fast my son!"

Now, <u>like attracts like</u>! Knowing this, successful folks mingle with like-minded folks who share similar interests. They share knowledge, thus mutually benefitting one another. "You become what you practice," thus mingling with successful folks can only make you successful. And I don't need to remind you what mingling with negative folks will turn you into.

Are you starting to see why the so-called, "Law of Attraction," only seems to work for some but not for others? Why do only few succeed in life, while the vast majority does not? Are you starting to see the reason why 95% of folks out there work for the remaining 5%?

The reason is simply that very few have the willpower, the courage, the initiative, the self-confidence, the unshakable strength of character necessary to achieve their goals. So the next time you see on TV famous successful folks such as Oprah, Bill Gates, Ellen DeGeneres, Warren Buffett, Steve Jobs, Mark Zuckerberg, Donald Trump, Michael Dell, Mark Cuban, Steven Spielberg, Elon Musk, and so on, instead of being jealous, do a Google search—and I guarantee you that in every instance, next to their net worth, you will find the words "Self-Made!"

It all truly starts—*and ends,* with you my dear reader friend! You are a "magnet" immersed in a sea of Magnetic-Sacred-Creative-Energy. Your thoughts, and more importantly your beliefs, continuously send-out magnetic vibrations—vibrations that go out and find matching—like energy, drawing it to you, thus giving you more of the same. So, reciting affirmation after affirmation, asking for wealth or health, concentrating on what it is that you want to accomplish, can only bring you the exact opposite of what it is that you are trying to achieve!

Read the above paragraph again, and see if you can spot where the problem lies. Here is a hint, it has to do with the "now" factor.

—**Question:** What are you "now" doing?

—**Answer:** You are (now) <u>asking</u>. You are (now) <u>wanting</u>!

Then what's your poor "Higher-Self" supposed to do, if that is what you see yourself doing now? It concludes that you do not "now" have it—hence, the obedient Higher-Self gives you more of the same, thus keeping you in a state of asking and wanting, a state of "not having it."

And most folks have their heads filled with conflicting ideas. On one hand they "wish," *wrong thing to do*, to be wealthy, while at the same time they harbor the belief that wealthy folks are greedy and evil.

They wish they had a huge bank account, but at the same time, do not want to be bothered with the responsibility of maintaining it, managing that wealth, investing, and keeping that money growing. And that's precisely the reason why most who do win at the lottery, will, within a short year or two, be back into whatever financial state they were prior to winning, or worse.

You must decide once and for all! One minute you get all excited and you want to open that business or get that better paying job, the next minute you begin to doubt yourself again. One minute you imagine yourself living in abundance, the next minute you curse at your unpaid electricity bill. Money is also, *of course*, a form of "Energy" and as such, must flow freely. So what can you do instead?

Start by being grateful for what you already have, no matter how small or how little. Bless and enjoy your money as you pay those bills, buy those groceries and meet your obligations. For when you do, you're allowing others to earn their money, pay their bills and meet their obligations, thus you create a positive "flow" that will benefit them as well as yourself. Begrudging spending money or paying bills can only create a bottleneck—a blockage in your natural and plentiful flow or energy, "money energy" in this case.

Be a grateful giver! Do not give—expecting to be rewarded later, but instead give for the simple joy of giving, for when you give gratefully, happily, freely and with no strings attached, the same experience will be mirrored back to you—not from a genie, but from your Higher-Self. As Seth bluntly reminded me, "if you despair, because you do not have enough money, start by gladly giving away some!"

Few have the mindset to handle great wealth. What would you do if you suddenly won the lottery? Would you hide it? Stash it away inside a mattress, to then spend sleepless night after sleepless night worrying about someone stealing it from you? For that clearly demonstrates that you're simply not ready to be wealthy! Or would you enjoy it and spend it with "gusto" creating your dreams and help others create theirs?

It all starts from you. Start by focusing on what you already have, no matter how little. Do not focus on what it is that you don't have—or what you wish to have.

Give thanks, give thanks, and give thanks again!

Be grateful for all the good things in your life—and also the not so good things, for they too are surely there to teach you something. Do not dwell on what is "wrong" with your friends, with people, with your country or with the world, focus on what is right instead! Start acting for what you are, a Co-Creator. At such, you are not only responsible for— but also entitled in the sharing, the beauty, and the abundance that flows naturally throughout the Universe. And above all, understand that you are never deprived when someone else gains, because abundance expands proportionally—to match desires, or better yet, state of mind!

Therefore, do not "ask" for things, simply "create," manifest them into your life. Do not wish for—but believe, <u>have faith</u> instead.

A Creator does not wish, ask or doubt—a Creator simply creates!

I am not implying that it is an easy thing to do. It is in fact extremely difficult to overcome indoctrinations, patterns, and habits that have made you into who you are today. For centuries, we have been conditioned to believe that we amount to nothing more than little undeserving, worthless sinners. We were told that there is a piper to pay for a sin that (provided there was one committed in the first place) we had nothing to do with. I am sure that by now you know the reasons.

And neither place the blame on others, for blaming keeps you having to do more of the same. For in the larger scheme of things, they did what they did—for they too are actors in a larger play. And no play ever existed that did not include good as well as bad guys. Truth be told, they served a greater purpose, for while playing the villain's role on the surface, they in fact showed you—in some cases forced you, to become a better you. They enriched your experience; you enriched theirs, and together you enriched the Creator's experience.

Now, contrary to the impression I might have given in the first part of the book, my "mission," is not to condemn those who are perceived to take advantage of the system, for I am very well aware that—as we said, it is all part of the larger movie script. Instead, my job is to help! Help those who want to be helped, those who want to know, those who want to better themselves, so that they can in turn help others. For information empowers!

What lies ahead in our future is nothing short of fantastic! It is true that on the surface it may appear as if some folks—misinterpreting the process, still prefer to steal, cheat, and lie, and they milk our beloved Mother Earth out of every last drop of natural resources. They too are slowly but surely vanishing, either dying of old age or passing the torch to their younger—more forward thinking heirs. The future is a future of sharing and co-operating at all levels. No longer there will be any room for those who wish to operate in the past. The time has come, a time of new beginnings, a time to let go of old limiting mindsets. It is time we finally realized and accepted "Who" we represent. We are all Sacred co-Creators living inside a Master Creator. The All-That-Is Gestalt.

Thus, Love is all there is—thus, All-That-Is, is Love!

If there were a single thing I wanted *this book* to achieve, is that it may have helped you to see that there is a lot more to <u>You</u> than you might have previously believed. Start from that realization! Accept "who" you are, or at the very least, Whom you represent! Love and honor yourself, for you are in fact a Sacred Being. And when in doubt, remind yourself of that little droplet of water that spent all of its life believing that it amounted to nothing more than an insignificant worthless little droplet of water, but then suddenly realized, that while it couldn't certainly call itself "the ocean," it was in fact an essential component of that magnificent ocean.

Now, there have been many Civilizations before us. Stop fooling yourself thinking that we are the first, the only and the last—because we are not! Civilizations have existed before, who knew WHO they represented. They had what we today would consider "superpowers," but not superman-like powers in the sense that they could fly, but superpowers in the sense that they knew their relationship with All-That-Is. They were aware of how precious and sacred their existence was. They did not, *as we do*, dismiss their dreams, visions, feelings, and imagination; they lived by them instead. They did not see them as "magical" as we do, for their life often depended on them. If their gut feeling told them that a saber-tooth tiger was hiding in that tall grass, it most likely was. There was a time when man knew how to use these and other tools, *tools that have always been available to us, but that we've forgotten how to use.* Tools like "sound" for instance. We use it mainly for entertainment, when in the past we used it to move very heavy objects, like for instance, the humongous blocks that built the Pyramids, and other impossibly heavy objects.

However, most of all we have forgotten our sacred God's given ways that are rightfully ours. It is surely not easy task to undo thousands of years of mental conditioning, but I urge you to try nonetheless. Simply start by waking up tomorrow morning and smile in the knowledge that you are not apart, but instead a sacred part of our Father and Creator. Get in the habit of doing so every morning. You are not going to believe the difference this alone will make.

Allow the All-That-Is God's given power of the Universe to work for you, but never at the expenses of someone else.

As often as you can, do not be afraid to re-awaken the inner-child in you, and act as if you were still one. For as a child, or when you act like one, you are as pure and as close to All-That-Is—as truest as you could possibly ever be. Thus do not spend too much time and effort trying to unravel the trivial things in life. Accept others—all others, no matter what their race, sexual orientation, personal beliefs or religion is.

And in case you are wondering what particular "religion" I subscribe to, or if you are trying to decide what religion you should choose. The answer is very simple. As I did years ago, ask yourself this question,

"Could God favor one religion over another?"

Therefore, it matters not which religion you are going to choose—or if any at all, simply bless! Bless all religions—as well as the atheist and the agnostic! And bless, even what may appear to you as against you, or your beliefs.

Do not acknowledge negativity; do not concentrate on trying to resolve it. And do not protest anything or partake in any demonstration against anything. For as you should know by now, "<u>that which you concentrate upon, you help in manifesting</u>." Hence, do not protest wars, for you will surely reinforce the experience of war, instead focus your energy on peace.

Do not predict a cure for any disease; instead try to envision a healthy world population. Do not concentrate or spend any energy speaking about what you do not want—or wish to go away.

Instead, concentrate; always speak about what you like.

Remember, "What you resist—persists," for it is the act of pushing against that gives strength to the problem you wish to eliminate.

Hence, when you declare war on drugs, poverty, or even obesity, you are fueling—spiritually adding to the strength of that which you want to eliminate. Thus, do not diet; concentrate on living a healthy lifestyle instead!

Remember that you're not a "Human Being having a Spiritual experience," but instead a "Spiritual Being having a Human experience!"

And above all, never forget WHO you represent!

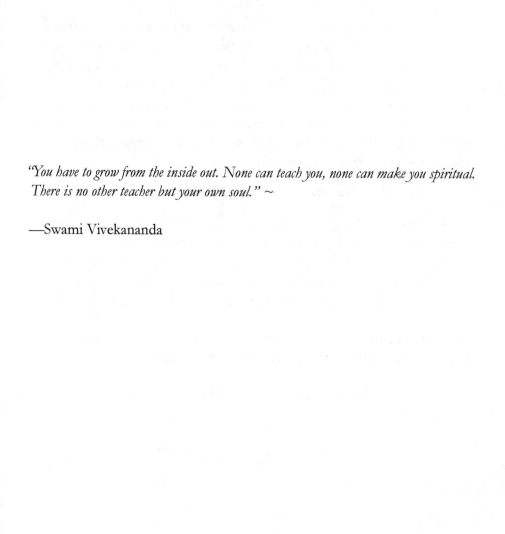

"You have to grow from the inside out. None can teach you, none can make you spiritual. There is no other teacher but your own soul." ~

—Swami Vivekananda

Chapter 11

Dr. Tyson's Dilemma

In these final pages, as promised, allow me to share yet two tremendously important and revealing pieces of information. However, let me first forewarn you, that some might see this next piece of information as disappointing or outright negative. We need to remind ourselves of the wider scope, the "Greater Design," only then will we understand that "it is all good" and as it was meant to be. Do you recall what I wrote at the very beginning of the book?

"From a human perspective, we're accustomed to think that a 'good versus evil' war is constantly being waged in the heavens—and by extension here on Earth. Think about it, what if—it were all One-Conscious-Intelligence, experimenting within, wanting to experience the full range of all that can be experienced?"

Now, throughout this book, we talked about "reincarnation," how we—each time we die—choose one particular life experience after another, and how each time we come back here to live that life. I know this will disappoint many, but I wish to remind you that I am only the "messenger," and if you paid attention to what you've been reading thus far in the book, I have hinted to what I am about to reveal, many, many times. Here it goes.

There is no "Re-incarnation" or "Coming back!" You are living it all now—simultaneously!

We simply cannot have it both ways. We couldn't possibly have a system where only the "now moment" exists—and also have a past and a future! You the Entity are simply projecting the entire sum-total of your experiences, <u>past and future included</u>—and everything in between, all at once, now, this very instant! You operate only and wholly from the "now moment!" Thus, from that now moment, you (the Entity) also conceive and project, both what you <u>from here</u> interpret as your "past," as well as, what you interpret as your "future."

<u>But only from here, not from the wider perspective of the Entity!</u>

As if a movie director, the Entity sees and knows the whole "movie" from beginning to end, at once—now! However, from the Human perspective you see your existence as a "spectator" would see that same movie, linearly, from beginning to end.

"Time" is an illusion, an illusion that affords us the experience of the "Past, Present and Future." Thus, everything exists only <u>now</u>! You are being born in—and living all of your lifetimes, simultaneously <u>now</u>! And you are also dying <u>now</u> and everything you have—and will ever do between these two points, all <u>now</u>! And for as incredible as it sounds, Dinosaurs, are still alive, now! So when you think of something in the past, or when a (real) psychic speaks of your future, what they are in fact doing, is tapping into your "now-pool," that holds all the things you did, are doing, and will do from a "time-based perspective." And when you go to a psychotherapist and have a "Past Life Regression" what you're really doing is "visiting" another of your lives. Not a previous life, but a concurrent one—"beside" this one.

And a so-called, "Deja-vu," is nothing more than a momentary un-syncing, a momentary glitch in the illusion of the passage of time. During a Deja-vu, you are not—as we normally think, "seeing something you had already done," you are instead briefly "peeping" through the curtain of "the illusion of time" so-to-speak, and you are actually seeing—if only for a moment, the true nature of time, past, present and future. All here, all at once! Simply put, you "perceive" the totality, the whole sum package of your total experience, now!

For it is all a dream, a vision, it therefore has no substance, no existence. "Life itself is only but a vision, a dream. Nothing exists; <u>it is all a dream</u>! The world, the starry sky, the sun and the moon, they have no existence, it is all but a dream! Nothing exists except empty space—and you the thought! But if you want to take it one step further, "you" also do not exist! Your body, your hair, your clothes, they're also but just a "thought," a dream actually. Do you recall what we said earlier?

All-That-Is, is simply "imagining" all of this, thus, you are simply put, being imagined!

But as disappointing as this may sound, look at the positive side of it. I don't know about you, but to me, dream or not—really makes no difference. Be it a "Dream" or even a "Simulation," I am enjoying every moment of it. And the best part is that because it is a dream, I have the power to change my own experience for the better, or any way I like, just by dreaming better dreams.

Just ask yourself this question. "How could have all of this been real? I mean, isn't this the strangest thing anyone could have ever imagined?"

We live a life, we work, we marry, we procreate, we play, we sleep, we drive our cars, we make our money, we spend it, and we do all of these things, all the while hanging by a thread—literally! And the amazing thing is, we do not know who or what is holding the other end of that thread! How could this have been real?

We live our life, struggling to get ahead, without knowing why—or if we will still be here the next day, or even the next minute. How can this be real?

A Universe so unimaginably large, so unimaginably inefficient and pointless, it could only exist but in a dream. How can this be real?

Consider this. We inhabit a planet; totally dependent upon a huge chunk of burning rock we call the Sun. And in its light, we live our life under the constant threat of extinction, and always one instant away from total annihilation. How could this be real?

This, while our beloved scientists do their best to reassure us that the Sun will keep on shining for yet many eons. But the truth is that no one has any clue about whether there will be a Sun—even tomorrow. For who or what could realistically stop it, if it, *for whatever reason*, decided to suddenly explode? How can this be real?

Let me ask you this, "if you had physically 'made' the Universe, is this how you would have made it?" Of course not! For the Universe is not being "made," but instead imagined. It is merely a thought in the mind of All-That-Is. These are all impossible impossibilities, except but in a dream. But am I implying that All-That-Is is also but a dream?

No! What is a dream, are the many gods we invented along the way. The gods who watch us suffer but do nothing about it, the gods we invented—to suit whatever argument we needed a god for—each time. That is a dream!

And that is precisely the reason why throughout this book I have been hinting to a larger God; "All-That-Is," that is not a dream! That is in fact, "Who" is doing all of the "dreaming!"

All-That-Is is a "State-Of-Being" where everything exists—including all man-made versions of deities and idols throughout history. Some were made in an attempt to comprehend "All-That-Is," some, where fabricated out of pure misinformation, but all because "that is what our movie script calls for." However, all exist within one larger-all-encompassing God. The movie director, All-That-Is!

—And last but not least, allow me to disclose the second piece of information I had promised earlier, and let me assure you that I am not exaggerating when I say that to those who understand its significance, this piece of information may very well represent—may I dare to suggest,

"The Holy Grail of Physics." Perhaps even "the Holy Grail of science." But allow me to remind you once again, that the information does not come from me, but from "Higher Sources"—from "Spiritual-Realms." Please bear that in mind all throughout this book, but especially now.

I was watching a documentary on TV one evening. The show commentator, the genius-scientist Dr. Neil deGrasse Tyson, said this.

"A recent scientific study shows that every time a particle (any particle) anywhere in the Universe changes—all the other particles in the Universe are instantaneously aware of the change."

In more mundane terms, what Dr. Tyson suggests, is that every time a particle in your body changes—all other particles in the Universe, including the particles that make up the Sun and the Moon, the zillions of stars, zillions of light years away, the particles that make the ice cream in your fridge, the particles that make the car parked in your neighbor's garage, and the particles making that bird, flying on the opposite side of the planet, are also aware of that change in you! At that exact same precise instant! This is a proven fact!

And our scientists have clearly established that, "All of the molecules in the Universe are somehow communicating to—and in direct-simultaneous contact with one another"—and we haven't got a single clue about "how" or "why" that happens.

And for as much as I admire him, not even Sir Stephen Hawking, who is widely considered to be the brightest scientific mind alive today knows the answer. And it may not be too farfetched to propose that this next piece of information may turn out to be the elusive, *"One simple, elegant equation that explains everything in the Universe,"* he is said to have been looking for, all of his entire life! It comes down to this.

The Universe is not made, *as it is commonly agreed upon,* "of an infinite number of Particles, all connected to, and all communicating to one another"—but instead:

A single Particle in an infinite void of nothingness. Nothing else but a single Particle!

And because it is but a single particle in an infinite void of nothingness, no pre-existing physical laws exist to interfere with it in any way—or that the particle needs to abide to, or be limited by. For "limitations" only appear in the aftermath—as "a result of."

Therefore, because there are no limitations, the single particle does not have to do—abide to, nor does it need to behave in any particular way. It is just there in an infinite void, with absolutely no limitations or hindering of any kind.

Therefore, if there are no limitations—hence nothing to slow it down in any way shape or form—and no laws of physics of any kind to hinder it in any way, then our beloved particle could—and is free to travel at infinite speed.

And because it is able to travel at infinite-unlimited speed, our particle is therefore able to appear everywhere and anywhere at once, everywhere and anywhere in that infinite void. And this appearing everywhere at once is precisely what causes the "filling-in" of every point in that void, all at once!

Hence, the resulting "infinite-multi-location," creates the illusion that an infinite number of particles existed, when in fact it was all one and the same original particle doing all of the work, all at once, but most importantly, all on its own!

Thus, one and the same particle appears at every point in the Universe next to itself, over and over, hence making-up—creating the illusion of a continuous—uniform Universe! But this, not only here in the "Physical Level," but in all Levels, in all Frequencies!

Therefore, the entire Universe, everything that surrounds us—including us, is all made by one single particle!

That is, my dear friends, not only how everything is connected to everything else, but also how everything is everything else! That is how we are one! That is how, **It is all All-That-Is**!

Therefore, feel the connection within. Feel the inner unity you have with the entire Universe. You are part of the fabric of existence, of the fabric of creation, and you are therefore inside the heart of All-That-Is.

You are the leading edge of God's life-force! Thus never feel unappreciated, and never feel unneeded.

For All-That-Is expresses through you, sees through you, laughs through you, cries through you. And All-That-Is loves through you!

What could be more valuable?

"As long as you believe that you live in a dangerous world, then, you must defend yourself from such a world. As long as you believe that your existence is 'flawed' and that your race is damned, then you must defend yourself from yourself. You need not say 'the Universe is safe,' all you need to say is 'I live in a safe Universe' and so you shall. Let us leave our priests to their hells and heavens, and confine the scientists to their dying Universe, with its accidentally created stars. Let us each dare to open our dream's door, and explore the unofficial thresholds, where we begin." ~

—Jane Roberts. (From the Seth Material)

Chapter 12

From the Ashes, A Phoenix

A nd so the book was completed!
Yes, the book was edited, reviewed several times over, corrected, formatted, signed sealed and delivered.

I emailed Steven (my Agent) and sent him the final copy of the book and cover design.

"Steven, I am finally done" I said, "25 years of work, and I can finally take a break from writing for a while—the book is now in your hands, make it great," I told Steven.

"Congratulations, get ready for great things! I will take it from here" Steven replied.

But only an hour had passed from that email, when behind a table in a corner of my office, an electrical spark started a fire.

It started as a very small flame, about five inches tall. Nothing to worry about, I thought at first. I grabbed a cup of drinking water from my desk, and poured it on the small flame. My son and a very good friend of mine were there with me. With the water, the small flame appeared to have died out—but it immediately surged up again, a few inches taller this time.

My son gave me a second cup of water, which again appeared to extinguish the flame. However, it immediately flared up again—much higher this time, about three feet tall. "Get me a fire extinguisher" I yelled, but in a split second, the flame shot all the way up to the ceiling and over my head—with such a speed, that within a second, I was completely enveloped by the now gigantic flame.

I turned around, the entire office now in total darkness from the very thick smoke. I found my way to the door by following my son's and my friend's voices—yelling at me to get out.

As I stepped out of my office, the glass side windows started to explode outwardly.

Someone—my son I believe—gave me a fire extinguisher, which, through the broken glass, I emptied aiming it at the base of the flame. It barely had any effect—a second fire extinguisher—and then a third. Nothing could stop the now gigantic flame, which had now spread in every direction, and into other adjacent businesses.

I don't know why, but my protective instinct for a business I really loved, made me want to go back inside. "I can still stop it" I foolishly thought for a second. But the moment I put my face in the door, I was faced with a solid wall of black smoke. I almost suffocated to death.

The many burning computers in my office—released an unbreathable burning plastic odor. I had no other choice but to turn back, and direct my efforts to helping other people abandon the now almost totally engulfed shopping mall. *(See photo at the back of the book)*.

There was nothing else we could do; the fire had taken over the entire building. Everywhere I looked, people screaming—people running for their lives. Some, trapped by the flames, had to jump from the at least 16 feet tall balcony.

The fire trucks—which I and several other people had already dialed—started to arrive, three at least. Ambulances, news trucks—total and utter pandemonium. An enormous disaster, an incredible tragedy.

In less than ten short minutes, many, many businesses, some still in the process of opening, some (like mine) which took decades of hard work and loving effort, simply vanished, reduced to nothing more than a pile of smoking ashes. The only thing we can all be grateful for is that no-one, absolutely and miraculously no-one got hurt.

And so here we are, in total shock, still unsure if it really happened, or if it is a terrible nightmare we are going through.

It has been five days now, and I still cannot stop crying. I can only sleep two or three hours per night. My doctor gave me sleeping pills, but even they are not enough to make that terrible image disappear from my mind.

It will eventually. "Time is the best medicine," they say. I know it will get better—much better. Rebuild we will! That is what we do, we fall, and we get up. We fall again—and we get up again.

Like a beautiful Phoenix, stronger, better, bigger, more prosperous and blessed than ever.

God Willing, إن شاء الله, Volendo Dio, S'il plaît à Dieu, Insha'Allah, Si Dios quiere, Gud Vil, השם בעזרת, Θεοῦ θέλοντος, Jumala Suo, 天意, Dá-li Bůh, ईश्वर की कृपा हो, 神の意志, Божий промысел, Jainkoaren Prest, по Божията воля, Als God het wil, Sa pahintulot ng Diyos, Ke Akua i kona makemake ana, Isten is úgy akarja, Guð Reiðubúinn, 신이 함게 있 길, So Gott will, خواست خدا به, InşAllah, Mungu Akipenda, Gud Villig, InsyAllah, ωεະເ¢້ຖເຕ້ມໃວທ້ອະ, كه خدای كول, Bi îzna Xwedê, Se Deus quiser, Jak Bóg da, ਰੱਬ ਦੀ ਇੱਛਾ, Божиja воља, God Villiga, Božja Volja, з божою поміччю, Božia Vôľa, Xudo Hohlasa, Thân săn sàng, Ngokwentando Kankulunkulu.

— *The End*

Sometimes the heart sees what is invisible to the eye.

I send you my warmest regards!

—Your friend Marco.

Reference Material

Seth, as depicted by Robert Butts. This is also how Seth appeared to Mark during the many "Teaching Sessions".

Jane Roberts and her husband Robert Butts. Jane channelled several books for Seth in a trance, while her husband Robert took notes.

As you can see everything is within All-That-Is!
All-That-Is is therefore the Source that creates everything - thus everything is All-That-Is.
At the Centre, is where the Gestalt (or System) is most "accelerated" hence pure Light.
The farther out you go - the more de-celerated - hence "solid" the System becomes.

Seth Speaks. The book Mark credits for starting the whole process. This is also the book which inspired Mark to write his own book "It Will Change You".

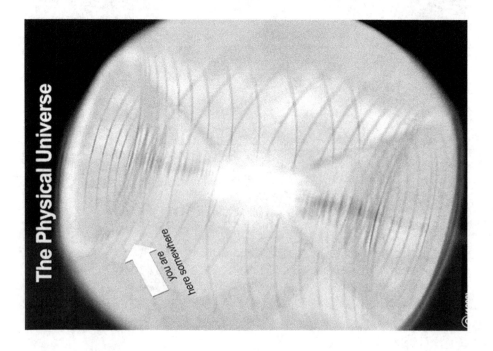

The Physical Universe

you are here somewhere

Photoshop rendition of the two lights Mark   and a passenger
in his vehicle witness together - floating out from the trees -
fifty yards in front of their vehicle, while on a hunting trip in the
Canadian Boreal forest.

This was my office.

Only a few hours had passed from when I had finished editing this book
and sent it out for publishing, when a catastrophic fire totally destroyed
my office, as well as several other businesses in our Mall.

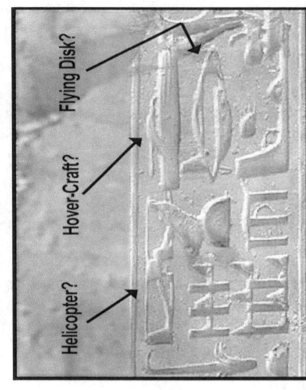

Helicopter? Hover-Craft? Flying Disk?

This pyramid hieroglyphics, as well as innumerable other sites, monuments and artifacts throughout the planet, clearly proves that other civilizations must have existed prior to ours - which achieved a remarkably high level of technological advancement, in some cases superior to ours even. *Note the (at least three) - clearly visible "flying vehicles" carved on the wall of this pyramid.

MARCH 2/94
DEAR MARK.
RE YOUR MOST REMARKABLE DREAMS, TO ME THE MOST
REMARKABLE OF ALL IS THE LONG ONE INVOLVING DRA-
WINGS 2+3. "THE UNIVERSE IN YOUR EYES", ETC.

YOU SEEM TO DREAM ABOUT JANE, SETH, + RUBURT MORE
THAN I DO, + AND VERY VIVIDLY. YOUR DRAWINGS ADD
A LOT, TOO, QUITE UNIQUE IN THEIR INDIVIDUAL WAYS.
TO ME, THEY TRANSLATE INTO PAINTINGS.

I WISH I HAD THE TIME TO GO INTO DETAILS ABOUT
YOUR DREAMS, IDEAS, ETC, BUT SADLY I DON'T- I'M
ALWAYS STRUGGLING TO KEEP UP WITH THE MAIL,
WHICH SELDOM EASES UP, SO I DO THE BEST I CAN,
I HOPE THAT MY EFFORTS AT LEAST ACKNOWLEDGE THE
CARING EFFORTS OTHERS SEND ME.

I WISH YOU THE VERY BEST.
YES, I'M STILL INVOLVED WITH JANE'S WORK, BUT
HERE AGAIN I HAVE TO BE CAREFUL ABOUT WHAT COM-
MITMENTS I MAKE, LEST I PROMISE MORE THAT I CAN
DELIVER. THIS INVOLVES SOME HARD CHOICES! I'M
ENCLOSING THE NOTICES I USUALLY SEND TO THOSE
WHO WRITE - IF YOU'VE SEEN ANY OF THEM BEFORE,
PLEASE PASS THEM ALONG, OR USE THE CIRCULAR FILE.

ONCE AGAIN - YOUR DREAMS + INSIGHTS ARE REMARKABLE
-THIS IS SOMETHING I DON'T TELL OTHERS SO STRONGLY,
USUALLY. SEEMS TO ME THAT YOU'LL HAVE A GREAT LIFE
EXPLORING WHAT YOU ALREADY KNOW!!

ROB

This is the letter Mark received in response to a letter he sent to Mr. Robert Butts.

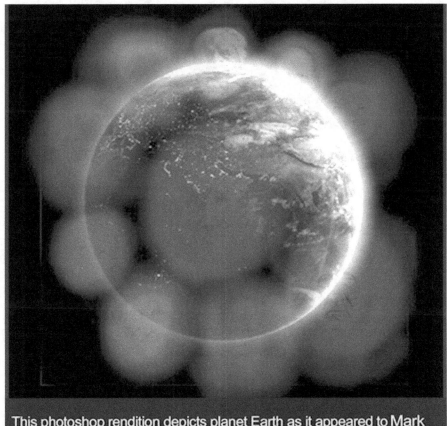

This photoshop rendition depicts planet Earth as it appeared to Mark in one of his interplanetary voyages with Seth. *Note the many ghostly faces (Earth Guardians) positined all around the planet.

For latest news, upcoming books and interactive blog please visit:
www.SethTeachings.org

Visit our YouTube and FaceBook Channels, Search for:
"Marco Governali"

Copyright Information. © 2017
All book contents are copyright of their respective owners. Nothing may be
reproduced in whole or in part without the express written consent of its owners. All
names, companies, trademarks, illustrations, photos and references are the property
of their respective owners.

CPSIA information can be obtained
at www.ICGtesting.com
Printed in the USA
LVHW050303030919
629675LV00009B/257